D0966271

JOHN E. FETZER

AND THE QUEST FOR THE NEW AGE

JOHN E. FETZER
AND THE QUEST FOR
THE NEW AGE

Brian C. Wilson

WAYNE STATE UNIVERSITY PRESS

DETROIT

ISBN 978-0-8143-4530-6 (jacketed cloth); ISBN 978-0-8143-4531-3 (ebook)

Library of Congress Cataloging Number: 2017956372

Except where noted, all photographs are courtesy of the Fetzer Institute.

Wayne State University Press
Leonard N. Simons Building
4809 Woodward Avenue
Detroit, Michigan 48201-1309

Visit us online at wsupress.wayne.edu

Soul Portrait of John E. Fetzer by Arthur Douët (1984)

Contents

Preface

If they ever write about me, the title will probably be *The Nine Lives of John E. Fetzer.*

—John E. Fetzer (1983)

John E. Fetzer indeed lived many lives. Born in 1901 and headquartered for most of his life in the small midwestern city of Kalamazoo, Fetzer was a pioneer broadcaster who helped bring the first radio station to southwestern Michigan in the late 1920s. An astute businessman, he grew with the industry, making millions by expanding his holdings from radio into television, recording, and then cable. During this time, too, he acted on a national stage, called on by the federal government and the industry to assume positions of leadership to help manage the many aspects of an electronic media that was swiftly evolving into the dominant form of communications in the United States. By the time he died in 1991, he had been listed in *Forbes* magazine as one of the four hundred wealthiest people in the United States. Today in Michigan, though, Fetzer is best known not as a media mogul but as the owner of the Detroit Tigers baseball team for almost thirty years beginning in 1956. There are still many people who in their mind's eye can picture the famous photograph of the man in the business suit laughing uproariously after being dunked in a whirlpool by his players after their 1968 World Series win.

Of Fetzer's many lives, there is one, however, that is not well known: that of his lifelong spiritual search, which led him from traditional forms of Christianity to an exploration of a variety of metaphysical religions culminating in the New Age. Although something of a misnomer, "metaphysical religion" refers to those traditions based on a monistic rather than dualistic cosmology, that is, one that posits that all is one, including God, as opposed to the radical separation of God and the cosmos that forms the basis for the Abrahamic traditions. In such monistic systems, the conception of God shifts from being transcendent and personal to immanent and impersonal, all of which tends to have major effects on the way one relates to the world. Despite Christian domination, there has been a continuous undercurrent of monistic thinking in the West from ancient times to the present. Indeed, in the United States, this current became fully established through a variety of traditions ranging from esoteric Freemasonry and Rosicrucianism to Spiritualism and Theosophy to the more recent spiritual synthesis called the New Age, which is simply one of the latest manifestations in the long history of spiritual monism in the West.[1]

Fetzer's interest in metaphysical religions began in the 1930s, but, a private man by nature, he was doubly circumspect about his study of these traditions because he was afraid it might jeopardize his business success in religiously conservative western Michigan, heavily influenced as it was by the powerful presence of the Dutch Reformed Church and its offshoots that made this part of the state a hotbed of Evangelical Christian activity.[2] And while Fetzer eventually gathered around him a small band of spiritually like-minded people in his hometown of Kalamazoo, discretion in these matters had by then become something of a habit. Even after he created the Fetzer Foundation in the 1970s to express his spiritual vision in service to the world, he was determined not to advertise this fact unduly, especially in his own backyard. Fetzer had a marked ability to compartmentalize his professional from his spiritual life, an ability that served him well in his desire for professional respectability. Because of this, however, the details of Fetzer's spiritual search have not been fully documented until now. It is for this reason that this book, while touching on aspects of Fetzer's life in business and baseball, focuses primarily on just one of his many lives: his spiritual life.[3]

Fetzer's quest for the New Age is made all the more significant because he used his wealth to institutionalize his spiritual vision in the Fetzer Foundation, later renamed the Fetzer Institute. For Fetzer, spirituality was a recognition that all is spirit, which he conceptualized as an eternal, conscious energy that, if one were open to it, would inevitably lead one back to the "great central source," which some people choose to call God.[4] The institute was thus born of Fetzer's desire to prove the reality of spiritual monism by funding research into the science of spirituality, which was its priority during the last years of Fetzer's life.[5] Fetzer also hoped that the institute would form a tangible and useful legacy of his spiritual search once he was gone. In this last, he was eminently successful, for long after his death in 1991, the Fetzer Institute continues to flourish, funding projects from alternative health care to holistic education to programs seeking to promote love and forgiveness around the globe. All of these activities still reflect John Fetzer's spiritual vision, even if the connection between that vision and its contemporary manifestations has not always been fully articulated. A major task for this book is, then, to make this connection clear, thus preserving it for the long stretch of the institute's projected five-hundred-year mission.

Beyond simply documenting the fascinating story of Fetzer's spiritual journey, which led to the creation of his foundation, I also argue that Fetzer's quest, for all its distinctiveness, nevertheless mirrored in fundamental ways that of thousands of Americans who sought new ways of thinking and being in the evolving metaphysical movements of the twentieth century. According to the historian J. Stillson Judah, one of the major attractions of metaphysical movements has always been the fact they provide a "practical type of philosophy" that draws from both science and religion, the reconciliation of which has been an abiding theme in the religious history of the United States since the late nineteenth century.[6] For John Fetzer, trained as a radio engineer but steeped as a young man in the fundamentalist dogmas of Seventh-day Adventism, figuring out how to effect this reconciliation became a burning question that led him to embrace metaphysical monism as the surest way forward to a coherent worldview that was both deeply spiritual and scientifically defensible. As I contend throughout the book, the reconciliation of science and religion was one of the primary goals of Fetzer's spiritual seeking and one of the primary motivations for the creation of the Fetzer Institute.

Another characteristic of metaphysical religion that many observers have pointed out is its inherent eclecticism, that is, the utter freedom with which its adherents pick and choose elements from discrete metaphysical traditions to craft worldviews of their own.[7] Nowhere is this better illustrated than in John Fetzer's spiritual search: from the 1930s until his death in 1991, Fetzer continuously evolved his worldview by combining and recombining elements from dozens of metaphysical traditions in a process he called "freedom of the spirit." Unlike the thousands of Americans who engaged in a similar process, however, Fetzer's synthesis can be documented step by step, thus providing us with a remarkably rich and detailed roadmap from the Spiritualism and Theosophy of the 1930s all the way to the New Age of the 1980s—and beyond. Recent polls show that the worldview of the fastest growing demographic in the United States today—those who identify themselves as "spiritual but not religious" (SBNR)—is shot through with an eclectic mixture of metaphysical ideas and themes, and indeed, SBNR can best be described as a hyperindividualistic evolution of the metaphysical and New Age movements of which Fetzer was an early pioneer.[8] Fetzer himself was definitely not an SBNR (as I argue later), but he and people like him—those of what might be called the "old New Age"—set the stage for the fluorescence of this new and influential form of metaphysical spirituality that is now swiftly reforming the American religious landscape of the twenty-first century.

Finally, by placing Fetzer's spiritual development within the broader context of the history of metaphysical religions in the United States, we also learn that his metaphysical interests were not atypical of the Midwest, which, despite conservative "heartland" myths to the contrary, was long a center of metaphysical activity. For too long, as the historian Philip

Jenkins has written, the "distinctiveness of California" in this regard has been "exaggerated" in both the scholarly and popular imagination to the detriment of regions such as the Midwest, which long hosted a thriving metaphysical subculture almost since its settlement.[9] As I document in detail in this book, when John Fetzer started his spiritual search among the metaphysical movements in the 1930s, he did not have to go far to encounter traditions as diverse as Spiritualism, Theosophy, esoteric Freemasonry, and Hermeticism, either in the flesh at such places as Indiana's Camp Chesterfield or in the books, magazines, and pamphlets churned out by the thousands by Chicago's many metaphysical presses. And this midwestern metaphysical subculture only grew during Fetzer's lifetime—in 1977, J. Gordon Melton, a historian of new religious movements, observed that there was "a larger psychic/metaphysical/mystical community functioning in Chicago than in either Los Angeles or San Francisco."[10] Fetzer did frequently reach beyond the Midwest for spiritual resources, but what is remarkable is how much of what he needed he found very close to home in Indiana, Illinois, and Michigan.

This is not to say, of course, that the metaphysical Midwest was the same as the metaphysical West and that a homogeneous metaphysical subculture pervaded both regions. That this was not the case is well attested by the specific details of Fetzer's developing worldview. A product of a small-town Hoosier boyhood, Fetzer never shed his midwestern sensibilities, and for this reason, certain heartland themes carried over into his New Age worldview in ways they probably would not have in other regions. These included an enduring pietistic belief in the importance of Jesus; an abiding concern for the integrity of community and the responsible use of wealth; and an unabashed patriotism that saw the American experiment as the herald of a New Age that never quite lost its Christian millennialist tinge. Thus, an exploration of Fetzer's spiritual search not only highlights the ubiquity of metaphysical currents in the United States but also begins the process of recovering the Midwest's distinctive metaphysical culture.

John E. Fetzer and the Quest for the New Age is thus both the story of one man's spiritual search and a window onto the rich and complex history of metaphysical religions in the United States. The historian of American religions Catherine Albanese once wrote that her years of research had convinced her that metaphysical traditions are "a normal, recurring, and pervasive feature of the American spiritual landscape."[11] The correctness of this assessment can well be judged in the spiritual life of John E. Fetzer and its afterlife in the Fetzer Institute.

Acknowledgments

Happily for the writing of this book, John Fetzer during his lifetime sensed the importance of the task of documenting his spiritual search and left behind a wealth of primary materials. The archives of the Fetzer Institute contain much of his correspondence, diaries, writings, speeches, and interviews, a record that stretches from his early life to his last years. All of this helps to illuminate his thoughts and feelings as he abandoned his childhood faith and embarked on his intensive study of spiritual alternatives. One of the greatest resources in this regard is Fetzer's library, which, while not completely intact, is nevertheless complete enough to chart his reading over decades. John Fetzer had a distinct style of annotating his reading, which reveals much about what he thought was wheat and what was chaff. Finally, the Fetzer Memorial Trust, which was created in part to preserve the legacy of John Fetzer, recognized early on the importance of documenting the Fetzer Institute's history. This resulted in a remarkable set of oral histories from family, friends, and colleagues who knew John Fetzer personally. These were collected in the 1990s by Dr. Philip P. Mason, Distinguished Professor of History, Wayne State University; and in the 2000s, by Larry Massey, an independent scholar and author of several local histories. Even more recently, the Memorial Trust has engaged in an extensive legacy project, spearheaded by Tom Beaver, whose advice and series of detailed memos have been invaluable for the present work.

In 2012, I was invited by the Memorial Trust to contribute to its ongoing legacy project by writing John Fetzer's spiritual biography. As a professor of US religious history with a focus on new religious movements and religion in the Midwest, I jumped at the chance to work on this fascinating figure who lived at the intersection of all of my research interests. For confidence in me for this undertaking, I would like to thank the Memorial Trust, especially Louis Leeburg, Chair and Treasurer; Bruce Fetzer, President and CEO; Tom Beaver, Senior Advisor for Founder's Legacy; and for unstinting support, Jimyo L. Ferworn, Manager of Finance and Grants. Due to a sabbatical leave granted by my home institution, Western Michigan University, not to mention a generous research grant from the Memorial Trust, I have been able to spend a year in residence at the Fetzer Institute working through the archival materials and concentrating on writing. During this wonderful time, I have been made to feel a welcome part of the Fetzer family, and for this, I would like to thank all the institute's staff, especially Robert Boisture, President and CEO of the Fetzer Institute; Robert Lehman, Chairman of the Board; and Dena O'Flynn, Information Specialist, whose efforts on my behalf have made my archival work at the institute a joy. At Wayne State University Press, I would like to thank my editor, Kathryn Wildfong, for her enthusiasm for the project and for making this the smoothest publishing experience I have ever had. In addition, I would like to thank Carolyn Dailey, Cleora Daily, Akram Elias, Christopher C. Green, Mary Hardy, Dirk Hughes, Denise Killick, Todd Jay Leonard, Vincent Mariani, Sister Elizabeth Reis, SSJ, Robert Rosenthal, Richard Merkel, and Caroline Yapp for sharing their time and expertise. Finally, I would like to thank my wife, Cybelle T. Shattuck, for her patience and love, and I dedicate this book to the memory of Tibault and Beryl, lost this year but never forgotten.

Meeting Jesus in an Elevator

Fetzer's Earliest Spiritual Influences and Experiences (1901–1920s)

As we go through my life story, you're going to find that the word "search" is one of the paramount activities of my life. I've been searching all my life—not essentially on one subject but on many subjects. . . . You're going to find practically in the whole history of my life that I've been searching and searching—the evolutionary search.

—John Fetzer (1983)

John Earl Fetzer was the product of the kind of early twentieth-century small-town Indiana so prominent in the nostalgic memories of much midwestern fiction. Indeed, many of the incidents in the young Fetzer's life could have been lifted from the pages of Booth Tarkington or Hamlin Garland. He was born at home on March 25, 1901, in Decatur, a village of little over four thousand people in the northeastern part of the state. Fetzer's father, John A. Fetzer, was the owner of a bicycle shop on Main Street who had an interest in the newly invented automobile. He was also

1. John with Della and Harriet ("Hattie") Fetzer (ca. 1906).

well known as the cornet and trombone player in the Decatur brass band. The senior Fetzer met his wife, Della Frances Winger Evans, on a train trip to play music in neighboring Fort Wayne, and after a brief courtship, they were married in 1899. Both had previous spouses and brought children into the marriage: Homer Fetzer and Harriet ("Hattie") Evans. To this ready-made family was added John Earl two years later. Another son, Walter Adam Fetzer, died in infancy in 1903.[1]

John E. Fetzer barely knew his father, who passed away from pneumonia when Fetzer was not yet two years old. In order for Della Fetzer to support her family, she converted her husband's store into a millenary shop. She enjoyed some success in her confection of hats, so when John was six, she moved her business to larger towns, first Frankfort and then, when John was eleven, to nearby West Lafayette, home of Purdue University. Della Fetzer soon began to supplement her income by buying and "flipping" houses, which meant that constant moving became a way of life for young John. Nevertheless, it was here in West Lafayette that Fetzer spent a typical midwestern boyhood: attending public schools, playing sandlot baseball, owning a mangy dog named Jack, and running with a tight-knit group of friends with such nicknames as "Chink" and "Hen Egg." Two photos from the period show a bright-eyed boy with a mischievous grin dressed in overalls sitting in a soapbox car and in knickers on a fishing expedition with friends. Another, later photo of his high school basketball team shows him towering over his teammates, John having reached his full height of six feet by early adolescence.[2]

In 1911, John's sister, Harriet, met and married a telegrapher for the Wabash Railroad named Fred Ribble. Ribble became something of a father figure for young John, teaching him Morse code and introducing him to the newly emerging field of radio. Ribble was also a rabid Detroit Tigers fan, a passion he passed on to his youthful brother-in-law. Years later, Fetzer cited Della, Harriet, and Fred as the "three great influences" in his life and West Lafayette as "the one real home" to him as a boy. Fetzer never outgrew his love of family and his small-town Indiana roots.[3]

Fetzer's Childhood Religious Upbringing

Growing up in the small-town Midwest, Fetzer could not help but be influenced by the optimistic go-getting entrepreneurial culture of these places. Long before the Midwest fell into the doldrums of the rust belt, it

2. John E. Fetzer as a boy (ca. 1908).

brimmed with the spirit of invention and innovation that was to become a hallmark of Fetzer's life. There was another spirit, however, that pervaded the small-town Midwest, a spirit that made an indelible impression on the young John Fetzer: Evangelical Protestantism. The ethos of Evangelical Protestantism can be identified by its intense focus on the Bible, on the person of Jesus, and on conversion, as well as an equally intense pietism, moralism, and missionary impulse. Since the first political organization of the Midwest as the Northwest Territory in 1787, Evangelical Protestants of nearly all stripes poured into the area. The fierce competition between Protestant denominations in the Midwest led to no clear winner, but it did succeed in stamping the region with a very particular religious culture shot through with the Evangelical ethos. Importantly, this generalized Evangelical ethos made it easy for people to switch back and forth between Evangelical churches in the Midwest, especially during the formative stages when churches were few and far between.[4]

Indiana's religious history represents a distinctive version of this generalized midwestern story. While French Catholics were the first Christians on the ground in Indiana in the 1700s, they were soon rivaled by large migrations of Protestants coming from the eastern United States beginning early in the nineteenth century. The majority were Methodists, Baptists, Presbyterians, and Quakers coming from the mid-Atlantic and southern states, with smaller numbers of Yankee Congregationalists and Presbyterians settling mainly in the northern counties of Indiana. Unlike the upper Midwest, Indiana settlement was largely from the South, which infused the state's culture—including its religious culture—with a fiercely egalitarian, individualistic streak. Added to this mix were Protestants of German extraction, primarily from Pennsylvania, who established Lutheran, Mennonite, and Amish congregations throughout the state. Indeed, Indiana sits squarely in the heart of what was called the "German Triangle" bounded by Milwaukee, St. Louis, and Cincinnati; it thus continued to attract migration directly from the Old Country throughout the nineteenth century, keeping Indiana's pockets of German culture vibrant well into the twentieth century.[5]

John E. Fetzer's own family tree reflected aspects of both the ethnic and religious history of Indiana and the Midwest. His father, John A. Fetzer, whose antecedents his son eventually traced back to the ancient German town of Denkendorf, came from a long line of Lutherans, so it is not surprising that when he settled in Decatur, he formally joined the Lutheran congregation there.[6] John E. Fetzer's mother, Della Winger Evans Fetzer, had a rather more complicated background. Her father, Joseph Levi Robinson Winger, was born a Mennonite, and her grandmother Nancy Jane Woods came from a long line of Pennsylvania Quakers and Scotch-Irish Presbyterians, although at the time of her marriage, she belonged to a German Brethren ("Dunker") church. During the couple's peripatetic life together, they attended a Christian (Disciples of Christ) church, a Lutheran church, a Winebrennarian Lutheran church (known simply as the Church of Christ), and when Joseph died in 1928, his funeral was held at a Congregational church. Della apparently followed the family as they switched churches, and she married John A. Fetzer in the Lutheran church in Decatur. More changes in denominations were in store for Della in the future; but far from eroding her piety, it apparently only intensified it, and throughout her long life, she not only thought deeply about her own spiritual condition but sought to inculcate her Christian piety in her children. Indeed, according to John E. Fetzer's recollections, the last words his mother said to him before she died were, "Pray, John, pray." She was, in John's words, "deeply spiritual."[7]

On October 17, 1901, despite the preponderance of German churches in the couple's backgrounds, the Fetzers decided to have young John E. Fetzer baptized by the Reverend C. G. Henderson of the local Methodist Episcopal church.[8] Thereafter, for most of his childhood, Fetzer attended Sunday school at the Methodist Episcopal church, later observing that "as a youngster," he was largely "raised in the Methodist Church." John attributed the choice of Methodism to the fact that no other church was available in town; but this was hardly the case, so the choice must have been a considered one, perhaps due to theological affinity, to social advantage, or simply to a friendship with the pastor.[9] However this may have been, his parents' choice had important consequences for John E. Fetzer's emerging spirituality.

Of all the varieties of Protestantism in the Midwest, Methodism was by far the most successful, and, as carrier of the Evangelical ethos par excellence, it had such an outsized role on the region's emerging religious culture that the historian Mark Noll has characterized the Midwest by its "enduring Methodist tinge."[10] Indiana's Methodist culture was especially vibrant, perhaps because early Methodist leaders were drawn from all three regions (North, South, and Mid-Atlantic) and therefore could appeal to Indiana settlers wherever they came from in the United States. Through practical means such as the vigorous preaching of circuit riders and religious revivals, Methodism grew apace in Indiana, such that by 1860, there were nearly one hundred thousand Methodists in the state organized into four conferences.[11] When John E. Fetzer was introduced to the church in the first decade of the twentieth century, Methodism was by far the dominant Protestant denomination in Indiana, boasting a quarter of all religious adherents in the state in 1906.[12]

Although by the time John E. Fetzer was baptized into the church, the flamboyant days of circuit riders and revival meetings were long gone, replaced by an atmosphere of prosperous respectability, the young John nevertheless would still have been exposed to the highly expressive piety that characterized the church since its founding by the mystical brothers John and Charles Wesley. Methodist Sunday schools were undergoing something of a renaissance precisely when John would have been attending one (with "Chink" no less).[13] Here John would have been taught the Arminian doctrine that all people are "free to resolve to improve their condition" and that if they do so, they will be "divinely assisted in their fulfillment, effecting their moral and spiritual transformation," especially if they heed the words of the Bible.[14] To this end, we find John writing in his 1914 diary about his efforts at reading the Bible; in one entry, he records that he was especially affected by the flood narrative and, in response, promised to "turn over a new leaf."[15] In Sunday school, too, John would have been exposed to the idea that while the quest for spiritual perfection—what Wesley called "perfect love"—was a lifelong task, God freely provided his grace through the Holy Spirit to aid the earnest seeker in the process. All it took to access this power or energy of God was nothing more than prayer.[16] Although the terminology might change, this idea of grace through prayer stayed with John for the rest of his life.

Of course, the centerpiece of Evangelicalism and thus Methodism is the religious experience of conversion, an experience to be cherished and remembered throughout life. Conversion is something to be worked for, but its occurrence is not always predictable and comes to people at unexpected moments. John Wesley himself was surprised when his attention wandered during a particular sermon to find his "heart strangely warmed," while in the days of Methodist camp meetings, people often found Jesus through powerful physical, sometimes visionary experiences. True to Methodist form, John E. Fetzer's conversion was a wholly unexpected happening. As a child of ten or eleven, he had found himself in an elevator at a local Decatur department store called Shortel's. Suddenly, he recalled, "I had this dream. I dreamed that I was in that elevator shaft and I was holding upon the leg of Jesus Christ. He was going up and I was hanging on going up the elevator shaft with Him. He was looking down at me. The connotation of that, as I interpret it, is that 'I will always be there for you.'" This vision had a powerful impact on Fetzer. The incident, which was recorded in a 1982 interview when Fetzer was eighty years old, seemed still to resonate with him with all the vividness and import that it had some seventy years before. Indeed, Fetzer offered up the anecdote to the interviewer as the key to his "religious life": the "first tip [of the iceberg] as to where I come from" spiritually.[17]

While Fetzer was not always consistent in his Sunday-school attendance, his Methodist faith nevertheless continued strong throughout his teen years and helped carry him through some very trying times, including constantly shifting homes, his family's hand-to-mouth existence, his mother's remarriage, and a lack of a permanent father figure for guidance.[18] The real test, however, came in Fetzer's senior year of high school, when he contracted the virulent Spanish flu. Although largely forgotten today, the Spanish flu was a global pandemic that killed upward of fifty million people worldwide.[19] When the flu came to West Lafayette, it hit the Fetzer household hard, but none harder than John, who was almost given up for dead. It was at this point that Fetzer's faith became paramount. He later recollected, "I thought from the remarks I heard that

I wasn't going to make it." Death had already visited the Fetzer family, carrying away his father and little brother, and in 1918, the country was embroiled in the unparalleled bloodshed of World War I. In such an environment, it would not have been surprising if the boy had simply resigned himself to the inevitable. However, instead, Fetzer reported, "I made a commitment at the time that if I were permitted to live, I would devote my life to the spiritual work of the Creator."[20] Although left with lingering and for a time debilitating aftereffects, he did survive the flu when countless others did not. True to his word, he never did forget his bargain with God, and while his subsequent life took him out of the Methodist fold, his devotion to God's "spiritual work" formed an unbroken theme for the rest of his long life.

Fetzer and Seventh-day Adventism

John E. Fetzer began during his teen years to cultivate those interests that came to dominate the rest of his professional life. His early mentor, Fred Ribble, introduced him to the telegraph when he was ten, and two years later, he and Fred built an even more marvelous device: the radio. Although radio was then in still a primitive stage of development, the fact that one could receive out of thin air first Morse code and then voices and music made radio something of an obsession with young John. He began to frequent the radio station and labs at nearby Purdue University, and while recovering from the flu, he spent hours studying his father's electrical engineering texts, which aided in his quest for the amateur radio license he received in 1919. After graduation from West Lafayette High School, Fetzer pursued further study in wireless classes at Purdue in 1921, allowing him to gain a commercial radio license a year later.[21] The university was indeed a fruitful place to study radio: in 1922, a class project at Purdue's School of Electrical Engineering led to the licensing of "Indiana's first non-commercial radio station," WBAA.[22] Witnessing this process was undoubtedly a valuable learning experience that impacted John's later career.

Religious changes, too, were on the horizon for young John. At some point, his mother, Della, joined the Seventh-day Adventist (SDA) Church, an apocalyptic sect originally headquartered in Battle Creek, Michigan.[23] It is not known when or exactly why Della converted to Adventism. The recent global traumas of World War I and the global flu pandemic, not to mention Della's continuing financial insecurity, could have easily conjured up images of the end of the world such as those narrated in the Book of Revelation. Moreover, apocalyptic thinking was a common theme not only of the time but also throughout the history of the Midwest. John's sister, Hattie, later told a comic story of just how deep-seated such end-of-the-world fears were for Della and her family. According to her recollections,

> There used to be a woman named Nan Plague. She used to come to Grandpa's a lot and tell about the end of the world coming. "When Gabriel comes through riding his white horse," she'd say, "that was the signal for the end of the world." Once, Grandma and Grandpa had gone to town to pay taxes and they left Momma and Uncle Frank there by themselves. They were six and seven years old. A man came driving in the barnyard on a white horse and blew a horn. It was a cowhorn. Momma and Uncle Frank were so frightened that they went upstairs and called out, "Are you Gabriel?" And he said, "No, I'm the assessor."[24]

Whether or not this early childhood experience predisposed Della to joining the Adventists, what can be said is that "Nan Plague" was hardly the only apocalyptic prophet to preach the imminent Second Coming and the destruction of the world to the willing ears of the farmers and townspeople of the Midwest. During the short career of the Mormon prophet Joseph Smith Jr., he preached the "latter days" from Ohio to Illinois, while other doomsday prophets, such as Benjamin Purnell of the Israelite House of David in Benton Harbor, Michigan, and John Alexander Dowie of Zion City, Illinois, preached their own brands of catastrophe. Many midwesterners, too, were open to the rhetoric of Chicago's Dwight L. Moody and Indiana-based Billy Sunday, both of whose biblical fundamentalism presupposed something called "dispensational premillennialism," that is, a literal reading of the Book of Revelation.[25]

By far, however, the most successful of these Midwest-based prophets of doom was Ellen G. White (1827–1915). Originally from Maine, Ellen G. White and her husband, James, were early followers of an Upstate New York farmer and Baptist preacher named William Miller (1782–1849), who in 1818 announced that he had "broken the code" of the apocalyptic books of the Bible. Because of this, Miller had concluded that the Second Coming was due sometime between 1843 and 1844. Slowly, through public lectures, pamphlets, and newspapers, Miller's calculations permeated the public's consciousness, and in time, Miller attracted a significant following. In the Midwest, Millerism centered in Ohio, especially in the cities of Cleveland and Cincinnati, although "Millerites," as the newspapers called them, could be found throughout the frontier. Excitement among Millerites grew throughout the 1830s and early '40s, and Miller made his predictions even more precise, eventually claiming that the Second Coming would occur between March 21, 1843, and March 21, 1844. When that fateful period had come and gone and nothing occurred, the date was recalculated to October 22, 1844. Again, nothing happened. Adventists still call this nonevent the "Great Disappointment."[26]

Dismayed by the "Great Disappointment," the bulk of Miller's followers fell away. Most returned to their denominations, while others abandoned religion altogether. A small group of Millerites, however, never lost faith in the imminent Second Coming of Jesus and, through a series of visions, were able to reinterpret Miller's teachings to account for events. They called themselves Adventists, not Millerites. One of these rump groups was led by James and Ellen G. White under the guidance of Mrs. White's prophetic trances, in which she spoke to God's angels and, occasionally, God himself. Along with apocalypticism, the Whites also made the restoration of the Saturday ("seventh-day") Sabbath and health reform (including vegetarianism) important doctrines in their new denomination. In the 1850s, sensing the possibilities of proselytizing the West, the Whites moved the headquarters of Seventh-day Adventism from Rochester, New York, to Battle Creek, Michigan, where they set up an extensive publishing operation, became involved in education, and launched missionary outreach to the rest of the United States and beyond. It was here, too, in 1863 that they legally incorporated what became called the Seventh-day Adventist Church.[27]

Small-town Indiana of the late nineteenth and early twentieth centuries proved receptive to the doctrines of Seventh-day Adventism. Just before the "Great Disappointment" of 1844, substantial numbers of Millerites could be found up and down the eastern counties of Indiana. Shortly after the 1863 incorporation of the Seventh-day Adventist Church in Battle Creek, missionaries came south into Indiana, and the Indiana Conference was founded soon after in 1871. While the number of Seventh-day Adventists was never large in Indiana during the first decades of the twentieth century (it hovered around two thousand during the 1920s), they maintained an active missionary program there, and SDA publications including newspapers, tracts, and books were readily available throughout the state.[28] Although the center of Indiana Adventism was found in and around Indianapolis, Lafayette could boast an Adventist church since 1888 and, since 1906, an Adventist hospital, probably founded under the auspices of Dr. John Harvey Kellogg's Medical Missionary and Benevolent Association. And while the Lafayette SDA did not have a permanent church building until 1930, the congregation was energetic, hosting in 1919 a series of tent meetings featuring the Elder Claude White at a number of locations around Lafayette, including one in West Lafayette. It is possible that during this revival, Della Fetzer was converted to the SDA Church.[29]

Just as we cannot be quite sure when Della joined the church, so, too, the exact date of John Fetzer's conversion to Seventh-day Adventism is also unknown. However, we do know that in part it was bound up with his love for radio. As John himself narrated it, sometime in 1921, when he was working at the Wolver Electric Company in West Lafayette, in walked a man who said, "I understand you are a wireless expert. I'm president of Emmanuel College in Michigan":

> To begin with, Emmanuel College was a Seventh-day Adventist institution, and my mother had joined the Seventh-day Adventists. I expect that's how he found out about me. So he said, "I understand that you are building equipment for some people down in Indianapolis, and I have an idea we'd like a wireless station up there at the college." I don't know whether he thought about the impact of advertising on the college or not, because advertising by radio had not been established then. So he invited me to build a station for him and I had a choice of whether to continue at Purdue and do what I was doing or to rough it and build this station for him.[30]

In the end, he decided to attend Emmanuel Missionary College, which was located in nearby Berrien Springs, Michigan. According to Fetzer, "I guess my mother was the reason I did it. She thought that it would give me some spiritual guidance—which it did. I was a pretty good Seventh-day Adventist at the time."[31] Apparently, his conversion predated his move to Berrien Springs in 1922, but it was there at Emmanuel that Fetzer threw himself into both the radio station and his new faith.

Now enrolled in classes at Emmanuel, John Fetzer built and ran the first radio station in southwestern Michigan from his dorm room in Maple Hall. Despite the fact that some people said "radio was a trick of the devil," soon the station had a commercial license under the call letters KFGZ (later WEMC) and was moved into separate quarters in the college's administration building. Fetzer worked under the head of the English Department, Paul Pearce, with whom he had something of a fraught relationship, and was responsible for everything including programming, announcing, and technical maintenance at the station. By the spring of 1923, Fetzer calculated that WEMC, "the Radio Lighthouse,"

3. John E. Fetzer with dorm-room radio station, Emmanuel Missionary
College, Berrien Springs, Michigan (ca. 1922).

was reaching some 250,000 listeners. The college now maintained that
"broadcasting by radio" was "one of the greatest blessings which the great
God has given the world" and that WEMC would serve as a bulwark
against "gross materialism" by bringing the "principles of the lowly Naz-
arene" to a broad listening audience. Daily broadcasts largely consisted
of news, educational programs, religious instruction, and edifying music
(and definitely "no jazz").[32]

These were busy, difficult years for Fetzer. In addition to studying and
running the radio station, he was also writing for student publications
and, as much as one could in such a pious environment, enjoying Emmanuel's social scene. During his junior year (1925), under the auspices of the
Seventh-day Adventist Church, he was given the opportunity of traveling to Europe to study advances in broadcasting there, all in an effort,
in John's words, to better "the promulgation of the Message through the
air." Staying primarily at Adventist institutions and sanitaria, John and
his traveling companion, Len Broner, toured radio facilities in England,
Germany, Switzerland, France, Belgium, and Holland. Time was given to
sightseeing, too, and John saw many of the great cities and monuments

of Europe. In Germany, he was particularly impressed by his tour of the Wartburg, especially the stain on the wall where Luther was said to have thrown his inkpot at the Devil.[33]

Throughout the trip to Europe, Fetzer carried on a lively correspondence with a young woman named Rhea Yeager, whom he had met at chapel in 1924. Rhea was occasionally employed as an on-air musician for WEMC and was featured as a cellist in the station's eight-piece orchestra, the Radio Lighthouse Music Makers. John found Rhea "a beautiful girl, talented, supportive, loving," and appreciated her blunt good sense and confidence. He also admired the fact that she had "courage enough" to talk to him "about God . . . with sincerity." "For," he said in a letter to her in 1926, "if our love was to last, God would have to rule us and I hope that you will always trust in God and point Him out to me when trouble comes." Before embarking for Europe, John requested that Rhea write him, and he remained on tenterhooks until he finally received two letters from her at the American Express Office in Paris. At this point, he said, "I made up my mind, as a result of those two letters, that when I got back I would propose to her, which I did. . . . She said yes so fast I didn't have time to clear my throat." They were married at the Vincent Hotel in nearby Benton Harbor on July 19, 1926, and honeymooned by taking a road trip in an old Model T to the Wisconsin Dells.[34]

On May 22, 1927, John Fetzer graduated from Emmanuel Missionary College. Popular and active on campus, "in the limelight a great deal," as he later recalled, Fetzer was chosen to be the class valedictorian.[35] Basing his remarks on the class motto, "faith of our fathers," Fetzer's speech was something of a sermon on the topic. According to Fetzer, the graduating class of 1927 had "reached the transition point in life," leaving the sheltered halls of Emmanuel to enter the real world. There, they would "come face to face with the task which every man and woman on this platform owes the world, that of facing a life that must be marked by noble achievement." However, "even though one may aim high" in this life, "he will meet utter failure, unless he takes with him, as an impetus to this noble achievement, the faith which has dominated the lives of honorable men

4. Rhea Fetzer playing the cello for the WEMC house orchestra (ca. 1926).

and women the world around." Indeed, "a successful life is impossible without this faith." Such a faith must be "a magnetic influence for the good, upon every life with which we come into contact." But what is this faith? According to Fetzer, it included a faith in oneself and one's abilities but also faith in one's fellow man, whose very faithfulness helps one keep one's own faith (and in this regard, Fetzer cited his mother). Ultimately, however, this faith was "faith in an all-seeing, all-powerful God," without whose "creative inspiration" the world would not have known the likes of Moses, Daniel, Milton, and Gladstone, not to mention Columbus, the Puritans, Franklin, Washington, Lincoln, and Garfield. Happily, "faith is not dead today": "it lives in this class." Fetzer concluded his address by envisioning his fellow graduates "encircling the globe" doing great things in the service of humanity, all the time repeating, "Faith of our fathers! Holy faith! We will be true to thee till death!"[36]

Although the speech was written when Fetzer was only twenty-six, it is interesting just how many of the themes in "Faith of Our Fathers" carried through his life. The emphasis on achievement and service, of course, were to be hallmarks of his later business ventures, as well as service to government, industry, and the community. Moreover, true to its title, "Faith of Our Fathers" focused on "founding fathers" throughout history but especially on the founding fathers of the United States. In time, the men who founded the nation became valuable touchstones for Fetzer, and one—Thomas Jefferson—took on a transcendental importance for him. Finally, another major theme in Fetzer's address was the divine origin of human inspiration and creativity. It was just such divine forces, Fetzer noted, that not only motivated founding fathers to high achievement but also made their personalities "magnetic" forces for good. The nature and availability of such divine forces eventually became a driving intellectual preoccupation for Fetzer, as did the faith that made such forces available. "I cannot deny my vision of faith," Fetzer announced in this address, and he spent the next several decades seeking a better understanding of how that faith could be achieved.

Just as interesting in this commencement address is what is not included. Although Fetzer praised Emmanuel Missionary College as the place where he and his classmates were "taught to aim high," there is nothing in the speech about the Seventh-day Adventist Church that had created the college. And while Fetzer lists a whole host of religious leaders—Moses, Paul, Martin Luther, John Wesley—none are from the Seventh-day Adventist tradition itself. Daniel, a key prophet in William Miller's calculations of the Second Coming, is mentioned, as is the medical missionary Wilfred Grenfell, who, while not a Seventh-day Adventist, was well known because of his visits to the Adventist Battle Creek Sanitarium. Nevertheless, no mention is made of James or Ellen G. White or of any contemporary Adventist luminary. Nor are any specific Seventh-day Adventist doctrines featured; indeed, one of the key ideas of the speech is that of a "faith which [is] social and universal, not entirely exclusive."[37] Perhaps Fetzer was instructed to make his speech nondenominational so as not to appear overly sectarian for those in the audience who were not Seventh-day Adventists. Just as likely, though, given other available evidence, this was an early hint about Fetzer's changing attitudes toward the Seventh-day Adventist tradition.

Fundamental Disagreements

Leaving Seventh-day Adventism
(1926–1930)

After graduation, decisions had to be made. Fetzer could continue at the college working for the radio station and teaching, or he could seek further graduate training elsewhere. For years now, Fetzer was having problems with his boss at the radio station, Professor Pearce. He attributed these tensions to the fact that while Pearce was an established figure at the school, Fetzer "was just a kid and engineering all this stuff"; thus, there was "some mental competition that was going on and maybe this is why Pearce wanted me off the air."[1] In the end, Fetzer chose to move on, and by 1929, the Fetzers could be found living in Ann Arbor, Michigan, where John enrolled in graduate classes in physics and mathematics at the University of Michigan.

Fetzer's move to Ann Arbor not only was a physical move from Emmanuel Missionary College but also signified a definitive spiritual move away from the Seventh-day Adventism that the college repre-sented. "At that time, I was becoming quite confused about the religious aspect of the institution," Fetzer remembered decades later. "Seventh-day

5. John E. Fetzer at the microphone at WEMC (ca. 1927).

Adventist people are highly doctrinaire. . . . I felt that wasn't the path I wanted to be on—there had to be another path."[2] Compared to Berrien Springs, Ann Arbor was a cosmopolitan city with the liberal atmosphere of a major university. Here, John could finally feel free to begin to explore and experiment without having to always look over his shoulder and risk the disapproving gaze of his coreligionists.

While the move to Ann Arbor intensified Fetzer's doubts about Seventh-day Adventism, apparently his concerns about the tradition can be traced back to at least 1926 and were perhaps catalyzed by an encounter with an Adventist minister named Sterling B. Slater from Charlotte, Michigan. Sterling had come that year to give a sermon over WMEC, and John struck up a friendship with the minister. In the wake of Sterling's visit, however, Fetzer was startled by some of his statements on the radio and equally so by what Sterling left out, as he apparently made no mention of key Adventist doctrines such as an imminent Second Coming, the Saturday Sabbath, or the belief in Mrs. White's revelations, known in the church as "Testimonies." Fetzer, who was clearly having doubts of his own, followed up with a letter to Sterling asking him about his seeming ambivalence to the church. This elicited a highly revealing response:

Dear Brother Fetzer,

I had not expected to say anything to you in regard to my future course but our acquaintance has gradually developed into an esteem and friendship that makes me feel as tho[ugh] I ought to write to you. I know something of the trial you are going through at this time, the falseness, hypocricy, and inconsistency which has caused you such bitter disappointment, and brought such perplexity to you that you have wondered if even God were true. I have been through your trial and I know what you have been suffering and I would have liked to help you but you will see from this letter that I could not, because of my position, make the necessary explanations to have straightened out your perplexities. . . .

You will meet up with this inconsistency as long as you are an Adventist and it will be a trial for you as long as you believe in the peculiar fanatical doctrines taught by them. Not that there are not many good people among the Adventists the same as there are among the Catholics but they are good people in spite of the systems to which they belong and not because of them. They have gotten their Christianity directly from God and not from these false systems. You will be surprised at such statements from me even as you have been disappointed that I did not preach the fanatical doctrines peculiar to Adventism over the radio. But I preached over the radio only those things which I know to be God's truth. There is much more that I might have presented over the radio but I did not, for courtesy's sake, present anything antagonistic to Adventist teachings. You will recall how reluctantly I took the radio work, how I objected to Elder Guthries about coming [to WMEC] and you will realize that my circumstances forced me into a very trying position which I tried to avoid and by this you will understand my reluctance to come to Berrien Springs, my refusal to consider it permanently, my refusal to preach the special doctrines of Adventism and some other things which have puzzled you. If circumstance forced me to come here as an Adventist minister when I no longer believed in the delusion, I have at least not pretended to believe it, neither have I perjured myself by preaching a lie after I found out it was a lie, as many Adventist leaders do whose actions show that they do not believe a word of what they preach.

. . . I can not show the fallacy of Adventism in the compass of one short letter, but if you wish to study into it you will find the book written by D. M. Canright a correct presentation of the fallacies of this system. Canright's book is entitled "Adventism exposed." You can get it from most any preacher of other denominations. Of course I know what the Adventists would say to this suggestion. For years I was prejudiced against this book because of the scoffing and ridicule of Adventists [and] I regarded [it] as one would regard a rattle snake. My opinion of it was that it was a book of weak, flimsy arguments so cunningly constructed that it was very dangerous, but you will find it a book not of arguments but a book of unavoidable facts. So if you want truth do not let anyone's scoffing keep you from an examination. I do not agree with Canright on the state of the dead, but I have followed out all his other positions in an unrelenting attempt to find him in error and was forced to yield point after point as I found his position impregnable.

Hoping that this may be the means in the hand of God in guiding you out of the anxiety of the bondage of Judaism into the peace that passeth all understanding as found in true Christianity, believe me,

Ever your sincere friend,
Sterling B. Slater.[3]

Slater's letter must have been a bombshell for John, although he did not act immediately on Slater's advice to read Canright, who at the time was the most powerful of Seventh-day Adventism's critics. Indeed, it took another two years for John to actively start questioning his faith, but by 1928, now graduated and contemplating leaving WEMC, he was openly expressing his concerns, at least to his mother. She responded in alarm:

Well my dear I am so sorry that you feel about Adventism the way you do I do hope and pray that the kind of proof you demand will come to you Of course I know nothing about philosophy and evolution and other thing[s] which have cause[d] you to lose faith in religion I am grieved about the whole thing and I suppose anything that I could say wouldent convince you any and all that I can do is to pray for you and Rhea I have always done that and I know nothing more to do or say. One thing I do know that life is so uncertain that it stands us all in hand not to tarry long and wonder about things that god never intended us to know anything about.[4]

A little later that year, while still living in Berrien Springs, Fetzer began to enter into correspondence with several anti-SDA activists and to collect in earnest anti-SDA booklets and pamphlets. Fetzer first contacted Thurber H. Madison, a music teacher from Virginia, Minnesota, and his wife, Agnes. Fetzer had met the Madisons when he was the director of the WEMC orchestra and professor in the Emmanuel Missionary College school of music and she was a secretary at the radio station.[5] Both had left the Church and were vocal SDA apostates.

There were many issues connected with Seventh-day Adventism that Fetzer hoped the Madisons might help clarify. Were Mrs. White's prophetic gifts genuine or was she a fraud? How trustworthy were the Adventist interpretations of the prophetic portions of the Bible that predicted the imminent end of the world and the Second Coming? Was the Saturday Sabbath indeed mandatory for salvation, and what about the health reforms? Was vegetarianism really necessary? And finally, what about the Church's teachings on science, especially Darwin's theory of evolution? Based in part on Mrs. White's visions, the Church had long supported biblical creationism over against Darwinism as the true origin of humanity, but the denomination's rejection had become even more uncompromising in the wake of the infamous 1925 Scopes Monkey Trial in nearby Dayton, Tennessee. The outcome of this trial made such fundamentalist rejection of modern science a national laughing stock, something John Fetzer must have been acutely aware of, as his mother's letter makes clear.[6]

In response to Fetzer's "purpose of ascertaining [SDA's] soundness," as he expressed it in his letter to the Madisons, they assured Fetzer that they had come to doubt the "Spirit of Prophecy" (i.e., Mrs. White's prophetic gifts) not through Canright or any anti-SDA materials but simply due to their detailed comparisons between the "S. of P." and the scriptures, which revealed "startling discoveries," especially regarding Sabbath observance and the apocalyptic interpretations of Daniel, which were at odds with SDA doctrines. This raised serious doubts in the Madisons' minds about the accuracy of the Spirit of Prophecy and therefore the entire Seventh-day Adventist tradition: "The S. of P. is a thread which runs through the whole cord of Adventist philosophy, and which permeates its every thought. It is only too true that when faith in that system is abolished that the rest falls easily. Too often one's faith in erroneous Adventist doctrines is settled by the knowledge that the S. of P. has endorsed such ideas, and for that reason we feel that it is necessary to give that a good share of discussion." It was for this reason, Madison wrote, that he and his wife had begun to circulate their ideas to like-minded friends and found that there were many in the Church who—like Fetzer himself—were in agreement with them.[7]

Ultimately, the Madisons encouraged John and Rhea to do all they could to free themselves from the Church: "We want you to know that we are deeply interested in your problems," they wrote, "for we went through the same thing. It is a wonderful thing to leave S.D.A.'s conscience-free, and we feel freedom from Adventism with its spiritual and mental bondage is freedom indeed." Moreover, having gone through the process and knowing the upset it caused for friends and family, the Madisons promised their absolute discretion: "It goes without saying that your correspondence will be held in the strictest of confidence. Our own folks here know nothing of it." In another letter sent to John and Rhea, now living in Ann Arbor, the Madisons sympathized with the mental anguish the young couple were experiencing: "The intense fear that you speak of, it seems to me can be attributed to a great degree to the incessant hammering which Adventists are continually at to keep people from even daring to think for themselves. We went through that stage and we know exactly what it is like."[8]

The Madisons had recommended that John Fetzer write a number of other dissidents, including George Mattison of Grand Rapids and John Kolvoord of Battle Creek, two of Michigan's leading critics of SDA. This John did, and Kolvoord quickly sent him a copy of his booklet, *The Vision of the Evening and the Morning: A Study of the Prophecy of Daniel VIII* (1907), written with Moses E. Kellogg. The book argued that the Book of Revelation was a historical document, recounting symbolically the fall of Jerusalem and not relating to future events, as Mrs. White had prophesied.[9] Fetzer read the work carefully, underlining and marking many passages. Around the same time, Fetzer also contacted E. S. Ballenger, the editor

6. Issue of the *Gathering Call*.

of the *Gathering Call*, a dissident SDA publication based in Riverside, California. Ballenger told Fetzer in his response that he would send him three issues of the magazine and suggested that he subscribe. Fetzer did, and the extensive underlining in each of Fetzer's issues of the *Gathering Call* suggests that he read them thoroughly. He was apparently especially interested in the shifts in doctrine among early SDA leaders that the magazine so assiduously documented.[10]

In July 1929, Fetzer wrote to the publishing arm of the conservative Moody Bible Institute to inquire whether it had materials related to critiques of Seventh-day Adventism. William Morton of the Moody Press replied, recommending the following: "Ought Christians to Keep the Sabbath" (Torrey); "Seventh Day Adventism Renounced" (Canright); "Adventism Refuted in a Nutshell" (a series of pamphlets by Canright in an envelope); and "Seventh Day Adventism" (Biederwolf), all of which Fetzer ordered and read closely.[11]

Mr. Morton also sent Fetzer a circular describing the Scofield Reference Bible, which was literally the Bible of dispensational premillennialism championed by Evangelical fundamentalists. It is not known whether Fetzer read the prophetic glosses of the Scofield Reference Bible, but he did read C. I. Scofield's *Rightly Dividing the Word of Truth* (1907),[12] and his profuse underlining of this book, which sets forth Scofield's dispensationalist premillennial position so different from Mrs. White's, indicates that Fetzer was at pains to discover the truth through this comparison. However, this procedure only increased his doubts: as he recalled in 1982, "when I began to have doubts about the efficacy of their [SDAs'] position, I started at the only starting point that you could and that was to keep at the fundamentalist research." The result was revealing: "When you start putting one fundamentalist outlook against the other, you run into controversy after controversy. Everything is a difference of opinion since all religions were formed from one little phrase in the bible."[13] From then on, a literal reading of the Bible dogmatically insisted on was something that Fetzer would never again abide.

In addition to Fetzer's theological investigations, it cannot be ignored, too, that Rhea must have had a powerful role in his doubts about the Church. Despite the fact that her parents were ardent Seventh-day Adventists and she went to SDA schools, Rhea, like her brothers, LaMont and LeVant, had become disenchanted with the tradition early in her life. "The matter of religion was always something that all the youngsters in the [Yeager] family argued with the older folks about," Fetzer wrote his mother in 1939.[14] That this was true is borne out in the existing Yeager correspondence from the period, in which all three children voiced criticisms about the narrowness of Seventh-day Adventism.[15] In a letter LeVant wrote to his parents complaining about the continual religious strife in the family since childhood, he said, "You mom and pop are word & letter good Christians; Rhea and I are not, Mont wasn't either but there is only one religion of any consequence, the religion of life itself."[16] By the time John and Rhea met in college, he was much more devout in his Adventist beliefs than was she, and it was Fetzer himself who insisted that Rhea finally be baptized in the SDA tradition, a procedure she "resented."[17] Fetzer, of course, must have been fully aware of his wife's beliefs before marrying her, and perhaps the fact that his questioning of the Church intensified after they were married has much to do with her influence.

Whatever the truth of the matter, the Fetzers finally did make a complete break from the Church sometime in January 1930. The next month, John and Rhea received a letter from Agnes Madison, which said in part, "We were very pleased indeed to know that you had resigned. Probably you think we are getting a little too personal in rejoicing over your affairs, but when you get out of bondage and know what it means to be able to express yourself in work and pleasure without having first to consult your neighbors, then you, too, will rejoice when you see another coming into his own."[18] Thurber Madison also sent a letter of congratulations that contains a remarkably optimistic take on humankind's spiritual quest that is worth quoting in full. "Dear John and Rhea," he wrote,

> I believe that the whole divine plan for mankind at this time is freedom in its truest sense. From all that I can see Biblical prophecy culminated within a short time after the crucifixion. No ceremonies, statutes, observances remain. All that man is to do is to obey the rule of common sense conduct toward his God and fellow men which He put in the mind of man as a fulfillment of Christ's plan. This I believe is the rule of the Holy Spirit.
>
> I disagree with this "weak as I am" philosophy which makes man dependent upon God every minute of the day. I

believe God plants into ALL human minds once and for all a law of conduct which if observed will usher him into a future life with all its rewards. Why some men don't get there is their own moral affair. With this in mind I cannot reconcile myself to the usual conception of prayer. I have always had some doubts in my mind about this. True, Christ prayed, but since his ascension He has given the Holy Spirit which (or whom) I fully believe is planted in every mind; as much a part of him as other physical and mental attributes; given to all to use and to exercise—there even without asking.

In other words, strange as it may seem, I think that man has the equipment to live without sinning; he doesn't have to bow and scrape and agonize to get into the right mental set. The will to do and succeed is there already. Man *can* mold his future (subject of course to heredity and environment) and can overcome through the power that IS there.

How about infallibility of Scriptures? What matters it? Man is free from the letter anyway. Personally I might question some things; not in a skeptical sneering way. Some of the things that Christ is quoted as saying in the N. T. echo some of the traditions and beliefs of the then prevailing sects and divisions of that time. I think some of the disciples may have unconsciously shared them. I wonder (I put this reverently) did Christ Himself become somewhat influenced by prevailing thoughts. He had the weight of humanity upon Him. Anybody who knows the all powerful influence that heredity and environment have upon the human mind knows what I refer to.

If this be skepticism make the most of it. I hope you are not horrified at some of the revelations. Yet you wanted to know, and I am telling you. I hope that in leaving Adventism some of these ideas (and others perhaps) which they hold up like so many boogie men and goblins to scare the delicate minds of the flock may not frighten you.

To sum my reaction, I would say that my mind is in a more wholesome and healthy state than ever before. I believe that I have sized up life's values better than ever. I feel the debris cleared away; old beliefs which in the last analysis amounted to pure superstition are swept out. Psychology and the study of the human mind can and does explain eccentricities and abnormalities, and the way to correct them is just as definite as the way to cure physical ills. Do this and prayer is relegated at best to the inward communings of the mind with itself and to the self-administration of better urges and ideals.[19]

In many ways, Thurber Madison's letter functioned as a kind of declaration of independence for the young John Fetzer. He seems to have internalized Madison's contention "that the whole divine plan for mankind at this time is freedom in its truest sense," for, given the fact that "the Holy Spirit . . . is planted in every mind . . . given to all to use and to exercise," there is no reason "to bow and scrape." Indeed, "man has the equipment to live without sinning" and "*can* mold his own future" and achieve a "healthy and wholesome state" if only he would look not to texts but "to the inward communings of the mind with itself and to the self-administration of better urges and ideals." These twin ideas of the freedom of the spirit and the mind as the place to seek the spirit were to become important guideposts in Fetzer's subsequent spiritual search.

Of all Fetzer's family and friends, it was his mother who took his alienation from Seventh-day Adventism the hardest. "It seems too me as if I would be the happiest woman and mother in the whole world," she wrote John shortly before his break in November 1929, "if you were only well spiritually and physically. What can I do for you[?] One thing I do I pray always for you."[20] And in January 1930, she was still trying to get him to listen to Seventh-day Adventist preaching: "[It will] set you right on the things that worry you." However, in the same letter, she observed, "The church here is going down so fast there is nothing to go [to] but empty seats and we never hear a sermon preached anymore so I feel that soon I shall go into the Baptist church."[21] Apparently, the church in Lafayette continued its decline, and Della did indeed join the Baptists.

Della always continued to worry about John's spiritual health and whether he continued to be a Bible-reading Christian.[22] In 1944, she wrote him, "[Never] forget [that] if you gain the whole world and lose your own soul you havent gained [or] accomplished anything. It shure behooves all of us to look on the other side of life eternal life I mean which is coming to all of us [since] we are here only for a very short time at the longest."[23] She need not have worried. John Fetzer never stopped thinking about the health of his soul and "the other side," nor did he cease being a Christian of a kind. However, his spiritual path was to be very different from the one that his mother had hoped for him.

Fetzer after Seventh-day Adventism

Sometime on or around April 21, 1930, John Fetzer gathered up all the letters and printed materials that had led him out of Seventh-day Adventism and placed them in a simple brown valise that was stored away and forgotten.[24] Fetzer was now ready to move on spiritually, although he would be called on occasionally to counsel others who wished to leave the tradition.[25] Fetzer, however, never forgot his time in the Church, and while his leaving it was painful, he bore no ill will toward it or its members. When, decades later, he was asked about Emmanuel Missionary College, he said that "it was not the place" for him, but he quickly followed up this statement with, "Not that it was a bad environment—it was a very good environment. The people there were excellent people—well-educated, far above average, . . . people who cared and were loving and generous."[26] Indeed, over the years, John and Rhea Fetzer remained in close contact with many of their schoolmates and professors, and once successful, they made significant financial contributions to their old college, renamed Andrews University in 1960.[27] When in 1980 Andrews University awarded Fetzer an honorary LLD degree at its June commencement, his remarks revealed a genuine affection and respect for the institution:

"By modernizing its communications and maintaining high standards of excellence in its curriculum, facilities and spiritual values this University has done its part in advancing the intellectual and moral values in America and throughout the world. As I look back upon my academic days, I must tell you that my past association here has given me a lifetime motivation. It's those fundamental lessons learned in this environment that have helped me to develop a code that has at least been satisfying in my quest to grow."[28]

Indeed, many of the themes of Seventh-day Adventism continued to preoccupy Fetzer for decades to come. While he was doubtful of Mrs. White's prophetic gifts, the idea that there were genuine prophetic individuals in the world was one he never shed. And while he became doubtful of the imminent Second Coming of Christ, he nevertheless held onto the millennial ideal that the world would soon be radically transformed and enjoy a long period of peace and prosperity—a new age of humankind.[29] Moreover, while he rejected the more ascetic aspects of Seventh-day Adventist health reform, the connection between health and the spirit continued to fascinate him and eventually became a major focus of his life's work. And finally, while he rejected the Church's stance on modern science, he nevertheless believed that science without spirit was lacking and, conversely, that true religion would harmonize with science, if not find its proof in it.

Once John Fetzer had broken with Seventh-day Adventism in 1930, he no longer felt he needed to be bound to a single religious tradition to seek the spirit. From then on, he ceased, as he put it, "to be addicted to church activity."[30] He did join the Presbyterian Church later that year, but he was very frank that he did so only for the sake of his business interests and was never active in the congregation.[31] Significantly, however, while he thereafter publicly identified as a Presbyterian for strategic reasons, this in no way stopped him from seeking out and sampling a myriad of other religious traditions. Having given up the exclusivism and dogmatism of Seventh-day Adventism, John Fetzer now had the confidence to launch out on what was to become a lifelong quest for a new worldview that would better express his evolving understanding of the relationship between humanity, spirit, and the cosmos.

3

Restless among the Spirits

Fetzer and the Spiritualist Mediums of Camp Chesterfield (1930s on)

In 1930, John Fetzer was given a business opportunity that changed his life. The powers that were at Emmanuel Missionary College had decided that WEMC, the Radio Lighthouse, was too expensive for the college to run and sought a buyer for its license. Fetzer managed to scrape together the $5,000 necessary to buy the station. Now a commercial operation instead of an educational service, Fetzer had to scramble to drum up the advertising business necessary to keep the enterprise afloat. This was made all the harder since, still located in Berrien Springs, he had to abide by Seventh-day Adventist strictures not to accept ads for "tobacco, meat, coffee, unethical medical practices, the theatre or dancing."[1] Undoubtedly in part to escape such limitations and to find a bigger broadcast market, Fetzer moved the station to Kalamazoo, a small but thriving city to the east of Berrien Springs. Now WKZO, the station went on the air in Kalamazoo in 1931, transmitting from the seventh floor of the Burdick Hotel, where John and Rhea Fetzer made their home for the next six years.[2]

Although a bigger market, Depression-era Kalamazoo was still a hard place for Fetzer to get the radio station established. Credit was tight, and in the beginning, WKZO broadcast only five or six hours a day during prime time. Finding advertisers was difficult too, in part because the city's newspaper, the *Kalamazoo Gazette*, was keen not to let a new technology steal its ad business. What is more, WKZO was originally licensed only as a daytime station, and when in 1932 Fetzer applied to the Federal Communications Commission (FCC) for a full-time license, he was stymied because of a federal law that mandated that multiple stations using the same frequency could not overlap at night. Already, two other stations in Boston and Omaha were broadcasting at WKZO's 590 kilocycles. A directional antenna had been developed to solve this problem but was not yet approved by the FCC. For the next seven years, then, Fetzer spent extended periods in Washington, DC, lobbying the FCC to approve the antenna and grant his request for a full-time license. After much frustrating delay involving not only the FCC but also Congress and the Supreme Court, the so-called "590 case" was finally settled in 1938 in Fetzer's favor. Fetzer's time in the nation's capital had paid off, assuring the survival of WKZO. Moreover, during the time he spent there, he met many powerful people, including Michigan's own senator Art Vandenburg and the future president Harry S. Truman.[3] Such contacts not only were important for the promotion of Fetzer's radio interests but also later brought him opportunities for high-level service to the government.

Fetzer's perseverance during this period is remarkable, and while some of his letters back to Rhea, who effectively ran the radio station in his absence, expressed keen disappointment, they also manifest a buoyancy of spirit that was a lifelong trait. He also found time to enjoy himself. Freed from the asceticism of Seventh-day Adventism, Fetzer developed an active social life and was something of a playboy during this period. In addition to Washington, DC, Fetzer also spent much time in New York City looking for business opportunities if the "590 case" went against him or WKZO failed. While there, his letters show that he often went to Broadway shows and frequented nightclubs such as the Cotton Club, and

7. John E. Fetzer in his WKZO office at the Burdick Hotel, Kalamazoo, Michigan, 1937.

he fell hard for the charms of the Rockettes at Radio City Music Hall. Back home in Kalamazoo, when not working on the radio station, he was not averse to the party life, and despite the national prohibition on alcohol, he knew Kalamazoo's speakeasies and had a taste for bathtub gin.[4] Although working exceedingly hard to make his radio station secure and learn his way around the seats of power that would make this possible, John Fetzer also knew how to enjoy himself.

Whither, then, John Fetzer's spiritual quest? In addition to being a time in which he enjoyed his newfound social freedom and laid the groundwork for his future business success and life of public service, the 1930s were also a time when John Fetzer was introduced to several metaphysical currents that were to have a tremendous impact on the evolution of his post-SDA worldview. One of the earliest of these was Spiritualism.

The Attractions of Spiritualism

In September 1930, John and Rhea Fetzer received a remarkable letter from John's mother, Della. "I have a *confession* to make to you," she wrote:

> You know that I never *believed* in the *fortune telling* or those astrologists but while you were in Washington I was so anxious about you and the things you were trying to do that I went up on Sixth Street to see that woman that Hattie went to see and I yielded to the temptation and had her read for me. Now don't take what I am going to tell you [to] be worth anymore than the paper that it was written on. The woman is a spiritualist and they talk too the dead. The first thing that she did was to talk to your father that is he talked to me threw her and the strange thing about it was the woman speled our names correctly that is Fetzer.

While Della's consultation with a Spiritualist was surprising, that she found one in West Lafayette was not. Almost from the beginning of this made-in-America tradition, Spiritualism had found a welcome home in the Midwest. The Spiritualist movement traces its origins back to the Fox sisters, who in 1848 began to experience communications with the spirits of the dead while living outside of Rochester, New York. Highly publicized in the press of the day, Spiritualism spread both east and west, and the séance, a ritual in which spirits spoke to the living through a medium, became commonplace.[5]

Spiritualism spread rapidly not only in the Northeast but also especially in the Midwest during the decade of the 1850s. In the wake of several tours by the Fox sisters to the region, innumerable Spiritualist "circles" sprang up, and many a "home grown" medium discovered his or her psychic ability to contact the dead and heal the living. Spiritualism was strongest in the growing cities of the region, where Spiritualist circles coalesced into incorporated Spiritualist organizations and then into state conventions. Spiritualism, too, had its representatives in the rural districts of many Midwest states, and here, borrowing from the revivalist tradition of Evangelical Christianity, Spiritualists sought to build community through the convocation of impromptu "camp meetings." In time, many of these Spiritualist camp grounds became institutionalized, with regular meeting times, boards of trustees, and elaborate infrastructure, including auditoriums and permanent housing.[6]

Although much of the popular interest in midwestern Spiritualism stemmed from the sensationalism of spirit manifestations and the like, among committed Spiritualists there was always an intellectual eagerness to explore the complexities of the metaphysical worldview behind the manifestations. Andrew Jackson Davis, the acknowledged "theologian" of American Spiritualism, was a frequent guest at both state and local Spiritualist conventions and traveled the same lyceum circuit that welcomed such luminaries as Ralph Waldo Emerson. Soon, printed material by Davis and others became extremely popular among the reading public, and importantly, the Midwest became a center for the publication of Spiritualist books, journals, and newspapers. According to one student of nineteenth-century Spiritualism, no fewer than seventy-five Spiritualist publications were issued from the Midwest, with Ohio alone accounting for a third of these. Most were short-lived and relatively crude, but some, such as the *Religio-Philosophical Journal*, published in Chicago from 1865 to 1895 (after which it moved to California), achieved international distinction as a sophisticated interpreter of the metaphysical worldview.[7]

Indiana was not immune to the lure of Spiritualism, and in time, it became one of the most active centers of the new religious movement in the Midwest.[8] Spiritualist circles had appeared as early as 1850, with the first Spiritualist churches built by Quaker converts in the southeastern portion of the state. By 1862, enough Spiritualist churches existed to warrant the creation of a state organization of Indiana Spiritualists, which proudly sent its first delegates to the national Spiritualist convention in Chicago in 1873.[9] By the time Della Fetzer had consulted the spirits in West Lafayette, Spiritualism was an old and established tradition in the region. Indeed, in the wake of World War I and the flu pandemic, Spiritualism had even undergone something of a revival during the 1920s, with the number of practicing mediums and their devotees steadily increasing over the decade. Formal membership in Spiritualist churches reached a high point of fifty thousand in 1926, while the number of unofficial believers was probably considerably higher.[10]

John Fetzer's initial reaction to his mother's visit to a Spiritualist was apparently disapproving, probably because the Seventh-day Adventist Church had long been a foe of the Spiritualist tradition and since Ellen G. White's visionary experiences resembled those of Spiritualist mediums or mesmerized subjects.[11] However, once he left that tradition, he likely felt freer to explore this forbidden fruit to see what all the fuss was about. Perhaps another clue as to why Fetzer came to explore Spiritualism has to do with his work with radio and his interest in one of radio's earliest and most enigmatic pioneers, Nikola Tesla (1856–1943). Late in life, when Fetzer was asked about how his earliest experiences in radio had impacted his spiritual life, he said quite emphatically, "Nikola Tesla was our bible."[12] Experimenter, visionary, and eccentric, Tesla was a pioneer of electronic invention, responsible for the rotating magnetic field necessary for an AC motor; the Tesla coil used for producing high-frequency alternating currents; and, most importantly for Fetzer, the wireless transmission of energy at a distance, the precursor to radio. In addition to these demonstrated technologies, Tesla also put forth ideas that even today seem like science fiction. For example, Tesla's ultimate dream was to harness electromagnetic radiation in such a way that he could use the entire earth as a capacitor that would deliver free and abundant energy to everyone on the planet.[13]

In light of Fetzer's early interest in Tesla, it is highly likely that Fetzer read his writings, such as his visionary article "The Problem of Increasing Human Energy," first published in 1900 and frequently reprinted thereafter.[14] Here, Tesla expounded on his rigorously holistic understanding of the nature of humanity:

> When we speak of man, we have a conception of human-
> ity as a whole, and before applying scientific methods to

the investigation of his movement, we must accept this as a physical fact. But can anyone doubt to-day that all the millions of individuals and all the innumerable types and characters constitute an entity, a unit? Though free to think and to act, we are all held together, like the stars in the firmament, with ties inseparable. These ties we cannot see, but we can feel them. I cut myself in the finger, and it pains me; this finger is part of me. I see a friend hurt, and it hurts me, too; my friend and I are one. And now I see stricken down an enemy, a lump of matter which, of all the lumps of matter in the universe, I care least for, and it still grieves me. Does this not prove that each of us is only a part of the whole?[15]

Indeed, Tesla believed that the interconnection of all human beings by invisible "ties inseparable" was the basis for all true religion: "For ages this idea has been proclaimed in the consummately wise teachings of religion, probably not alone as a means of insuring peace and harmony among men, but as deeply founded truth." And while the "Buddhist expresses it in one way, the Christian in another," they "both say the same: We are all one." Moreover, "metaphysical proofs are . . . not the only ones which we are able to bring forth in support of this idea": "Science, too, recognizes this connectedness of separate individuals, though not in quite the same sense as it admits that the suns, planets, and moons of a constellation are one body, and there can be no doubt that it will be experimentally confirmed in times to come, when our means and methods for investigating psychical and other states and phenomena shall have been brought to great perfection."[16] Characteristically, Fetzer interpreted such Teslan statements to mean that just as there were "energy waveforms" such as radio that connected human beings by sound, so there might be "more subtle waveforms" yet to be scientifically detected that connected people directly mind to mind.[17] Thus, it was perhaps Tesla's endorsement of the reality of such "psychical states and phenomena" that piqued Fetzer's curiosity about Spiritualism, the most convenient tradition in which he could experience such psychical phenomena.[18] Whatever the spur, just a few years after Fetzer scolded his mother about consulting the spirits, we find him doing the same himself at a place long known to him due to its proximity to West Lafayette: Camp Chesterfield.[19]

Camp Chesterfield, Indiana

Spiritualists emulated the revivalist techniques of their Evangelical neighbors and adopted the practice of camp meetings as a means to associate with like-minded people and to proselytize the curious. Inspired by an 1883 visit to an exceptionally successful and long-lived example of such a Spiritualist camp in Vicksburg, Michigan, several Spiritualists from the Indianapolis area banded together to organize what was to become the Chesterfield Spiritualist Camp, located on a thirty-four-acre site on the banks of the White River. The first camp meeting, which occurred in 1888, was an ad hoc affair, more picnic than camp. However, by 1891, an inn and a dining hall were now available for the comfort of visitors, tent cabins were erected for staff, and a little later, a large canvas auditorium was constructed to host the displays of the "physical" mediums for which the Camp became famous.[20]

While physical demonstrations always remained popular, the philosophical side of Spiritualism was not neglected at the camp. A lyceum was organized that featured speakers who expounded on the works of Andrew Jackson Davis and other Spiritualist thinkers, as well as mediums who described in florid Victorian detail their time among the spirits. By 1900, Camp Chesterfield was firmly institutionalized, with activities now extending beyond the summer season. Frequent visitors now constructed permanent cottages with gas and electricity, and the grounds were serviced on a regular basis by interurban trolleys from Indianapolis. Given the camp's longevity—it remains active to this day—Camp Chesterfield by the 1920s had become the most important Spiritualist camp in the

Midwest, rivaled only by New York's Camp Lily Dale and Florida's Camp Cassadaga in national prominence.

It is not known exactly why John Fetzer first ventured to Camp Chesterfield; he himself simply said he went "just out of innate curiosity": "Heard about it. Everybody in Indiana had heard about it."[21] Apparently, his first trip there was in 1934.[22] Something or someone there must have made a positive impression on him, because he was hooked and made frequent pilgrimages to the camp for readings well into the 1970s.[23] Not all the mediums there lived up to his expectations, and later in life, he claimed that he could easily spot a fake one;[24] but apparently there were some, such as Lillian Johnson, Charles Swann, and Clifford Bias, whom he came to trust implicitly and to whom he went back year after year.[25] Some were physical mediums who conjured up for John the spirit manifestations of such notables as Abraham Lincoln, Sitting Bull, and Babe Ruth.[26] Others were trance mediums who would enter altered states of consciousness to allow the spirits of the dead to communicate through them by voice, writing, or drawing.

Spiritualists often believe that one is assigned a series of five types of spirit guides, sometimes known as guardian angels. These are the teacher who aids in one's spiritual learning; the Master who represents the highest spiritual level attainable for human beings; the doctor chemist responsible for one's spiritual and physical health; a gatekeeper and protector, often an Indian spirit; and finally, a joy guide, typically a chattering child who helps one find happiness in life. According to an undated note card in Fetzer's hand, probably from the 1960s, his spirit guides were identified as Dr. Ray Fyfe; an anonymous Master; Mary Teresa of Avila, the Carmelite mystic; Pierre Goulan (perhaps the doctor chemist); two Indian protectors, Chief Thunder Cloud ("Apache") and Running Red Fox; and, as joy guide, a little girl named Red Robin. Of these, Fetzer received written communications from Dr. Fyfe, Pierre Goulan, Thunder Cloud, and Running Red Fox, the last two of which bear colored-pencil portraits of their spirit authors. It must be said that the wisdom proffered by these guides was hardly profound ("Remember that temperament is temper that is too old to spank," opined Dr. Fyfe), but these spirit encounters must have been important for Fetzer since he carefully preserved the record of them in his papers.[27]

Especially meaningful for John Fetzer were undoubtedly the spirit communications he received from deceased family members at Camp Chesterfield. Through one medium, John Fetzer heard from his baby brother, Walter, and his father, John A. Fetzer. Both expressed their undying love for John and pride in his accomplishments, and they implicitly confirmed that they were together in the afterlife, united as a family again. Because John had not known his father well in life, communication with him from beyond the grave reinforced for John the importance of family connections, strongly suggesting that these connections were eternal, stretching from the distant past to the unseen future. Perhaps it was for this reason that during this period Fetzer became seriously interested in tracing his family's genealogy. Fetzer devoted the next several decades to the project, resulting in two books, one on his father's side, *One Man's Family* (1964), and another, *The Men from Wengen and America's Agony* (1971), tracing his mother's. Fetzer apparently developed a deep spiritual conviction that by tracing his family tree he was in some sense "liberat[ing] family members," thus "allowing them to move on in the after life."[28] According to Judy Skutch Whitson, Fetzer told her that "the reason he was so intent on doing [genealogy]" was that it allowed him to "go into the darkness of those people's lives wherever they were held in darkness, where their thoughts were keeping them enslaved in darkness," and to "bring them to the Light and lead them out; so it was like a service."[29]

Over the years, the mediums of Camp Chesterfield came to function as resources of last resort when Fetzer's archival research reached dead ends. On several occasions, he consulted them for leads, especially Lillian Johnson, Charles Swann, and Luigi de Paolo.[30] At least twice Fetzer asked for and got portraits of long-lost ancestors for use in his book projects. One was a spirit drawing of Johanna Bunz Fetzer by de Paolo and reproduced in *One Man's Family*. Other portraits came from spirit photographs most likely produced by the medium Charles Swann. According to Fetzer's recollection,

This medium would get people in a circle and they would stand around and hold litmus [photographic?] paper against their solar plexus and after you'd go through the exercise, you'd get a picture. So I obtained these four pictures this way and when they came through I was told who they were. . . . You have to remember these pictures would be from the 16th century, long before photography. Yet these were all obtained through mediumship. . . . I was asking for pictures that were long since gone and I went in and asked for a picture of Christian Winger and this is what I got. And then I asked for his mother and got [it].[31]

Fetzer then turned over the spirit photographs to a professional artist, who rendered them as pastel drawings for publication in *The Men from Wengen and America's Agony*.[32]

The ability of Camp Chesterfield's mediums to put John Fetzer in contact with his dead relatives was one of the attractions of Spiritualism, but the worldview soon came to intrigue him as well. From his first visit on, Fetzer said he read everything he could get his hands on: "Camp Chesterfield had a book shop with a lot of literature in it and I think that every time I went down there I would buy three or four books."[33] It was through this reading that Fetzer was first introduced to a fully articulated vision of life, death, God, and the cosmos very different from his Christian upbringing.

Spiritualism's worldview evolved out of several metaphysical currents then popular in early nineteenth-century America. Two of the most important of these were Swedenborgianism and mesmerism. Swedenborgianism was based on the writings of the mystical Swedish seer Emanuel Swedenborg (1688–1772). Swedenborg was a trained scientist who specialized initially in mining and metallurgy but who later sought to master and extend all the known sciences. At age fifty, he began to experience a series of religious visions that allowed him to travel in higher worlds, where he conversed with spirits of the dead, angels, Jesus, and God

8. One of Fetzer's spirit photographs from Camp Chesterfield.

himself, who was symbolized as a great central sun. In the last years of his life, Swedenborg produced a stream of books such as *Secrets of Heaven* (1749) and *Heaven and Hell* (1758) describing his visionary experiences in great detail. Here he related how it was revealed to him that the material and spiritual worlds were simply mirror images of each other, intimately connected and sustained by the continual circulation or "influx" of divine love throughout the cosmos. Further, Swedenborg taught that physical and mental health here on earth were available to all those who sought to live in harmony with God through his divine emanations, and that after death, one chose where one went based on the character one developed in life. Salvation in Swedenborg's system was a continual process in which the spirits of the blessed ascended through the three levels of heaven by making more perfect their harmony with God and cosmos.[34]

Swedenborg's writings caught on in the English-speaking world, and the first Swedenborgian church—known as the Church of the New Jerusalem or simply the New Church—was founded in England in 1787. By this time, Swedenborg's works were already available in the United States, leading to the founding of the first Swedenborgian society in Philadelphia in 1792. This was followed by vigorous proselytization efforts into the interior of the nation. In the Midwest, the most famous Swedenborgian missionary was, of course, John Chapman (1774–1845), who, as "Johnny Appleseed," scattered Swedenborgian tracts along with his seeds as he traveled the back trails of Ohio and Indiana. (Johnny Appleseed's burial place in Fort Wayne, Indiana, is now something of a minor tourist attraction.) A more substantial, if less colorful, contribution to the extension of Swedenborgianism was made by a host of more conventional missionaries, men such as the Reverend George Field, who, from 1838 to 1850, planted congregations in Illinois, Missouri, and Michigan. Indeed, so popular a vogue did the writings of the Swedish seer have in Michigan during the 1840s that there was a serious proposal to name the capital of the new state "Swedenborg." In Indiana, too, Swedenborgianism had an early presence, again thanks to Rev. Field: both Goshen and La Porte emerged as centers for this tradition in the state, with the La Porte congregation, founded in 1842, now the longest continually operating church in the city.[35]

The second element leading to Spiritualism as a religious movement was the popularity of mesmerism and the belief in animal magnetism. Franz Mesmer (1734–1815) was an Austrian physician who posited the existence of an ethereal electric "fluid" permeating the universe. He called this fluid "animal magnetism." By concentrating and manipulating animal magnetism, certain gifted individuals could place others in mesmeric trances, during which, among other things, spiritual healing could be effected. By the early nineteenth century, the practice of mesmerism had been brought to the United States, where itinerant "magnetizers" made the rounds of the lyceum circuit giving demonstrations of the power of animal magnetism, all to great acclaim. In addition to healing, one of the curious phenomena noticed by professional magnetizers was that occasionally entranced persons would begin speaking in voices not their own and reporting ideas and information beyond their ken. This phenomenon was soon attributed to contact with the spirits of the dead, and it was soon asserted that the mesmeric subject was acting as a "medium" through which the spirits spoke. Such a sensational by-product of mesmerism made mesmeric demonstrations even more popular with the American public, hungry for wonders of all kinds.[36]

Swedenborgianism and mesmerism soon became indissolubly linked during the 1840s and coalesced in the theological writings of the "Seer of Poughkeepsie," Andrew Jackson Davis (1826–1910). It is Davis, not the Fox sisters, who probably should be seen as the true beginning of the Spiritualist movement in this country. Davis began his career as a mesmeric healer but soon found that while in a mesmeric trance, he could travel in the spirit world and meet with many of the great spiritual Masters of previous generations, the most important of whom were the Roman physician Galen and Emanuel Swedenborg himself. Through dozens of books such as *The Principles of Nature* (1847), Davis articulated a complicated system he referred to as Harmonialism. Harmonialism stressed a number of Swedenborgian ideas, such as the divine central sun that emits a constant flow of spiritual energy throughout the concentric spheres of the cosmos; the microcosmic nature of mind, body, and soul; and the possibility of continual spiritual perfection after death. Importantly, unlike Swedenborgianism, Davis stressed the availability of spirit revelation to all, thus giving an impetus for the experiences of mediums everywhere, such as the Fox sisters. Later, Davis emphasized the compatibility of his system of Spiritualism with science; after all, this was the era in which invisible natural forces were being harnessed for communication, for example, the electric telegraph, an instrument every bit as mysterious to the general public of the day as was the Spiritualist séance.[37]

By the second half of the nineteenth century, the works of Swedenborg and Andrew Jackson Davis came to function as sacred scriptures for the Spiritualist movement.[38] Fetzer may have read some of Swedenborg and Davis during this period (he certainly could not have avoided hearing about them in discourses at Camp Chesterfield), and we do know for a fact that later in life, he read such key twentieth-century Spiritualist texts as F. W. H. Myer's *Human Personality and the Survival of Bodily Death*

(1903) and the works of Arthur Findlay, including *The Rock of Truth or Spiritualism, the Coming World Religion* (1933).[39] However, during his early sojourns at Camp Chesterfield, the version of the Spiritualist worldview that Fetzer was most likely exposed to was the Spiritualist creed developed by the National Association of Spiritualist Churches (NASC), with which the camp was loosely associated. The creed essentially simplified the metaphysical and theological concepts of Swedenborg and Davis into a form that easily explained the rudiments of Spiritualism as a religion.

Nine Principles of the National Association of Spiritualist Churches (NASC)

1. We believe in Infinite Intelligence.

2. We believe that the phenomena of Nature, both physical and spiritual, are the expression of Infinite Intelligence.

3. We affirm that a correct understanding of such expression and living in accordance therewith, constitute true religion.

4. We affirm that the existence and personal identity of the individual continue after the change called death.

5. We affirm that communication with the so-called dead is a fact, scientifically proven by the phenomena of Spiritualism.

6. We believe that the highest morality is contained in the Golden Rule: "Whatsoever ye would that others should do unto you, do ye also unto them."

7. We affirm the moral responsibility of individuals, and that we make our own happiness or unhappiness as we obey or disobey Nature's physical and spiritual laws.

8. We affirm that the doorway to reformation is never closed against any soul here or hereafter.

9. We affirm that the precepts of Prophecy and Healing contained in all sacred texts are Divine attributes
proven through Mediumship.[40]

Though few in number, the nine principles of the NASC provide all
the doctrinal elements found in most religions: theology, cosmology,
anthropology, ethics, and soteriology. The first three principles outlined
the cosmo-theology of spiritual monism of the Spiritualist worldview.
Unlike the dualistic Judeo-Christian view of God and the universe as
completely separate (since God created the universe ex nihilo) or the
Godless monism of materialist science that viewed everything as matter, Spiritualists saw everything existing as part of "Infinite Intelligence,"
essentially an impersonal God of spirit that emanated itself to create both
the spiritual and physical universe. John Fetzer was already conversant
with the philosophical distinctions between monism and dualism since
one of the earliest books in his library, James H. Ryan's *Introduction to
Philosophy* (1924), was largely structured around this metaphysical question.[41] Based on his frequent underlinings and other annotations, it is
obvious that Fetzer thought long and hard about this issue and therefore grasped that such a spiritual monistic worldview held out hope for
the reconciliation of science and religion. For example, with regard to
anthropology, spiritual monism meant that human beings were so consti-
tuted that their happiness entailed obedience to the laws of both nature
and spirit (principle 7), laws that could be discovered not only in revealed
texts (principle 9) but also "scientifically" through the use of human reason (principle 5). Moreover, such discovery was humankind's moral obli-
gation (principle 7), which could all be summed up in the ethics of loving
kindness as found in the Golden Rule (principle 6).

There were other aspects of the Spiritualist worldview that Fetzer found
attractive. For instance, despite the fact that we are all part of an impersonal
God, Spiritualism nevertheless taught that human personality is eternal
and survives death (principles 4 and 5); and while the Judeo-Christian
religions see death as a prelude to final judgment and punishment for

the wicked, Spiritualism sees no time limit for salvation or any postmortem punishment: souls after death have an eternity in which to progress to final perfection (principle 8). After the anxiety engendered by the orthodox Christian belief that if perfection were not achieved in this life, one might be damned to hell for all eternity (or simply annihilated, as in SDA theology), Fetzer must have found the Spiritualist notion of endless progress in the afterlife liberating. Years later, when Fetzer was in the last decade of his life, an interviewer asked him about his thoughts of life after death. His response echoed many of the ideas he first encountered in Spiritualism and the NASC creed:

> I don't believe that man comes into this life to have a shallow experience, make some improvements and developments, only to fade away to nothing. There's something more. Five minutes after man discards his material body in this world, he could assume another body, another form. He could be operating on another channel, a new frequency, a new plane of existence. I think that every person will transfer to that new plane, but he or she will be precisely in the same place or life status as when the person was in the previous plane. The kind of life you had in the old channel will have nothing to do with the new channel. However, you may be able to take advantage of the mistakes you've made. The next channel will bring great opportunity for all of us.[42]

It is clear that much of the NASC creed was constructed to point up differences between Spiritualism and the reigning orthodoxy of Christianity. It is important to point out, however, that while Spiritualism defined itself over against mainstream Christianity, as did its chief theorist, Andrew Jackson Davis, Spiritualism as a movement was not anti-Christian. Principle 9 ("We affirm that the precepts of Prophecy and Healing contained in all sacred texts are Divine attributes proven through Mediumship") was added in 1944 to make this explicit, for, according to B. F. Austin in his *The A.B.C. of Spiritualism* (1920), "The Bible so far as it is inspired and true is based upon Mediumship and therefore, both Christianity (the simple and beautiful teachings of Jesus—real primitive Christianity) and Spiritualism rest on the same basis." Thus, "Spiritualists as a body venerate the name and character of Jesus and regard him as the world's greatest Teacher and Exemplar," albeit "one of many Savior Christs, who at different times have come into the world to lighten its darkness and show by precept and example the way of life to men."[43] For Fetzer, not wholly willing to give up on the Christian pietism of his childhood, such sentiments must have also been welcome, cushioning the fact that Spiritualism discarded most of the orthodox Christian doctrines he imbibed in his youth.

Spiritual Healing and Divination

Many of the practitioners at Camp Chesterfield did not limit themselves to the role of medium contacting the dead but also claimed other psychic powers, such as spiritual healing and divination. Spiritual healing was frequently practiced at Camp Chesterfield, and indeed, Spiritualism itself developed in part out of earlier forms of mesmeric healing. Typically, mediums would enter into a trance that allowed them to clairvoyantly diagnose the source of a person's physical ailment and then make recommendations for its treatment. Although Fetzer was beginning to suffer from ailments such as ulcers that were probably related to the stress of building his broadcast business, there is no record that he took advantage of the opportunities for spiritual healing at Camp Chesterfield. However, we do know that it was here that he first heard of America's most famous trance healer, Edgar Cayce.[44] Cayce, known as "the sleeping prophet," gained a following during the 1910s and '20s not only because of his ability to diagnose patients clairvoyantly at great distances while in a trance but also because of the novel remedies that he prescribed. Fetzer never met Cayce, who died in 1945, but he was fascinated by the transcripts of his trance sessions and read the several biographies written about him. Later in life, Fetzer made contact with the Association for Research and

Enlightenment (ARE), which was set up to preserve and study Cayce's teachings, and eventually he submitted to medical treatments based on those teachings.[45]

Of more immediate interest to Fetzer were the various kinds of divination he saw practiced at Camp Chesterfield. Divination is an ancient practice that involves the use of psychic means to predict events or to guide a person's future actions. Divination can be done either through simple clairvoyance or through the use of any number of ritual tools such as astrology, Tarot cards, and the modern Ouija board. Fetzer at various times in his life used all of these means and more, and it is likely that he first encountered them being used seriously during his visits to Camp Chesterfield. Fetzer, for example, often cited the prediction of a Chesterfield clairvoyant in 1934 that late in life, a young woman would appear at a critical time and would make an admirable secretary. Looking back on that in 1982, Fetzer claimed that that was exactly what happened in 1972 when he hired Carolyn Dailey in the wake of the unexpected death of his longtime secretary, Wilma Berteema.[46]

Astrology, too, became an important tool for Fetzer. Astrology had undergone a revival in the United States during the 1920s.[47] During the 1930s and '40s, when Fetzer was residing in Washington, DC, his letters occasionally speak of consulting the local astrologers.[48] In a letter of 1938, for example, he wrote to Rhea, "Yesterday had some fun consulting an astrologer. She said we would win this case and that the whole thing would be settled in eight months or less. Told me a lot of other things which will be interesting to see if they happen."[49] Apparently, this was not unusual among the denizens of the nation's capital: in another letter from 1948, he wrote, "Incidentally while in Washington I ran into Ella McClaren, the astrologist. As you know about half the US Senate consults her. I really got a kick out of what she told me."[50] In yet another letter, this time from 1952, Fetzer mentions, "yesterday I stopped in to see a Fortune Teller who reads cards," and he was quite intrigued by the results.[51] What is more, during the early 1930s, perhaps after Fetzer's first visit to Camp Chesterfield, WKZO began to feature El Haren, who advertised himself as a "world famous astrologer" who would "answer questions on Business, Finance, Love, Marriage, and Other Important Matters."[52]

Perhaps the most useful form of psychic technology that Fetzer encountered was the Ouija board. A combination of the letter boards used by nineteenth-century Spiritualists to translate raps and taps into letters of the alphabet and the planchette used for automatic writing, the modern Ouija board was patented by William Fuld in 1890, the name simply a combination of the French and German words for "yes." Since its introduction, the Ouija board has sold millions of units and continues to be popular today, one of the most widely used divination tools by Spiritualists and non-Spiritualists alike. Consisting of a board with the alphabet printed at the top, numbers along the bottom, and "yes" and "no" at the corners, users of the Ouija board place their fingers lightly on the tripod planchette and wait for the spirits to move the pointer along the board.[53] Again, it is quite possible that Fetzer first saw one in use at Camp Chesterfield and took up the practice himself, since the beauty of the Ouija board was that one could operate it anywhere without the need of a medium or clairvoyant (although Fetzer was careful never to use it alone, lest it evoke powers he could not control).[54] Over the years, Fetzer used it again and again to make business and personal decisions and especially to find leads for his genealogical research.[55] Indeed, according to Judy Skutch Whitson, the spiritual purpose of his genealogical research—to lead the dead out of darkness toward freedom in the afterlife—was only revealed to him after a session with the Ouija board.[56]

With all forms of divination, however, Fetzer evinced a critical spirit, not accepting everything predicted. Of one session with an astrologer, he observed, "She had the faculty of conveying the impression that she knew more than she actually does"; and of another, a former "chorus girl," he said, "I saw her on numerous occasions and she was giving me names of ancestors to look for and not any of those were accurate—it was a complete waste of time. It led me down a lot of alleys."[57] This was true too of some Tarot sessions: "I don't know if these things are worth while or not. It becomes quite confusing and probably is a waste of time."[58] Indeed, after much experience with such people, Fetzer said. "I could really tell when I got through with them how many were bluffing."[59] Nevertheless, Fetzer must have found at least some of the results useful, since he continued to consult "fortune tellers," Tarot cards, and the Ouija board many times in the years to come.

Spiritualism and divination had a decided impact on Fetzer's spiritual quest, but it was only the beginning of his investigations into metaphysical traditions and techniques. After his experience with SDA, never again would Fetzer be tied down to one belief system, and indeed, from this point forward, a fundamental pattern developed in his spiritual quest in which Fetzer acted as the consummate *bricoleur*, sampling many spiritual traditions, accepting some of their elements and rejecting others, all in the attempt to create a worldview that would work for him.[60] In this sense, Fetzer's worldview was always a work in progress, with one discovery leading him on to another and new discoveries continually enriching his approach to life, the universe, and God. Indeed, while Spiritualism provided him some very durable ideas, it also served as a gateway to other metaphysical ideas and movements. It was not long before Fetzer was exploring the constellation of ancient wisdom traditions, to which we turn next.

Finding Ancient Wisdom in the Midwest

Freemasonry, Hermeticism, and Rosicrucianism (1930s on)

The late 1930s and '40s were a period of immense work for John E. Fetzer. Radio had now become mainstream, and competition between stations and networks was fierce. Despite his position as president of only a small outlet in a small midwestern town, Fetzer continued to fight his way forward. In addition to stabilizing and then expanding the advertising base for his radio station, WKZO, in Kalamazoo, Fetzer became active in trade organizations such as the Michigan Association of Broadcasters, of which he was elected vice president in 1936, and the National Association of Broadcasters, to whose board of directors he was elected two years later. By 1940, WKZO was transmitting eighteen hours a day, and in 1945, the Fetzer Broadcasting Company won a license for WJEF in Grand Rapids, which eventually became western Michigan's first FM station.[1]

9. John E. Fetzer on the air at WJEF, January 1, 1949.

Meanwhile, Fetzer's contacts in Washington led to opportunities for government service during World War II. The first was an appointment in 1944 by President Franklin D. Roosevelt as assistant director for broadcast censorship, which meant an extended stay in the nation's capital, where he and Rhea lived for a year. Then, in the wake of the German surrender in 1945, General Dwight D. Eisenhower tapped Fetzer to accompany a group of broadcast executives and journalists to survey the state of radio in postwar Europe.[2] This was the first time that Fetzer had returned to Europe since his trip twenty years before, and the changes he saw wrought by the war were dreadful, especially in Germany, where destruction was everywhere. For someone of his spiritual sensitivities, Fetzer must have found aspects of the trip somewhat disconcerting: from the center of evil that was Hitler's Berlin bunker, where he was allowed to wander at will, he traveled to the splendor of the Vatican, where he toured the Sistine Chapel and met with Pope Pius XII, whom he found "a man of spirit and a man totally, totally, dedicated to his function." Later, Fetzer said that this trip was one of the most formative experiences of his life.[3]

Although the 1930s and '40s were years of increasing personal success, Fetzer nevertheless understood that the economic dislocations of the Great Depression followed by the carnage of World War II signaled that—morally and spiritually—the world was headed in the wrong direction. This was especially depressing when one noted the great advances in science and technology that these two decades produced, including radio. In the dedicatory address for WJEF, Fetzer observed,

> Living in this enriched world, released from so many of his former physical burdens, blessed with enlarged opportunities for greater knowledge and understanding, with an increasing margin for leisure for enjoyment and inspiration, surely man had reason to look forward to an era of enlightenment and peace among the nations of the world. And yet, the unhappy fact is that today we find man once again using instrumentalities of destruction. Discoveries of science, dedicated to prolonging and enriching life, are being used to wipe out human beings on a scale and a manner so wanton as to eclipse the most barbaric episodes of recorded history. The ingenious and powerful machines by which we have linked together the furthermost corners of the globe are now devoted to service in the wholesale destruction of life and property.[4]

It was against this backdrop of global insecurity, violence, and the misuse of science that John Fetzer continued his spiritual quest. To some degree, Spiritualism helped to put recent history into perspective and to offer some hope for the future, but something more was needed. Humankind had developed science and technology to a high state, and the results were powerful; but the human race lacked the wisdom to use it correctly. It was clear that more guidance was needed, but guidance from whom and from

10. John E. Fetzer and other broadcast executives meeting with Dwight D. Eisenhower at SHAEF headquarters during European tour, 1945.

where? Thus, it was during this period that Fetzer began to explore other metaphysical traditions that not only promised a more robust plan for the future than did Spiritualism but, like Christianity, could also claim roots in the wisdom traditions of the humankind's ancient past.

Fetzer and Freemasonry

Sometime in 1933 or shortly before, John Fetzer became a Freemason, joining Kalamazoo's Anchor Lodge in Strict Observance (S.O.) No. 87 of the Free and Accepted Masons. He remained a member in good standing of this lodge for the rest of his life.[5] Perhaps prompted to join by his half brother Homer, who was a lifelong and very active Mason,[6] Fetzer probably joined the lodge in part for the contacts he would make there, which would help him break into Kalamazoo's social, political, and business elites. Membership in a lodge also conferred some advantage in his dealings in Washington, DC, where many of the powerbrokers were Masons: in at least one instance, an FCC commissioner, Governor Norman S. Case, indicated his support for Fetzer during a hearing on the 590 case by flashing him a Masonic sign.[7] However this may have been, Fetzer found much more in Freemasonry than simple fellowship and commercial and political advantage. Among other things, Freemasonry provided him with a set of teachings and symbolism that resonated with his developing worldview, as well as a set of rituals that filled a deep need in his life for spiritual practice.

The history of Freemasonry is complex, and its reputed origins in medieval guilds of itinerant ("free") stonemasons are still hotly debated. However, in its modern form, Freemasonry sprang from a meeting in London of four existing lodges to form the Grand Lodge of England in 1717. In the wake of the formation of the Grand Lodge, new Masonic lodges spread throughout the British Isles and the European continent during the eighteenth century. As one writer has described early Freemasonry, it was "largely a product of the Age of Enlightenment," with "lodges commonly [meeting] in the upstairs rooms of pubs—accessible but private venues that enable men from different classes to meet 'on the level' for nonsectarian philosophical discussions supplemented by much food and ale."[8] So popular did these meetings become that soon Freemasons were building separate buildings dedicated to the purpose. Such Masonic "temples" now became commonplace in many towns and cities. True to the spirit of the Enlightenment, any freeborn white male was eligible for membership, provided he was of good character, acknowledged monotheism and the brotherhood of man, and could find a sponsor among existing members. This meant that for the first time, Protestants, Catholics, and Jews could meet on equal terms and engage in rational debate—although not on religion or politics, which were regarded as topics too contentious for gentlemen to engage in without rancor. As the Masonic "Anderson's Constitutions" of 1738 put it, it was enough that a prospective initiate "adhere to that Religion in which all Men agree (leaving each Brother to his own particular Opinions) that is, to be Good Men and True, Men of

Honour and Honesty, by whatever Names, Religions or Persuasions they may be distinguish'd."[9]

In North America, Freemasonry enjoyed great popularity at the end of the colonial period, spreading throughout the thirteen original colonies and then into the hinterland shortly after the Revolutionary War.[10] For many members, Masonic lodges provided a continuity of fellowship and a source of intellectual stimulation lacking on the frontier. It is not surprising, then, that we find lodges popping up in the Northwest Territory, the heart of what was to become the Midwest, almost as soon as the earliest settlements were platted. Settlers from New England, Upstate New York, and Kentucky organized the first lodges in Ohio in the 1790s, and from there, Freemasonry quickly spread throughout the region.[11] The earliest Masonic lodge in Michigan dates from 1764, when a military lodge was warranted among British troops in Detroit, and by 1794, six more lodges could be found in the city. In 1826, there were enough new lodges in Michigan and Wisconsin to necessitate the creation of the Grand Lodge of Michigan, again in Detroit.[12] The number of lodges grew apace throughout the state during the nineteenth century (423 by 1899), and by 1900, even the smallest towns could boast a Masonic temple. By this time, Kalamazoo had two "blue lodges," that is, lodges where the first three initiatory rituals are performed: Kalamazoo No. 22, chartered in 1849, and Anchor Lodge of S.O., chartered in 1857.[13] By 1922, Masonry was so popular in Michigan that Masons throughout the state contributed to the building of the neo-Gothic Detroit Masonic Temple, still the largest such temple in the world. The growth of Masonry in Michigan reflected trends in the nation at large: in 1930, over three million men were members, some 12 percent of the native white adult male population of the United States.[14]

When John Fetzer joined Kalamazoo's Anchor Lodge in the early 1930s, he was joining what was arguably the most successful fraternal order in the United States. Like millions of other American men, his reasons for joining were many. Fellowship and status within one's community played a part, but so too did an attraction to American Freemasonry's growing emphasis on civic service and philanthropy. Patriotism, too, was another strong motivation. A number of the nation's Founding Fathers such as George Washington, Benjamin Franklin, and Paul Revere were Freemasons, and Masonic mythology had long claimed that Masons had played an outsized role in fomenting the Revolution and establishing the American Republic. Many Masons continued to believe that the craft would be instrumental in realizing the sacred destiny of the nation (such was the meaning of the purportedly Masonic symbol of the all-seeing eye above the unfinished pyramid on the back of the dollar bill).[15] The Masonic contention that the United States had been founded to perform a sacred mission to the rest of the world was one that Fetzer wholeheartedly embraced.

All of this undoubtedly had an appeal for John Fetzer, but the fact that he chose to join Anchor Lodge of S.O. No. 87 over Kalamazoo's older Lodge No. 22 signals that his interest in Freemasonry went beyond simply fellowship, charity, and patriotism to something deeper. One of the reasons men in the thousands joined Masonic lodges in the nineteenth century was that many were seeking the spiritual experience that comes from meaningful ritual, something that America's ritual-poor Protestantism did not provide.[16] Thus, Masonic rituals developed into highly formal and complex acts that required special rooms fitted out with specific symbols and elaborate props and costumes in order to be performed. There also developed during the period complex philosophical and religious interpretations of the rituals.[17] In the twentieth century, however, there was a notable slackening in interest in the rituals to the point of perfunctoriness, and most lodges came to emphasize informal good fellowship, patriotism, and charity at the expense of ritual.[18] Not so the Strict Observance blue lodges. They continued the early emphasis on ritual performance, insisting on proper dress and behavior, formal atmosphere, ritual precision, and a fairly deep understanding of the meaning behind both the rituals and the symbols they employed.[19] The fact that all of this took more time and effort than required in other blue lodges meant that John Fetzer's choice of a Strict Observance lodge was not an idle one.

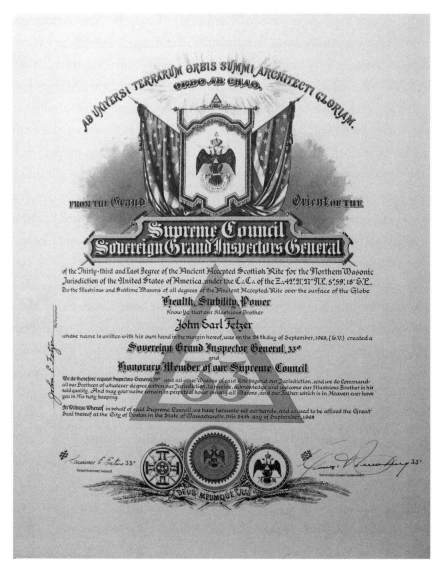

11. John E. Fetzer's Scottish Rite 33° Certificate.

And what were the rituals and teachings that attracted Fetzer? As a blue lodge, Anchor Lodge provided Fetzer with the first three degrees of Masonry: Entered Apprentice (1°), Fellow Craft (2°), and Master Mason (3°). To achieve each of these degrees, which correspond to body, mind, and spirit, respectively, the initiate is required to memorize the ritual, understand the symbols and vows used in the ritual, and then correctly perform the ritual in the presence of the Masters of the lodge. Each of these rituals is performed in the lodge room, whose symbolism makes it a re-creation of Solomon's Temple. Indeed, Solomon's Temple plays many roles in Masonry. Masonic mythology traces the origins of the order back to the ancient stonemasons who built that edifice, a fact reflected in the Order's logo, a crossed square and compass with the letter *G* for "geometry" in the center. Even if one does not take this mythology literally, however, Solomon's Temple remains important due to its multiple levels of symbolic association: for some, it is a microcosm mirroring the macrocosm, but for others, it symbolizes the human mind. For, just as the innermost chamber of Solomon's Temple—the Holy of Holies—was the meeting point between humans and God, so too the innermost recess of the human psyche can play this role, if properly purified through ethical conduct consisting of the Masonic virtues of "faith, hope, and charity; brotherly love, relief, and truth; temperance, fortitude, prudence, and justice."[20] As Fetzer went through the three rituals, the presence of Old Testament motifs and the emphasis on traditional virtues must have appealed to his abiding Christian pietism, while the emphasis on the connection between macrocosm and microcosm, along with its psychological interpretations, fit well with the spiritual monism he was imbibing in Spiritualism.

What is more, the blue lodge rituals highlighted another virtue that also appealed to Fetzer: secrecy. In the third degree, the initiate plays the role of Hiram Abiff, the legendary master mason who built Solomon's Temple and who allowed himself to be murdered rather than reveal the password to Masonic secrets to the unworthy. For his faithfulness unto death, Hiram was rewarded by being raised from his grave, signaling to the initiate not only that he has progressed to a new level on his spiritual quest but also the importance of secrecy to the successful pursuit of that quest.[21] This was a teaching that Fetzer took to heart. In later years, he told confidants that he kept his spiritual interests a secret so as not to jeopardize his business interests, but it is hard to ignore the contribution of this core Masonic teaching to Fetzer's reticence about his spiritual path. Only once did he comment in print about his commitment to Freemasonry and then only obliquely: in his ruminations at the end of *One Man's Family*, he said that his philosophy of life is based on "that which is *deeply* and *subtly* hidden in the *wisdom philosophy* enunciated in the distant past" and that his readers "may require the prolific use of the square and compass in order to comprehend its geometric proportions."[22]

John Fetzer achieved the status of Master Mason on November 13, 1933. He must have found the experience worthwhile, since he quickly went on to the higher degrees. European Freemasons had devised a whole host of additional degrees beyond the third, which in the United States during the nineteenth century were gathered together into two "appendant" orders, the York and Scottish Rites.[23] Fetzer avidly participated in both. In the York Rite, Fetzer rapidly rose through the lower degrees of the Kalamazoo Royal Arch Masons (Chapter No. 13): Master Mark Mason (October 8, 1935), Most Excellent Master (October 29, 1935), Royal Arch Mason (February 25, 1936). He was then created a Knights Templar by the Peninsula Commandery No. 8 on April 8, 1936 (his Knights Templar hat and cloak are still preserved in the Fetzer archives). Once the York Rite was completed, he made even faster progress in the Scottish Rite, which was headquartered in Grand Rapids: initiated on October 20, 1936, he achieved the 32° two days later. Fetzer then went on to join the Grand Rapids Saladin Lodge of the Shriners later that year. Despite his rapid progress, Fetzer remained loyal to all the Masonic bodies that he joined, achieving life-member status in each during the 1960s. This culminated in his elevation to the rank of Sovereign Grand Commander 33° and Honorary Member of the Grand Council of the Scottish Rite in Boston on September 24, 1969. To the end of his life, Fetzer wore a gold Masonic ring with pride.[24]

Importantly for Fetzer's spiritual development, the higher degrees of Freemasonry probably brought him into contact with an even greater range of spiritual ideas and symbols than ever before. Ostensibly, the degrees of both the York and Scottish Rites were simply expansions of the mythology of Hiram Abiff, Solomon's Temple, and other Old Testament motifs, with medieval Knights Templar legends added for good measure.[25] However, ever since the higher degrees were created in the eighteenth century, many Masons were tempted to find deeper meanings in them, seeing echoes of other, more esoteric mythologies and symbol systems such as Hermeticism, Rosicrucianism, the Jewish mystical system of the kabbalah, and the thought of the ancient Greek philosophers Pythagoras and Euclid. Further, given impetus by the newly emerging field of comparative religion in the nineteenth century, some commentators such as the American Albert Pike sought to find in Freemasonry the epitome of all world religions past and present. Some even claimed that the elements of Freemasonry had been passed down through the generations by bands of hidden Masters whose lineage stretched back to the days of Noah or even Adam. It is not known where or when John Fetzer first learned of these esoteric interpretations of Freemasonry. We do know that Fetzer owned Mackey's two-volume *An Encyclopedia of Freemasonry* (1927), a standard work that extensively treated these subjects.[26] Moreover, throughout his life, Fetzer remained attentive to works that developed the esoteric background of Freemasonry, such as Corinne Heline's *New Age Bible Interpretation* (1946) and the works of Manly P. Hall, whose monumental *The Secret Teachings of All Ages* has remained a favorite of esoterically inclined Masons ever since its first publication in 1928. It was a book Fetzer knew well.[27]

Hermeticism and Rosicrucianism

It is highly possible that Fetzer's interest in esoteric Freemasonry led him to two modern works in the Western esoteric tradition that we know he read and annotated: *The Kybalion: A Study of the Hermetic Philosophy of Ancient Egypt and Greece* (1908), attributed to "Three Initiates"; and *Soul! The Soul-World: The Homes of the Dead* (1872), by Paschal Beverly Randolph.[28] The former Fetzer probably read in the late 1930s and the latter in the 1960s.[29] Both were to have a profound effect on his thinking, and interestingly, both were products of the Midwest.

Although published anonymously as the work of "Three Initiates," *The Kybalion* is most likely the work of a Chicagoan, William Walker Atkinson (1862–1932), a noted writer and publisher of dozens of extremely popular books on metaphysical spirituality, yoga, and popular psychology. *The Kybalion* was by far the most successful of these, becoming "one of the most important and influential occult texts written in America."[30] Published by the Yogi Publication Society, located in Chicago's massive Masonic Temple, *The Kybalion* purports to be a primer on the Hermetic philosophy as expounded by the legendary Hermes Trimegistus (the "thrice great"), to whom the book was dedicated. According to the introduction, Hermes "dwelt in Old Egypt in the days when the present race of men was in its infancy." Here he taught "the fundamental and basic teachings" to a group of Masters who in turn formed the "Great Lodge of Lodges" to secretly pass the teachings down through generations of hidden adepts, belief in which Fetzer came to share.[31] What we actually know of Hermeticism with any historical confidence, however, is to be found in the *Corpus Hermeticum*, a series of anonymous ancient texts that present a form of Neoplatonism clothed in the symbols of ancient Egypt. Since their rediscovery and publication during the Renaissance, the monistic philosophy of the *Corpus Hermeticum* formed the basis for most of the Western esoteric movements that developed thereafter. Atkinson's own presentation of the Hermetic tradition reflects this long tradition tracing back to the *Corpus Hermeticum*, although *The Kybalion* mixes in concepts gleaned from Spiritualism, Theosophy, and New Thought, an influential American movement emphasizing the power of mind over matter that developed out of nineteenth-century mesmerism and Christian Science. Ideas from contemporary psychology and natural science were used as well.[32]

The Kybalion is organized around the exposition of seven principles or laws, all of which emphasize the unity of the cosmos. The most important of these are the principles of mentalism (everything there is in the cosmos is mind or sentient spirit), correspondence (everything is a microcosm that reflects the macrocosm), and vibration (all is in motion and vibrates).[33] Fetzer undoubtedly heard variations on these laws of spiritual monism from the Spiritualists at Camp Chesterfield, as they echo similar themes in Swedenborg and Andrew Jackson Davis. *The Kybalion*, however, reduced these laws to a level of abstraction and systematicity that must have appealed to the engineer in Fetzer.[34]

Fetzer, for example, specifically marked the chapter on the principle of vibration: in it, Atkinson postulates that matter and energy are the same things, only at different rates of vibration. Atkinson also postulates that thought and emotion, which are manifestations of mind, are simply forms of energy at such extremely high rates of vibration that they appear to be more spirit than matter. As a radio pioneer, Fetzer was, of course, fascinated by energies of all kinds, and his reading of Tesla already suggested to him that the "energy waveforms" such as radio might indicate the existence of "more subtle waveforms" we cannot measure.[35] According to *The Kybalion*, in a passage marked by Fetzer, "the Plane of Energy (A) . . . comprises the ordinary forms of Energy known to science," while "the Plane of Energy (B) comprises seven sub-planes of higher forms of energy not as yet discovered by science, but which have been called 'Nature's Finer Forces' and which are called into operation in manifestations of certain forms of mental phenomena and by which such phenomena becomes possible."[36] The ultimate importance of all this is, if mind is all (the principle of mentalism), and mind, energy, and matter are all connected, then mind could control both energy and matter. *The Kybalion* terms this process "mental alchemy."[37] Fetzer had already witnessed many such psychic events during his visits to Camp Chesterfield; now he had a theoretical model by which he could understand them, accept them as real, and hope that he, too, could aspire to their creation. It is perhaps because of *The Kybalion* that Fetzer soon became fascinated with the American "mind over matter" movement known as New Thought and, later, with parapsychology.[38]

At one point in *The Kybalion*, the author observes that "much of these Inner Teachings is held by the Hermeticists as being too sacred, important and even dangerous for general public dissemination." It is for this reason that "the knowledge regarding these Planes has been kept in the Holy of Holies in all Esoteric Fraternities and Occult Orders,—in the Secret Chamber of the Temple."[39] Freemasonry, as Fetzer knew well, was long implicated as one of these "Esoteric Fraternities," but the modern archetype of such "Esoteric Fraternities" was Rosicrucianism, a perhaps-fictitious seventeenth-century secret society of master Hermetic alchemists led by Christian Rosenkreuz ("rose cross"). The putative existence of this society was revealed to the world through the writings of the German Johannes Valentinus Andreae, setting off a scramble throughout Europe to contact the adepts and join their group.[40] In the nineteenth century, the legend of the Rosicrucians was revived in Europe by the novel *Zanoni* (1842) by Edward Bulwer-Lytton (recommended in *The Kybalion*),[41] and in the United States through the writings of the African American Spiritualist and occult author Paschal Beverly Randolph (1825–1875). According to Randolph's own report, he was initiated into a Rosicrucian lodge while in Paris, and this formed the basis for his foundation in 1858 of the American Fraternitas Rosae Crucis, the first of several such Rosicrucian organizations in the United States. Born and raised in New York City, Randolph resided in numerous cities, from New Orleans and San Francisco to Paris and Cairo, but spent much time in the Midwest, dying in Toledo in 1875.[42]

Only one of Randolph's works, *Soul!*, made it into John Fetzer's library, but given the quantity and exuberance of Fetzer's annotations in his copy of the book, it made a great impression on him.[43] *Soul!* is a record of Randolph's experiences in the afterlife or, as he called it, the "Soul-world." Randolph entered the afterlife through a process of meditation that allowed him to "blend" with the spirits of the dead, specifically a nineteenth-century woman named Cynthia and Thotmes, an ancient Egyptian king of the Second Dynasty, now lord of the "Imperial Order of the Rosy Cross." With the help of these beings, Randolph saw the true nature of God, the cosmos, and humanity. God is pure mind, a "great central sun" endlessly radiating thought waves by which the cosmos and everything in it—mind, spirit, matter—is created. Indeed, "man is the crystallization of the waves of thought which proceed from God." Randolph, given a God's-eye view of the universe, saw that everything is flame (or radiation or energy). He saw, too, that the human soul is a winged globe or sun constantly generating an aura of varied colors. And during sleep, the soul, like the "great central sun," retreated behind the "electric moon" of the solar plexus, where it accessed "the great telegraphic system of all Being, connecting its remotest points." Such was the nature of intuition, according to Randolph, and the source of all true knowledge. It is through intuition that God has guided humanity's soul on its countless transmigrations through the mineral, animal, and human realms. Eventually the soul will evolve to the point that it can leave the material world behind and achieve its final freedom in a "disenthralled spirit body." At this point, the soul will be able to access consciously the radiating knowledge of God that most embodied beings can access only fitfully in sleep, for only "a small minority of the race," such as Swedenborg, could ever hope to access this knowledge consciously while in the body.[44]

Despite the fact that *Soul!* is concrete and anecdotal, whereas *The Kybalion* is abstract and philosophical, both present nearly identical monistic worldviews clothed in the symbols of Western esotericism and nineteenth-century science. (Indeed, the author of *The Kybalion* may well have been influenced by Randolph's works.) Thus, Fetzer responded to certain aspects of both books in much the same way. As in *The Kybalion*, Randolph's assertion that soul, spirit, and matter were different waveforms of the mind-energy of God fascinated him, for it ineluctably brought to mind the metaphor of radio: "The carrier wave is the spirit!" Fetzer wrote in the margins of *Soul!* "The modulation of the carrier wave is the *soul!*" And later, he mused in another marginal note, "If spirit is substance . . . it seems that it is vibrating at a different *frequency* than that of the material." Thus, the soul "can occupy the same space as the original body *at the same time* or *not*. [A]ll material objects could pass through it, or it could pass through objects."[45] Soul and matter were like two light waves projected through each other at right angles, and because they are at different frequencies, they would not interfere with each other. (Fetzer drew a diagram to illustrate this principle.) This clarified for Fetzer the relationship between spirit and matter: spirit is the primary substance of the universe; at high rates of vibration, it can carry mind and thus form a soul ("conscious spirit"), and at lower rates of vibration, it coagulated into matter. Importantly, the fact that matter was simply spirit at low vibration suggested that spirit at any energy level might be susceptible to scientific investigation and demonstration. This was an idea that became a cornerstone of Fetzer's later mission: integrating science with spirituality to develop evidence of the spirit.

While the two books share the same worldview, there are, however, marked differences in approach between them. Unlike *The Kybalion*, *Soul!* is as much interested in personal soteriology as it is in abstract theology and cosmology, and it is clear from the material Fetzer underlined that he was again comforted by Randolph's assertions of the imperishability of the soul, the survival of human individuality, and the absence of judgment or punishment, as well as the prospect of postmortem learning and progress. Additionally, given *Soul!*'s focus on the afterlife, it is less interested in using knowledge of the monistic structure of the cosmos for developing psychic powers than is *The Kybalion*.[46] In this sense, the two books complement each other, for while Fetzer would always worry about what would happen to him after death, he nevertheless always remained intensely interested in the reality and attainability of psychic powers here in this life. Indeed, in his mind, the importance of these two things were linked, since the former could be used to prove the reality (or at least the likelihood) of the latter. Thus, while Fetzer would always be interested in the this-worldly, pragmatic benefits of psychic powers, the real benefit of such powers would be as an empirical demonstration of the reality, ubiquity, imperishability, and freedom of the spirit.

5

The Ascended Masters' Call

Fetzer Explores the Theosophical Cosmos (1930s on)

That John Fetzer responded so positively to *Soul!* was probably due to the fact that by the time he read Randolph's book in the 1960s, he was already very familiar with another metaphysical tradition that was, at least in part, an outgrowth of Randolph's revived Rosicrucianism.[1] This was Theosophy, which Fetzer first encountered in the 1930s around the time he first began his studies of Spiritualism, Freemasonry, and Hermeticism.

In 1874, Helena Petrovna Blavatsky (1831–1891), a Russian-born medium newly arrived in the United States, met Colonel Henry Steel Olcott (1832–1907) while both were investigating spirit manifestations in Vermont. The pair soon found that, beyond Spiritualism, they shared an interest in the esoteric teachings of the religions of the world. The following year they founded the Theosophical Society in New York City in order to pursue the unification of all religions through a recovery of ancient wisdom from East and West. The first fruit of the Theosophical Society was the publication of Blavatsky's *Isis Unveiled* (1877), part 1 of which argues for an occult science to complement modern science and part 2 of which argues for the harmony between Western spiritual monism and the esoteric teachings of ancient India. The work was only partly Blavatsky's, for she made it clear that she had long been in contact with a number of transcendent spiritual Masters, or "mahatmas," who lived in Egypt and Tibet, members of the "Great White Lodge or Brotherhood." It was they, she reported, who psychically conveyed much of the information that appeared in *Isis Unveiled*.

In 1879, Blavatsky and Olcott relocated the headquarters of the Theosophical Society to Adyar, India, in order to more adequately study the ancient texts of Hinduism and Buddhism. In time, this eventuated in Blavatsky's magnum opus, *The Secret Doctrine* (1888). Here again, with the psychic help of the Great White Brotherhood, Blavatsky synthesized Western with Eastern monism to create a grand cosmological scheme in which the human race was destined to evolve to higher levels of consciousness under the guidance of the Masters. According to *The Secret Doctrine*, part of this process occurs on earth, where humankind is in the process of evolving through seven "root races," the first two of which inhabited the legendary islands of Lemuria and Atlantis. *The Secret Doctrine* sparked much interest and controversy upon publication and remains today a spiritual classic for many metaphysical groups both inside and outside the Theosophical tradition.[2]

Despite Blavatsky's and Olcott's early removal to India, Theosophy became firmly established in the United States, with Theosophical lodges founded across the nation in the decade that followed. Perhaps in part because of the excitement over Asian religions generated by the World's Parliament of Religions, held in conjunction with the Columbian Exposition in Chicago in 1893, Theosophy found a home in the Midwest—indeed, the US headquarters for the Theosophical Society was Chicago and, later, Wheaton, Illinois.[3] In addition to formal lodges, informal associations of Theosophists popped up throughout the region, especially where Spiritualist groups already existed. In Fort Wayne, Indiana, for example, the Spiritualist Occult Science Society was joined in the

1890s by a chapter of the Theosophical Society, and there were soon two more branches of the Theosophical Society in Indianapolis and Bluffton. Theosophy had its followers as well in Michigan: branches of the American Theosophical Society could be found in Detroit, Grand Rapids, and Jackson. All told, there were some twenty-five lodges in the Midwest during the 1890s, and the Theosophical Society reached a nationwide membership high point of 8,520 in 1926.[4]

So popular did Theosophy become in the Midwest that it came to challenge the older Andrew Jackson Davis–inspired Spiritualism as the most popular metaphysical system in the region. Even in strongholds such as Indiana's Camp Chesterfield, Theosophical ideas became so prevalent that by the 1910s and '20s, longtime camp secretary Mabel Riffle attempted unsuccessfully to ban the discussion of such ideas as the Masters, spiritual evolution, and especially, reincarnation. By this time, however, besides the various branches of the Theosophical Society itself, several correspondence schools, such as the College of Universal Truth in Chicago and the College of Divine Metaphysics in Indianapolis, were offering courses in Theosophical subjects to those who wished to go beyond Spiritualism.[5] What is more, Chicago, already the Midwest center for esoteric and occult book publishing, was the location for the Theosophical Press, which evolved from the earlier Theosophical Book Concern to become the nation's largest producer of Theosophical materials.[6] By the end of the Roaring '20s, the Midwest was no stranger to Theosophy.

It is entirely possible that John Fetzer first encountered Theosophy at Camp Chesterfield, either through conversations with Theosophically inclined mediums or through materials purchased at the camp's bookstore. Unfortunately, Fetzer himself never said exactly when he came within the Theosophical orbit, and any Theosophical books he may have purchased at Camp Chesterfield before 1960 have not come down to us in his personal library. Moreover, we do not know whether John Fetzer ever read the foundational texts of Theosophy, Blavatsky's *Isis Unveiled* or *The Secret Doctrine* (although copies of the latter dating from the 1970s exist in the Fetzer Institute library). We do know that he read some of the chief authors of the second generation of Theosophists, Charles W. Leadbeater, C. Jinarajadasa, and Ernest Woods, but this was not until the 1960s and '70s.[7] It appears, then, that Fetzer's earliest introduction to Theosophy that we can document came through the literature a Theosophical splinter group, the "I AM" Religious Activity of Chicago, Illinois.

The "I AM" Religious Activity

Four of the earliest Theosophical books still extant in Fetzer's personal library are the distinctive green leatherette-bound books of the "I AM" Religious Activity: *Unveiled Mysteries* (1934), *The Magic Presence* (1935), *The "I AM" Discourses* (1935), and *Ascended Master Light* (1938).[8] While all four volumes have John Fetzer's annotations, intriguingly, the first three volumes bear the signature of his half sister, Harriet ("Hattie") Ribble. Although Hattie was always much more of a mainstream Christian than her half brother was, she nevertheless was something of a seeker too, visiting fortune-tellers and Spiritualists, not to mention maintaining a keen interest in her brother's spiritual development.[9] It is not surprising, then, that if Hattie happened onto a spiritual group that she thought would interest John, she would pass the materials on to him.

And what materials they were! The founders of the "I AM" Religious Activity were Guy and Edna Ballard. Throughout the 1910s and '20s, the Ballards were active in Spiritualist and Theosophical circles in Chicago, where Edna taught music and worked in her brother's occult bookstore, The Philosopher's Nook, while Guy, who was a mining engineer by training, promoted his oil and mining interests. Guy Ballard's work often took him west, and beginning in 1928, he spent two years in California, landing first in Los Angeles, where he continued studying Theosophy. At some point, according to Ballard, he was directed by a voice to travel to Northern California to visit Mount Shasta. On the slopes of that mountain, he reportedly met the mysterious Comte de Saint Germain, an eighteenth-century European often cited in modern Rosicrucian and Theosophical literature. Saint Germain explained to Ballard that he was an immortal "Ascended Master" and representative of the "Great White Brotherhood," the divine hierarchy that ruled the destiny of the solar system. Saint Germain was one of many such Ascended Masters who, after an earthly existence, had returned and now dwelt in secret chambers in western mountains such as Mount Shasta, the Grand Tetons, and the peaks of the Colorado Rockies. The Masters' mission was to reintroduce humankind to the "Mighty 'I AM' Presence," a boundless source of transformative spiritual energy radiating from God himself, the "Great Central Sun," which, when dwelling within each individual, was the "Christ Self." Once the "Mighty 'I AM' Presence" was made permanent, the earth would enter the "Seventh Golden Age," and humanity would be able to exercise stupendous powers simply through the medium of thought. Further, Saint Germain told Ballard that the United States was destined to play a special role in this divine drama and that the Ballard family had been specially chosen to bring the "Ascended Master Light" to the nation as "Accredited Messengers."[10]

Once returned to Chicago, which Saint Germain designated "the Permanent Atom at the heart of the world," Guy and Edna Ballard, along with their son, Donald, set about spreading the Mighty "I AM" Message by establishing the Saint Germain Press and the Saint Germain Foundation. Guy Ballard wrote up his experiences in two books, *Unveiled Mysteries* (1934) and *The Magic Presence* (1935), which he published under the pseudonym of Godfré Ray King. Meanwhile, both Edna and Guy Ballard began receiving psychic messages from Saint Germain and a host of other Ascended Masters such as Jesus, the Archangel Michael, Sanat Kumara, the Goddess of Liberty, and the Tall Venusian (Masters from other planets were commonplace in many varieties of Theosophy), as well as Kuthumi and Morya, who were Blavatsky's Masters.

The bulk of these communications enjoined on humankind an endless series of decrees, affirmations, and invocations, which, if recited with conviction, would transform the world through the power of thought. The twelve volumes of these communications were supplemented by a monthly magazine, the *Voice of "I AM,"* and, beginning in 1937, regular radio broadcasts featuring both Guy and Edna Ballard. It is interesting to note that Fetzer's radio station, WKZO, began broadcasting these programs in September 1939. At this point, the movement claimed to have a million members nationwide, and while this most likely was an exaggeration, the historian Philip Jenkins estimates that "there were at least tens of thousands prepared to support a sizable merchandizing operation, which included books, records, pins, rings, posters, and portraits of the Masters, including Saint-Germain and Guy Ballard himself."[11] In light of this, the historian Robert Ellwood is undoubtedly correct in observing that the "I AM" Religious Activity, "at its apex in the late thirties," "must have represented the greatest popular diffusion [of] Theosophical concepts ever attained."[12]

Judging by the annotations, which are extensive, there was much in *Unveiled Mysteries* and *The Magic Presence* that interested Fetzer. On the one hand, many of the ideas resonated with concepts and scenarios with which he was already familiar in other guises. Both books read like the Tom Swift "boy inventor" adventure stories that John read in his youth, and he duly noted much of the technology described, whether plausible (radio, television, airships, and Tesla-like wireless lamps) or fanciful (machines to read the human aura, an atomic accelerator that cures disease by raising human vibration to the level of the "Pure Electronic Body," a telephone to other planets and beyond, etc.). As for spiritual ideas, there were Hermetic elements in the books that Fetzer must have recognized. These included the mirroring of microcosm/macrocosm and the Ascended Masters' ability to control atomic structure to create vast supplies of gold and diamonds, wealth that only the Masters had power not to misuse. (In fact, it was the dire psychic effects of the hoarding of gold, according to Saint Germain, that caused the Great Depression, for gold can only energize humanity if it circulates.)[13] Meanwhile, the idea that the United States was destined to play a sacred role in the ushering of the Golden Age of political and spiritual freedom was straight from Freemasonry, while the prediction that the Golden Age would be resisted by a "sinister force attempting to create chaos" and preceded by "extraordinary physical disturbances" must have echoed for Fetzer the apocalypticism of Seventh-day Adventism. Finally, the central role of Jesus Christ as the Master Jesus, the Great Cosmic Christ who first returned the "Mighty 'I AM' Presence" to humanity, must have appealed to Fetzer's still-strong Christian piety, as did the presence of "Guardian-Angels" such as the Archangel Michael.[14]

On the other hand, the "I AM" books introduced Fetzer to a wealth of new Theosophical concepts, albeit in Ballard's own distinctive terminology: these included the "Etheric" (*akashic*) record in which every event is cosmically recorded and available for playback; "Projected Consciousness" (astral projection) through which human beings can travel out of body at will; and the body's "seven ganglionic centers" (chakras) through which "Universal Substance," God's radiating energy, or *prana*, is "channeled" if, like a radio, the body is correctly tuned. Additionally, the Blavatskian contention that the human race is far older than previously thought, stretching back to the inhabitants of Atlantis and Mu (a Pacific Ocean counterpart to Lemuria), formed a part of Ballard's narrative. The idea of the remote antiquity of humanity was something that Fetzer came to believe implicitly. Karma and reincarnation also form prominent themes in the "I AM" material, with an emphasis on the distinctive notion of group reincarnation. Group reincarnation posits that groups of people work out a collective destiny by reincarnating together; relationships between the group may change, as may the sexes of the individuals, but none are released from the wheel of birth and death until all are successful in eliminating their karmic debt. As we shall see, this idea had a great influence on Fetzer's subsequent personal and professional relationships.[15]

In addition to dovetailing with parts of Fetzer's existing worldview and introducing him to Theosophical ideas, there is perhaps another reason why he was so taken with the "I AM" materials. During the 1930s and '40s, Fetzer, after much hard work and sacrifice, was finally beginning to experience some financial success as a businessman. Wealth was now a real possibility. But how was Fetzer to fit the inherent materialism of wealth and business into his spiritual thinking? Both his childhood

Methodism and the Seventh-day Adventism of his teens and twenties strongly warned against the temptations of wealth and the distractions of a life devoted solely to money getting. The "I AM" Religious Activity, however, saw business as an opportunity for spiritual growth and saw wealth as a sign of the Master's favor.[16] At one point, Saint Germain tells Ballard (in passages triple underlined by Fetzer), "No one in the world ever accumulated a great amount of wealth, without the assistance and radiation of some Ascended Master," and when one does, "such an experience is a test and an opportunity to expand their Light." To illustrate this, near the end of *Unveiled Mysteries*, Ballard uses the "Mighty God-Power Within" to deftly conclude a lucrative mining deal, which then allows him to convert all the parties to the "Great Cosmic Laws of Life": love, harmony, perfection, and service to humanity. Significantly, unbeknownst to Ballard, he was then being tested by the Great White Brotherhood, and having passed with flying colors, he was initiated as its Accredited Messenger.[17]

In *The Magic Presence*, another model of a successful businessman aided by the Masters is presented in the person of the fabulously wealthy Daniel Rayborn, whom Ballard meets at his opulent ranch house in Wyoming. Of him, Ballard remarks, "I never ceased to marvel at the power of Love to bless men and their business, when they really accept and live it," adding, "Rayborn was a living proof of its efficacy and wisdom, in the practical daily experience of the business world." Eventually, after a lifetime of discrete philanthropy and service, Rayborn himself is allowed to become an Ascended Master, servant of the Great White Brotherhood.[18] While it is impossible to know how literally Fetzer took these narratives, the idea that business and wealth could be spiritually uplifting if used for love and service appealed to him greatly.

John Fetzer is a good example of Ellwood's assertion that the "I AM" movement was the most effective popularizer of Theosophical ideas during the 1930s. After reading the "I AM" materials, which were apparently the earliest Theosophical materials Fetzer encountered, he was hooked. For the rest of his life, Fetzer would seek out different iterations of the

Theosophical worldview. He avidly read and annotated the books that inspired the "I AM" Religious Activity (for example, *A Dweller on Two Planets* [1905] by Phylos the Tibetan and *The Impersonal Life* [1914] by Joseph Benner), as well as those that were inspired by it (for example, the four *Books of Azrael: Teachings of the Great White Brotherhood* [1960?–1967], which, judging by a bookplate, he bought at Camp Chesterfield in the 1960s).[19] He also came into contact with another "I AM" offshoot, the Magnificent Consummation of the Ruby Focus, an Arizona group that claimed Nikola Tesla as an Ascended Master.[20]

With regard to other non-"I AM" versions of Theosophy, Fetzer also diligently made his way through the four dense volumes of the *Harmonics of Evolution* (1956) by the Chicago-based Theosophist Florence Huntley, as well as Nancy Fullwood's *Song of the Sano Tarot* (1929) and Vera Stanley Alder's *The Initiation of the World* (1939), the last of significance because of its chapter on the theory and technology of energy healing, a subject that became a vital interest of Fetzer's in later life. Fetzer was especially captivated by Theosophical stories of ancient civilizations such as Lemuria, Mu, and Atlantis and their connections to ancient Egypt, and so it is not surprising that we find in Fetzer's collection W. P. Phelon's *Our Story of Atlantis* (1937), Edgar Cayce's *Edgar Cayce on Atlantis* (1967), and Paul Brunton's *A Search in Secret Egypt* (1936).[21] Indeed, Fetzer looked forward to the time in the future when underwater cameras would provide irrefutable evidence of this "previous modern civilization" now "at the bottom of the sea."[22]

Alice Bailey and the Arcane School

From all Fetzer's later reading on Theosophy, there are two writers that stand out with regard to their impact on his later thinking: Alice Bailey and Baird T. Spalding. Bailey died in 1949, and Fetzer apparently encountered her thought by reading *The Unfinished Autobiography*, most likely shortly after its publication in 1951.[23] Alice Bailey was born into a wealthy English family in 1880. As a young women, she became a conservative Christian and spent time in India as a missionary with the YWCA. After marrying in 1907, she moved with her husband to Cincinnati, Ohio, where he studied for the ministry in the Episcopal Church, after which they settled for a time in Pacific Grove, California. Soon separated from her husband, she rejected her conservative Christian roots and became attracted to the Theosophical Society in 1915. Two years later, she moved to its headquarters in Hollywood, where she met and eventually married Foster Bailey. Judging by Fetzer's annotations, he identified with Bailey's transition out of conservative Christianity, underlining passages in the book in which she talked about how she had come to realize the futility of a literalist interpretation of the Bible in favor of a more universalist understanding of the scriptures and the role of Christ. Indeed, like Fetzer, far from giving up her childhood Christian pietism, it remained an indelible part of Bailey's evolving worldview, albeit integrated with such things as reincarnation, the religions of the East, and the spiritual hierarchy of the Masters.[24]

As with the "I AM" materials, Fetzer was fascinated by Bailey's encounters with the Masters. Alice Bailey claimed that as child of fifteen, she had met a mysterious turbaned stranger who had told her she had a special mission in the world. She interpreted this at first to be a Christian mission, but upon joining the Theosophical Society, she saw a picture depicting Kuthumi, one of Blavatsky's mahatmas, and recognized him as the man she had met years before. Bailey was contacted soon after by another Master, Djwhal Khul ("the Tibetan"), who enlisted her aid in channeling a series of books, the first of which was *Initiation, Human and Solar* (1922).[25] The following year, Alice and Foster Bailey were ejected from the Theosophical Society for her unauthorized channelings, after which they relocated to New York City, where they founded the Lucis Trust and the Arcane School.[26]

While retaining many Theosophical ideas, the key teaching of the Baileys' Arcane School is the imminent inauguration of the New Age through the Second Coming of Christ, also identified as Maitreya, the bodhisattva and world teacher prominent in many sects of Buddhism. According to

Alice Bailey, human beings must prepare the way for the New Age and the world freedom that will characterize it, by projecting spiritual energy into the planet and all its peoples. To this end, the Arcane School created the Triangles Program (1937), which encouraged the formation of small meditation groups, typically groups of three ("triangles") to act as "points of light" to channel energy by chanting the "Great Invocation" during the full moon of each month. Fetzer was intrigued by the idea of small meditation groups for esoteric study and was impressed by how Alice and Foster Bailey had used their initial meditation group to develop the Arcane School and the Lucis Trust into prominent organizations. Moreover, the "Great Invocation" became a favorite of Fetzer's, reproduced in later writings and recommended to many friends.[27]

The Great Invocation

From the point of Light within the Mind of God
Let light stream forth into the minds of men.
Let Light descend on Earth.

From the point of Love within the Heart of God
Let love stream forth into the hearts of men.
May Christ return to Earth.

From the centre where the Will of God is known
Let purpose guide the little wills of men—
The purpose which the Masters know and serve.

From the centre which we call the race of men
Let the Plan of Love and Light work out
And may it seal the door where evil dwells.

Let Light and Love and Power restore the Plan on Earth.[28]

It was the Master Kuthumi who initially put Alice Bailey on the path to discipleship under Djwhal Khul, and it was this idea that "average humanity of all degrees" could be called to serve the Masters, first as disciples and then as initiates, that interested Fetzer greatly. As Fetzer carefully noted, many of the Masters resided in far-away places such as Shamballa (a secret city in the Gobi Desert) or in the mountain fastnesses of the Himalayas, while others, notably Master Jesus, Saint Germain, Hilarion, and Master P., were said to be active in Europe and North America. Indeed, Fetzer noted that it was Hilarion who first promoted Spiritualism and psychical research, that it was Master P. who promoted New Thought, and that it was Saint Germain, under the name of Master Rakoczi, who led the Freemasons. The fact that Fetzer was already active in some of these groups perhaps encouraged him to think that he, too, may someday be called by the Masters to enter the Path of Discipleship. Bailey gave added life to this hope through her observation that while "a large number of the initiates and those who have obtained adeptship in the last cycle, have been orientals, . . . the time now comes when a period of attainment by occidentals will be seen, . . . [attainment] suited to their type of mind."[29] What she meant by "their type of mind" greatly excited Fetzer, judging by his exuberant marks on this passage: "It is interesting to note that the oriental type attains its objective through meditation, with a modicum of executive organization and ritual, and that the occidental will achieve largely through the organization which the lower mind produces, and a type of meditation of which intense business concentration might be considered an illustration. The one-pointed application of the mind by a European or American business man might be regarded as a type of meditation. In the purification of motive lying back of this application will come, for the occidental, his day of opportunity [for initiation as a disciple]."[30] Of course, "one-pointed application of mind" is only the beginning: one must also prove purity of motive. As in the "I AM" Religious Activity, Bailey specifies that for the successful businessman, this meant understanding "the occult value of money in service," that is, its use not for oneself but "as a means to bring about the fruition of the Master's plans as he senses those plans." For "only he who desires naught for himself can be a recipient of financial bounty, and a dispenser of the riches of the universe. In other cases where riches increase they bring with them naught but sorrow and distress, discontent and misuse."[31]

Having thus established that discipleship was a real possibility, even for Western businessmen, much of the rest of *Initiation, Human and Solar* is given over to detailed discussions of the various steps through which the successful aspirant, once he has proven himself, is inducted into the Great White Brotherhood of the Masters. Fetzer read this material carefully. Much of what followed undoubtedly reminded Fetzer strongly of Freemasonry since it involved rising from a lower blue lodge to the higher white lodge through a series of secret initiations. Like Freemasonry, these initiations entailed the memorization of copious secret teachings (an "Esoteric Catechism" is provided), the spiritual understanding of a variety of esoteric symbols (prominent among which was the triangle), the giving of the secret word (AUM), and the memorization of complex rituals employing oaths and sacred implements (the "rods of power").[32] It was "thus by a graded series of steps" that "the initiate [is] brought face to face with Truth and Existence," leading to three "basic realisations": "faith for ages is justified" and doubt banished; "the immortality of the soul and the unseen worlds [are] . . . proven and ascertained"; and the true "meaning and source of energy" is understood, thus allowing one "to wield power with scientific accuracy and direction."[33] As a summary of John Fetzer's spiritual goals, this list could hardly be bettered.

Baird T. Spalding

Of equal importance to the works of Alice Bailey for John Fetzer was Baird T. Spalding's *Life and Teachings of the Masters of the Far East*, the first volume of which was published in 1924 and the fifth and last in 1955.[34] So impressed was Fetzer that after reading these volumes, he contacted the publisher, Douglas K. DeVorss, for more information about Spalding. He was disappointed, however: DeVorss was dead by 1953, and his company could supply very little concrete information about the author or his claims.[35] Baird himself said variously that he was born in England those who have obtained adeptship in the last cycle, have been orientals and those in Hindu bodies. This cycle has been dominated by the sixth ray, which is just passing out, and the two preceding. In the preservation of equilibrium the time now comes when a period of attainment by occidentals will be seen, and this upon a ray suited to their type of mind. It is interesting to note that the oriental type attains its objective through meditation, with a modicum of executive organisation and ritual, and that the occidental will achieve largely through the organisation which lower mind produces, and a type of meditation of which intense business concentration might be considered an illustration. The one-pointed application of the mind by a European or American business man might be regarded as a type of meditation. In the purification of motive lying back of this application will come, for the occidental, his day of opportunity.

By availing themselves of the present day of opportunity, and by conformity to the rules for treading the Path, will come to many in the West the chance to take these further steps. That opportunity will be found by the man who is ready in the place where he is, and among the familiar circumstances of his daily life. It will be found in attention to duty, in the surmounting of tests and trials, and in that inner adherence to the voice of the God within, which is the mark of every applicant for initiation. Initiation involves the very thing that is done from day to day by any who are consciously endeavouring to train themselves:—the next point to be reached, and the next bit of work to be accomplished is pointed out by the Master (either the God within or a man's Master if he is consciously aware of Him) and the reason is given. Then the Teacher stands aside and watches the aspirant achieve. As He watches, He recognises points of crisis, where the application of a test will do one of two

12. A page from Alice Bailey's *Initiation, Human and Solar* with Fetzer's pencil markings.

or India and that he graduated from the University of Calcutta at the age of seventeen. After further education in the United States and Germany, he was invited in 1894 to form part of an eleven-man team sent by an Ivy League university to the remote regions of Persia, India, Tibet, and China (specifically the Gobi Desert), there to conduct archaeological and philological research.[36]

While in the Himalayas, the team reportedly was introduced to the Masters. The Masters then proceeded to teach them profound spiritual truths by allowing them to translate ancient religious texts preserved on precious gold tablets and by demonstrating to them phenomenal psychic powers and fantastic new technologies. The Masters told Spalding that soon the "great Law" of the "Christ Consciousness" or "I AM" necessary for the further spiritual evolution of humankind "will be brought forth in America" in preparation for "the New Age."[37] Spurred by this declaration, Spalding returned to the United States and began to speak and write about his experiences. (A mining engineer by trade, Spalding was Guy and Edna Ballard's houseguest in Chicago during the early 1920s.) In the wake of Spalding's involvement with a San Francisco–based New Thought group called the Comforter League of Light, a privately published version of the first volume of *Life and Teachings* became popular among metaphysical circles in the West and Midwest. Soon, the 1924 DeVorss edition launched it to even greater fame, followed by three more books in the series (volume 5 was a posthumous production). In between Spalding's mining ventures, he continued to lecture on his supposed encounters with the Masters and their spiritual philosophy until his death in 1953.[38]

It is easy to see why Fetzer was so taken by Baird Spalding's *Life and Teachings of the Masters of the Far East*. Written like an adventure story with plenty of action, *Life and Teachings* is replete with lost cities, mysterious ancient texts, and exciting encounters with bandits and abominable snowmen.[39] It is also, however, one of the most engaging and enduringly popular introductions to a wide range of Theosophically inspired teachings available. Almost every page of Fetzer's copies of volumes 1, 2, 4, and 5 bear his annotations and underlinings, and it is clear that he read and reread the books several times. From the time he first encountered them in the late 1950s, Spalding's books became a crucial resource for the development of Fetzer's spiritual worldview.

Like the "I AM" materials and the teachings of Alice Bailey's Arcane School, Baird's work is premised on the basic Theosophical concepts of a monistic cosmos in which God, the "Universal Mind," radiates his energy, the "Universal Mind Substance," which is used by a divine hierarchy of reclusive Masters, the "Great White Brotherhood," to direct the spiritual evolution of humanity through successive reincarnations toward "Christ Consciousness." Too, throughout the volumes of *Life and Teachings*, Jesus plays a prominent role as "the Great Master and Teacher" of humankind, although much in the Theosophical mold. Indeed, at one point, Spalding and his colleagues are treated to an audience with Jesus in the flesh, who tells them of his travels as a young man to the far East, where he studied at the feet of the ancient Masters. (This reconstruction of Jesus's lost years closely echoes the 1907 *Aquarian Gospel of Jesus the Christ*, reportedly channeled from the *akashic* records by the Illinois Disciples minister Levi Dowling.)[40] Thus, as both Jesus and the other Masters never tire of telling Spalding's expedition, Jesus's mission was not to remit sins (the mistaken teaching of the Apostles) but to preach the immutable "Law" that God is one and all is God. Once human beings realize this through the practice of "silence" (meditation), they will recognize the "Christ Consciousness" or "I AM" within, after which God's power will flow through them and all things will be possible.[41]

As in the "I AM" Religious Activity and, to a lesser extent, Alice Bailey's Arcane School, *Life and Teachings of the Masters of the Far East* also prophesied a leading role for the United States in the work ahead, a theme that always interested John Fetzer keenly. On July 4 during the first year of the expedition, the Master Emil treated Spalding's group to a peroration on the United States' divine mission. According to Emil, it was God who guided Columbus and Pilgrim Puritans to the New World, and it was God who, through his "Universal Mind Substance," inspired the Declaration of Independence, the signing of which signaled the beginning of "one of the greatest epochs since that of the advent of Jesus into the world." Indeed, the two events are intimately related in their sacredness: "Cannot those that signed the Declaration of Independence that day, be likened unto the Wise Men from the East who saw the Star symbolizing the birth of the Babe in the Manger, the Christ Consciousness in man?" Is not the very motto *e pluribus unum* the perfect expression of the Christ Consciousness, the idea that all is one with God? In time, "with the Christ Consciousness fully developed in [this] nation, whatever is undertaken by it, or by its people, must work out for the good of all; for the very root or heart of all government is the consciousness of those governed." Emil assured his listeners that this process had already started: on the day the Founding Fathers first struck the Liberty Bell, it "magnified and sent out the vibrations" of the Christ Consciousness, "until some day they will penetrate the deepest and darkest corners of the whole earth, and thus enlighten the darkest consciousness." The United States, according to Emil, is thus the capstone of the evolution of nations, and "while [g]reat mistakes have been made by your nation," its destiny is guided by "great souls," and "[w]hen your nation does recognize its true estate, or mission, and joins hands with the Spirit . . . we can see for your great nation a marvel far transcending the power of any human tongue to describe."[42]

It should also be noted that in addition to the Theosophical framework, much of the language in *Life and Teachings* reflects that of the "mind over matter" thinking reminiscent of the New Thought and Christian Science movements of which Fetzer was well aware.[43] For example, as one of the Masters tells Spalding, "Through the power or process of thought we can transmute and evolve our bodies, or our outer conditions and surroundings, through recognition of this Christ Consciousness within ourselves, so that we will never experience death nor any change called death. This is done wholly through man's power to visualize, idealize, conceive, and bring forth that which he gazes upon." Thus, while "fear thoughts, pain thoughts, and grief thoughts create the ugliness of old age," "joyous thoughts, love thoughts, and ideal thoughts create the beauty called youth." Indeed, by nightly affirmation that "divine Love in demonstration is eternal youth," one's "inner alchemist" will cause the body's "dead and worn out cells to fall, and the gold of new skin to appear with perpetual health and loveliness." Since the body is fundamentally a microcosm reflecting the cosmos, all one needs is a positive attitude to channel the healing rays from God, the great "central sun" of the universe.[44]

It is possible that Fetzer also recognized in such pronouncements Teslan themes. For once the power of thought is realized, the Masters claimed, adepts will command extraordinary psychic abilities and enjoy enormous inspiration and creativity, which in turn will lead to great advances in science and technology (perhaps Fetzer wondered if that had been Tesla's secret).[45] Moreover, as human beings learn to tap into "Universal Power," it will be available to "turn and move every mechanical device, furnish transportation without consumption of fuel in any way, and will also furnish light and heat." This indeed would be confirmation of Tesla's dream, for the Universal Power "will be everywhere present without money or price, and can be contacted and used by all."[46]

Finally, as the foregoing indicates, Baird Spalding's *Life and Teachings* made it clear that there was no fundamental conflict between science and religion, once it is correctly understood that spiritual laws are complementary to natural laws. As Emil's mother puts it, "You will find that in the spiritual there is a higher law, and when you abide by that law, you will receive benefit; for the spiritual is just above and around the mechanical or material." However, despite this, spiritual law is every bit as scientific, and "you will find there is no more mystery in the spiritual than there is in the mechanical or the material." This is because all is energy, and the only difference between physical energy and spiritual is the rate of vibration, something that, according to Spalding, is only now coming to be grasped in the West through quantum theory. Of course, since all energy is essentially mind, it is also true that all energy is conscious and responds to the fundamental law of the cosmos, the Law of Love. This is an idea that also became a fundamental conviction for John Fetzer.[47]

The Impact of Theosophy on John Fetzer

In considering the elements that went into the creation of John Fetzer's later worldview, it is hard to overestimate the impact of Theosophy in its various forms. Beginning in the 1930s, when Fetzer first encountered Theosophy, until the end of his life, Theosophical or Theosophically inspired literature continued to be some of his favorite reading.[48] Fetzer, of course, had already encountered in Spiritualism, Freemasonry, Hermeticism, and Rosicrucianism many of the spiritual ideas that he found so attractive: a monistic cosmos composed of conscious energy; the conception of the body as microcosm; the reality of psychic powers and the possibility of scientific discovery of spiritual laws; the operation of karma and reincarnation; the continuing centrality of Jesus; the contemporary relevance of ancient wisdom from past civilizations such as Atlantis, Lemuria, and Mu; the divine destiny of the United States under the watchful eye of a brotherhood of secret Masters; the harmony of science and religion; and the impending global spiritual transformation leading to the New Age.[49] However, of all the wisdom traditions, it was Theosophy that wove these concepts and themes together into a comprehensive cosmic mythology that Fetzer found uniquely compelling and through which everything he learned subsequently would be filtered and judged.

6

Unorthodox Science

Fetzer, UFOs, and the Paranormal
(1950s on)

The 1950s were a time of accelerating growth for John Fetzer's media empire. Having expanded his radio operations into FM, Fetzer moved into television, with WKZO-TV3 going on the air in July 1950. Three years later, he expanded his operation yet again by acquiring two television stations in Lincoln, Nebraska, one of which, KOLN-TV, he donated to the University of Nebraska in 1954 for use as a public television station. By 1958, Fetzer Broadcasting had moved out of the Burdick Hotel into a brand-new stand-alone facility on Maple Street that came to be known as Fetzer Broadcast House. During this decade, Fetzer also branched off into the music business and into television production, but his most noteworthy business decision was to organize an eleven-man syndicate to purchase the Detroit Tigers baseball team, which he did in 1956. Over the next five years, he bought out his partners, emerging as the sole owner of the Tigers by 1961. It was under Fetzer's watch that the Tigers succeeded

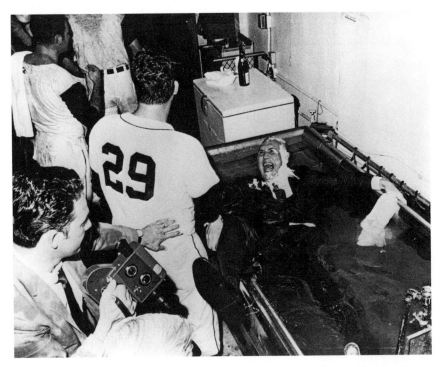

13. John E. Fetzer dunked in locker-room whirlpool by Tigers players after World Series win, October 10, 1968.

in winning the World Series in 1968, the first time in twenty-three years (and only the third time in the history of the franchise).[1]

All of this made Fetzer a very wealthy man, although this did not dampen his public spiritedness. In 1952, Fetzer chaired the CBS Radio Business Standards Committee and was named the first chair of the Television Code Review Board of the National Association of Broadcasters (NAB). In recognition of his longtime service to the NAB, Fetzer was awarded the 1969 Distinguished Service Award, the highest award of the broadcasting industry.[2] In addition, Fetzer continued to lend his expertise to government service, specifically in supporting the Crusade for Freedom Program, which included traveling on an inspection tour for Radio Free Europe in 1956.[3] Philanthropy, too, became a growing concern for Fetzer. In 1954, the John E. Fetzer Foundation was established "to give grants for religious, charitable, scientific, library, and/or educational purposes."

It was incorporated in 1962, and over the next decades, Fetzer worked to develop its focus and goals.[4]

Meanwhile, Fetzer's spiritual journey continued unabated. Fetzer's trusted secretary, Carolyn Dailey, stated that his spiritual search intensified after his mother's death in 1958.[5] He continued to periodically visit the Spiritualists at Camp Chesterfield, from whence he brought back more books on spiritual topics to stock his expanding library at his modest home on Clovelly Road, where he and Rhea had moved in 1946. He also began ordering Spiritualist, Hermetic, Theosophical, and other metaphysical books through the book service of *Chimes* magazine. Advertised as the "largest psychic monthly magazine," this California publication had close ties to several of Camp Chesterfield's most prominent mediums and was a clearinghouse for information on a wide variety of metaphysical movements. Fetzer was also a reader of the Chicago-based *Fate* magazine, which featured articles on a variety of paranormal subjects such as unidentified flying objects (UFOs) and extrasensory perception (ESP), both of which became major interests of Fetzer.[6]

While study was important for Fetzer's spiritual search, equally important was travel beyond Kalamazoo. A 1952 trip for journalists organized by the State Department took him and Rhea to Europe and the Middle East, including a visit to the sacred sites of the Holy Land. Later trips took the Fetzers to the Caribbean and Latin America, where Peru's Machu Picchu made a profound impression on them both. Perhaps the trip that had the most impact on John Fetzer occurred in 1962, when the Fetzers accompanied the Detroit Tigers to Japan for a goodwill tour and exhibition game. Once in Asia, the Fetzers took the opportunity to travel not only in Japan but also to Hong Kong, the Philippines, Thailand, India, and finally Egypt.[7] Religious sites were especially interesting to John Fetzer; Rhea's diary records that they visited several Buddhist and Shinto shrines in Japan and Buddhist temples in Thailand, and while in India, they visited the Ramakrishna Mission, a Jain temple, the Taj Mahal, the ruins of Sarnath, where the Buddha delivered his first sermon, and the holy city of Benares, where the couple toured the myriad temples and ghats

14. WKZO Broadcast House on Maple Street, Kalamazoo, Michigan, 1958.

of one of India's holiest cities. Perhaps spurred by his Theosophical readings, Fetzer had become interested in Hinduism and Buddhism, which he knew primarily through Western interpretations such as Paul Brunton's *A Search in Secret India* (1935) and Lobsang Rampa's *The Rampa Story* (1960).[8] Now, however, Fetzer had a chance to interact with actual practitioners of these traditions. For example, while in Calcutta, he spent an hour discussing Hindu philosophy with S. B. Dasgupta of the University of Calcutta, whose book *Aspects of Indian Religious Thought* (1957) Fetzer ultimately bought and read. According to Rhea's diary recollections, "One point [Dasgupta] brought out was [that] religious philosophy is universal but interpreted differently by each religion. Divine spirit is in all men. He also said that spirit is in matter or something living could not have been created from matter. John said he completely confirmed his conception of the divine mind."[9]

The Fetzers' round-the-world trip ended in Egypt, a land that had long fascinated Fetzer. Here they visited the pyramids, the Sphinx, and the mummies of the Cairo Museum, before venturing out to see Luxor and the Valley of the Kings. Especially awe-inspiring was the magnificent Temple of Karnak, whose portals are dominated by the winged solar disk flanked by rearing cobras. Having recently read Paul Brunton's *A Search in Secret Egypt* (1936), the symbol must have powerfully conjured a variety of Freemasonic and Theosophical connotations for Fetzer, making a lasting impression. Coincidentally, while staying in Luxor, the Fetzers met and befriended the psychiatrist Shafica Karagulla, whose interests in the esoteric history of ancient civilizations and the paranormal paralleled Fetzer's own. Karagulla was in Luxor gathering information for a book on parapsychology. After nearly a month and a half on the road, the Fetzers flew back to Kalamazoo, undoubtedly exhausted but exhilarated by their experiences overseas.[10]

Of course, Fetzer did not need to leave the United States to find sacred spaces and spiritual experiences. In 1948, he purchased a ranch property outside of Tucson, Arizona, and for decades, he and Rhea would retreat there, ostensibly to escape the Michigan winters and to allow Rhea to keep horses.[11] However, the Tucson property had a special significance for Fetzer, for he believed that the Catalina Mountains above the ranch were home to a group of Ascended Masters once visited by Guy Ballard of the "I AM" Religious Activity. Moreover, Fetzer recalled in an interview that a psychic once told him that the "area was a very sanctified area during the time of Lemuria. That there was a lot of activity in that area and it was sort of holy ground," adding wryly, "It's interesting to see what will come out of that." A later psychic even saw the etheric city of Shamballa hovering above Fetzer's Tucson property.[12] Long before Sedona became the metaphysical hub of Arizona in the 1970s, the state in general had been attracting people like John Fetzer who found its stark landscape and ancient past spiritually inspiring.

Fetzer and Unorthodox Science

When Fetzer decided to build a home on his Tucson property in the early 1950s, one of the major problems he encountered was water. He had a cistern built, but shortly before the house was ready for occupation, the water source failed. Told by geological experts that a well was impossible, Fetzer dealt with the problem in typical Fetzer fashion: he called in dowsers. Fetzer was skeptical at first, but he tried out the divining rod himself and felt the magnetic pull that the "water witches" said he would feel. When they told him that if he drilled in a certain spot and to a certain depth (two hundred feet), he would get a flow of twenty gallons per hour, he did not hesitate to call in a driller to test their prediction. Fetzer loved telling the story of the subsequent battle he had with the well driller who told him he was crazy and wasting his money—that is, until the driller struck water at nearly the exact depth and flow indicated by the rod. From then on, having witnessed it empirically, Fetzer was a believer in the power of dowsing, and he challenged the geological experts to explain scientifically what he had experienced with his own eyes.[13]

From Fetzer's days as a radio technician, he was predisposed to believe that the universe was brimming with unknown powers and phenomena that, like dowsing, had not yet been explained by science. Today we would call these phenomena "paranormal," that is, "the psychic, mental, or spiritual phenomena that are believed to fall outside the range of the 'normal,' as defined by current scientific knowledge."[14] Of course, the operative phrase here is "current scientific knowledge," for Fetzer, like many others, was firmly convinced that someday science would indeed come to a full understanding of these powers and anomalous phenomena, rendering the paranormal normal. In fact, Fetzer was part of a larger movement that gained strength after World War II that pushed for greater scientific engagement with the paranormal, leading to what one scholar has called the rise of "unorthodox science."[15]

A grass-roots movement, unorthodox science not only seeks to bring the rigor of scientific investigation to phenomena long dismissed by mainstream or "orthodox" science but is characterized by the willingness to entertain theories that run counter to received scientific wisdom. Indeed, looking to the history of science, especially Thomas Kuhn's construction of it as a series of paradigm shifts, unorthodox scientists assume that some of their theories, which today might seem outlandish, will tomorrow become part of science's routine theoretical inventory or perhaps even the basis of a new paradigm. Some unorthodox scientists, moreover, reject the materialism of the scientific method as dogmatic and wrong-headed: they believe that only when science admits the reality of the spiritual and incorporates it into its method will science advance to the next level. In fact, they believe that advanced science can only be the product of advanced spirituality.[16] Given that John Fetzer's career in radio and television was based on the discoveries of mavericks such as Nikola Tesla, it is no mystery why unorthodox science had a great appeal for him.[17]

Fetzer and UFOs

Judging by the number of volumes on this topic still extant in Fetzer's personal library (thirty-three, fourteen having extensive annotations), one of his central unorthodox science interests during the 1950s and '60s was unidentified flying objects, or UFOs. In this, he was not alone. Ever since UFOs were first widely reported after a sighting by a pilot named Kenneth Arnold in Washington State in 1947, they have become a paranormal fixture on the American landscape, with millions of Americans convinced of their existence. Urgent calls for scientific investigation came early, but few believers in the phenomenon were satisfied with the government's and military's dismissal of UFOs as natural events misinterpreted. Therefore, as sightings increased and as stories of alien encounters evolved from simple contact to alien abduction, there was no shortage of unorthodox scientific theories that took aliens and UFOs seriously and tried to account for their sudden presence on earth. These theories varied from space aliens as advanced humanoids controlling vastly superior technology to pan-dimensional beings commanding unheard-of psychic powers to spiritual beings heralding the advent of a new religious dispensation. Over the next decades, groups coalesced around these theories, ranging from those purely interested in UFOs from a phenomenological and technological standpoint (e.g., the Aerial Phenomena Research Organization) to those who were drawn to their religious implications (e.g., the Saucerians). Moreover, a multimillion-dollar media industry grew up to supply the public's hunger for UFO information, thus ensuring that the phenomenon would long remain in the public eye despite dismissal by orthodox scientists and government officials.[18]

UFOs had been on John Fetzer's "radar" ever since he served as assistant censor for broadcasting in 1944 and heard stories of "flying disks over London" and the mysterious "foo fighters" shadowing allied planes during World War II.[19] But it was apparently in the early 1950s with the multiplication of sightings that he became seriously interested in the phenomenon. He even went so far as to contact Major Donald E. Keyhoe, one of the most prominent UFO investigators of the period and founder of the National Investigations Committee on Aerial Phenomena (NICAP), in order to champion a UFO sighting by Bruce Glycadis, an employee at WJEF in Grand Rapids.[20] For the most part, however, Fetzer was circumspect about his UFO fascination at this point, and what we know about it comes primarily from his reading, which was wide-ranging and eclectic.[21] He read and annotated the earliest book-length reports that debated the existence of flying saucers, both pro (e.g., Keyhoe, Ruppelt) and con (e.g., Menzel).[22] He was also apparently a personal friend of Coral Lorenzen, who with her husband, Jim, directed the Aerial Phenomena Research Organization (APRO). Founded in 1952, APRO was one of highest profile and longest lasting such UFO research organizations, which since 1960 was located in Tucson, where Fetzer probably first met the Lorenzens.[23] And true to his commitment to unorthodox science, Fetzer also read with keen interest the early speculations on UFO propulsion, which generally involved some kind of novel energy system that generated antigravity.[24]

The year 1966 saw an upsurge of UFO sightings in western Michigan, culminating in the incident at Dexter, Michigan, where some forty people witnessed what they said was a flying saucer landing in a nearby swamp.[25] Famously, the sighting was discounted as "swamp gas" by J. Allen Hynek, a professor of astronomy at Northwestern University then consulting for the US Air Force on its report on the UFO phenomenon, Project Bluebook.[26] Hynek's assessment of "swamp gas" was widely derided within the UFO community, simply confirming its suspicions of a government cover-up. Even congressman Gerald R. Ford, whose district included Dexter, called for a congressional investigation of UFOs, citing his lack of confidence in the Air Force's investigation (the hearings never took place).[27] Later in 1966, the Air Force commissioned the University of Colorado to do an impartial investigation, but the resulting "Condon Report," published in 1968, satisfied no one.[28] In the wake of the Condon Report, Hynek broke with the Air Force and, in his book *The UFO Experience* (1972), publicly accused it of suppressing the truth about UFOs.[29]

Fetzer, who later became a friend of Hynek (a signed copy of Hynek's *The UFO Experience* is in Fetzer's personal library), was also skeptical about the government's impartiality about UFOs.[30] Perhaps mindful of his own personal experience with government suppression of the rumors of "foo fighters" during World War II and prompted by another outbreak of UFO sightings in 1973, Fetzer decided to speak publicly about the issue. This was a major step in light of his concern for his reputation and is a good indication of his strong conviction that UFOs were real. In May 1974, at a meeting of the Outlook Club, a social club meeting in downtown Kalamazoo at the Park Club, Fetzer read a carefully prepared speech called, in homage to his friend Coral Lorenzen of APRO, "The Flying Saucer Hoax."[31] In what must have been a long talk—forty pages with some eighty slides—Fetzer first reviewed and rejected the Project Bluebook and Condon Reports, and then, using data from the files of APRO, detailed what he felt were the most credible sightings and contacts with UFOs from around the world and throughout history (including the visions of the Prophet Ezekiel).

Far from UFOs being a hoax, Fetzer maintained in his Outlook talk that it was imperative "to voice a concern of urgency" because the "existence of a species of superior beings in the universe could cause civilization on earth to topple," for "even on earth, societies have disintegrated when confronted by a superior society." Therefore, Fetzer counseled, "It's high time we mustered the top scientific talent in this country, even at the expense of changing the NASA program, and begin a hard scientific study to determine the existence and purpose of the UFOs which are assumed to be extraterrestrial vehicles." Indeed, scientists must be willing to push the boundaries of what is acceptable in "orthodox science" and take comfort in the fact that "history is filled with examples of great men whose 'unconventional work' made them, in their own time, the subject of controversy at best and scorn, ridicule at worst." In any case, humanity must be prepared, and if UFOs do represent higher beings, which Fetzer apparently believed they did, then "let us recognize and welcome the men from other worlds. They are here among us. Let us be wise enough to learn from those who can teach us much—who will be friends if we will but let them."[32]

In addition to the "nuts and bolts" scientific approach to the phenomenon of UFOs, John Fetzer was also open to the early contact literature about UFOs, that is, the stories of people who had not just seen a UFO but claimed they had met their occupants and in some cases been taken on space trips in flying saucers. Fetzer read all the early contact accounts, such as those of Truman Bethurum, George W. Van Tassel, and the most famous of all, George Adamski, of whose 1955 book *Inside the Space Ships* Fetzer owned a signed copy.[33] Adamski had given a talk in 1954 at the Detroit Masonic Temple, so it is possible Fetzer heard him speak there and met him then.[34] This was not the last time Fetzer sought out a contactee: in November 1968 in Tucson, he went to a talk by the Reverend Frank Stranges, who claimed to have been introduced to a Venusian at the Pentagon in 1959.[35]

Unlike later contactee accounts of alien abductions, these earliest accounts report the aliens as friendly and concerned with the welfare of humankind. Indeed, the "Space Brothers" almost uniformly said that they appeared on earth because of the development of the nuclear bomb and the rise of the Cold War. They desired to warn humanity that it would have to evolve beyond its present war-like state to achieve a new age if it wished to survive. Importantly, much of this was couched in the language of the Ascended Masters of Theosophy and the "I AM" movement. This is not surprising since many contactees, such as Adamski, came from strong Theosophical backgrounds, as did many of his followers, who undoubtedly saw in Adamski's story empirical proof of the existence of the Great White Brotherhood, as perhaps did Fetzer himself.[36] Many of the UFO contactees said that they communicated with aliens via telepathy.[37] What is more, they often further claimed that such telepathic communication could continue even when the aliens had left earth, in other words, that the contactee could function as a "channel" for alien intelligences. Indeed, the words "channel" and "channeling" were first used in this sense in relation to the telepathic abilities of some UFO contactees.[38] For Theosophists and "I AM" followers, not to mention Spiritualists, the idea that the beings they had been channeling had been Space Brothers all along was not a hard one to assimilate, especially since the Space Brothers' messages were so similar to those of the Ascended Masters and discarnate spirits previously.[39] This was certainly the case for John Fetzer. For example, he read and studied the revelations received by contactee George W. Van Tassel, who channeled not only the space alien Ashtar from the Pleiades but also Nikola Tesla; and later in the 1980s, Fetzer avidly studied the channelings of Van Tassel's successor, Tuella (Thelma B. Terrell), who in addition to Ashtar, channeled a number of "I AM" figures, including Saint Germain and the Archangel Michael.[40]

Of all the documents channeled from space aliens, however, the one that had the most impact on Fetzer was the *Urantia Book* (1955). The *Urantia Book* has a curious history, a history that in some ways intersects with John Fetzer's own. Sometime after 1906, the Chicago psychiatrist William Sadler, a onetime Seventh-day Adventist and protégé of John Harvey Kellogg, was called in to observe a neighbor who was talking in his sleep. The content of the "sleeping subject's" utterances suggested to Sadler and others that the man, later identified as Wilfred Kellogg (a nephew of Dr. Kellogg), was actually channeling a series of higher beings from other planets. Over the following decades, Sadler hosted a forum in his home to discuss the insights revealed by Wilfred Kellogg, now gathered together as the Urantia Papers ("Urantia" being a name for earth).

While much in the Urantia Papers is unique, some of it strongly echoes both Seventh-day Adventism and Theosophy. For instance, in addition to incorporating Jesus and the Archangel Michael as central characters and featuring some distinctive Adventist doctrines such as postmortem unconsciousness or "soul sleep," the Urantia Papers also continue the early Adventist belief in intelligent life on other planets, something insisted on by Ellen G. White in the Testimonies. However, the fact that these extraterrestrials function in the Urantia Papers as "Ascended Masters" who have made contact in order to guide the evolution of human beings through a vast and intricate cosmos strongly suggests a Theosophical influence. Finally published in 1955 by the Urantia Foundation as the *Urantia Book*, the 2,097-page "fifth epochal revelation" appeared at the height of the UFO craze in the United States, which boosted its exposure to the nation. Since that time, it continues to capture the imaginations of people like John Fetzer who are entirely comfortable with the blending of Christian pietism with Theosophy and ufology.[41]

Whatever one may think of the UFO phenomenon, Fetzer was not alone in his keen interest in it, for the possibility of alien visitation has taken a tenacious hold over the American psyche. Today, over half the population of the United States believes that intelligent extraterrestrial life exists, and slightly less believes that the planet has been visited by such beings, despite the fact that reliable evidence still remains elusive.[42] Perhaps this is because, as none other than Carl Jung asserted in 1959, UFOs function as a modern mythology. For Jung, this mythology articulates not only humans' delight in technology but also our fears of its misuse. It thus calls into question the reigning wisdom of orthodox science and calls for a holistic, "unorthodox" alternative that is open to the transcendent possibilities of spirit, in other words, a spiritualized science. Furthermore, Jung believed that even if UFOs were not real and there were no Space Brothers to guide us, UFO mythology nevertheless signaled the psychic transition of humankind from the age of Pisces to the new age of Aquarius.[43] There is no evidence that Fetzer read Jung, but it is clear from his reading and subsequent statements that he, too, sensed that UFOs had a meaning beyond simply their empirical reality (although proving this remained a priority). The appearance of UFOs portended that something new and wonderful was happening to the world, perhaps even the promised New Age that Fetzer had been reading about in Theosophical literature since the 1930s.

Fetzer and Parapsychology

UFOs were not the only paranormal phenomena that John Fetzer thought needed to be subject to scientific study. He was also keenly interested in the developing field of parapsychology, that is, "the scientific study of [psychic] experiences which, if they are as they seem to be, are in principle outside the realm of human capabilities as presently conceived by conventional scientists."[44] Such experiences typically include extrasensory perception (ESP), psychokinesis (PK), and the survival of human personality after death, among many others. The reasons for Fetzer's interest were many. Much of the UFO literature that Fetzer was reading at the time speculated widely on the psychic nature of the phenomenon, especially when it came to telepathic communication with aliens and their supposed abilities to control human minds.[45] However, Fetzer's interest in such phenomena long predated the UFO craze, starting in the early 1930s with his attendance at the spiritualist séances and psychic readings of Camp Chesterfield and then continuing with his extensive study of Theosophical and ancient wisdom teachings, all of which alerted him to the possibility that the occult powers of the mind were greater than ever imagined. Moreover, during his time as radio censor in Washington, DC, during World War II, Fetzer said he was in "contact with the Russians constantly concerning sensitive military matters" and was made "aware at that time the use the Soviets were making of ESP in their determination of clandestine matters": "From that day to this I have watched the Soviet activities in this field and it has become abundantly apparent that their surveillance of top secret matters in this country is amazingly accurate."[46] Thus, from the early 1940s, Fetzer was interested in psychic phenomena not only for its own sake but also for its national security implications.

Fetzer's interest in parapsychology intensified throughout the 1960s, which not coincidentally saw a renewed acceptance, if not adoration, of individual "celebrity" psychics in the United States. It was during this period, for example, that the reputation of the United States' most famous psychic, Edgar Cayce, underwent something of a renaissance, especially in the wake of the publication of Gina Cerminara's *Many Mansions: The Edgar Cayce Story on Reincarnation* (1959) and Jess Stearn's *Edgar Cayce: The Sleeping Prophet* (1967). Fetzer read both books carefully, as well as others devoted to Cayce the prophet and Cayce the psychic healer, many of which were put out by the resurgent Cayce organization, the Association for Research and Enlightenment (ARE).[47] What is more, sometime before 1966, John Fetzer met the psychic Jeane Dixon, who was nationally famous for predicting the Kennedy assassination, the veracity of which Fetzer believed implicitly. Over the next decade, she and Fetzer became close friends. Fetzer even went so far as to help her fund-raise for her Children to Children Foundation, which sought to build the Jeane Dixon Medical Center in response to one of her visions. Fetzer thus went out of his way to introduce Dixon to some of his influential friends in the broadcasting business. As part of this effort, Fetzer invited Dixon and her husband, James, to be his guests at the 1969 NAB ceremony, where he received the Distinguished Service Award. Conversely, Dixon would give Fetzer psychically derived personal advice, at one point recommending a visit to the alternative healer Henry G. Belier, when Fetzer complained of ulcers. Fetzer's assessment of Dixon was that she was "a most delightful person . . . [who] has an uncanny record for accuracy in her prophetic utterances," while she cited him as "a most realistic businessman"

15. John and Rhea Fetzer with the psychic Jeane Dixon at the NAB ceremony where he received the Distinguished Service Award, 1969. (Photo by de Kun International News, courtesy of the Fetzer Institute)

who nevertheless "never allowed his realistic attitude to blind him to the spiritual core of life or phenomena of the psychic world."[48] From then on, Fetzer would never be without a personal psychic on whom he could rely for personal and professional advice.

Perhaps the major reason why psychic phenomena captured and held John Fetzer's attention for as long as they did was that, unlike ufology, the study of psychic phenomena had achieved a modicum of academic respectability as the field of parapsychology. In other words, here was an "unorthodox" science that had almost become "orthodox." Early in the twentieth century, what was then called "psychical research" was introduced into US universities, first at Stanford in 1911 and then, with more lasting results, at Duke University in 1930. Here, J. B. Rhine and others created the first parapsychology laboratory, which sought to take paranormal phenomena such as ESP out of the realm of the anecdotal and qualitative into that of statistical, quantitative research. It was here, for example, that Zener cards with their cross, square, circle, star, and wavy lines were first popularized. Rhine's methodology was widely criticized, but his series of popular books such *Extra-Sensory Perception* (1934) and *New Frontiers of the Mind* (1937) made "parapsychology" a household word and helped to legitimate the new field. This stimulated research at other institutions that was published in a growing number of scientific journals. This in turn led to the creation of a professional organization, the Parapsychological Association, in 1957 and, in 1969, the grudging acceptance of parapsychology as a legitimate field by the American Academy for the Advancement of Science.[49]

Undoubtedly, John Fetzer was aware of the development of academic parapsychology; as a reader of *Fate* and *Psychic* magazines, whose pages were replete with digested accounts of parapsychological research, he could have hardly been unaware. However, it is clear that Fetzer did not start reading seriously in the field until the late 1960s and '70s. His entrée into the world of parapsychological research was apparently the work of Shafica Karagulla, whom he and Rhea had met at Luxor in 1962. Born in Turkey in 1914 and trained as a psychiatrist in Lebanon and Scotland, Karagulla became interested in Edgar Cayce after moving to the United States in 1956, when she took a position on the faculty of the State University of New York's Department of Psychiatry. Soon, however, she decided to leave academia to pursue research on what she called "higher sense phenomena" (HPE), with which she believed people such as Cayce were endowed. Her research took her around the world, including Egypt, where she met the Fetzers, seeking material for a book that was eventually published in 1967 as *Breakthrough to Creativity*. Karagulla remembered Fetzer's interest in her work and sent him an inscribed copy of the book.[50]

Breakthrough to Creativity describes Karagulla's decision to abandon orthodox psychiatry in order to investigate parapsychological phenomena and her early attempts to locate and study people with HSP or, as she also called them, "sensitives." Much of the first half of the book is taken up with anecdotes about people with ESP and PK abilities, including discussions of psychometry, clairvoyance, and dowsing (indeed, John Fetzer's story of dowsing for water in Tucson was reported verbatim, with Fetzer appearing under the pseudonym "Perry").[51] However, the most persistent theme of the book is the paranormal diagnostic and healing power of sensitives. Karagulla had concluded that most paranormal abilities came from the fact that psychically gifted people could sense and manipulate naturally occurring energy fields, especially the energy fields surrounding human beings. Since the 1950s, several theories were developed regarding the true nature of psychic power ("psi"), with the "energy field" theory, which posited psi as an "undiscovered or unrecognized form of physical energy," being one of the more popular.[52] Karagulla's research had further shown that these energy fields were frequently seen by sensitives as either colored auras or lines of force emanating from certain portions of the body and that the quality and intensity of these could be used to diagnose with uncanny accuracy the health or debility of the body's various organ systems. In addition, she also found that some sensitives had the ability to heal by channeling subtle energy back into the affected areas of the body, using either the sensitive's own energy or that of specially organized materials such as crystals or magnets. Ultimately, Karagulla postulated, if the nature of these subtle energies and the means by which sensitives came to manipulate them could be more thoroughly understood, then psychic diagnostic and healing abilities could be systematically developed and taught, or perhaps even machines could be created to do the same things. Either way, Karagulla believed, medicine would be revolutionized.

Fetzer found Karagulla's work exceedingly exciting, especially since, as we shall see in chapter 7, it coincided with much of his thinking on the subject. Karagulla's research program seemed to offer a way forward in empirically proving these contentions, and her focus on healing was especially attractive to Fetzer. There were roadblocks, however. In the beginning of *Breakthrough to Creativity*, Karagulla talked at length about how her abandonment of orthodox science led to difficulties of financing her research: "The research project I was about to embark upon was unlikely to attract a grant or fellowship at first. Most foundations would not risk financial commitments for such a 'far out' project. Who could evaluate a project when there was so little knowledge about it?"[53] Who indeed? Ever since Fetzer incorporated the Fetzer Foundation in 1962, he had been searching for a worthwhile field of unorthodox science in which to invest his resources. It appears that Karagulla's book (and most likely conversations with Karagulla herself) were beginning to convince Fetzer that, as "far out" as the field was, parapsychological research—unorthodox science par excellence—just might be the direction his foundation should pursue.

7

Articulating a Worldview for the New Age

(1960s and 1970s)

The 1960s and '70s marked a profound shift in John Fetzer's spiritual quest. For the preceding thirty years or so, he had been reading and studying a variety of monistic traditions, from Spiritualism to the ancient wisdom traditions of esoteric Freemasonry and Rosicrucianism to Theosophy and its offshoots. And in more recent years, his engagement with the UFO phenomenon and parapsychology convinced him beyond a doubt that the spiritual worldview behind these traditions was indeed real. Moreover, everything that Fetzer had been reading and feeling led him to believe that he lived in an age of major transition, a conviction that the turmoil of the 1960s did nothing to dispel. If he were to play a role in that transition beyond that of a mere spectator, like those who attended his ballgames, it was time to begin the shift from contemplation to action. Now in his sixties, financially secure and a business success, Fetzer sensed it was time for him to articulate what he had learned into an explicit worldview and then, before it was too late, put that worldview into action in service to the country and the world.

One Man's Family [1964]

Despite Fetzer's heavy work schedule and the demands of his growing businesses, he had continued to collect materials for a genealogy of his father's side of the family. Again, Fetzer's devotion to this project had long developed beyond that of a simple hobby, although when and why he started it is not entirely clear. Late in life, Fetzer said that it was originally due to the fact that he had lost his father at a young age and that tracing his father's lineage was an attempt to know him better. Fetzer, however, also characterized the work as a spiritual mission that he hoped would serve as "a guide for [his ancestors] in corrective learning about the oneness of mankind and the oneness of all of us . . . connected [as we are] with the universal intelligence."[1] Whatever his true motivations were for beginning this work, what is interesting about the project is that when it came to publishing his findings in 1964 as *One Man's Family: A History and Genealogy of the Fetzer Family*, John Fetzer decided to devote the last chapters to briefly articulating his worldview. Thus, not only do the final chapters of *One Man's Family* offer a valuable window onto his thinking at the time, but they are also important because they formed the kernel for Fetzer's later, more elaborate statements of his spiritual beliefs.

After surveying the past five hundred years of the Fetzer clan, John Fetzer concluded that he feared for humanity because of its deplorable psychological state. This was due, Fetzer opined, to a dreadful ignorance about our true psychological makeup and to a trend in contemporary American society for "every constructive element" to be "deprecated to the point that the average person had lost his confidence and has no conception concerning his God-given powers of success, accomplishment and a balanced life."[2] This had created a situation in which "psychiatric problems have reached such a chaotic state that it is the unhappy prospect that one out of every twenty persons will have to undergo institutional treatment." And while he recognized that it was "presumptuous" on his part "to discuss such profundity," nevertheless he was sure that there were at least three "progressive solutions" that humankind must employ to achieve permanent mental balance.[3]

First, Fetzer counseled the rigorous adoption of "a *positive, constructive,* approach to life," "an attitude of expectancy, a belief in accomplishment," and faith in oneself. Second, Fetzer believed it was imperative "for the average person to accept the idea that all is in the mind within," for "it is the image created in his mind that gives man reality to the world outside of him." In other words, contentment "is a state of mind which we, ourselves have the power to control, and that control lies with our thinking." And third, we must understand that what ultimately determines our thinking is our subconscious mind. Once this is fully understood, there is nothing that cannot be brought to "materialization and solution" through the techniques of meditation, affirmation, and the use of the "pictorial imagination" (i.e., creative visualization), all of which can reinforce one's positive outlook. The reason this works, according to Fetzer, is that the human body is actually an "intricate electronic device, with a delicate set of transistors built in from head to toe," all of which is controlled by the master component, the subconscious mind: "The subconscious mind annihilates time and space, and acts as a powerful transmitting and receiving station, communicating with the physical, mental and cosmic forces to supremely unify all energy into intelligent use by the conscious mind." Indeed, due to the "cosmic wholeness of every atom in space, including our own physical and mental make-up," the subconscious can tap into nothing less than the mind of God. To make this fact plain, here Fetzer quotes the entirety of Alice Bailey's "Great Invocation": "From point of light within the Mind of God / Let light stream forth into the minds of men," and so on.[4]

Fetzer had great hopes that this philosophy of psychology would reconcile religion and science and thus convert the "pure religionist" and "pure scientist" into the "scientific religionist" who would finally understand "the wholeness of the universe."[5] Once this occurred, all of society's great ills (poverty, crime, war, etc.) would be abolished, the globe unified, and great strides in science and medicine achieved through an "intellectual explosion." Not only would technological marvels such as 3-D television and spaceflight become commonplace, but hitherto rejected ideas such as ESP, telepathy, and astral travel would be proven properties of the subconscious mind, and extraterrestrial life, UFOs, and the ancient civilization of Atlantis would be established as empirical scientific realities.[6]

Although John Fetzer put his own unique spin on these ideas (for example, humans as an electronic device composed of transistors and capacitors was a favorite trope), his sources for these ideas are fairly clear. At the end of his philosophical musings, he stated that this psychological "system" of the subconscious was nothing new. It had been "exported through the ages by those in tune with the ancient wisdom of the past, dating several thousand years, through the thread of Egyptian history," and carried into the modern period by authors such as Baird Spalding and Shafica Karagulla. Fetzer also mentioned Norman Vincent Peale and Claude Bristol, whose inclusion in his list of practitioners of his subconscious system gives another clue to his sources.[7] During the 1940s, Fetzer had begun avidly reading books on the "mind over matter" philosophies of New Thought, then most famously represented by Peale, whose book *The Power of Positive Thinking* he extensively annotated.[8] Even more important for Fetzer was Claude Bristol, an equally important figure in this genre but one who explicitly linked his positive-thinking philosophy to the paranormal and the parapsychological research of J. B. Rhine.[9] Specifically, in his best-selling *The Magic of Believing* (1948), Bristol taught that the kind of positive thinking that changes reality is based on the power of the subconscious mind to channel the higher forces of the universe through a process much like extrasensory perception.[10] If we could only learn to go beyond the limitations of the conscious mind by developing our subconscious through "concentration" (i.e., meditation), then by means of this new "super-consciousness," humanity would be rewarded with untold happiness, mental stability, and boundless creativity.[11] Although Fetzer first encountered such ideas about the infinite power of the subconscious in his readings of Theosophy and the ancient wisdom traditions, Bristol expressed them in the modern idioms of New Thought and parapsychology. Fetzer perhaps found this language more up-to-date or at least thought it more acceptable to his readers. Thus, when Fetzer championed the powers of the subconscious to solve individual and social problems in *One Man's Family*, he downplayed his more esoteric influences in this regard and expressed himself instead using Bristol's language of the "power of positive thinking" and parapsychology.[12]

"This I Believe" (1967)

John Fetzer returned to the articulation of his worldview sometime in 1966 or 1967. The reasons for this are unclear, but the result was an essay titled simply "This I Believe" (perhaps inspired by the 1950s CBS radio series of the same name).[13] Here, for some reason, Fetzer felt more comfortable employing his esoteric sources in this latest expression of his beliefs. Fetzer was still concerned with outlining a correct understanding of human psychology in "This I Believe," but now he did so by situating it more thoroughly within a complex esoteric cosmology that he derived from a variety of sources.[14]

Fetzer began "This I Believe" with the announcement that "scientific and spiritual forces find unification in the cosmos of outer space." Fetzer came to this conclusion by giving the cosmological "Big Bang" theory a Theosophical gloss.[15] Thus, the essays starts with a description of the "gigantic central sun," which sits at the center of a rotating "galaxy of ninety-one universes," just one of one hundred million such galaxies stretching to infinity.[16] Fetzer's evocation of this scene at the cosmic center borders on the ecstatic:

> Around the central Sun of our Universe is a huge electronic ring composed of the seven colors of the rainbow which flashes with perpetual motion and brilliancy, as though a thousand million suns were being woven into it, to feed

its transcendent luster. From every part of this rainbow-ring dart long broad shafts of light, sometimes forming into circles, small or great, whirling around the enormous girdle of the intelligent, scintillating, jewel-like, opal-tinted flame of the Central Sun within. *It is this nucleus of the great Sun-Globe itself, revolving upon its own axis, that constitutes the sublime scene—the Center of the Universe—the Cause of all Creation, the Universal Mind, the Supreme Principle, the Primal Cause, the Cosmic Field, the Divine Spirit, Infinite Intelligence, God the Father!*[17]

From this Universal Mind come "throbbing, pulsating, harmonious emanations of electronic energy," pervading everything, including "*Man [who] has been created from and is a counterpart of this Source of Power.*"[18] Indeed, "each and every cell [of the human body] is a permanently adjusted and resonate miniature receiver of perpetually intelligent, electronically modulated wave-forms from this Central Source—the Infinite Intelligence."[19] Moreover,

the aggregate of all these body cells, from first to last, is connected through the nervous system to the more sensitive cells of the brain, which culminates in a concentrated center in the dome of the head. This, in the East, is known as the "Thousand Petaled Lotus," but in the West as a high-gain parabolic antenna of supreme sensitivity, which is electronically tuned to the incoming rays of the Infinite Intelligence. This high-gain antenna maintains resonance and sensitivity so long as an understanding of its mechanism is held within. Lack of knowledge or negative thinking detunes this antenna to almost complete detachment so that awareness of reception from Primal Cause is practically nil, or you can tune in the channel-control of understanding and electronic wave forms will come through loud and clear. You are then one with the Source.[20]

The "Thousand Petaled Lotus," however, is only one of seven such centers in the body; another such receiver is the "electronic marvel" of "the ganglionic cellular mass at the back of the stomach, known as the solar plexus or abdominal brain." Taken together, the seven centers, each of which vibrates with one "of the seven colors of the rainbow," compose the subconscious mind, which "is in complete attunement with and has every attribute of the Universal Mind at all times." Thus, it has access to "the sum total of all past, present, and future knowledge because of its resonance with the great storehouse of information, the Universal Mind," not to mention the "thought-forms received telepathically through space radio transmission." These come "not only from mankind on the physical plane but from entities on all planes of existence," such as "Friends, Relatives, Guides, Teachers and Masters." Conversely, "through control of the body cells of the subconscious mind," individual human beings "can cause these same seven centers or reflectors to act telepathically as electromagnetic space transmitters, sending [one's] own constructive thought-forms to reinforce the great cosmos as well as personalities on every plane of existence, individually and collectively, to the benefit of all mankind." Indeed, "as you give out affirmative power, more of the same is pressed upon you," and "you will find that you cannot deplete the supply."[21]

However, the central problem for all humanity is to learn how to make the best use of the subconscious by the conscious mind, which through years of incorrect training and conditioning has lost touch with this cosmic conduit. The goal, as Fetzer saw it, was to coordinate the two minds through "efficient and automatic amalgamation" to achieve "unified cosmic consciousness" and "possess the magic of believing." This cannot be done through following "creeds and dogma" but through cleansing the subconscious of its "negative power" and then employing, among other techniques, *creative prayer*. Creative prayer consists of visualization of one's desires "as on a television screen," followed by "audio enunciation to make the picture completely vivid and clear." By thus "modulat[ing] the electronic waves of radiation, which bathes your being, into picture form," "a whole new line of communication is opened between you and the

Father of Radiation through the Central Sun." Moreover, by "speak[ing] affirmatively of love, life, peace, [and] harmony" using such affirmations as "This day in every way Cosmic Force is making me better and better" or "I am God Power; I am all abundance and free from all limitation," the cosmic connection is strengthened, thus allowing one to "take conscious constructive control" of one's life.[22]

In addition to creative prayer, one must also practice meditation. This can be done primarily by the conscious mind "exercising balanced concentration" on "the umbilical center of the abdomen" in order to awaken "the seven vibrating primal forces" that "lie dormant in the solar plexus."[23] Indeed, the road "to Masterhood is to assimilate and amalgamate one force after another until you have reached Adeptship."[24] At this point, "one achieves divinity, which some choose to call Superconsciousness or Christ Consciousness," and with this "arrives a sense of amazing new freedom." One "becomes a mobile center of consciousness, becoming the 'single eye' or I AM." Moreover, "in this state, the healing Force is now converting every cell, tissue, nerve, muscle and bone according to the excellence of the pattern established in the subconscious mind, and the vitality of the life principle is manifest in every atom of [one's] being which restores health, harmony, and peace." Having achieved this, one will "understand the true meaning of the assertion of the Master of Masters, when he said that all, along with him, are Sons of God." At this point, the saying "'I and the Father are One,' becomes a truism."[25]

The road to Masterhood is not easy, though, and in a handwritten addendum to the essay, Fetzer made it clear that he had "personally attained far too little of this science." Fetzer lamented the fact that, "compared to the total population of the West, very few have reached a status of total commitment," unlike those in the East, "where comprehension of the whole comes to them as a matter of course." In part, this is due to the fact that "the West cannot segregate itself from every earthly desire as the East prescribes."[26] However, "in spite of the fact that ill-conceived western orthodoxy is still a great barrier, the coming of the electronic and space age is rapidly bringing scientific and spiritual facts into focus." One of these facts is that the "seven planes" of the cosmos "have a governing body often referred to as the Hierarchy or Hermitage," "an orderly government with many divisions and departments," "with departmental chiefs, as well as the Supreme Cabinet of Ministers, manned by Masters, [who] exercise great influence over the people of our planet."[27] Indeed, "through the Alchemy of internal personal control, that is the conscious mind directing the subconscious, the Masters affirmatively transmute the vibrations of the Universal Mind Substance or vortices of energy to produce a variety of protective images." These "fortify not only themselves, but members of the human family against an array of negative experiences of life."[28]

Importantly, given this orderly organization of the cosmos and the protection of the Masters, every human being can aspire to Masterhood. Many of the great men of history, such as Washington, Franklin, Lincoln, Edison, Einstein, and Tesla, were Masters.[29] And even if one cannot hope to equal these great men, it is nevertheless important to make the attempt, for "the degree of conscious development attained on the earth plane determines which plane you join after you have discarded your earthly body."[30] However, "if you do not make satisfactory progress" here on earth, "you may exercise the option to return through birth into earthly life, often referred to as reincarnation." By this means, even if it takes multiple lifetimes, everyone eventually can acquire the "Divine Monitor" necessary for self-mastery and the integrated consciousness of a Master.[31]

Fetzer ended "This I Believe" on an exceedingly optimistic, if not ecstatic, note. "In the new age that lies immediately ahead," he predicted that, "through electronic instruments, direct communication between persons on the earth plane and those on higher planes will become commonplace," proving once and for all "the reality of life in other vibratory forms and the eternity of the human soul." Moreover, "a new race of thinkers under the influence of the Divine Mind and that of the Masters is coming into being with herculean strides" who "will combine the finest qualities of the scientific intellect with that of the trained transcendental consciousness." Such people will sweep away for all time the dualistic "delusion of orthodoxy."[32] For in the end, Fetzer proclaimed at the conclusion of "This I Believe," "there can be no true science, religion, social structure, nor successful living, outside the indisputable fact that there is a oneness in all things. . . . THIS IS THE TRUTH OF GOD. THIS IS THE NATURAL LAW OF SCIENCE. THIS IS THE ROAD TO ETERNITY. GOD I AM. I AM THAT I AM."[33]

In April 1967, Fetzer finalized an extensive revision of "This I Believe," simplifying and greatly shortening the essay. He added a brief introduction in which he stated that while these were his firm beliefs, he would not attempt to prove them and that people could accept or reject them as they wished. And yet, given "the utter contempt for the status quo in the World today," he felt his remarks were important. He then proceeded to reproduce his theology, cosmology, anthropology, and soteriology much as in the original essay, but he toned down most of the overtly esoteric elements. For example, the extended discussion of the body's "seven centers" and its color vibrations was dropped, as was all mention of the Masters, Masterhood, the seven planes, and reincarnation.[34] It is not clear exactly why Fetzer made these changes, but considering he received the Masonic Scottish Rite 33° in 1969, it has been suggested that he decided to submit the revised "This I Believe" as part of the nomination process. He therefore stripped out elements that he feared might be misunderstood by his Masonic brethren.[35] If this were the case, it indicates that even at this late date, Fetzer was still very cautious about exposing the totality of his beliefs to public scrutiny.

The Men from Wengen and America's Agony (1971)

Four years after John Fetzer's revised version of "This I Believe," he published his second work of genealogy, *The Men from Wengen and America's Agony*.[36] Most of the book was taken up with tracing his mother's family line, but as with *One Man's Family*, he took this opportunity to articulate his worldview again, this time in five chapters that were set apart in the book as "America's Agony." Much of "This I Believe" was reproduced in these chapters, but significant material was added.

16. John E. Fetzer in his Broadcast House office working on *The Men from Wengen and America's Agony*, 1970.

As the title "America's Agony" suggests, Fetzer believed that the country had entered into a crucial period, a period that he thought would last another fifty years. He came to this conviction because he believed it had been foretold in a series of visions reportedly received by George Washington while wintering at Valley Forge in 1777. According to an account of "Washington's Vision," published by the journalist Wesley Bradshaw in the *National Tribune* in 1880, the future president had been surprised in his study by a mysterious female figure who commanded, "Son of the Republic, look and learn!" (a refrain repeated throughout the story). She then proceeded to show Washington three visions of crises or "perils" that the new American nation must pass through. It is clear from context that the first two crises were the Revolutionary War and the Civil War, but the third "most fearful" crisis still lay in the future when Bradshaw reported the story in 1880.

Fetzer first encountered "Washington's Vision" in the 1930s, and it obviously made a distinct impression on him.[37] Thus, writing in 1969, the acme of the counterculture, the antiwar movement, student unrest, and racial strife, Fetzer interpreted all this as the beginning of the chaos long ago predicted to Washington. Given his roots in the apocalyptic tradition of Seventh-day Adventism, Fetzer was perhaps predisposed to read prophetic meaning into the signs of his times, even without "Washington's Vision," but the story emphasized to Fetzer that while the "destiny of the United States of America is to lead itself and the world into the era of peace on earth," this sacred mission was currently endangered, not only by the social unrest but, ironically, also by the "complacency, apathy and dependency" of many Americans of his time, a state aggravated by the constant pessimism emanating from the universities and the mass media.[38] Significantly, however, despite Fetzer's establishment bona fides, his assessment specifically of the student unrest of the day was more than a little sympathetic. It was no wonder, Fetzer wrote, that students were revolting against "the establishment" since it represented to them nothing more than institutionalized war, poverty, depersonalization, overpopulation, environmental degradation, racism, and materialism. With regard to this last, students were also "rebelling against the scientific culture" of the day in order to go beyond the "reign of technocracy." In other words, "they want to seize control of technology before it irreversibly seizes control over them." And while much student protest was misguided and divisive, and some downright subversive, such dissent nevertheless indicated to Fetzer a healthy and genuine "impatience with social structures, an impatience which portend[ed] change." Indeed, "today as never before there is a longing for some degree of liberation from America's agony," for which "the Establishment" was in part to blame.[39]

What was needed to realize this liberation, Fetzer believed, was a respite: a respite from the negativity and extremism of the age—a respite to realize that Americans were still "morally strong and spiritually responsible," "a generous people," and that the institutions of the "establishment," while desperately in need of reform, were still the best agencies there were for "constructive change." Most importantly during this respite, the older generation must take time to communicate to the young "a positive, constructive and forward looking *action drive*," for "they must be shown that evaluations of our country, whether true or false, will materialize if they are *believed* by enough people."[40]

With this familiar theme of the power of positive thinking, Fetzer returned to ideas and themes already elaborated in his previous essays, specifically the necessity of tapping into the "Energy Intelligence" behind those positive thoughts emanating as "low frequency radiation" from "God, the Scientific Father," the Great Central Sun at the center of the cosmos. To do so, of course, one must meld together the conscious and unconscious minds until they are *electronically tuned to the incoming rays of Infinite Intelligence*," thus conferring on the individual "creative powers [that] are unlimited," "making no problem too big to defy solution." Again this could be done by creative visualization, repeated affirmations, and meditation, especially novel forms of scientific meditation guided by such new technologies as biofeedback. However one does it, though, through biofeedback or older forms of meditation, one must become "conscious of the unfathomable—the complete totality of God," for it is "in this state [that] one develops the force of mind, heart, faith, hope, material wealth, inspiration and love" that will "[pour] out [the] quickening spirit" necessary "to uplift humanity" into "a reformed society."[41]

Fetzer ended "America's Agony" with "A New Age Epilogue." Here Fetzer returned to "Washington's Vision" and the "third peril," which he predicted would "be America's darkest hour." However, Fetzer was confident that "when the third peril is finished and man has discovered that science and spiritual forces through Meditative Wisdom have led him to the path of attainment and complete personal fulfillment, he will then discover a new world of peace, the Golden Era of Earth." Social problems will be solved; the impending crises of environment and population will be resolved into balance; "new age education" will be "totally relevant"; new forms of communication—even with extraterrestrials and the souls of the dead—will be perfected; new forms of safe energy will be discovered

THE MEN FROM WENGEN

AND

AMERICA'S AGONY

The Wenger-Winger-Wanger History

including

Christian Wenger, 1718

By

John E. Fetzer

with additional family notes
on
Barnhart, Barr, Brandon, Coble, Deitrick, Dittmore, Eby,
Evans, Fetzer, Foster, Geaubaux, Gilbert, Hager, Hess,
Hoenie, Keeler, Lawrence, Limes, Marker, McGrew, McKee,
Mendenhall, Passwater, Pierstorff, Pyle, Ribble, Robinson,
Sipes, Smith, Thomas, Watters, Woods and Yeager.

Published
by
JOHN E. FETZER FOUNDATION, INC.
of
Michigan

17. The title page of *The Men from Wengen and America's Agony*, 1971.

through the power of "spiritual intuition"; and "through [new] spiritual dynamics, the necessity of armed conflict will be eliminated." Ultimately, "science and spiritual forces will unite under the aegis of Energy Intelligence," "the earth will be resurrected, re-formed and raised into a higher dimension," and "all the people of the world will unite to express the truths central to all major religions" in a "New Age spirituality."[42]

Fetzer's Worldview

Fetzer's genealogy books were largely intended to be given away to family and friends and never did reach a wide audience. Stacks of them can still be found on the shelves of the archives at the Fetzer Institute. Nevertheless, Fetzer's several iterative attempts to articulate his worldview during the 1960s and early '70s are invaluable to understanding his spiritual evolution, for it is possible now to define the basic contours of his conception of a "New Age spirituality" according to the basic categories of theology, cosmology, anthropology, soteriology, ethics, and eschatology. With regard to theology and cosmology, Fetzer was resolutely monistic, and his "concept of God goes far beyond the anthropomorphic concept of God in that He encompasses the total universe as One Being."[43] Everything that is, is formed by and with God's "Intelligent Energy," which some people call "consciousness" or "mind," others "spirit," and others "love." As for religious anthropology, the human being, too, is formed entirely by this divine energy, and therefore God dwells in all of us and is always available as a source of power and wisdom. However, in most human beings, the channel of the subconscious is blocked, and God's "Intelligent Energy" cannot flow through us. The ultimate goal of human life, therefore, its soteriology, so to speak, is to transform one's consciousness into super-consciousness or Christ Consciousness by completely unblocking the flow. Once this is achieved, then health, happiness, prosperity—perhaps even psychic powers—will be ours. For many individuals, achieving this state of complete openness to God's energy might require reincarnating through multiple lifetimes, but once achieved, our afterlife journey back toward our cosmic source will continue forever unimpeded.

Despite the initial gloominess of "America's Agony," Fetzer's worldview was fundamentally, relentlessly optimistic. He was certain that all people could eventually achieve superconsciousness. This was almost all but guaranteed not only by the very structure and laws of the universe but also because of the presence of those superior beings, the Masters, who would always be available to help us on our way. Throughout history, these Masters have appeared at crucial times, for example, the Buddha, Lao-tzu, and Jesus, whose true gospel was that of Christ Consciousness, not atonement. Moreover, in Fetzer's mind, the Masters also functioned as ethical exemplars since their unconditional compassion toward us modeled how we should behave toward others. Ultimately, it was not enough that we unblock ourselves: we must also open ourselves to the free flow of God's energy or love through and between all people, and this by means of a compassionate forgiveness that acts like so many acupuncture needles in the body politic. And, finally, once humanity had reached a critical mass of superconsciousness—primarily through the leadership of the United States, whose sacred destiny it was—Fetzer prophesied great things: a now spiritualized science would make unimaginable intellectual and technological progress, social relations would be perfected, a lasting peace would be achieved, and the earth would be totally transformed for the better. Earlier in life, Fetzer might have called such an eschatology millennial, but now it was nothing less than the promise of the New Age.

Although the term "New Age" did not come into common use for another decade, John Fetzer's worldview closely followed what became the "soft orthodoxies" of the New Age movement.[44] In this, he was anticipating a worldview that millions of Americans and others embraced in the 1980s and 1990s, and that precipitated the "spiritual revolution" of the first decade of the twenty-first century.[45] John Fetzer may have been a conservative businessman from Kalamazoo, Michigan, but he was also an intuitive soul who caught the zeitgeist of the coming era with uncanny clarity.

The Science of Spirit

The Fetzer Foundation and Parapsychological Research (1970s)

John Fetzer, having thought deeply about his worldview and its values, now began to think seriously about how he could actualize those values in larger service to the world. Perhaps providentially, a change in the tax code prompted Fetzer to begin considering how his foundation could play a role in addressing the challenges and bringing about the changes he had talked about in "This I Believe" and "America's Agony." Indeed, as a February 1973 letter reveals, Fetzer intended "America's Agony" to guide the reorganization of the foundation, which he was contemplating as he wrote.[1]

The Fetzer Trust had been established back in 1954 and incorporated as a private foundation in 1962, but changes in the tax codes in 1972, resulting in what Fetzer termed "confiscatory taxation," led him to convert it into a "semipublic" foundation in order to preserve its capital. This change meant that Fetzer now had to identify worthy projects more aggressively and to open seats on the board to representatives of the institutions that he chose to fund. When the trust was originally created, its mission was "to give grants for religious, charitable, scientific, library and/or educational purposes." With its conversion to a public foundation, such a broad mission was no longer appropriate, both because the law demanded a more focused purpose and also because Fetzer wished to make sure that the outside people who joined his board shared his worldview and its values and wished to spread them. Indeed, guided by the voice of the Holy Spirit, Fetzer believed that the foundation's reorganization was his "'call' to service."[2] Happily, at this point in his life, John Fetzer knew precisely what the focus of that service would be: parapsychological research.

Fetzer and Parapsychological Research

John Fetzer had, of course, been fascinated by paranormal phenomena and parapsychological research for decades. His participation in Spiritualism and divination, his work with the pendulum and the Ouija board, and his interaction with psychics such as Jeane Dixon and scientists such as Shafica Karagulla had convinced him not only of the reality of the phenomena but of the possibility that psychic powers might be understood scientifically. Thus, the reality of such powers became a cornerstone of his spiritual vision as articulated in "This I Believe" and "America's Agony." In fact, Fetzer always suspected that he himself had some psychic powers, at least to a limited degree. In a 1974 interview with *Psychic* magazine, "Testing for Executive ESP," Fetzer attributed his business successes and his ability to pick good people to his intuition, which, in the context of the article, was clearly seen as a form of extrasensory perception.[3] And in addition to his belief in ESP, Fetzer also believed in his personal power of psychokinesis (PK). Fetzer used to carry a simple pendulum on his person, and when he needed to make a decision about which there might be some debate, he would suspend the pendulum's bob from his index finger and thumb and ask simple yes/no questions. The subsequent deflection of the bob either left or right would supply the answer. The pendulum figured in one of the more celebrated stories that highlighted Fetzer's belief in PK. In 1976, the Tigers' star pitcher Mark "the Bird" Fidrych began to feel self-conscious because of his habit of talking to the baseball, telling it where to go before each pitch. To deal with the problem, Fetzer invited Fidrych to his office for a session with the pendulum, instructing the pitcher that, if they concentrated, they could "make that pendulum move with the power of [their] minds." The experiment, according to Fidrych's later recollection, was successful, the two of them making the bob move at will in one direction and then the other. Fetzer's point here was not to answer any question but to demonstrate to Fidrych that we all have the power of PK and that that was the secret behind the effectiveness of his unique pitching style.[4] Such powers, Fetzer believed, were our natural birthright and a key to humanity's survival. It would take science, however, to teach us how to use them efficiently.

In November 1972, the board of the John E. Fetzer Foundation met to ratify the new mission of the newly public foundation.[5] After a "motion duly made and seconded, a program of research in the field of parapsychology was approved as the initial program to be undertaken," and it was stipulated that "eight institutions who would agree to cooperate in such research [would] be selected as those to be supported." Funded programs would place "particular emphasis . . . on initiating research on natural means of enabling men to live and grow as persons, and contribute to the propagation of the highest human values." Moreover, "tools of modern technology, which require full involvement of the person as a volitional being, would be utilized," and the results of the research would be disseminated through "courses, seminars and workshops" offered by the chosen institutions and made available to the community at large "for extension purposes."[6]

At an earlier board meeting, some institutions had already been identified. These included Duke University and the University of California, as well as the local schools Kalamazoo College, Western Michigan University, and Nazareth College. Meanwhile, looking for further guidance, Fetzer entered into "extensive correspondence" with the American Society for Psychical Research, J. B. Rhine's Research on the Nature of Man Foundation, and Edgar D. Mitchell and Associates. This latter organization had been created shortly before by the mystically inclined Apollo astronaut to pursue investigation into the "nonphysical aspects of the universe" and "to bring about a transformation of human consciousness . . . for the purpose of planetary survival." Later, the organization formed the basis for the Institute of Noetic Sciences, or IONs.[7]

Inspired by this correspondence, Fetzer spent the first week of January 1973 traveling to make personal contacts within the world of parapsychological research.[8] He went first to New York City, where he met with Marian Nester of the American Society for Psychical Research and Eileen Coly (daughter of the famous psychic Eileen Garrett), who headed the Parapsychology Foundation. Next, in Durham, North Carolina, Fetzer met personally with J. B. Rhine, the dean of parapsychological research in the United States, and toured the facilities of his Foundation for Research on the Nature of Man, which Fetzer thought was "an outstanding organization." Also in Durham, Fetzer met the poltergeist researchers William R. Roll and Robert Morris of the Psychical Research Foundation and William Joines of the Duke University Department of Electrical Engineering, all of whose approaches to psychic phenomena as fundamentally electrical in nature fascinated Fetzer. Finally, Fetzer wound up his trip with a visit to the University of Virginia School of Medicine to confer with Ian Stevenson and J. G. Pratt, whose research into reincarnation was soon to become widely cited and debated.

While in New York, Eileen Coly had suggested that Fetzer meet Jeanne Pontius Rindge, who directed the Human Dimensions Institute of Rosary Hill College in Buffalo, New York.[9] Fetzer was already in contact with the institute, having read an article about it in *Psychic* magazine.[10] Fetzer was impressed not only by the research being conducted by the institute (for example, into psychic healing and Kirlian photography) but also by the institute's concerted efforts at education and practical outreach.[11] Fetzer apparently did not find the time to visit Rosary Hill on his first fact-finding trip east, but he soon was in contact with Rindge, with whom he entered into a long correspondence. He sent her a copy of "America's Agony," whose remarks on "new age education" she approved and asked to reproduce in her *Human Dimensions* magazine. Fetzer had also written Rindge that while he was "a complete neophyte when it comes to basic knowledge of parapsychology," he was convinced "that one day much of the unknown will be explained in electronic terms."[12] In response, Rindge sent Fetzer the "Letter to the Scientist" from Alice Bailey's *Esoteric Healing* (1953), which likewise characterized psychic power ("psi") as electrical in nature and therefore amenable to scientific understanding.[13] The Bailey excerpt must have confirmed for Fetzer that he and Rindge were indeed on the same wavelength when it came to the nature of psi.

By May 1973, the Fetzer Foundation board had expanded to include representatives from nine outside institutions, including Rindge from Rosary Hill, Joines from Duke University, and Stevenson from the University of Virginia.[14] From the beginning, however, there was considerable debate among the board members about what kinds of parapsychological projects should be funded. By the 1970s, the variety of topics pursued and the range of methods being used by parapsychological researchers had become overwhelming. Reaching a consensus about which to support was a struggle. At the September 1973 board meeting, therefore, in order to break the impasse, John Fetzer volunteered to "produce a digest of some of the reported research which had been previously reported in India" in order to "stimulate new reactions amongst [the board's] members which would be helpful in reducing [the foundation's] programs to a meaningful effort."[15] The "reported research" Fetzer had in mind was none other than Baird Spalding's *Life and Teachings of the Masters of the Far East.* Fetzer duly produced a twenty-page summary of Spalding's books.[16]

In Fetzer's introduction to what came to be called the "Spalding Memo," he wrote that he was excited by recent discoveries by the Nobel Prize–winning physicist Carl Anderson, whose research on "anti-electrons" seemed to indicate the existence of the "anti-physical—a channel to another dimension of the cosmic." Fetzer believed that this recognition of "anti-matter" was a prelude to new discoveries in "metaphysics and parapsychology."[17] What is more, Fetzer had been "astonished to find that the same thesis seems to be alluded to in the writings of the Far East," as translated and communicated by Baird Spalding. Fetzer then proceeded to reproduce excerpts from the five volumes, followed by his personal commentary. Fetzer began the memo with Spalding's report of the existence of "marble tablets" hidden in Tibet on which were recorded advanced cosmological knowledge, long anticipating Einstein and quantum theory. According to the tablets, the cosmos is continually created by a "wise intelligence" that emanates "Universal Energy," which is the spiritual (high vibration) and physical (low vibration) basis for everything. Indeed, "cosmic rays," newly identified by astrophysicists, are simply a pure form of this "Universal Energy." That such advanced knowledge was already recorded thousands of years ago, perhaps in the age of Atlantis, indicated to Fetzer that some of Spalding's more incredible claims might be true and bear investigation. These included a camera that recorded past events and the idea that the cosmos was filled with "inaudible sounds," which, if properly projected, could produce in people "emotional feelings such as love, peace, harmony, and perfection that benefit the whole world."[18]

Spalding's most important discovery from the Masters, according to Fetzer, was that human beings were electronic amplifiers who, when properly instructed, could receive and "transform God-power and send it out with such force that it is irresistible." Once "the body become[s] a generator through which this Great Creative Radiating Principle flows," one will have complete control over matter by means of the power of consciousness. Individuals will now enjoy something akin to ESP, which is probably due to "amplitude modulation through the mind" by means of which "wave forms [are] modulated into intelligible characters of transmission" (i.e., information). Given the antiquity of these discoveries, why have these truths not been rediscovered before, Fetzer wondered? Perhaps it was because, as Spalding points out (in Fetzer's paraphrase), "in order for [scientists] to make discoveries, [they] must definitely work with Principle [i.e., belief in God as Universal Energy] and that if they do so, their research will be more effective and the time frame will be considerably reduced." Thus, the Spalding Memo signaled not only the types of metaphysical and parapsychological research topics Fetzer was interested in funding but also the ideal attitude of the investigators doing the research.

The Spalding Memo was apparently sent out to board members in September, and a compilation of ten replies (without names) was made available to the board at the November 1973 meeting.[19] Perhaps not surprisingly, several of the responders were highly skeptical of the historicity of Spalding's Tibetan expedition, and one found its metaphysics confusing or, at best, "speculative and theoretical and a lot of it metaphorical." Another stated flatly,

> In general, I do not see documents like Spalding's as highly likely sources of important ideas for influencing scientific understanding of the paranormal. Apart from questions of accuracy, they are, I think, too abstract and remote from the possibility of observational test. . . . Researchers in the paranormal are certainly likely to be increasingly aware of ideas and practices developed in India and Tibet, and their work is likely to be much more fruitful for it. But for the development now of substantial verified knowledge and understanding of the paranormal, I think increased support of pertinent scientific research is the most central factor.

Others, however, while still rejecting the veracity of his narrative, were nevertheless intrigued by Spalding's metaphysics—or at least Fetzer's interpretation of it. Since "metaphysics underlies and shapes empirical inquiry," one responder "welcome[d] new paradigms as stimulating and potentially productive." He thus found that "Eastern religious and philosophical thought" contained "data of great relevance" for parapsychological investigation today. And a few apparently had no problem with the fantastic nature of Spalding's reports: "Spalding certainly suggests experiences," one respondent wrote, "which are amazing just as many of the insights that grow out of quantum mechanics are amazing. It seems desirable to put these kinds of insights together to form a new viewpoint which would provide more understanding and less pain in the world."[20]

Fetzer stated that he considered these responses "to be invaluable toward the establishment of a future policy for the John E. Fetzer Foundation." However, it is hard to see how they gave much guidance, since they reproduce one of the fundamental cleavages that had bedeviled parapsychological research from the beginning. Put simply, should such research be conducted, as one responder put it, on purely objective ("demonstrational") grounds, seeking at most to establish, "though without absolutely repeatable evidence, the presence of phenomena but not advancing very far our understanding of them"? Or should such research be open to a spiritual science based on recognition that "man's potentials and his place in the world are much broader and deeper than some contemporary views would imply"?[21] The first promised very slow progress but acceptability to the mainstream scientific world, while the second seemed to promise faster results but at the cost of credibility to those who did not share the spiritual worldview.

This dilemma continued to be discussed by the Fetzer board well into 1974, when R. A. McConnell, a parapsychologist at the University of Pittsburgh, forwarded to Fetzer a paper titled "Parapsychology: Its Future Organization and Support."[22] In a reference perhaps to Fetzer himself, McConnell framed the issue this way: "Recently I was approached by a successful businessman of evident intelligence and discernment who wanted to do something for parapsychology. I asked him: 'Are you interested in parapsychology as a science, that is, as a quest for understanding using the theoretical-empirical method in the tradition of Western science, or are you concerned with how parapsychology may provide support for the ethical aspirations that, in large measure, you and I share with most thoughtful members of our culture?' I have not yet received his answer." McConnell's own answer to his question was unequivocal: "Progress in basic science requires a disciplined separation of non-scientific ends from scientific activities. Particularly in a pioneering field, one cannot afford to be a softhearted scientist any more than in the medical arena one can be a softhearted surgeon. A distant vision may provide motivation, but the hope for quick salvation is of no help in the conduct of frontier research." In other words, he supported research that was "scientific," not "inspirational."[23] Fetzer circulated the paper to his board and solicited their comments. Predictably, some on the board applauded McConnell's approach ("it is time we moved away from mysticism to scientific research"), while others felt it evinced a "spiritual blind spot":

> I venerate the awesome power of man's intellect, but I know that its powers and its inspirations flow from deeper sources, and it is precisely those spiritual sources which best suggest how to carry out detailed research into parapsychology, mysticism, and the occult. McConnell seems, unfortunately, not to understand this and he, therefore, makes suggestions about how to best further parapsychology which omits the most potent sources of wisdom. His intellectual arguments are erudite and highly polished and he makes valid points with which reasonable persons may agree or disagree. But in the cold brilliant light of the intellect the flickering candles of spiritual illumination can easily be overlooked. This is my greatest concern; because it would severely limit progress and understanding in parapsychology.[24]

In addition to the disagreement over what kind of science (materialist versus spiritual) should be employed in parapsychological research, a different but related issue was whether parapsychology should focus primarily on quantitative bench science or whether more effort should be put into qualitative research, investigating so-called spontaneous phenomena as it is actually experienced by people out in the world. Rindge replied, citing a paper by D. Scott Rogo that appeared in *Fate* magazine (a copy of which she sent to Fetzer),

> I will say that I feel there is much to commend in McConnell's views, but I am concerned, as many of us are who are more on the "firing line" where people live, with the apparent cul-de-sac which the professional "elitism" and purism have engendered in the (commendable) effort to conform psychic phenomena to conventional scientific procedures. The results are minimal, while, at the same time, psychic

experiences are blossoming out all over the place. . . . I wonder if D. Scott Rogo . . . may not be thinking more appropriately when he says, "I am not arguing against laboratory results and methodology but I am pointing out that after more than 30 years some basic objections still have not been met. The growing dissatisfaction with the meager and disputable results in the laboratory show that this area no longer offers parapsychology the new horizons it seemed to offer 40 years ago—especially since gifted sensitives seldom have been able to channel their abilities into the laboratory. There seems to be only one direction for psychical research to take—actually only one area to explore; psychical phenomena themselves. This means leaving the laboratory to explore what is occurring in real life."[25]

The battle between laboratory research and field research was long standing in parapsychology and can be traced back to the very beginnings of the field. Indeed, J. B. Rhine in part promoted his brand of laboratory research as fundamentally better than the "old fashioned" field research carried out by, for example, the Society for Psychical Research. Ironically, however, Rhine's wife, Louisa, who was a noted researcher in her own right, spent most of her later career doing fieldwork on spontaneous paranormal phenomena, thus indicating that this was not an issue easily solved even by the experts.[26]

Not having reached a consensus among the American investigators on the board about the best approach to parapsychology, Fetzer decided to make a paranormal study tour of Europe, ostensibly to identify possible partnerships but perhaps also hoping he could find among European parapsychologists the consensus that he could not find at home. Rindge provided Fetzer with several introductions and suggested others he should visit. The minutes from the October 1974 board meeting before his trip listed parapsychologists working in England, France, and Germany.[27] It is not entirely clear from the record whether Fetzer met with all who were on his list, but we do know that on October 17, in addition to meeting with the staff of the British Society of Psychic Research in London, Fetzer met with Marcus McCausland and his wife, and with Joan Grant. McCausland was partner in the creation of one of the first holistic health organizations in the United Kingdom, Health for the New Age, while Grant was a well-known psychic, famous for novels such as the *Winged Pharaoh* (1937) reportedly based on her past life experiences as an Egyptian priestess. Grant and her psychiatrist husband, Denys Kelsey, operated consulting rooms in London using a form of past-life regression as therapy. The next day, Fetzer met with Ena Twigg, then arguably Europe's most famous clairvoyant.[28] Fetzer's next recorded visit was on October 25 with Hans Bender at his laboratory in Freiberg, Germany. Bender was famous for his research regarding poltergeist phenomena and was an excellent example of the qualitative case-study approach to parapsychology.[29]

Returning to Kalamazoo, Fetzer reported that the "entire investigatory trip was most satisfying" and that he hoped to develop the contacts he made in Europe. However, it is not clear what impact this had on the policy problem of which kinds of parapsychological research should be funded.[30] A review of the funded research throughout the 1970s shows a continued willingness to fund an eclectic mix of parapsychological research projects on a variety of topics and utilizing a variety of methodologies (lab versus field research) but no clear focus.

Early Funded Research

The first funding cycle for the Fetzer Foundation under its mandate to support research in parapsychology was 1973.[31] That year, small incentive grants were given to Rindge's Human Dimensions Institute to fund its magazine and to two local Kalamazoo institutions, Nazareth College (principal investigator Jim Keating) and Bronson Methodist Hospital (principal investigator Doyle Wilson), both for the promotion of awareness of the paranormal and parapsychological research. The following year, Kalamazoo College got a like grant, and the foundation continued to fund parapsychological workshops and talks at the college until 1982.[32] The bulk of the foundation's grants, however, went to fund high-profile academic research programs in parapsychology at major universities. In 1973, these included grants to Ian Stevenson at the University of Virginia (UVA) to investigate cases of reincarnation and to William G. Roll of Duke University for research on Kirlian photography and the nature of the human aura. For the next several years, both UVA and Duke continued to receive Fetzer grants ranging from $500 to $7,500 for a variety of projects, including investigations of reincarnation, PK, and near-death experiences at UVA; and PK, poltergeists, and hauntings at Duke and the nearby Psychical Research Foundation. And by the end of the decade, large Fetzer grants ranging from $12,000 to $30,000 were being awarded to Robert Jahn of the Princeton Engineering Anomalies Research (PEAR) Lab, which investigated a variety of paranormal phenomena including PK and remote viewing.[33] Because of the potential national defense uses of remote viewing, Fetzer touted Jahn's research as the United States' best antidote to the progress being made in psychical research by the Soviet Union.[34]

One of the longest running projects funded by the Fetzer Foundation was research on biofeedback at the Langley Porter Neuropsychiatric Institute at the University of California, San Francisco. In 1967, Fetzer's brother-in-law, Charles LeVant ("Vant") Yeager, was a medical researcher at the institute when Fetzer sent him a letter asking for information on current ESP research.[35] This prompted Yeager to send Fetzer a brief overview of research at the Langley Porter Institute on the then-new technique of biofeedback. Biofeedback, which was to become something a scientific fad in the following years, was based on the idea that certain autonomic processes of the body (e.g., heart rate, blood pressure, muscle tension, skin temperature, brain waves) could be put under conscious control by the power of mind. Subjects were exposed to machines that audibly or visually reproduced the rhythm of particular autonomic functions such as brain waves, and then by concentrating on the audio or visual signal, they were reportedly able to affect the speed or frequency of the function's rhythm, thus leading to greater calmness and physical health. The Langley

Porter project was specifically aimed at training astronauts in biofeedback to make the isolation of spaceflight bearable.

Fetzer was impressed by what Yeager sent him, writing that if such a "technique could be developed to maintain unlimited periods of self-containment, or as referred to in metaphysics as 'meditation,' the end result could bring about a complete revolution of attitudes."[36] In 1970, Fetzer visited Yeager at Langley Porter and was introduced to the staff, including Joe Kamiya, one of the pioneers of biofeedback, and submitted himself to having traces of own brain waves made. (Yeager characterized Fetzer's brainwaves as "well integrated.")[37] By 1973, when the foundation was looking for projects to support, Fetzer suggested to Yeager that biofeedback might be a good prospect. Yeager, however, was on the verge of retirement,[38] and while he long remained involved in the project, the principal investigator at Langley Porter became James Hardt, who began to receive foundation funding for biofeedback research that year.[39]

With Fetzer's support, Hardt soon became one of the premier exponents of biofeedback in the United States. Over the following twelve years during which the foundation funded his research, Hardt maintained a lively correspondence with his benefactor. He shared John Fetzer's interest in the paranormal and parapsychological research, believing that biofeedback could "bring about a quantum level increase in Human Consciousness."[40] In addition to its medical uses, Hardt was keenly interested in using the technique to explore human consciousness and the spiritual and psychic aspects of human beings, believing that the "core of the alpha experience" is "the mystical."[41] To this end, he did research in India on yogis and firewalkers and on psychics and Zen meditators in San Francisco.[42] Hardt suggested in a letter to Fetzer that biofeedback might be a way to develop shared consciousness among human beings and perhaps even to free the astral body.[43] Hardt saw Fetzer as a mentor, writing that Fetzer inspired him "to a very high path" and that Fetzer's "example and instruction" had taught him "to believe and share with [Fetzer] in the working of miracles."[44] Fetzer, for his part, returned the complement, commenting to his secretary, Carolyn Dailey, "I would say Dr. Jim Hardt is 'right on.'

What more could one say. I would like to see more of this man and I would like all people in our Foundation inspired by this man's spiritual awareness and enthusiasm. This is what we have needed, this is what it's all about. I was impressed before by his communications, but more impressed now and enthused now that I have actually looked [at] specific examples of his spirituality and cosmic awareness and goals for the benefit of mankind."[45] Fetzer, too, came to believe that biofeedback had tremendous potential for "transcendental breakthrough events," perhaps becoming the means by which "alternate consciousness can be spread most effectively and rapidly throughout the cultures of mankind." Indeed, in 1978, Fetzer took the time to listen to a series of biofeedback training tapes produced by Hardt, which he said induced in him "an intense feeling of well being, relaxation and sense of attunement," including a mystical "feeling of communication with another mind." Fetzer eventually underwent extensive alpha biofeedback training with Hardt at his Tucson ranch in 1988.[46] Fetzer also attempted to stimulate biofeedback research at the local level, providing money for workshops at Kalamazoo College under the supervision of psychology professor Lonnie Supnick and, in 1978, financing a Center for Biofeedback and Mind Control at Western Michigan University (WMU) under the supervision of Richard R. Williams in the College of Health and Human Services. A year later, Williams, with Fetzer's support, partnered with Bronson Hospital to develop a full-blown program in holistic health at WMU, with biofeedback as a key component.[47]

In addition to Langley Porter, the Fetzer Foundation partnered closely for a time with the Institute of Noetic Sciences (IONS), "noetic" meaning "intuitive mind" or "inner knowing." Founded in 1973 by the astronaut Edgar D. Mitchell and Paul Temple, IONS's mission was to support "research and education in the processes of human consciousness to help achieve a new understanding and expanded awareness among all people."[48] To this end, IONS funded several projects in parapsychology that paralleled those of the Fetzer Foundation. Apparently, John Fetzer had heard through newspaper accounts about the telepathy experiments that Mitchell had run from space during Apollo 14 and invited him to a

Tigers game in 1973. The two hit it off, and when Mitchell formed IONS, he asked Fetzer to be on the board.[49] It was through the board that Fetzer met such luminaries as Marilyn Ferguson, author of the New Age manifesto *The Aquarian Conspiracy* (1980); the future Fetzer Foundation president Glenn Olds; and most importantly, Judith Skutch Whitson, who soon came to play an important role in Fetzer's spiritual life.[50] As with the Fetzer Foundation, it was several years before the IONS board settled on a specific research agenda, so it was not until 1976 that it received its first grant from Fetzer. By 1978, however, the Fetzer board had decided to undertake a major collaboration with Mitchell's foundation, with the Fetzer Foundation supplying funds and IONS handling program selection and administration. Thus, an officer of IONS, Brendan O'Regan, took on the role of project director for the Fetzer Foundation at IONS.[51]

Unfortunately, perhaps due to the still-inchoate nature of both foundations, collaboration with IONS did not go smoothly. Differences in opinions eventually led Fetzer to decide to back away from providing sustaining support to IONS at that time. He thus stopped attending IONS board meeting and by 1979 was only listed on its board roster under "Members Emeritus."[52] The Fetzer Foundation continued to work with IONS for years to come, but Fetzer had concluded from this experience that, for the time being at least, he should be careful to keep his foundation independent from other organizations, no matter how much they shared in outlook. As Fetzer put it, "I have concluded that each one of us, as we listen to the Voice [of the Holy Spirit], [should] find our own vineyard in which to work."[53]

What this specific vineyard would be was slowly becoming clearer to John Fetzer. While Fetzer would always remain interested in parapsychological research, he soon became "disappointed in [many parapsychological] programs which seemingly are repetitious and very short on definition and purpose." His board echoed his frustration: "More and more it seems to us that [funded parapsychological] research to date seems to be quite repeatable but compounding more of the same kinds of evidence in more or less an endless circle."[54] The parapsychology programs that did continue to generate the most enthusiasm in Fetzer and his board were those

18. John E. Fetzer and Edgar Mitchell, ca. 1979. (Courtesy of Judy Skutch Whitson)

that had some connection to health, such as Hardt's biofeedback project and the local work being done by Williams in the Holistic Health Program at Western Michigan University. Both demonstrated empirically that there was a parapsychological aspect to health and healing, and the biofeedback projects in particular held out the promise that practical new technologies based on this were now possible. Fetzer had always been concerned with his health since a young man, and he came out of a tradition, Seventh-day Adventism, that closely linked physical and spiritual health.[55] What is more, Fetzer himself was fascinated by new technologies of all kinds, stimulated, as he said, by his childhood reading of the Tom Swift stories.[56] Thus, by the end of the 1970s, a major shift in the foundation's funding priorities was about to occur, from pure research in parapsychology to research into the parapsychological aspects of health and the development of alternative medical technologies.

John Fetzer's Personal Practice

While John Fetzer was reorganizing his foundation, he continued to explore his personal spiritual path, especially with regard to practice. For example, although finished with his family genealogies, Fetzer continued to consult the Ouija board at the behest of the English medium Ena Twigg, who at their 1974 meeting suggested that he use it to explore his past lives through a spirit guide named Ibrahim. Taking her advice, perhaps because this seemed to him a logical extension of his genealogical work, Fetzer subsequently contacted not only Ibrahim but also Jesus, the Ascended Master Hilarion, a being called Tamud, a host of other entities identified only by initials (A.T., C.T., A.Z., N.M., etc.), and the Great White Brotherhood itself. The voluminous transcripts of these Ouija sessions, which lasted until 1982, record that the various entities related in great detail the facts of Fetzer's past lives, including those as Amnusta M-Alamaz from Mu; Ra, a high priest in ancient Egypt; St. Paul the Apostle; and the Spanish mystic St. John of the Cross. Moreover, the entities also confirmed that many of Fetzer's closest friends and associates had reincarnated with him through these lives. Although Fetzer was never completely uncritical of what he learned by this method, he nevertheless put a great deal of stock in these communications and relied on them not only for information about his and others' past lives but for continued guidance in his present life as well. During this period, Fetzer made few decisions about his media businesses, the Tigers, and the foundation, not to mention his personal and professional relationships, without first consulting the Ouija board.[57]

It was back in 1974, too, that Fetzer encountered Transcendental Meditation (TM), a Hindu meditation practice brought to this country by Maharishi Mahesh Yogi in the 1960s. TM is the practice of meditation fifteen to twenty minutes a day in order to achieve a deeper, "transcendental" form of consciousness that not only is "physically and mentally refreshing" but also "energizes a person to use a vastly wider range of mental powers, and therefore become more creative, as well as happier." Originally a physicist by training, the Maharishi presented his meditation technique in the context of a simplified form of Vedanta, and the practice itself was tailored to Westerners. TM eschewed complicated Sanskrit terminology and years of ascetic practice in favor of short trainings by a guru, mostly Westerners themselves, who would assign a unique mantra to each student at initiation, after which students were free to practice TM in small groups or individually. There was also a societal aspect to TM, for the Maharishi claimed that if a critical mass of TM meditators was achieved, the world would instantly be transformed into a more peaceful and loving place. TM caught on in the United States, becoming what Ellwood characterizes as "a cultural phenomenon, initiating a million people in its first two decades."[58]

John Fetzer had touted meditation as early as *One Man's Family* but admitted in the 1974 *Psychic* interview that he himself did not practice it.[59] Soon, however, after reading about TM in a book,[60] he and Rhea began attending a TM center in Tucson.[61] The following year, Fetzer was practicing TM regularly and recommending it to others, including his broadcast employees and, most famously, the Detroit Tigers at their 1974 spring training. According to newspaper articles at the time, several of the Tigers players found the practice useful to reduce stress and increase focus, and one paper even reported that the Tigers were "on the spiritual route to success." Not all approved, however, and at least one western Michigan minister attributed the Tiger's 1975 losing season to the introduction of this dangerous form of "disguised Hinduism."[62]

In April 1975, Fetzer and his wife traveled to Los Angeles to attend a lecture by the Maharishi, after which Fetzer had a private interview with him. Fetzer advised the Maharishi on the effective use of TV to promote the TM message in the United States, while the guru implored Fetzer to use his influence to get President Ford and Henry Kissinger to practice TM, since TM "was the plan for the new age, and America has to be in the vanguard of this effort." Fetzer left greatly impressed, commenting that the Maharishi was both "a scientist and a holy man, a rare combination in the history of the world." "Through his knowledge of the combined disciplines," Fetzer wrote later, "he was able to evolve an understanding of meditation which leads to scientific conclusions that establish the efficacy of TM as a physiological and mental aid to the human anatomy."[63] Fetzer subsequently directed his broadcast company to promote programming featuring TM and its founder, although he carefully specified, "anything we do, either on a commercial or promo basis or public service contribution, should strictly adhere to the scientific aspect of the subject and if possible, play down completely the Far-Eastern matters, which have a such a dilatory effect on the West." Ever mindful of his privacy and public image, he also made it clear that he did "not wish to publicize . . . personal participation in this subject either as a foundation, company, or the baseball club."[64] Nevertheless, Fetzer himself continued to practice TM for the next several years.

The 1970s were also important for Fetzer's personal practice because it was during this decade that he discovered *A Course in Miracles*. During the 1960s, Dr. Helen Schucman, a professor of medical psychology at the College of Physicians and Surgeons at the Columbia-Presbyterian Medical Center in New York City, began spontaneously to channel an "inner voice." In October 1965, the voice announced to her, "This is a course in miracles. Please take notes."[65] This she did, reluctantly, for over seven years, producing a manuscript of over fifteen hundred pages. Despite her years as scribe, Schucman contended that she never believed in the channelings, although she and her colleague Bill Thetford approached Judy Skutch Whitson about possible dissemination of the *Course*. Whitson, who at the time was involved in parapsychological research through her New York–based Foundation for Parapsychological Investigation, secured funding to publish the *Course* as a three-volume set, which she did in 1975 through a new organization, the Foundation for Inner Peace, located in New York City. This brought the *Course* to a wide audience. Its popularity proved phenomenal, becoming, in the words of one scholar, "the most obvious choice" if one had to choose the "'sacred scripture' of the New Age movement." By 2016, nearly three millions copies were said to be in circulation around the globe.[66]

A Course in Miracles, which is purported to be the words of Jesus as communicated by the Holy Spirit, is organized into a main text, a workbook of 365 lessons, and a brief "Manual for Teachers." The central teaching of the *Course* is summed up in its famous opening lines: "Nothing real can be threatened. Nothing unreal exists. Herein lies the peace of God." Despite its rather traditional theistic language, the *Course* rests on an absolute spiritual monism in which the world is fundamentally an illusion and the ego is as illusory as the world. Spiritual progress in this system comes by getting beyond the ego to an inner spiritual "awareness of perfect oneness, and the knowledge that there is nothing else." The first workbook provides a series of spiritual exercises that gradually prepare one for "the undoing of the way you see now," and the second, for "the acquisition of true perceptions."[67] As the scholar Jon Klimo points out, "many of the exercises parallel traditional psychotherapeutic approaches such as working to undo 'negative self-programming' acquired from past experience and learning to be 'in the now.'"[68] Once this correct awareness is achieved, the *Course* promises to lead students to greater happiness through a loss of fear and anxiety in favor of God's perfect love and peace.

John Fetzer first encountered *A Course in Miracles* through Judy Skutch Whitson, his fellow IONS board member. Two weeks after Whitson received the manuscript of the *Course* from Schucman and Thetford, she asked for permission to send it to Fetzer. As luck would have it, Fetzer had suffered a mild heart attack and was recovering at his ranch in Tucson. With persistence, Whitson managed to locate him and send him the *Course*. Fetzer always had had an interest in channeled texts such as Alice Bailey's works, the *Urantia Book*, the *Aquarian Gospel of Jesus* of Levi Dowling, and Jane Roberts' Seth material,[69] but he apparently found the *Course* much more compelling. According to Whitson, his immediate response to the *Course* was overwhelming: "I've looked here and I've looked there and I've poked under all sorts of debris . . . and I have found some nuggets of gold in some of the ancient wisdoms and the perennial philosophies, but I have never, ever, ever imagined I would find it all in one place, and written just for me."[70] Soon Fetzer was recommending the *Course* to friends and colleagues, often sending them a set of the *Miracle* books once they were published, and he relished sharing insights with other *Miracle* devotees.[71] Together with his personal secretary, Carolyn Dailey, Fetzer intensively studied the text, reading it over several times. Indeed, Fetzer's personal copies of the three published volumes show heavy use and extensive annotations.[72] In a letter to a family friend, Fetzer summarized the *Course* in this way:

Gone is ego, guilt and fear as I am sustained in perfect health by the love of God within and thus become one with the Light of the World. Knowing that as I give I receive, I forgive all mankind, including my adversaries without rancor or attack. My freedom from conflict being the miracle of forgiveness of all personal negation, and the solution to the collective problem of life. I am still and undisturbed as God's reality and solely function with love through creative intelligence within (Holy Spirit). I therefore accept with eternal gratitude the peace of salvation which is mine forevermore.[73]

After Judy Skutch Whitson introduced Fetzer to the *Course*, she became an important advisor to him and a close personal friend. (Characteristically, Fetzer once told her that they had been married in a previous life; Whitson, for her part, told Fetzer that she thought he was a Lamed Vovnik, one of the thirty-six hidden Masters that Jewish lore maintains are always present on earth, but Fetzer demurred).[74] By 1976, Whitson had become a member of the Fetzer Foundation's board, on which she served for the next twenty years.[75]

It was through Whitson that Fetzer enormously expanded his contacts in the psychic and metaphysical subcultures of the Untied States. The two, for example, held a number of informal meetings in Detroit and Chicago at which Whitson introduced Fetzer to important figures in the world of parapsychological research, such J. Alan Hynek, the ufologist; Brendan O'Regan and Willis Harman, both of whom became associated with IONS; and Andrija Puharich, famous for his promotion of Uri Geller and an expert on Nikola Tesla. Fetzer also traveled to visit Whitson at her home in New York, where she would host other luminaries from the paranormal world. These included, in addition to Helen Schucman[76] and William Thetford, Stanley Krippner from the Maimonides Dream Lab, Karlis Osis of the American Society for Psychical Research, and William McGarey of ARE. In July 1978, en route to the IONS board meeting at Asilomar, California, John and Rhea Fetzer stopped in San Francisco to visit with Whitson (who relocated there that year) and to visit the nearby offices of the Foundation for Inner Peace. Here the Fetzers met Jerry Jampolsky, a psychiatrist who made use of the *Course* in his "attitudinal healing" work with children, and Michael Murphy, the cofounder of the Esalen Institute. Whitson also took him to visit the Stanford Research Institute (SRI), where he met Russell Targ, Ingo Swann, and Hal Puthoff, all of whom became known for their work on remote viewing. Finally, Whitson wrangled an invitation for Fetzer to be included in the influential December 1978 Quail's Roost Conference in Durham, North Carolina, which brought together thought leaders such as Willis Harman, Robert Jahn, Marilyn Ferguson, and the congressman Charlie Rose, all to discuss spiritual transformation in service to the US government.[77]

So close did Fetzer and Whitson become that in March 1978, when Rhea Fetzer had a major heart attack, Whitson was one the first people John Fetzer called. Fetzer asked that she pray for Rhea, and several weeks later, when she had improved sufficiently, John and Rhea both began going through exercises from the *Course* workbook twice a day in her hospital room.[78] Perhaps the best example of how much Fetzer trusted Whitson, however, was that he had her arrange for him the opportunity to experience LSD. First synthesized in 1938, LSD was touted in the 1960s by such cultural icons as Timothy Leary as a kind of "shortcut" to transcendent experience, becoming the psychedelic drug of choice for the counterculture. According to Whitson, Fetzer had confided to her that he had never had a sustained mystical experience and was eager for one. Eventually she suggested the drug as a possibility, and despite being seventy-eight years old, he agreed.

On February 17, 1979, at the Smuggler's Inn Motor Lodge in Tucson, Fetzer and Whitson met with three others including Willis Harman and Al Hubbard, both of whom had done LSD research and were skilled in the controlled use of the drug. After a brief discussion about what Fetzer hoped to gain from the experience, the group gathered in a circle, where Fetzer recited a prayer from *A Course in Miracles*, followed by a ten-minute meditation. Then, left alone with Harman and Hubbard, who administered

19. Judy Skutch Whitson and John Fetzer, 1987.

a low dose of the drug, Fetzer spent twenty-four hours under its influence. According to Whitson, Fetzer spoke for much of this period in a deeply altered voice, beginning with, "I am the Holy Spirit. I will tell you about your race." The voice then proceeded to narrate the creation of the universe and the history of the world up until the founding of the United States, at which point it dwelt on the writing of the Declaration of Independence and the role of Saint Germain in the process. The voice also told Fetzer about his spirit guides and assured him that he would always have spiritual help in his further journey. Despite this assurance and despite the fact that the drug had no lingering aftereffects, it is reported that Fetzer found the entire experience unsettling, if not embarrassing, although why is not exactly clear. Fetzer had written ten years earlier in "America's Agony" that many people maintained that LSD only led to a "perverted consciousness" ending in "disillusionment," and apparently at some level, his drug experience confirmed this. In any case, Fetzer was never again tempted to experience LSD for spiritual insights. For these, he remained content to rely on psychics whose natural abilities allowed them to contact the transcendent world without chemical stimulation.[79]

Continued Spiritual Exploration

While John Fetzer found much in TM and *A Course in Miracles*, he never stopped seeking, and he continued assiduously investigating new spiritual resources, including those that existed in and around Kalamazoo, which, by the 1970s, had a vibrant metaphysical community. One close friend remembered that Fetzer would often attend the meetings of a variety of such groups in the area, although as unobtrusively as possible.[80] His primary entrée into the local psychic scene during this period was through James Keating, a student counselor and part-time instructor at Nazareth College, a Catholic institution under the direction of the Sisters of St. Joseph. Keating had been informally offering courses on topics in parapsychology at Nazareth since the late 1960s, and when Fetzer sent a letter to the college's president, Sister Mary L. Bader, inviting her to nominate someone for the Fetzer board, she suggested Keating.[81] Keating subsequently received one of the earliest grants from the Fetzer Foundation, $1,000 to design a course in parapsychology for undergraduates and to put together a library on parapsychological topics. Keating hoped this would lead to a program in which students would be trained "experientially in esp, astral projection, psychokinesis, etc., so that there will be an abundance of evidence available for scientific study."[82] Thus, in preparation for this program, he made an effort to identify and network with as many like-minded people and "psychic groups" in southwestern Michigan as he could find, becoming in the process one of the best connected and most well informed individuals on the region's "psychic underground." Keating thus served as an invaluable source of introductions for Fetzer.[83]

In July 1974, Keating submitted a "Proposal for a Mid-West Center for Research and Development of Psychic Sciences" to the Fetzer Foundation. Keating envisioned the center to be a clearinghouse for current research on parapsychology and a catalyst for educational outreach, but he also sought funds to do research on, among other things, "out of body experience[s] including dematerialization and teleportation." In the proposal, Keating stated that he had been working with a group called Les Initiés, "forty people in Canada who have been claiming to practice out-of-body travel for anywhere from five months to five years." Keating found out about the Montreal-based Les Initiés (known there as the Société Montréalaise D'Ontologie, Inc.) through his Kalamazoo friend and colleague Joe Bourdages, whose brother, Gaston, was the Montreal group's leader. After meeting Gaston Bourdages in 1973, Keating helped found a southwestern Michigan branch of Les Initiés (whose first president, a local businessman named Lloyd Swierenga, later came to play an important role in the development of the Fetzer Foundation).[84] And even though Keating's proposal for a Mid-West Center for Research and Development of Psychic Sciences was not funded, he nevertheless continued to correspond with Fetzer about his activities, especially with Les Initiés, going out of his way to introduce Fetzer not only to Gaston Bourdages and Lloyd Swierenga but also to one of the primary spiritual advisors to Les Initiés, a self-educated engineer and psychic named Kenneth Killick.[85]

Kenneth Killick was originally from England but immigrated to Canada in 1954, where he worked in the electronics and aviation industries, including work on the AVRO car, essentially a two-man hovercraft that bore more than a passing resemblance to a flying saucer.[86] Killick also apparently had a wide reputation as a clairvoyant and expert on UFOs, having reportedly conversed on many occasions telepathically with the Space Brothers of the Great White Brotherhood. Sometime in the early 1970s, Gaston Bourdages asked Killick to advise his group on how to develop psychic abilities through mental exercises, which, according to Killick, depended on the ability to see and hear faster-than-light tachyon energy. It was through this initial contact with the Montreal Les Initiés that brought Killick into the orbit of the Michigan branch. Under Killick's guidance, the Michigan Les Initiés separated in 1976 to form an independent spiritual organization based in Grand Rapids.[87]

Ever since meeting Killick in 1975, James Keating had been keen to introduce him to John Fetzer.[88] The meeting finally took place the following year and then under rather unusual circumstances that originated in an October 1968 UFO sighting by the Hardy family of Allegan, Michigan. Ever since that encounter, the Hardys had begun to experience a mysterious presence at their Allegan home every Sunday night. Seeking answers, in 1974, Mary and Dean Hardy took a course in Silva Mind Control at Nazareth College, where they met James Keating, who introduced them to Les Initiés, which they soon joined.[89]

Using Silva Mind Control, a method to increase one's clairvoyance through a form of meditation, along with the mental exercises of Les Initiés, the Hardys soon realized that their Sunday-night experiences were actually attempts at contact by the space beings they had encountered on the road years before. Now able to more fully communicate with the aliens, the Hardys came to understand that the aliens wanted them to build a pyramid in their backyard to cure their son's acute dyslexia through the application of "pyramid power." The space beings telepathically provided the Hardys with the outlines of a design, which they supplemented with ideas gleaned from *The Kybalion*, Theosophy, and the work of Nikola Tesla. Repeated experiments in the pyramid with their son, however, were unsuccessful. Therefore, in July 1975, Mary and Dean Hardy journeyed to Canada to seek the aid of Kenneth Killick, who helped them refine their plans and build a series of small but reportedly effective pyramids using wood, Styrofoam, fiberglass, and aluminum foil.[90]

Knowing John Fetzer's interest in parapsychology, Egyptology, UFOs, and Tesla, James Keating invited Fetzer to visit the Allegan pyramids while they were being built. It was probably there that Fetzer first met Killick.[91]

Fetzer was soon impressed with Ken Killick's psychic abilities, and the fact that Killick was a self-taught but accomplished engineer must have made him seem a kindred spirit. Over the next year or so, Killick became something like a "house psychic" for Fetzer, visiting Fetzer when he came down from Canada for his periodic visits with Les Initiés.[92] Unfortunately, their conversations were one-on-one, and little of their correspondence survives. One 1980 letter hints that Fetzer wanted Killick's input on a new reorganization of the Fetzer Foundation that he was then contemplating. Moreover, Fetzer thanked Killick for his "generosity in offering commentary on financial investments" and assured Killick that he was planning "careful investments in the stock market along lines that [Killick had] suggested." Finally, Fetzer also reported on such sensitive subjects as his plan to sell the Tigers and the state of his health, evidence that Fetzer quickly put a great deal of trust in Killick.[93]

It is clear from this letter that Fetzer intended his association with Killick to be a long one,[94] but sometime after October 1981, Fetzer abruptly stopped seeing him. It is not at all clear why this occurred; perhaps Killick's financial predictions did not pan out, or his advice about how to manage the 1980 baseball strike was counterproductive, or perhaps Killick, who had to rely on financing from the Michigan Les Initiés to underwrite his trips to Kalamazoo, overstepped his friendship by asking Fetzer to buy him a car.[95] Whatever the reason, on October 3, 1981, Killick wrote a farewell letter to Carolyn Dailey. Probably aware of Fetzer's shifting priorities with regard to the foundation, he encouraged the foundation to stop funding purely academic research and instead focus on programs that "terminate with a useful product, be it a computer system, program or a new electronic device or again some other method or manner where human despair is replaced by radiant hope and health." Killick was especially keen that the foundation fund research in "bioelectrics," which he defined as "the use of electrical fields and currents with the view to bring an end to any form of human suffering" ("pyramid power" was undoubtedly an example of this). He then ended the letter by saying, "For my own part I feel that my work is done," and as "I entered quietly . . . [I] shall leave in the same manner."[96]

20. Kenneth and Marjorie Killick (*left*) with Dean and Mary Hardy in front of the Allegan pyramids, ca. 1980. (Courtesy of Mary Hardy)

Whatever the reason for the break with Killick, Fetzer's reliance on his psychic abilities, as short-lived and problematic as the episode was, made him receptive to the idea of a full-time personal psychic advisor. After spending the 1970s in determined investigation of the psychic and the parapsychological, Fetzer was as convinced as ever before of the reality of paranormal phenomena and that his foundation should be devoted to some aspect of its study. Now, in the wake of his encounter with Killick, Fetzer was also convinced that direct psychic guidance was indispensable for determining correctly what the future direction of the foundation should be. This was a conviction that was to have a profound impact on both Fetzer and the Fetzer Foundation over the course of the 1980s, Fetzer's last decade.

9

Fetzer's Psychic Advisor

Jim Gordon and the Channelings (1980s)

Born almost with the century, John Fetzer entered his eighties in the decade of the same number. This was to be a period of great changes and final decisions, both for the man and for the foundation. Despite his heart attack in 1975, Fetzer still enjoyed relatively good health, although he did not have the energy he once had, and he knew that moderation in his working day would have to be his watchword. The body, indeed, was getting old, even if the mind remained keen. The same could not be said, however, of his wife, Rhea, whose body and mind were failing alarmingly. By the early 1970s, Rhea was experiencing balance issues that led to accidents and hospitalization, and her heart attack in 1978 was followed by a series of strokes that robbed her of her mobility and speech. Alzheimer's soon took her memories and the mind itself. By the early 1980s, Rhea needed round-the-clock nursing care, and after a major weeklong ice storm knocked out the power to their Clovelly Road home in 1984, John Fetzer made the painful decision to place her in a nursing home. Fetzer remained philosophical, however. He had long believed that Rhea and he had spent many past lives together and that her illnesses were part of a karmic debt that both needed to pay.[1]

Fetzer, faced with his wife's and his own mortality, began to think about what to do with his business interests while he was still competent to do so. Without children and with the likelihood that his wife would predecease him, Fetzer decided to liquidate his holdings and devote the bulk of the proceeds to his foundation.[2] The process was not an easy one for him.[3] Fetzer had spent a lifetime building up his businesses, and he wanted to make sure they landed in the right hands. The first to go was his ownership in the Detroit Tigers. Fetzer was proud of what he had made of the team, but the burdens of managing the manifold problems of the Tigers, including building a new stadium, negotiating the challenges of free agency, and weathering the baseball strikes of 1969, '80, and '81, all took their toll, making the "last ten years of owning that ball club," Fetzer remarked sadly, "literally hell on earth."[4] Not wanting to sell to just anybody, Fetzer was pleased to find a spiritual kinship with Tom Monaghan, the founder of Domino's Pizza, whom, it was said, Fetzer believed he had known in a past life.[5] Fetzer sold the Tigers to Monaghan in 1983.[6] This was followed by the sale of the television station in 1985, his cable operations over the next two years, and then finally his remaining interest in the Fetzer Broadcasting System in 1989.[7]

With the sale of Fetzer's major businesses during the 1980s, he was finally free to devote more and more time to his spiritual exploration and development. The money generated by the sales, moreover, finally gave the foundation the financial freedom necessary to accomplish a far more ambitious program than in the 1970s.[8] Both the intensification of Fetzer's spiritual search and the expansion and redefinition of the foundation's mission became the primary foci of Fetzer's last decade.

Jim Gordon and the Monday Night Group

It seemed to John Fetzer that every time he revealed his metaphysical beliefs in public, he would inevitably get grief for it. A good example of this occurred in 1981, when he gave an interview to Nancy Kool for the *Detroit Monthly Magazine*.⁹ The article that resulted, "Enlightenment and the Oldest Tiger," played up in a rather tongue-in-cheek way his interests in UFOs, the paranormal, reincarnation, and Eastern religions, especially Buddhism (indeed, referring to a statue Fetzer had in his office, the tagline for the article was, "The man who owns the Buddha also owns the baseball team"). After reading the article, Fetzer's sister, Hattie, wrote him with concern: "I see you have embraced Buddhism. I read you have studied it for a good many years. You are an unusual intelligent man and I feel you know what you are doing. It is your priviledge and right to believe as you see fit. I relize you have been trying to tell me by the books you have been sending and I have been unable to read." Hattie evidently reiterated her concern for John's spiritual direction in a phone call, so he wrote back, stating that she "completely misinterpreted the article": "A case in point, you seem to indicate that I have become a Buddhist and have abandoned Christianity. Nothing could be farther from the truth. The fact that I have studied world religions and have talked about these various aspects of other religions in other parts of the world has nothing to do with my overall philosophical beliefs. The fact remains if you study most of these comparative religions, there is little to choose from between any of them and the real [tenets] of Christianity."

So far, this must have been a comfort to Hattie, but then John continued:

> There is everything in history to show that Jesus himself was in constant touch with the Hindus and was exposed an awful lot to the Hindu philosophy before he established the precepts of his own Christian philosophical thinking.
>
> Out of all the world religious leaders, I regard Jesus Christ as the prime developer of the Truth which is evolutionary, guiding mankind onto greater and newer heights. Then too knowing a great deal about my prior history in the world, I have had considerable intimate exposure during the time of Christ when he was on earth to the events of that period.

Moreover, I have been identified with other periods of world history long before the appearance of the Christ, although the so-called inner circle of religious development has been in constant contact [with Christ]. . . .

I recognize much of this is a little bit foreign to you and foreign to a lot of fundamental Christian concepts; on the other hand, there can only be one Truth, and that, of course, is what we are all seeking. It is up to each one of us to seek the truth as we see it, to know it and to live it.[10]

It is hard to say what Hattie made of this. Without an understanding of the Theosophical and other esoteric literature that Fetzer was steeped in—which she admitted she "was unable to read"—it is doubtful that Hattie could make heads or tails of these beliefs. It would have probably been easier for her to understand if Fetzer had indeed simply admitted to being a Buddhist!

Given the likelihood of such misunderstandings among the uninitiated, Fetzer eagerly sought out opportunities to discuss and develop his beliefs privately with people who shared his worldview and who knew (or were willing to study) the esoteric literature that he knew. Thus, in the last years of his life, he sought to assemble small, handpicked groups of like-minded people with whom he could intelligently converse, perhaps influenced in this by Bailey's "Triangles Groups." One of the most important of these centered on *A Course in Miracles*. Sometime after Fetzer received the *Course* from Judy Skutch Whitson in 1975, he began to study "The Workbook for Students" with his personal secretary, Carolyn Dailey. At some point, the two decided that they would get more out of the *Course* in a group setting, so they invited from among their friends Jim Keating and his wife, Clare; Marion Jager, a local healer associated with the Unity Church; Leonard Fouche, a local psychiatrist; Curt Butters, an instructor in Silva Mind Control and director of a Fetzer-funded program at Kalamazoo College; and Janice Anders, a local schoolteacher and friend of Dailey's. The group met for about five years at the Fetzer Broadcast

House, diligently studying the three parts of the *Course*. However, despite the progress made by the group, at some point, Anders was diagnosed with cancer, and the emotional fallout from her death led to the group's dissolution in 1980.[11]

Nevertheless, Fetzer was still keen for group study and practice. On an informal basis, then, he kept meeting with Dailey on Monday afternoons to continue with *A Course in Miracles*, now joined by Fetzer's personal lawyer, Michael Gergely.[12] Sometime early in 1981, however, a chance meeting between Gergely and an Austin-based clairvoyant named Jim Gordon changed the direction of this little study group in ways they could not have foreseen.

Jim Gordon was born in 1949 and raised in San Antonio, Texas.[13] As a child and adolescent, he had an unusual interest in things spiritual. Early on, he was subject to out-of-body experiences, visions, auras, and premonitions. When he was eighteen, he met his first spiritual teacher, Cash Bateman, a onetime student of Edgar Cayce who was then part of the Inner Peace Movement (IPM), an organization based in Iowa promoting better communication through psychic development.[14] Bateman allowed Gordon to feel more comfortable with his psychic gifts and taught him how to control them for the benefit of others. Soon, Gordon was doing psychic counseling for friends and others who heard about his abilities through word of mouth. Never charging for his counseling sessions, he worked days at a frame shop and art gallery in San Antonio, while carrying on his informal practice in the evenings and on Sundays. A serendipitous encounter in 1976 led him into the Coptic Fellowship of America, a Christocentric neo-Theosophical organization founded in 1937 by Hamid Bey, who claimed to have undergone training with the Masters while a child in Egypt.[15] Gordon soon began communication with the spirit of Hamid Bey, who had died that year. Bey offered to cure Gordon of the cancer from which he was suffering if Gordon would take over Bey's work on earth. Gordon agreed, was cured, and was soon engaged by the Coptic Fellowship (now based in Grand Rapids, Michigan) to speak at its annual conferences, first in Fort Wayne, Indiana, and then, after 1981, at Albion College in Albion, Michigan.[16]

During the May 1981 conference at Albion, Jim Gordon was the houseguest of a Coptic Fellowship member named Mike Wunderlin, and Wunderlin invited Mike Gergely to meet with Gordon while he was in town. According to Gordon, his typical method of counseling was "to call on the Lord and . . . say a prayer for protection, for clarity of Spirit." He then would answer "questions, sharing what the Spirit brings in, in whatever way they do through guides, teachers, the archangel, an angel, or a guardian angel, whoever." In many cases, he channeled the Archangel Michael. It was the Archangel in fact who instructed Gordon to share with Gergely an information packet he created in 1972 for a prospective organization called the American Medical and Psychic Research Organization (AMPRA). The purpose of AMPRA was "to focus energy from [the Archangel's] level of consciousness" in order to use these "spiritual energies" for "physical healings on an individual level." Moreover, another goal of AMPRA was the invention and development of "non-surgical healing instruments . . . [to] screen to detect problems in the chakra system and problems in the aura." AMPRA, however, never got off the ground, so Gordon filed away the information packet until 1981, when the Archangel Michael told him to take the materials with him to Michigan. Upon being presented the AMPRA materials, Gergely was immediately struck by "the emblem of the Archangel Michael" on the cover. Such emblems, Gordon later explained, were "given by teachers, archangels and guides as a symbol of themselves, so that when they come in Spirit, you'll know that this is who they really are and not someone pretending to be them." Gergely was well aware of John Fetzer's intense interest in the Archangel Michael, having spoken to him about it shortly before. He was therefore incredulous at the coincidence. Days later, at a meeting at Broadcast House, Gergely gave the AMPRA packet to Fetzer, who, when he saw the emblem, reportedly exclaimed, "My God, this is it. I've been having dreams about this. Where did you get this?"[17] Gergely told him

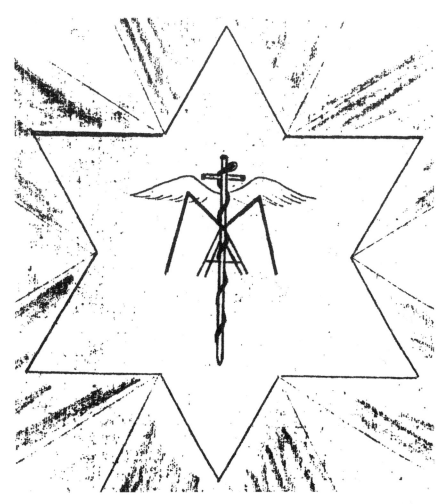

21. AMPRA symbol.

Gordon's story, whereupon Fetzer demanded that Carolyn Dailey get him on the phone immediately, which she did.

Fetzer quizzed Gordon about his psychic abilities and AMPRA and especially about the emblem of Archangel Michael. Gordon explained that the emblem's central "Star of David was used as a focus because it represents the two triangles of life—one of the energy coming downward as he and the Masters on the inner planes focus it down and then [one for] those receiving the energy on the physical plane [to] begin to focus the energy upward." In addition to the Star of David, the caduceus, explained Gordon, was an "ancient symbol of the snake representing the kundalini," and "the wings [represent] a certain spiritual power of an initiate of spiritual truths," especially those "ancient principles in Egypt and in India." And finally, superimposed on the caduceus were "AAM," the initials of the Archangel Michael.[18]

Suddenly, in the middle of the phone call, Gordon said that he was feeling dizzy. Did Fetzer have any problems with his carotid artery, Gordon asked? Plainly astonished, Fetzer said yes: a blockage had just been detected, and he was soon going to the Mayo Clinic for surgery. Gordon told him not to and to try chelation therapy first, which Fetzer did, apparently with success. From that point on, given the impact of the emblem and this demonstration of Gordon's power of distant psychic diagnosis, Fetzer developed a deep spiritual trust in Jim Gordon.[19]

In December 1981, John Fetzer again called Gordon, who was now working as a manager of a health-foods store in Austin, Texas, and invited Gordon to visit Kalamazoo to do a session with him in person. Gordon met with Fetzer, Gergely, and Dailey in Fetzer's office at Broadcast House. Gordon later observed, "When I walked in, I was taken by a spiritual presence that I had never really felt with other people, not even with Cash. Cash Bateman had a spiritual presence, but not the magnitude that John had. There was something about his aura that . . . when I walked into his office, I was in another world" (Gordon later recognized Fetzer as a "Master Soul of the Spirit," although of this Fetzer was skeptical). After some brief chat about AMPRA and a psychic reading concerning Fetzer's family background, the conversation was interrupted by loud popping noises from a nearby TV. Gordon interpreted this as one of Fetzer's spiritual teachers making his presence known. This impressed Fetzer as a favorable sign, so he asked Gordon then and there to be his personal spiritual guide and act as a paid consultant for the foundation to help rethink its mission. Gordon, however, was loath to leave Texas for the cold winters of Kalamazoo, so a compromise was reached whereby Gordon would make occasional trips to Kalamazoo or Tucson when his work schedule permitted or when he was in the Midwest lecturing for the Coptics. Fetzer and Gordon also pledged to stay in touch regularly by telephone and letters.[20]

During the first face-to-face meetings in 1981, Jim Gordon worked intensively with John Fetzer. Indeed, instead of simply reporting to Fetzer what he was told by Spirit privately, Gordon began to channel Spirit directly during the session, something he had never done before. The practice of channeling was becoming something of a spiritual phenomenon in the United States at this time, so it was perhaps not a surprise to Fetzer that the Texas psychic had this ability.[21] The process, Gordon found, was easy: "I would close my eyes and go into meditation and just start speaking what Spirit brought forward." Thus, "a lot of information came forward for [Fetzer], and the development of the [foundation] that way—from Spirit. It was just sort of like a telephone to [Spirit]." According to a later channeling, Spirit told Fetzer that, in addition to "serv[ing] as a communication link," Gordon would be a "confirmation point for much of what you, John, . . . receive from us, but sometimes doubt." In other words, Fetzer should treat Gordon as both channeler and interpreter for the channelings. Fetzer must have found this a useful arrangement, for Gordon's channelings for Fetzer continued periodically for the next five years.[22]

At Gordon's suggestion, Fetzer, Dailey, and Gergely invited a small circle of friends to meet on Mondays to study and discuss Gordon's channelings.[23] Included were Margaret Zolen, Rhea's physician, and her husband, Frank Henry, with whom Fetzer did chelation therapy.[24] Another couple was Cleora Daily and Charles Spence. Daily, an astrologer by vocation, had met Dean and Mary Hardy on a metaphysical tour to Egypt in 1981, and they in turn had introduced her to Ken Killick, who then introduced her and her husband to John Fetzer.[25] A few months after the group's first meeting on December 20, 1981, Sister Elizabeth Reis of Nazareth College was also invited to join. Zolen and Henry had taken a Silva Mind Control course from Reis and recommended it to Fetzer, who took it along with Carolyn Dailey and Charles Spence.[26] Fetzer was impressed

22. John E. Fetzer with Jim Gordon, 1989.

by "Sister Liz" and soon brought her into the group. Finally, Bruce Fetzer began attending in early 1982. Bruce Fetzer had recently come to Kalamazoo to work closely with his great-uncle and to get his MBA at Western Michigan University and intern at Fetzer Broadcasting. Often, Bruce would come on Sundays to the Clovelly house, where he and John would study the *Course*, the *Urantia Book*, and other channeled materials. Bruce's eagerness for the materials made him an obvious candidate for membership in the group.[27]

The friends called themselves simply the "Monday Night Group" and later the "Spiritual Advisory Core Council Group of the Fetzer Foundation," meeting weekly from three to six p.m., first at Broadcast House and then at the foundation's offices in downtown Kalamazoo. Fetzer had decided, based on a channeling by Gordon from the Archangel Michael, that the purpose of the Monday Night Group would be twofold and evolve over time:

> The first few meetings are going to be devoted solely to [Gordon's channelings] and complete assimilation of the

instructions given [in them] so that each and every one of us know precisely the entire story. We will then undertake to carry out those matters of spirit that will teach each of us how to find the alternate state. After this step we can then begin to structure the foundation, the whole process of which will take five years. The first year is devoted to our self-advancement, followed by the next two years of foundation structuring, and then two more years to round out the five year program to make an initial beginning.

In a letter to Gordon the following year, Fetzer further specified that the Monday Night Group would function as a "spiritual board" to complement the foundation's "physical board," and while "this is the only foundation in the history of foundations to have two boards of directors," Fetzer was convinced that this was "the only way [the foundation could] possibly succeed in the future."[28]

The Monday Night gatherings were loosely structured around a ritual called the "Master of the Heart," which Jim Gordon developed in part from elements from Alice Bailey's Arcane School teachings. Meetings opened with everyone in the group placing their personal crystals together and the lighting of a candle to call in the light. Next was a brief meditation and then a sharing of individual concerns and insights among the group, followed by study of a selection from *A Course in Miracles* or *The Aquarian Gospel of Jesus*, after which the group settled down to discuss the latest channeling from Jim Gordon. At first, Gordon did live channelings, or occasionally he would speak to the group during the meeting on speakerphone. Mostly, however, the channelings would be sent from Austin as letters circulated in advance or recorded on tape. Once discussion of that week's channeling was exhausted, the meeting would end with a recitation of Alice Bailey's "Great Invocation," and then all would repair to a nearby restaurant called Chicken Charlie's for dinner.[29]

Gordon's Channelings

The first of Jim Gordon's channelings or "soul transmissions" were delivered to the Monday Night Group on December 20 and 21, 1981. Through them, the group was introduced to the six Masters of the Planetary Hierarchy who would be their spiritual guides: Jesus, the Holy Spirit, Saint Germain, Zoser and Cato (both of whom had been Egyptian priest-kings), and, of course, the Archangel Michael. Later, Gordon would also channel another group of Masters called the Boddhisattva Council, which included Kuan Yin and Samatabhadra, the latter whose job was to nurture the "Divine Spark" of the foundation on the astral plane. Each of these Masters had reportedly already worked with members of the group during past lives. Indeed, it was believed by Fetzer due to his Ouija sessions, and subsequently confirmed by Jim Gordon, that the core group had been destined to be reincarnated together in this life so that they could now fulfill through the common mission of the Fetzer Foundation the missions that each of them had been pursuing through countless prior lifetimes.[30]

The Fetzer Foundation's overall mission, according to the Masters, was to catalyze the further spiritual growth of humankind so that it could achieve its next evolutionary level. This was especially necessary today, the Masters said, because recent medical interventions, far from benefiting humankind, had actually "disrupted much of the evolutionary process" at the genetic level. To put humanity back on track to positive spiritual evolution, what was needed was an entirely new way of "healing through a nonmedication and non-surgical means, through working with certain vibrations and sounds, [and] working with machinery that can change and alter vibrational patterns of the aura and the chakras" (such machines, the Masters asserted, had been commonplace in Atlantis and Lemuria, and many more "have been developed over the centuries at Mt. Shasta"). "Through the protection of the foundation," great minds would be able to "find ways of manifesting that which is needed to change and alter the healing procedures of man today," which in turn would alter "the genetic factor towards

23. Fetzer Foundation's first logo.

a more healthy oriented physical body." Ultimately, this will "change the karmic pattern of [humankind's] spiritual development and begin once again to open up the spiritual identity of the 'I AM' within." It is clear that what the Masters intended for the Fetzer Foundation was that it become the new embodiment of AMPRA, a fact made clear by the Masters' permission to adopt the Archangel Michael's emblem as part of the foundation's new logo.[31]

Many of Gordon's later channelings would deal with the specifics of how the reorganization of the foundation should be effected (see chapter 10). However, also covered was the role of the core group in the reorganization process and the means by which each member could become more spiritually worthy of the task. The Master Cato likened the creation of the Fetzer Foundation to the founding of the United States and the core group to the Founding Fathers; for just as the Founding Fathers brought about political freedom, so would the foundation bring about "soul freedom." This parallel greatly pleased John Fetzer, but it implied great responsibilities: "As father of the foundation," he said, "I cannot emphasize too strongly the sanctity of this spiritual group."[32] Individuals in the group were thus enjoined to practice sacrifice, detachment, and the "Master of the Heart" meditation in order to open the aura of the crown chakra for the inflow of Spirit. This was important because the core group and the Masters, Gordon reported, formed a complicated series of triadic karmic relationships, symbolized by the two triangles of the Star of David, through which the energies of the cosmos would flow in and out of the foundation. In a metaphorical sense, then, the reorganized foundation would be like a collective child born of the core group. Thus, when conflicts arose within the group or when a member was out of spiritual balance, the energies would not flow and the child would starve. Many of the channelings therefore urged the individuals of the core group to practice harder and to always call on the aid of the Masters in order to overcome both ego and doubt. Only in this way would the spiritual conduits remain unblocked and the foundation thrive on the influx of divine energy.[33]

In 1982, the Archangel Michael strongly urged the core group to develop "a declaration" that would "announce to the universe" their "ideals and intentions for the group and the foundation." Such a declaration would help to "align" their "energy with the universal energy that wishes to aid and support" their activities.[34] In response, the group developed the following list of "personal goals," all of which reflect ideas and statements taken from the channelings:

> To strive every day to live and be full of the spirit of God, manifesting it in truth and harmony with our fellow men.
>
> To look to today and say this is what we must do today, and to succeed in each day and know that the tomorrows will take care of themselves.
>
> To take it day by day, breath by breath, moment by moment to succeed in our stated goals. Doubt will not enter

our minds, only success will be there, for the Masters of Light have envisioned success for us and success is meant to be.

To begin to develop the healing flow of force within, and to become aware of it and feel it flow through our bodies as we are communicating with others.

To walk this path of Truth and service because we know it is a path of reward and redemption; redemption in the sense of liberation of the soul and freedom from the rebirth cycle.

To find that principle "I am" within our own hearts and minds and become one with it before we can share it with others upon a physical level.

To become channels of Light, channels of the Spirit; and to open our hearts, minds and souls and allow the Light to come forth.

To strive for unity and detachment with love so that we will not be sidetracked and confused. We ask for inner knowing and inner strength and know that as we ask we shall be told; as we seek, we shall find; as we knock, the door shall be opened.[35]

In addition to being the attitudes that the core group wished to cultivate among themselves, these, too, were to be the attitudes of anyone working in the foundation in the future.

In subsequent channelings, the Masters also made it clear that if Gordon were to fulfill his spiritual destiny in this life, he would need permanent financial support.[36] In a channeling from 1983, for example, Cato contrasts the life of Fetzer, who was destined for great things in the physical world, to Gordon, whose great work was to be in the spiritual world. For "just as you [Fetzer] have been veiled of some of the higher so you can be of better service to the physical, so Jim must open to the spirit more and more, moving his focus from this physical world and concern so he can truly manifest his service to humanity." Indeed, "the less he focuses on spirit and the more he concerns himself with the physical world—the less he can truly accomplish."[37] Furthermore, the channelings revealed that Gordon was the mouthpiece not simply of the Planetary Council but for even more exalted beings, the Masters of the Inner Light, who exist on the "inner planes" beyond karma and whose message was that of "soul liberation" and "freedom of the spirit" for the achievement of "soul transcendence." Gordon's special mission was to impart this message to the world.[38] To facilitate this mission, therefore, Gordon was put on the foundation's payroll as a consultant in 1982, and the following year, a new division was created to fund the writing and publication of Gordon's books. Called Inner Light Publications, it was located in Gordon's hometown, Austin, Texas.[39] A little later, a new channeling suggested that, since the Fetzer Foundation would be dealing with practical spiritual approaches to the physical world, there should be a separation between "the foundation and the Spiritual Path," to which end John Fetzer should set up "a church or non-profit organization" for Gordon. Only in this way could he "achieve physical liberation so God might [allow Gordon to] do his work [exclusively] on spiritual planes."[40] Hence, Inner Light Publications soon morphed into the Inner Light Institute and, later, Inner Light Ministries, which, endowed personally by Fetzer through large cash donations, eventually became an entity wholly independent from the Fetzer Foundation.[41]

A New Spiritual Influence: John-Roger and MSIA

While Jesus, the Archangel Michael, and Cato were the Masters that Gordon most consistently contacted through his channelings, other beings would come through regularly as well. These included the Holy Spirit, Saint Germain, the Egyptian Zoser, and the bodhisattvas Kuan Yin and Samatabhadra. Occasionally, these Masters were also joined by, among others, Gautama Buddha, Mother Mary, Master Jupiter, Kuthumi, Paul the Venetian, El Morya, Hilarion, Abraham Lincoln, Sir Arthur Conan Doyle, Thomas Edison, and a Native American named Little Fox.[42] The kind of beings channeled, their names, their roles in the cosmic hierarchy, the cosmic planes that they were said to inhabit (physical, emotional, causal, mental, astral, etheric), and the spiritual places mentioned (e.g., Mount Shasta, Shamballa, Clarion, the great Central Sun),[43] not to mention the overall emphasis on human spiritual evolution, all suggest the strong influence of Spiritualism and various Theosophical currents such as the Arcane School and the Coptic Fellowship, with the addition of a few themes from Edgar Cayce (e.g., Atlantis and Lemuria) and elements from *The Urantia Book*.[44] There is another tradition, however, that also appears in the channelings, and its influence grew over the years: this was Radhasoami.

The Radhasoami ("Soul Master") tradition, a variation on Sant Mat ("Path of the Saints"), originated in Agra, India, in the 1860s with the teachings of Shiv Dayal Singh. Like the Sant Mat tradition, Radhasoami emphasizes personal devotion to a master (guru) who, after initiation, guides one in daily meditation to access higher states of consciousness. However, the particular form of meditation practiced by Radhasoami is called Surat Shabd Yoga, sometimes known as the Path of Sound and Light, so called because it is said to allow one to sense as sound or light the universally permeating energy current that is sent out from the Supreme Being (Shabd). Uniting with this current can lead one through the five inner planes of the cosmos toward God-realization, resulting in liberation from karma and reincarnation at death. Eventually, the Radhasoami tradition spawned a myriad of offshoots, some of which reached the United States in the early twentieth century. One of the largest of these is the Radhasoami Satsang Beas, which expanded to over a million initiates worldwide under the leadership of Charan Singh.[45]

The fact that key Radhasoami themes such as the sound and light current and the inner planes appear throughout Gordon's channelings is not surprising since as a young man he had studied the tradition and even sought initiation from Charan Singh in 1973. Singh, however, told him that he was not destined to be Singh's disciple but encouraged Gordon to continue searching for his "particular spiritual teacher." In the meantime,

Gordon continued to revere Charan Singh and practice elements from the Radhasoami tradition.[46] Significantly, John Fetzer himself already knew about the Radhasoami tradition before meeting Gordon, having read about it in both Paul Brunton's *A Search in Secret India* (1935) and Julian Johnson's extremely popular introduction to the tradition, *The Path of the Masters* (1939).[47] So, when elements of it showed up in Gordon's evolving "Master of the Heart" ritual or in the channelings, Fetzer most likely recognized its source and welcomed its inclusion.[48]

In 1984, as Gordon was traveling in Egypt with a Coptic-affiliated group called Spiritual Unity of Nations (SUN), he met John-Roger Hinkins, the leader of the Movement for Spiritual Awareness (MSIA), a Westernized variant of the Radhasoami tradition.[49] Born Roger Delano Hinkins in 1934, he had a spiritual awakening in 1963 in which a new "spiritual personality" emerged whom he called "John." Now calling himself John-Roger, he briefly studied Eckankar, one of the first Westernized versions of Radhasoami in the United States, before striking out as a teacher in his own right. John-Roger began offering seminars throughout Southern California in 1968, and their success led to the founding of MSIA in Los Angeles in 1971. Although clearly within the Radhasoami tradition, MSIA mixed in elements of both Christianity and Western esoteric traditions, resulting in several distinctive doctrines and practices. For example, John-Roger taught that he was the most recent embodiment of the Christ Consciousness, also known as the Mystical Traveler Consciousness. As such, he was a "wayshower" who could guide people to soul transcendence by means of a series of spiritual exercises that attune one to the divine sound current. What is more, again reflecting the eclecticism of the movement and perhaps reflecting Hinkins's early background in psychology, MSIA developed a series called Insight seminars, which were designed to remove psychological blocks to one's personal and spiritual development. For would-be disciples, the Insight seminars were typically done before embarking on the study of John-Roger's "Soul Awareness Discourses," which prepared one for initiation into the five inner planes where dwell the "Silent Ones," spiritual forces emanating from God.[50]

Upon meeting John-Roger in Egypt, Gordon instantly recognized him as the spiritual master he had been waiting for and was soon initiated into the tradition. Shortly after, specific MSIA concepts and vocabulary (e.g., Mystical Traveler Consciousness, wayshower, the Silent Ones) began appearing in the Monday Night Group's channelings, as did explicit mentions of John-Rogers and MSIA.[51] Moreover, both Gordon and Cleora Daily, who had met John-Roger on the same trip, were soon encouraging John Fetzer to explore this new tradition. In October 1984, a meeting was arranged between Fetzer and John-Roger at the MSIA headquarters in Los Angeles, and they met later in May 1985 in Fetzer's home in Kalamazoo. Fetzer at this time received all five initiations from the Mystical Traveler at once, a highly unusual procedure since most initiations were done separately and only after working one's way through the Discourses. Fetzer continued to meet occasionally with John-Roger when "J-R" was in Kalamazoo visiting the MSIA group formed by Cleora Daily, and Fetzer went on to take the first two Insight trainings. Although he apparently had some misgivings about John-Roger himself, Fetzer nevertheless found the teachings profound, contributed money to the organization, and encouraged Fetzer Foundation board members to seek "soul awareness." He also practiced the MSIA spiritual exercises until the end of his life.[52]

The End of the Monday Night Group

In September 1985, John Fetzer suffered a second, more severe heart attack and decided to go to Arizona for treatment and recovery.[53] Fetzer eventually regained some of his energy and returned to work, but it took an extended period for him to convalesce. Meanwhile, the Monday Night Group continued for a time without him, looking forward to his return. In May 1986, Margaret and Frank Zolen wrote him a letter wishing him a speedy recovery and hoping he would return to the group soon. But in reply, Fetzer said that his recurring health problems would make it "very incompatible" for him "to attend meetings or be in any conference

24. Bruce Fetzer and John E. Fetzer at MSIA Insight seminar, 1987.

of considerable length," although he did promise to try to meet at least periodically with the group for lunch when he returned to Kalamazoo. Nevertheless, without Fetzer's drive and leadership, the group gradually faded away, disappearing entirely by 1987.[54]

As spiritually enriching as the Monday Night Group was for Fetzer personally, it was always primarily a means to an end: to smooth the process of reorganization of the Fetzer Foundation using the guidance of Gordon's channelings. By the time the Monday Night Group dissolved, the reorganization of the foundation was well under way, and the group had served its purpose. As will be seen in chapter 10, the Gordon channelings largely reflected a shift in emphasis that was already under way in the foundation, although, without the transcendental affirmation of that shift that Gordon's channelings provided, it is difficult to say how thoroughly the reorganization would have been carried out. Indeed, Fetzer himself stated that had the channelings "not precipitated in the initial stages [of the reorganization], there is a great probability that the foundation would not have taken the direction that it did and had the degree of success that it did." In other words, as Bruce Fetzer put it, Gordon's channeling's formed nothing less than "the esoteric blueprint" for the evolution of the Fetzer Foundation in the 1980s.[55]

Building for the New Age

The Fetzer Foundation's New Mission and Headquarters (1980s)

The Fetzer Foundation's reorientation during the 1980s affected the organization at all levels. In the wake of Fetzer's business divestments that allowed him to dedicate an even larger share of his fortune to the foundation, one of the first tasks was to create an infrastructure adequate to his vision. For the most part, the foundation during the 1970s consisted of a filing cabinet and desk at Broadcast House; the board of trustees was largely a rubber stamp; and much of the actual legwork was done by one person, Fetzer's secretary, Carolyn Dailey.[1] At the October 1981 meeting, however, it was announced that the foundation would be leasing an office at 130 North Park Street in Kalamazoo and that Charles E. (Chuck) Spence would be hired as executive director to run this office and serve as project analyst for the foundation.[2] Spence, who was the husband of Cleora Daily and a member of the Monday Night Group, had a PhD in social work and had worked in health care administration. He was initially introduced to Fetzer by Kenneth Killick as a person who could advise him on Rhea Fetzer's home health care but was soon asked to help develop the foundation, especially now that its focus was shifting toward holistic medicine and health care. What is more, it was Spence's rather-unglamorous job to work with the foundation's lawyer, Jerry Luptak, to make sure the foundation stayed within IRS guidelines. This was not always an easy task, since the laws were constantly changing during this period.[3]

Over the next few years, additions were made to the staff, and the office moved twice due to the growing need for more space, first in 1983 to the Comerica Building on South Rose Street, during which time Bruce Fetzer joined the staff to oversee finances; and then to the Skyrise Building on South Burdick Street the following year.[4] In addition to secretarial staff, Lloyd Swierenga was retained as a consultant "to determine future organizational needs." Eventually, he was appointed executive director of administration and education for the Fetzer Foundation.[5]

True to Fetzer's own evolving interests and the channeled advice of the Masters, the early 1980s saw the Fetzer Foundation's decided shift away from the funding of parapsychological research to what was eventually called "energy medicine," that is, the harnessing of subtle energies through techniques and technologies to conquer human disease, whether physical, psychological, or spiritual in nature.[6] As a part of the larger "alternative health care" movement that was beginning to catch on in the United States, this new focus on "energy medicine" anticipated and in part sparked the widespread public enthusiasm for such research in the 1980s.[7] Indeed, even before the Gordon channelings, this shift was already under way at the foundation. As the September 1981 minutes of the Fetzer Board of Trustees observed, "Several of our members have called attention to the fact that preliminary study of force field radiation [i.e., subtle energy], either created by instrumentation or that which is radiated from a natural body force, indicates considerable healing results are evident and such subjective phenomena needs further investigation. All of this seems to be an added dimension in the study of healing as a result of electronic radiation as contrasted with that of chemical and mechanical studies which for the most part have been a preoccupation in an enormous amount of [medical] research and development." In particular, "there is unanimous agreement [among the board] that henceforth our purpose should be redefined to initiate new scientific research which will study, design and produce electronic instrumentation to be used as an aid to diagnose, treat, and prevent illness."[8] As Fetzer himself put in a 1981 letter to Brenda Dunne, "We are aware of a number of individuals who have produced and developed electronic equipment having great promise in connection with holistic health programs," but "the medical community, for the most part, has denied even elementary examination of this great resource." Thus, "there is an opportunity to fill this void . . . and find the worthy instrumentation for healing and pain relief to promote health and well-being for a large segment of humanity."[9]

Two years later, the foundation board wished to formalize this new direction and called for the development of a new mission statement and program overview. This Spence and Bruce Fetzer did, taking into account, of course, advice from Jim Gordon's channelings. As stated in a working document called "Potential Goals from the Channelings," the new mission of the foundation would be to "form a network throughout the world of light" so that "the energies of this world will be changed to a higher vibrational growth, and the evolution of man shall be changed through our interactivities, the love of God, and the physical instrumentation that [will be] share[d] throughout the medical industry." In line with this mission, according to a diagram channeled by Gordon, the foundation should have three goals: "1. Treatment of patients (non-surgical) [and] Development of [subtle energy] instrumentation[;] 2. Present ideas for development by industry and present them to [the] medical industry[;] 3. Educate medical industry of alternative treatments [and] Research for validity." To achieve these goals, the foundation should be divided into six programs: a research center for the development of holistic technology to manipulate the aura and balance the kundalini energies of the chakras; a holistic health care center (presumably in Kalamazoo); other healing centers (presumably beyond Kalamazoo); an education center; a psychic research center; and a center for spiritual teaching.[10]

Of the six programs proposed by Gordon in the channelings, the psychic research center was not to be, as John Fetzer had moved beyond any interest in an exclusive focus on purely parapsychological research.[11] Moreover, the center for spiritual teaching, while initially created within the foundation as Inner Light Publications, eventually was spun off from the foundation as Inner Light Ministries in 1988. Nevertheless, the other four programs in some form or another became the primary foci for the Fetzer Foundation for the rest of the decade and well into the 1990s. As such, they figured prominently in the final version of the "Statement of Mission and Goals and Program Overview," which Spence presented to the board at its July 1983 meeting.

According to this document, "The John E. Fetzer Foundation is dedicated to identifying and supporting innovative research concerning holistic health care delivery systems and techniques . . . which recognize the important role the dimensions of body, mind, and spirit play in the healing process." Of special interest will be "research which emphasizes the bioelectric or bio-magnetic nature of the human body." To this end, the new goals of the Fetzer Foundation would be to "encourage constructive and scholarly scientific investigation of all health care philosophies and techniques regardless of cultural origin or historical knowledge base." These would be primarily "holistic health care techniques" and especially "force field radiation healing therapy, including either instrumentation or natural body radiation techniques as related to physiological or psychological health maintenance and restoration." In addition, the foundation would "facilitate the dissemination of health care research findings to academic and professional institutions . . . and the general public," while also "encourag[ing] development of public health education programs advocating a wellness philosophy which incorporates both total personal involvement and recognition of the inherent natural healing ability of the body." The board duly approved the new "Statement of Mission and Goals and Program Overview."[12]

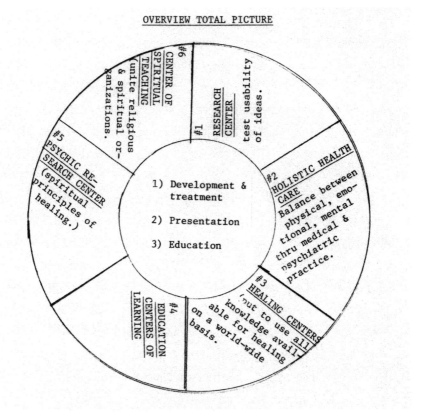

25. Channeled diagram of Fetzer Foundation mission.

Funded Research under the New Mission

To some extent, the new mission did not entail a complete shift of the foundation's funding activities since some of the previous projects easily fit within it. These included William's Holistic Health Program at WMU and Hardt's biofeedback studies (which continued to receive Fetzer funding until 1985).[13] Another such project that received funding before the new mission was approved was that of Herbert Benson from Harvard. One of the pioneers of mind/body medicine, Benson had done work on Transcendental Meditation, which formed the basis for his best-selling 1975 book *The Relaxation Response*.[14] Fetzer contacted Benson after reading about *The Relaxation Response*, and this eventually led to an invitation to speak at Kalamazoo College in 1980 as part of a Fetzer-funded lecture series.[15] Soon after, Benson wrote to Fetzer requesting financial assistance for a new project that he and his team were planning involving Tibetan Buddhist monks. Through his contact with the Dalai Lama, Benson had gained access to monks who practiced *g Tum-mo* yoga, or heat yoga, which allowed them to raise their body temperatures at will, supposedly by drawing in *prana* (subtle energy) from the "inexhaustible 'pranic' reservoir of Nature." The rise in body temperature, it was reported, was enough to dry sheets doused with ice water. Due in part to Fetzer support, Benson and his team were able to travel back to Dharamsala, India, to study and film this meditation practice, the results of which were published in *Nature*.[16] John Fetzer was thrilled by this research, as it confirmed his confidence in *Life and Teachings of the Masters of the Far East*, commenting, "finally what Spalding said is being done."[17] Further funding followed, this time to underwrite a trip to China to investigate the work of Qi Gong masters in that country.[18] Benson's work continued to receive foundation support until 1991.[19]

Another project during this period was related in many ways to Benson's work with Tibetan monks. This was the work of Elmer Green at the Menninger Foundation, who was brought to the attention of the Fetzer Foundation by WMU's Richard Williams, whose mentor Green was.[20] Green was a pioneer in the field of biofeedback and was one of the first to study this phenomenon in yogis and other spiritual adepts. In the 1980s, Green, who was fascinated by Spiritualist and Theosophical literature, was inspired by comments about meditation practices in the Theosophical classic *The Mahatma Letters to A. P. Sinnett* (1924). According to the words of Master Kuthumi recorded in that book,

> The methods used for developing lucidity in our chelas (student monks) may be easily used by you. Every temple has a dark room, the north wall of which is entirely covered with a sheet of mixed metal, chiefly copper, very highly polished, with a surface capable of reflecting in it things as well as a mirror. The chela sits on an insulated stool, a three-legged bench placed in a flat-bottomed vessel of thick glass,—the

lama operator likewise, the two forming with the mirror wall a triangle. A magnet with the North Pole up is suspended over the crown of the chela's head without touching it. The operator having started the thing going leaves the chela alone gazing on the wall, and after the third time is no longer required.[21]

Green interpreted the use of the magnet and the copper wall to mean that there were "measurable electric fields associated with a particular method of meditation," and he wrote a research proposal in order to test this "copper wall" method of meditation. As Green tells it, Fetzer was instantly intrigued by the project after talking to him on the phone, and the board soon approved funding.[22] Green tested both "regular subjects" and "exceptional subjects," that is, people who were noted sensitives or psychic healers. He found that while the "regular subjects" did not generate "anomalous voltage spikes" in the copper wall, the healers did, occasionally up to sixty volts. This strongly suggested to Green that he was witnessing what he called a genuine "MIOMA" (mind over matter) phenomenon, although years of testing and research, funded by the foundation through 1987, failed to isolate exactly how and why this phenomenon occurs.[23]

In addition to these two researchers, the Fetzer Foundation renewed its ties to the Institute of Noetic Sciences (IONS). In 1983, John Fetzer proposed creating the "John E. Fetzer Fund" within IONS to underwrite projects of which he specifically approved.[24] The first of these was a purely parapsychological project, the Life Beyond Death Foundation's Spiricom, an electronic voice phenomenon (EVP) device invented by George Meek, by which Meek claimed he could contact the dead.[25] In keeping with the new mission, however, the major programs funded through IONS were oriented more toward alternative medicine. One such was the Inner Mechanisms of the Healing Response Program, an umbrella under which several mind/body research projects were pursued that Fetzer believed were congruent with Gordon's channelings. These included the then-new fields of psychoneuroimmunology (that is, the impact of emotional states on immune system effectiveness) and dissociative states research (that is, the healing potential of altered states of consciousness).[26] Another project funded through the IONS Fetzer Fund was to the Higher Sense Perception Research Foundation of none other than Shafica Karagulla, who now finally benefited from her early lobbying efforts to get Fetzer to support paranormal research, although in this case with a healing focus.[27]

Perhaps the most ambitious project was the creation of the John E. Fetzer Institute of Energy Medicine Research in conjunction with the ARE Clinic in Phoenix, Arizona. The clinic, founded in 1970 by William and Gladys McGarey, was designed to apply the holistic health ideas of Edgar Cayce as revealed in his trance readings. The Association for Research and Enlightenment (ARE), the original Cayce research foundation, was located in Virginia Beach, Virginia, and the clinic operated in conjunction with it under a "Covenant Relationship." The McGareys had met Hugh Lynn Cayce, Edgar Cayce's son, while he was on a speaking tour in Arizona in 1955. It took them a while to accept Cayce's holistic approach to health and healing, which was based on the trinity of "Spirit is the life. Mind is the builder. The physical is the result." Once they did, however, they created the ARE Clinic to promote and test his ideas, such as the medicinal use of castor-oil packs and techniques to manipulate subtle energies.[28]

In May 1984, Chuck Spence visited the clinic on a fact-finding trip to "gather information regarding current activity in electromagnetic research and instrumentation." After a tour led by Harvey Grady, the head of Education and Research for the ARE Clinic (and a psychic in his own right), Spence returned enthusiastically recommending some kind of affiliation to the clinic, stating, "The ARE Clinic model could serve as the beginning point of our efforts to establish a network of holistic health clinics, develop a central laboratory for energy medicine research, and develop a central base for a high technology information/education system concerning spiritual/mental/physical healing principles." Long interested in Cayce's readings, John Fetzer was soon visiting the clinic himself and was likewise impressed. (It probably helped that in conversation with Fetzer,

Grady characterized the ARE Clinic's work as a continuation of similar work begun in Atlantis.) Grady was encouraged to write a grant proposal, which he did, calling for the creation of the Fetzer Energy Medicine Research Institute (FEMRI). At the August meeting of the Fetzer board, $311,846 was approved for the ARE project. By June, the Fetzer Foundation signed a twenty-five-year "Covenant Relationship" with the clinic, and in September 1985, FEMRI was up and running. Soon, too, Fetzer staff began to attend the annual ARE Clinic symposia held in Phoenix.[29]

During FEMRI's first year of operation, one of its most important projects involved research into the "Kervran Effect" by Edward Stanton Maxey and the biochemist Justa Smith. This was based on the research of the French engineer Louis Kervran, who claimed to have demonstrated the ability of plants to utilize subtle energies to effect biological transmutation of basic elements at the atomic level. Maxey and Smith sought to replicate Kervran's results as part of a larger study of electromagnetic effects on biological systems, both plant and animal. Maxey had great hopes for this "unorthodox scientific" research, for he believed that "once the weak energy transmutation of atomic elements is replicated and announced simultaneously in several countries, the scientific community will be hard-pressed to prove or disprove it, thereby stimulating open discussion of the energy transactions associated with it." This, in turn, would "advance research into the subtle energy domain, which [would] help to legitimize later research into the study of healers and the healing process."[30]

Another important FEMRI project was the evaluation of the effectiveness of an "apparatus for measuring the functioning of meridians and their associated internal organs" (AMI, for short) invented by Japanese parapsychologist Hiroshi Motoyama. Based on Chinese acupuncture and the idea of the importance of the free circulation of chi (subtle energy) for bodily health, Motoyama's AMI reportedly could measure chi-energy flow at the body's twenty-eight meridians and, through computer analysis, diagnose energy blockages that could then be cured through acupuncture.[31] In addition, the institute also conducted an "Electro-Medical Device Evaluation Service" designed to test scientifically existing subtle-energy healing devices then in use at the ARE Clinic, as well as creating a computerized energy-medicine library and database.[32]

Of all the projects pursued by FEMRI, perhaps the most fascinating to John Fetzer were those involving the development of new technologies to diagnose and treat disease through the manipulation of subtle energies. As he put it later, his early reading of the Tom Swift books, which chronicled the exploits of the eponymous boy inventor, had primed him to anticipate great advances in all technology. He was indeed thrilled that he had lived long enough to see science catch up with science fiction in this regard, especially as it related to healing through advanced electronics.[33] As early as 1980, on the advice of Ken Killick, Fetzer had bought a device called the Pathoclast, which according to its manufacturer was "capable of influencing and adjusting energy fields which surround every living organism."[34] Killick perhaps also recommended to Fetzer the Lakhovsky Multiple Wave Oscillator, which was said to be able to cure cancer through the electromagnetic emissions of a specially designed Tesla coil. Research on the Lakhovsky device and other like devices was continued by FEMRI.[35] What is more, this research was given a boost when the Fetzer Foundation underwrote much of the cost of the first Energy Medicine Conference in Madras, India, in 1987.

The brainchild of T. M. Srinivasan, a professor of biomedical engineering at the Madras Indian Institute of Technology, the Energy Medicine Conference brought together an international group of scientists working in the area, including staff members from the ARE Clinic and FEMRI. Several members of the Fetzer Foundation staff such as Chuck Spence and Jim Gordon also attended. Srinivasan, who at the time of the Madras conference was working on perfecting a sophisticated biofeedback device, was invited to relocate to the ARE Clinic in Phoenix as research director of FEMRI. There, he edited the proceedings of the Madras conference and began work on the Pulsed Electromagnetic Field (PEF) Coil, which functioned much like the Lakhovsky device, as well as a version of the Motoyama AMI machine called the FEMRI Acupuncture Meridian Evaluator (FAME). The following year, 1989, Srinivasan traveled to Kalamazoo, where he was tasked with setting up the in-house energy-medicine-device research laboratory for the Fetzer Foundation. John Fetzer was especially keen on this project, since he believed that such devices would only be developed in spiritually focused private labs where "hard science" can be employed by "minds which are inspired by the voice of divinity within."[36]

So promising did the FEMRI research appear to be, and enjoying the approbation of Jim Gordon's channeled Cato, John Fetzer envisioned an even closer connection with the McGareys and the ARE Clinic.[37] As early as 1986, plans were laid for a stand-alone John E. Fetzer Life Sciences Laboratory in Phoenix and for an enlarged energy-medicine treatment facility associated directly with the ARE Clinic.[38] Moreover, for the next two years, the Fetzer Foundation explored legal options for closer ties to the ARE Clinic, including the incorporation of something called the John E. Fetzer Medical Institute, which apparently existed only on paper but was designed to ease some kind of merger.[39] None of these ambitious institutional projects ever came to fruition, but the relationship between the Fetzer Foundation and the clinic nevertheless remained strong for the rest of the 1980s. By the time the Fetzer Foundation ceased its funding in late 1989, $1.5 million had been awarded to the FEMRI and the ARE Clinic.[40]

The Fetzer Foundation Building

Sometime in 1983, John Fetzer decided that the foundation needed its own administration building if it were to continue to grow. Now that he had sold many of his businesses, the foundation had a significant endowment from which to draw for such a project, and he was being urged by Jim Gordon's channeled Masters of the Inner Light to take the "next step" toward "the development of land and building" for the foundation.[41] Fetzer had earlier provided $1 million of the $4.8 million for the Western Michigan University Fetzer Business Center, which was inaugurated in November 1983. The successful completion of this building perhaps inspired Fetzer to create a similar facility for the foundation, especially after Jim Gordon channeled Paul the Venetian, who reported that he

and six other Masters had attended the dedication of the WMU building in order to "ensoul" it with the consciousness of the angel Ishna.[42] If
the Masters approved of this Fetzer building, how much more blessed
would be a Fetzer building dedicated solely to spiritual tasks? By 1984,
the Fetzer board had committed the foundation to a serious exploration
of a stand-alone administration building.[43]

One of the major questions debated was where the building should
be located and what it should look like, and in this, Fetzer and the core
group looked to Jim Gordon for advice. In one of Gordon's channelings,
the Archangel Michael debated whether the foundation's headquarters
should be located in Kalamazoo—which benefited from a "great vortex of
energy" that had been set in motion by John Fetzer himself and that could
be stepped up by the activities of the foundation—or in Arizona, "because
Shamballa focused in the higher planes over this area" had "created [there]
a chakra center of great importance to the world and its development."
The Archangel Michael also suggested that a building of "crystal design"
would be "a truly great idea and can be a very inspiring structure as well
as a good focus for higher light to . . . manifest in the physical realm."
The Archangel realized, however, that such a structure might not be fea-
sible, in which case "a large crystal sculpture in a water fountain" should
be incorporated into the "center of the building" for this purpose. In any
case, Michael said, "Use your imagination and let the spirits of nature
guide you on proper flow of energy within the land, surrounding plants,
the use of water, and in this way the proper flow can be created which
will also harmonize with our flow of Light." Ultimately, Michael left "the
final decision" about all these issues "in [the] hands and minds" of the core
group who simply needed to use the "gift of discernment and judgment
and go within and ask God's guidance."[44]

To help with the site selection for what was now being called the "Fetzer
Foundation Administration and Research Complex," the Fetzer board
hired Joseph ("Joey") Jochmans. Jochmans was a psychic and dowser with
ties to the Coptics and a business associate of Cleora Daily, with whom
he ran a New Age travel agency, World Light Travels. Jochmans was also

well acquainted with Jim Gordon. The board's brief for Jochmans's work was short but comprehensive: "Recognizing the mission of the foundation as bridging the physical and spiritual dimensions of humankind through energy medicine research, Mr. Jochmans will consider: geographic location; structural design; and appropriate use of color, sound and light." With regard to location, Jochmans's original preference was for Bimini since Edgar Cayce had identified this Caribbean island as a last remnant of Atlantis. However, it was decided early on that the foundation would stay in Kalamazoo, and so several local sites were considered, including an undeveloped parcel across the street from the Fetzers' Clovelly house and property across from Broadcast House on Maple Street. Jochmans felt that the Clovelly property would be good for a retreat center and a chapel but not for the administration building. Instead, based on his pendulum dowsings, Jochmans decided that the Maple Street property would be ideal because its configuration of ley lines, tracks of subtle energy said to crisscross the surface of the earth, created the potential for "new energy vortices." To "amplify and anchor" these power centers, Jochmans subsequently held a series of ceremonies on the property. These involved readings of rune stones and Tarot cards, in addition to burying pieces of Aswan granite brought back from Egypt and thirteen crystals from Arkansas.[45]

While favoring the Maple Street location (and Bimini, at least for the foundation's research center), Jochmans also dowsed two properties on the outskirts of Kalamazoo, one of which was a fifty-six-acre parcel on Dustin Lake. Located in rural Oshtemo township, the heavily wooded parcel with its small spring-fed lake was extremely attractive, and Jochmans determined that the land possessed "potentially healing energy properties" and was "an energy balance point for this entire region." Jochmans's opinion about the Dustin Lake property was seconded by the Archangel Michael, who, in a Gordon channeling, said that "the property will suit the needs of the foundation quite well," especially since "the water on the property will help greatly in raising the energies of the land and the buildings because of the deva [i.e., nature spirit] activity and the cleansing effect that water devas have." This, plus the fact that the Dustin

26. Participants in the Summer Solstice crystal-laying ceremony at the Maple Street property across from Broadcast House, June 21, 1984: *left to right*, Frank Henry, Margaret Zolen, John E. Fetzer, Mike Gergely, Lloyd Swierenga, Carolyn Dailey, Joey Jochmans. (Photo by Bruce Fetzer, courtesy of the Fetzer Institute)

Lake property would allow for almost unlimited expansion, seems to have clinched John Fetzer's decision to build there, culminating in the foundation's purchase of the land in August 1984.[46]

The responsibility for coordinating the building of the Fetzer Administration Building fell to Lloyd Swierenga. Swierenga soon threw himself enthusiastically into the building project, arranging for the initial site surveys, contacting contractors, and working to identify an architectural firm in tune with both the physical and spiritual demands of the project.[47] In addition to the practical necessities of creating a usable workspace, the building also had to address the concerns of Jochmans and the Archangel Michael that it be in "balance with the flow of the deva kingdom as well as the natural electrical field of the property."[48]

Moreover, Jochmans prepared a document titled "Guiding Design Principles for the Fetzer Foundation Centers," which made recommendations based on what he called "terramonics" and "archemonics," that is, the correct placement and architecture of a building to maximize harmony with natural earth energies. Many of Jochmans's specific "terramonic" recommendations, such as situating the building according to the property's ley lines and solar, lunar, and celestial alignments, were indeed respected as far as possible, and many of the specific "archemonic" suggestions made it into the finished building. These included the use of natural material, the incorporation of "energy forms" (particularly triangles, spheres, cones, and pyramids), the creation of spaces conducive to meditation through sound and color, and the inclusion of carefully chosen symbolic art and artifacts. In addition, the building was to enjoy natural lighting; ionized air, created either artificially or through use of a running-water feature such as a waterfall; copious use of plants and flowers; and, of course, the placement around the interior of lots of crystals.[49]

In the end, the Southfield, Michigan, architectural firm of Harley, Ellington, Pierce and Yee Associates (HEPY) was chosen for the Fetzer Administration Building project.[50] In a meeting with the architects, John Fetzer was adamant "that this building not be just another rectangular thing stuck up there" and that it reflect in some way the esoteric nature of the energy-medicine work championed by the foundation. Fetzer was also clear that the overall feeling of the place had to be one of peace and serenity, "something of a world to set yourself aside from the physical world in which we live." Moreover, philosophically, the building must express "a oneness and wholeness that brings it all together. Because if you have a oneness outlook, you then are beginning to come to the source of all creative matter." He explained what he meant by this last statement:

> Perhaps, somewhere out of this Universe there is a super-creative intelligence that brought all of this together. That all of this, this Universe in which we live, is not just a grand slammed accident. But we feel there is a creative source in back of all those things in which you're looking, and, if you could bring it all together, that those . . . in our own group or,

at least, those that could be coming into this place for business transactions or otherwise say, "Hey, there's something different about this. This is a place to come and get some rest. This is a place not in the norm of things, of this world but here is something that's a little bit different that contributed to the well being of man." Now those are the things that I would be thinking about if I were to be walking in here.

More specifically, Fetzer wished the building to reflect in some way the durable architecture and symbolism of ancient Egypt, which had so impressed him on his trip down the River Nile, especially the Great Pyramid and the archways and pillars of the Temple at Luxor (some of which also figured in the higher degrees of Freemasonry). And finally, he wished the building to express something of the great personalities of history who had special meaning for him: Alexander the Great, Ramses II, Louis XIV of France, and the US Founding Fathers Benjamin Franklin and Thomas Jefferson. With regard to Jefferson, he thought that Monticello could also be an inspiration.[51]

Designing a building that would take all of this into account was a tall order, but the HEPY architects did a masterful job synthesizing these disparate elements into a harmonious whole. Seen from the air, the building was to be a two-story, 57,500-square-foot equilateral triangle, the sides of which would be sheathed in polished gray granite with black-and-white granite trim reminiscent of the facing of the Great Pyramid of Cheops. Visitors would arrive up a winding walkway flanked by a serpentine Jeffersonian wall and pass through red-granite "pylons," carved into the lintel of which would be the great winged solar disk flanked by two cobras like that which Fetzer had seen in Luxor. Visitors would then enter a two-story atrium, awash with sunlight and the gentle sound of falling water from a long black-granite interior waterfall. Here, too, they would see a strikingly large quartz cluster, and throughout the building, they would encounter rare natural gem specimens ranging from celestite and ammonite to petrified wood and meteorite. Moreover, the triangle motif would recur frequently in the building, from the terrazzo floor tiles to the brass banisters around the stairways to the second floor. The hallways leading to the upstairs library and offices would be in the shape of gothic arches, and the offices themselves would be lighted by a combination of clerestory and low horizontal windows, giving it all a somewhat monastic feel. Upstairs, too, at one of the angles of the building would be a room set aside for meditation, acoustically designed for serenity with a large selenite crystal as a focal point; and at another angle of the building, John Fetzer would have his office, which would feature a large circular window echoing one of similar design at Monticello. Finally, as visitors exited out the back employee entrance, flanked by the Egyptian goddesses Isis and Nephthys carved into the rose-marble walls, they would see to their right a large black obelisk. Pierced at the top by two large holes, the obelisk would be oriented in such a way that on March 25 of each year—John Fetzer's birthday—the first rays of the rising sun would be focused on a copper disk set into the side of the building.[52]

Taken as a whole and viewed from the air, the entire building would echo in a stylized way the new logo for the Fetzer Foundation, which was designed by Jim Gordon.[53] The new logo was much simplified from the older symbol, whose six-pointed star, it was thought, might ultimately lead to misunderstandings. Rather, the new logo was to be an inverted triangle with the stylized letters "J" and "F" dependent from the triangle's upper horizontal base. The triangle, of course, is a primary symbol that appears in a multitude of spiritual traditions, from ancient Egypt all the way to more recent traditions such as Freemasonry, Rosicrucianism, and Theosophy. However, according to Jim Gordon's Cato, the inverted triangle was specifically chosen because it "represents the downward flow of knowledge from the higher regions to the lower, to manifest in the physical realm for the upliftment of mankind"; and the entwined letters represent "the two energies—the two symbols of flow," "one coming down from the higher regions, flowing down; another reaching up from the point in time and space that is the Foundation, and merging with the energy flowing downward." What is more, when the logo appeared in gold (as a later internal memo explained), this was the symbol of "Christ Consciousness coming

27. The completed John E. Fetzer Foundation Administration Building with obelisk in foreground, 1989. (Photo by Lance Ferraro, courtesy of the Fetzer Institute)

into manifestation on the physical plane," and when in blue, the "balancing of physical and auric energies." In this sense, the logo was more than a logo but an icon; and as with any icon, it has inspired multiple interpretations. For example, an internal foundation document from 1986 interpreted the three legs of the triangle as representing either body, mind, and spirit or, from a Christian perspective, the Father, Son, and Holy Ghost. John Fetzer himself also interpreted the three legs of the triangle as the three goals of the foundation: research, education, and service. Whatever its final meaning, the triangle logo would appear throughout the building, and a specially designed flag featuring it would fly out front alongside the American flag and the Michigan State flag.[54]

Perhaps one of the more intriguing (and ultimately controversial) features of the Fetzer Administration Building was to be the Hall of Records.[55] Near the center of the building on the first floor would be built a replica of half the dome of Monticello covered in gold leaf, under which, arranged in a semicircle, would stand eight busts done in bronze by the local artist Kirk

28. New Fetzer Foundation logo.

Newman. The busts would represent Socrates, Ramses II, Francis I, Joseph of Arimathea, Louis XIV, St. John of the Cross, Henry II, and Thomas Jefferson, all of whom, according to the booklet prepared for visitors, "John Fetzer believes helped nurture and bring humanity forward to a new level of awareness and potential."[56] Beyond their historical importance, however, the eight men had a deep esoteric meaning for Fetzer, for he believed that he was the reincarnation of at least some, if not all, of the figures memorialized.[57]

The Hall of Records design also called for other symbolic elements to be present to underscore the esoteric importance of the room: upon entering, one would pass between two pillars (reminiscent perhaps of those in a Masonic lodge) and underneath a stained-glass depiction of the Great Central Sun by the artist Dawn Doüet. Moreover, the arrangement of the busts would echo a similar display of religious founders that Fetzer had seen at Camp Chesterfield.[58] And finally, the very name—Hall of Records—would have rich esoteric overtones. Edgar Cayce frequently predicted in his readings that such halls, said to contain the ancient history and lost spiritual knowledge of Atlantis, would be discovered in Egypt, Central America, and Bimini as humanity transitioned into the Age of Aquarius. Fetzer was familiar with this from his readings of Cayce, but his association with Joey Jochmans, who wrote extensively about the Halls of Records, undoubtedly reinforced the notion.[59]

It is clear that Fetzer was extremely proud of the Hall of Records when it was completed, and he believed that it was not only the heart of the Administration Building but the spiritual key to his thinking about the balance between the physical, emotional, mental, and spiritual aspects of human life. Fetzer realized that for most people, the Hall of Records would be an "enormous challenge," but he hoped that "for just the few, not the many, even just the few spiritual seekers that go through [it], . . . a gleam of light [will] penetrate that will teach them just one more little step toward their own spiritual development."[60]

Construction on the Fetzer Foundation Administration Building commenced on December 6, 1985.[61] During the next several months, Lloyd Swierenga attended to the myriad details necessary to complete a project of this complexity. Reportedly, John Fetzer had told Swierenga "to build a monument," and he took this injunction very seriously, worrying about every phase of the construction process and demanding the highest possible quality in every aspect of the building.[62] Unfortunately, a couple of months before the start of construction, Fetzer suffered his second heart attack and retreated to Arizona for recovery and treatment at the ARE Clinic.[63] He did not return to Kalamazoo for several months. In the meantime, Swierenga, whom Fetzer soon appointed executive vice president of the foundation, forged ahead with the project, and despite the inevitable setbacks and delays, the building was ready for occupancy in March 1987.[64]

Some acquaintances said that John Fetzer was a bit embarrassed at first by the grandeur of the new Fetzer Administration Building when it was finally done, but it is clear that he very quickly became comfortable and then delighted by what his vision had wrought.[65] On March 25, John Fetzer's birthday, in preparation for the staff move-in the following month, Jim Gordon presided over a simple dedication ceremony in the atrium of the new building. He asked that all the people present join hands around a table with a single lighted candle flanked by the red rose of love and the white rose of wisdom. Invoking the Holy Spirit, Gordon asked that blessings be bestowed on Fetzer, his foundation, his staff, and the land on which the new building stood. He also asked that the

29. Interior of the Hall of Records, 1989. (Photo by Baltazar Korab, courtesy of the Fetzer Institute)

"Masters of the hierarchy and the host of angels" be always present and that the "ringing radiance" of the "sound and light current" would "beam forward from this land throughout all levels, throughout all existences, to lift all back to the heart of God."[66]

At the conclusion of the ceremony, John Fetzer himself was asked to say a few words, and what he said reflected both his pride in the accomplishment and also something of the weariness he was feeling as he entered into his eighty-sixth year. "I think we have that which can be a beautiful beginning," he said, "a beginning of something in which we could find a sense of direction that is over and above and beyond any ideas that we may have here. I believe what has been established into this Foundation has been ordained from the highest order." Looking around the circle of his staff, he continued,

> We all know there is a light and there is a force and there is
> an energy that is present here. And everybody here in this
> room, if he so desires to grow, can become something far

superior than that which you are at the moment. Because there is light, and the light will carry you to balance—the balancing of the physical, the emotional, and the mental, and the spiritual, so that you can become balanced men and women, and you truly can make your contribution and be instrumental in bringing others in who will make contributions to the great hopes of the world as time goes on.

I'm glad to be here. I'm glad that I have been permitted to stay awhile longer, for the last two years have been difficult times. I was glad to see the spot, Lloyd, on the side of the building, and the sun shining through it on the morning on March 25. And I hope that, when March 25 rolls around from time to time, there will always be a rising sun.

At this point, sensing that the occasion was becoming overly solemn, Fetzer smiled and concluded puckishly by asking, "Well, can somebody tell a joke now?"[67]

Finally, on June 25, 1988, an elaborate public dedication ceremony was held for the Fetzer Administration Building, now called the John E. Fetzer Foundation World Headquarters. The event included notables from local government and area educational institutions, as well as a representative from the United Nations. A children's group from a Kalamazoo elementary school was also on hand to dedicate the building on behalf of "the future." The invocation was given by none other than Sister Elizabeth Reis from the Monday Night Group, and the Litany of Dedication was given by the Reverend David McShane, the pastor of Fetzer's Presbyterian church and a longtime supporter of holistic health. John Fetzer said in his dedication remarks that after "a lifetime of hope," he was "gratified beyond words, to commit this building as a permanent and living servant to the purposes for which it was created" and that it was his "earnest prayer that it will ever embody and inspire the vision of the whole and healthy persons in the service of a whole and healthy world, that truth may be its cornerstone, and love its life."[68]

11

The Last of the Nine Lives

Fetzer's Transition and Legacy
(Late 1980s to 1991 and Beyond)

With the Fetzer Foundation's mission set and its World Headquarters built, John Fetzer may have felt at this point that his work was done and that his legacy through the foundation was secure. However, the sun was to roll over the World Headquarters' brass dot nearly four more times for Fetzer, and during those years, both he and his foundation faced great challenges and continued to experience great changes. Fetzer by this time was becoming increasingly frail, often using a cane or a walker, and his wife Rhea's death in May 1988 hit him especially hard, undermining his health even more. Nevertheless, at least until 1990, he dutifully went into his office at the foundation for a few hours every day. During these last years, Fetzer was aided greatly by the presence of Tom Beaver, who, after Fetzer's second heart attack in 1985, lived with him at the Clovelly house and served as his companion. Originally from Grand Haven, Michigan, Beaver had worked as an aerospace engineer and math teacher. It was his deep interest in and knowledge of metaphysical traditions, however, not to mention his psychic abilities, that led Jim Gordon to recommend him to Fetzer. Moreover, Beaver was active in Surat Shabd Yoga, having been initiated into the tradition in 1975, and he also had experience with MSIA. Together, he and Fetzer maintained the Radhasoami sound-and-light meditation practice assiduously.[1]

Such spiritual centering was especially important at this point in Fetzer's life. Throughout his career, Fetzer had prided himself on his close control of his various businesses, and it is clear that he maintained the same desire for control over the foundation. "I constantly hear multitudinous voices purporting to give advice and counsel as to how the Foundation should be run," he wrote during this period. "To all this, I have turned a deaf ear, for always I have been my own man and certainly will continue to do so."[2] What is more, Fetzer apparently believed that throughout his multiple reincarnations, his mission had been to use his wealth to create an institution that would transform the world through spiritual freedom and that since this was his last incarnation, now was his last chance to fulfill this destiny. Thus, his desire for control reflected not only his particular psychology but also his conception of his spiritual destiny.[3]

Control, however, became more and more difficult to achieve as John Fetzer weakened and the foundation grew and became more complex. From an organization with a rubber-stamp board and two full-time employees in the early 1980s, the foundation had evolved to have a professional board and dozens of employees by the end of the decade. By this point, the board meeting minutes are full of discussions about bylaws, health insurance, retirement plans, and all the other colorless details of a burgeoning corporate structure. Perhaps because more and more people were joining the foundation whom Fetzer did not know personally and about whose spiritual orientation he was unsure, at his insistence, the foundation instituted the "John E. Fetzer Foundation Commitment":

> We manifest the universal Christ Consciousness in order
>   to bring true healing and harmony to ourselves and
>   humanity.

30. John E. Fetzer with Tom Beaver at the Fetzer Foundation Retreat, Traverse City, Michigan, June 1989.

> We affirm the universal Christ light radiates through our body, mind, and spirit within the John E. Fetzer Foundation.
>
> Today we affirm our mission of sacred service to humanity.[4]

The commitment was often recited by employees at staff meetings and by board members before board meetings.[5] By the 1980s, the ideas of Christ Consciousness and Christ Light were commonplace in the New Age movement, having originated in earlier Theosophical circles and used extensively by such figures as Alice Bailey, Guy Ballard, and Edgar Cayce and more recently by Jim Gordon, John-Roger, Joey Jochmans, and the Coptics.[6] In some ways, the commitment functioned as a simple creed for the foundation, a distillation of Fetzer's spiritual vision. It thus served to indicate (and perhaps inculcate) the kind of spirituality Fetzer expected (or at least hoped) all foundation staff would share.[7]

Issues of control also surfaced after the May 1987 vote by the board to convert the foundation's legal status from a supporting foundation, which allowed major funding recipients to control the election of the foundation's leadership, to one which enabled the foundation to determine its own directors.[8] This was done to ensure the foundation's continued autonomy in line with John Fetzer's long-term goals, but it also coincided with the formation of a professional board, which, as it turned out, was much more independent of Fetzer's specific wishes.[9] Indeed, the new "Statement of Purpose" approved that November was notably more vague than the previous statement of four years before: "The John E. Fetzer Foundation supports and provides research, education, and action designed to discover and enhance the integral relationships of the physical, mental, emotional, and spiritual dimensions of experience fostering human growth, service, and responsible improvement of the human and cosmic condition."[10] It was for this reason that Fetzer often felt he had to reiterate at board meetings his specific wishes that the top priority of the foundation should now be laboratory research, either by funding others' basic research or through the creation of an in-house laboratory for applied research. This was a theme he tirelessly rehearsed, suspecting that, if he was not entirely clear on this, "little by little the Foundation [would] lose its Founder's purpose." However, in the face of a board with different priorities, he feared that he no longer "had the health and strength necessary to get in [there] and swing as [he] once did" in order to make sure that the board assumed responsibility for this "principal purpose."[11]

In Fetzer's last years, he also attempted to reassert his control over the foundation by replacing presidents. In June 1987, ostensibly because of cost overruns on the new Administration Building, Lloyd Swierenga was replaced by Glenn A. Olds.[12] Olds, who had spent a lifetime in academia and government, had met Fetzer when both were members of the IONS board back in the 1970s. He impressed Fetzer with his knowledge, connections, and energy, and Fetzer believed that he had the national stature that would give the foundation the credibility it needed. Olds's tenure began well, spearheading, for example, the creation of new fellowships such as the Fetzer Pioneers and Fetzer Associates and the organization of the large "Helping Heal the Whole Person and the Whole World" conference

31. John E. Fetzer addressing the "Helping Heal the Whole Person and the Whole World" conference at the Fetzer Foundation World Headquarters, June 25, 1988.

in June 1988. Very quickly, however, tensions developed between Fetzer and Olds. Not only did Olds have little use for Jim Gordon and his channelings, but his autocratic leadership style and spending left Fetzer again feeling an acute loss of control. By June 1989, therefore, Olds was out, and Robert Lehman from the Kettering Foundation was tapped to be the new president of the Fetzer Foundation.[13]

Lehman, who came from a position as vice president of the Kettering Foundation, brought a wealth of experience in charitable foundation administration and a leadership style that was quieter than Olds's. His presidency ushered in an extended period of change and innovation at the Fetzer Foundation (indeed, he remained in this office until 2000).[14] It was during Lehman's first year in office that the name of the foundation was changed to the Fetzer Institute to emphasize its educational mission; and while this move had been under discussion during Olds's tenure, Fetzer took this as a propitious sign that with a new name and a new president, his organization was finally on the right track.[15] Fetzer also created another organization called the Memorial Trust, a private, non-operating foundation designed to aid the institute in maintaining Fetzer's legacy and vision after his death. As a mark of his faith in his new president, Fetzer named Lehman as the chair of the trust as well.[16]

Despite this positive turn of events, the stress of the past few years had taken a toll on John Fetzer's already-fragile health. His last public appearance at the Fetzer Institute World Headquarters was on November 13, 1990, for the dedication of the Hologram, an esoterically rich sculpture by the artist Vincent Mariani. Fetzer was visibly infirm and confined to a wheelchair, and the assembled guests had to gather close to hear his words.[17] Fetzer was still suffering from the lingering effects of pneumonia contracted at a Tigers exhibition game a month earlier in Kalamazoo, and it was clear to many people around him, but especially to Jim Gordon and Tom Beaver, that if Fetzer had to go through another Michigan winter, he would not last out the year.[18]

Final Days in Hawaii

With Rhea gone and the Fetzer Institute now in good hands, Fetzer saw the wisdom of moving to a warmer climate, if only so he could eke out a few more years of life to see the institute grow.[19] Tucson unfortunately was out of the question due to its altitude and relatively cool climate, and Fetzer was not interested in going back to Florida, where he had spent so many seasons at the Tigers' spring training. He finally decided that Hawaii was where he wanted to spend his final days, so Jim Gordon and Tom Beaver were dispatched to Oahu, where they found two homes near Diamond Head, one for Fetzer and Beaver, another for Gordon. Shortly after the Hologram dedication, Fetzer flew by chartered jet to his new home. According to both Gordon and Beaver, Fetzer loved being in Hawaii, delighted by the warmth and sunlight and tropical foliage. He continued his regular meditation practice with Beaver and saw Gordon daily. Fetzer loved nothing better than being chauffeured around

32. John E. Fetzer at the Hologram dedication ceremony at the Fetzer Foundation World Headquarters, November 13, 1990.

the island by the pair, sightseeing in his new Mercedes Benz; or he would simply sit comfortably in his bedroom watching the whales play and the navy ships coming in and out of Pearl Harbor. Here in Hawaii, far from the cares of Kalamazoo, John Fetzer had finally found a sense of peace. Looking out his window one day, Fetzer claimed he saw Jesus walking on the ocean. It is perhaps a measure of his spiritual equanimity at this point that, while he found the experience interesting, it did not hit him the way that his youthful vision of Jesus in the elevator had so many years before.[20]

The institute's leaders, acknowledging the absence of their founder, decided to have their February 1991 board meeting in Oahu.[21] Since Fetzer would be the guest of honor, he set to work drafting his address to the board, but the strain of this was too much. His health began to fail precipitously several days before the meeting, and by the time the board arrived at the Kahala Hilton on February 12, Fetzer had already been admitted to the hospital. Gordon and Beaver kept vigil in shifts in his hospital room along with a private nurse. His strength and energy were fading fast.

Three days after the board meeting, the end came early in the morning on February 20. Jim Gordon was alone with the nurse when Fetzer suddenly sat up and said that he was in pain. The nurse administered a dose of morphine, allowing him to relax. Gordon told Fetzer, "Just chant the names of God. Just focus on the name of God and go inside." As Gordon related later, "In the spiritual tradition we practiced, we were taught to chant the unspoken names of God inside in meditation, which is a process of letting go of the physical when an initiate is moving through the levels of awareness." Silently but with lips moving, John Fetzer began to chant, and soon, while still in prayer, he passed over.[22]

For years, Fetzer had been telling friends that he thought the afterlife would be a "great adventure" and not something to be feared. In his later years, he said, he had achieved a "philosophy of serenity" in the face of death, for while heaven was very real for him, hell was just "a product of our society." He believed that the transition would be natural and easy and that people will be "surprised how normal it is." As he told a niece, Svea Yeager, "this life it is just the beginning, not the end": "This life is just a school of continued learning that develops into a new posture and conditioning which completely prepares us for the great things to come in the next life. Actually our physical being is in a certain octave of existence, i.e., it is a vibratory state of the physical and after we ascend into the next life, we go into a higher octave that is made of finer material, lighter-weight, and completely sustained in the light of the creative intelligence who made all things in all phases of the universe." Fetzer's only concern was that he might be made to come back for a further reincarnation. He told Judy Skutch Whitson that this was something he hoped he would not have to do, for it would indicate that his great mission as represented by the institute would, after so many lifetimes, still not be successful. He had a good feeling, though, that he would not be called back.[23]

The Evolution of the Institute's Mission

In the years after Fetzer's death, the Fetzer Institute has grown, and its programs have diversified. Throughout the 1990s, the institute continued to pursue programs in energy medicine and holistic health broadly conceived. Significantly, the idea of an in-house research laboratory aimed at developing subtle-energy devices was shelved as impractical, although the institute continued to fund for a time subtle-energy research, for example, that of Jan Walleczek at the Bioelectromagnetics Laboratory at Stanford University. More and more focus, however, was directed toward mainstream studies of the emerging field of mind/body health, which resulted in the funding of David Eisenberg's groundbreaking study of the widespread use of "unconventional medicine" in the United States and later, in collaboration with the National Institutes of Health, rigorous empirical studies on the impact of spirituality on various facets of health and wellness. Too, the institute focused on mind/body health education, which became an increasingly important component of the institute's programs. Funded under this rubric were the popular PBS documentary series and book *Healing and the Mind with Bill Moyers*, the "Courage to Teach" program of the spiritual educator Parker Palmer, and the work on education for emotional intelligence by Daniel Goleman.[24]

Around the turn of the millennium, the Fetzer Institute moved further away from scientific research on subtle-energy healing toward the promotion of a practical spirituality for individual health and social transformation. Called the "Common Work," this spirituality was based on an understanding of Fetzer's concern for "freedom of the spirit," which, according to a working document from 1997, "emerges through becoming conscious of our wholeness and [breaking] the emotional patterns that generate the illusion of separateness" from "the presence of God, the Spirit of Love." Thus, through research, education, and service (but primarily the latter two), the institute would attempt to transform the world by "nurturing communities of freedom" to achieve "freedom of the spirit." Along these lines, funding continued for the projects of Parker Palmer and Bill Moyers but expanded to include organizations promoting spiritual practice such as the Center for Contemplative Mind in Society of Northampton, Massachusetts. It was during this period as well that the institute built Seasons, an elegant conference and retreat center adjacent to the administration building. Finally, the institute recommitted itself even more strongly to the idea of developing the institute staff into a working "community of freedom," and from this point on, individual staff development of "freedom of the spirit" became a highly visible part of the institute's culture.[25]

In the wake of the terrorist attacks in September 2001, the spiritual mission of the Fetzer Institute was honed even more, this time to focus specifically on the "power of love and forgiveness" in the formation of "communities of freedom." As stated in 2007, the Fetzer Institute's new intent was "to reveal, serve, and inspire the global awakening that is turning the tide of our times from fear and violence to love and forgiveness." This would be accomplished through publicizing the idea of a global awakening, promoting transformative practice with individuals and groups, and exploring ways in which science and spirituality could be reconciled. This last included funding projects to use neuroscience to study the brains of "exemplary practitioners of compassion and forgiveness" in the hope that this might lead to better "ways to cultivate prosocial capacities that might lead to transformation." More typical of the projects funded, however, were qualitative studies of the role of love and forgiveness in community building or workshops and dialogue meetings on the theme. The most important of these was the Fetzer Global Gathering in Assisi, Italy, in 2012, which brought together spiritual leaders from around the world to raise consciousness of the global awakening and to develop new networks for the promotion of love and forgiveness. By this time, scientific research within the institute was now confined to that which was being funded by the Memorial Trust.[26]

What might John Fetzer think about the evolution of the mission of the institute that bears his name? There is no easy answer to this question, for at the heart of Fetzer's spiritual journey were two distinct projects. After a lifetime of deep reading and thinking about several metaphysical traditions and after years of personal practice from Spiritualism to Surat Shabd Yoga, Fetzer had gained an unshakable faith in the reality of spirit and the monistic nature of the cosmos. Thus, one of his projects was to introduce the world to this spiritual outlook—indeed, at one point, he literally dreamed that he was the spokesman for a new religion.[27] And yet, despite his deep faith, he remained perpetually anxious to seek empirical evidence of spirit through science and thus give his spiritual beliefs scientific respectability. Ultimately, this desire can be traced back to early skepticism of traditional Christianity and to his lifelong understanding of spirit as energy. His second project, therefore, was to somehow reconcile materialist science with spirituality, thus creating the spiritualized science that he felt was so necessary for global transformation to the New Age. As he put it in his speech to the 1988 "Helping Heal the Whole Person and the Whole World" conference, "The challenge . . . is that often hard line science dares spirit to become evidential and, at the same time, a spiritual minded philosophy often looks at science as an unnecessary evil. We must recognize that both viewpoints have a right to exist where there is a mutuality of purpose, and the integration between concepts is a crying need." Unfortunately, "both classical sciences and classical religion are, more often then not, looking in the wrong directions, to find compatibility." It would thus be the goal of the Fetzer Foundation to discover both the new spirituality and the new science that will work harmoniously to improve "the human and cosmic condition."[28]

In Fetzer's 1989 "Founder's Statement," which has come to be seen as his definitive word on what he wanted for the institute's future, the two projects are front and center. The "Founder's Statement" emphasized that the institute's "core program" should be scientific "research of subtle energy . . . as it applies to the physical well being of humankind." In this regard, the in-house laboratory again figured prominently as the venue where "applied science" would lead to a wealth of new "electronic diagnostic and healing devices." However, Fetzer was also quick to point out that "energy scientific research that is not accompanied by the spirit is suspect," and indeed, most of the document deals with Fetzer's second project, the institute's responsibility to nurture a specific kind of spirituality. Individually, this meant cultivating the "freedom of the spirit" that liberates one from the "downward turn in a spiral of consciousness, and brings one into higher focus, back into your higher self." Collectively, this meant coming together to use these higher selves to channel spirit for the good of the planet. "It seems apparent to me," Fetzer said in the "Founder's Statement," "that there has been a great outpouring of energy and that humankind, on a mass level, is [now] seeking to bring into embodiment [a] greater balance, individually and collectively" that will lead in the end "to a world peace, a world government, a world financial system, a world language, a world religion, a world of one mankind." By "creat[ing] a community of freedom," the institute should seek to tap into this through "a certain consciousness of synthesis, that brings forth light, that some refer to as the 'avatar symmetry,' that is here, ready to assist all who are connected with the [institute] to delineate its mission." However the "community of freedom" comes about, though, it was important that it have a solid foundation in "unconditional love," for that "is the unifying energy field that mobilizes the physical, emotional, mental and spiritual resources in the caring and sharing with one another" that is so necessary for the future.[29]

In this, Fetzer's last major statement, it is easy to see the germ of the Fetzer Institute's current mission of "helping build the spiritual foundation for a loving world" by "catalyz[ing] and support[ing] a broad-scale, spiritually grounded transformation from an ego-centered way of being grounded in separation and fear to an all-centered way of being grounded in oneness and love."[30] However, the Memorial Trust continues to emphasize the founder's concern for developing a new spiritual science by funding, for example, the Fetzer Franklin Fund which is designed to encourage continued exploration of "the frontiers of scientific knowledge and to advance breakthroughs toward scientific views of reality that are integrated and relational."[31] Indeed, the trust believes that John Fetzer intended spiritual science to be a perpetual funding priority for the institute. Admittedly, however, both approaches can be found in Fetzer's "Founder's Statement," and since Fetzer himself envisioned a life span for the institute of several hundred years, perhaps its mission will continue to oscillate between these two projects depending on the evolving interests of the board, the needs of the times, and the breakthroughs of science.

The Fetzer Legacy

What, then, is the most important legacy of John Fetzer's spiritual search? To answer this question, we must again briefly review his search within the larger context of spiritual developments that occurred during his lifetime. While Christianity with its theological and cosmological dualism predominated in the West at the beginning of the twentieth century, there has been a remarkable shift among many segments of the population toward Western spiritual monism.[32] A current of spiritual monism had always flowed in the West, manifesting itself in the nineteenth century as esoteric Freemasonry, Hermeticism, Rosicrucianism, Spiritualism, New

33. John E. Fetzer in his office at the Fetzer Foundation World Headquarters, 1989. (Photo by *Encore* magazine, courtesy of the Fetzer Institute)

Thought, and Theosophy and eventually coalescing in the middle of the last century into the spiritual movement called the "New Age."[33]

As this book has made clear, John Fetzer's spiritual search followed precisely this path to the New Age, and as such, his journey should be seen as part of the larger spiritual transformation experienced by many people in the West—not to mention the Midwest. In fact, his intellectual trajectory hit nearly every mark on the road to the New Age, and his mature interests coincided almost exactly with those of the New Age movement of the 1980s. Although definitions of the movement are still debated, we are nevertheless distant enough from its heyday that many of its elements have been generally agreed on by scholars. According to Wouter Hanegraaff, these included the cosmo-theology of spiritual monism in which all is spirit, variously expressed in the metaphors of energy (because of its dynamism), love (because of its intentionality), or mind (because spirit is inherently conscious). It was also widely believed by New Agers that spirit was made manifest to humanity through channeling. Moreover, unlike the Judeo-Christian tradition, there was a marked emphasis in the New Age movement on the freedom of individuals to direct their own spiritual development (i.e., seekership), confined only by the presuppositions of spiritual monism and the widespread belief in reincarnation as a means of spiritual evolution. And while this liberal approach to spiritual development tended toward anti-institutionalism, this was counteracted by a marked tendency for New Agers to participate in group work and other means of securing community. Indeed, as the label implies, the New Age movement, at least in its beginnings, was predicated on nothing less than the coming collective spiritual transformation of the planet, advancing humanity as a whole in the next step of spiritual evolution.

Finally, many people within the New Age movement believed that such a global transformation would only be effected by converting the dominant intellectual force in modern society—science—from materialist monism to spiritual monism. Medicine, as one of the most successful branches of science, was a principal target for this conversion, and thus New Agers were keen to promote "holistic health" through new transpersonal psychologies and new medical practice (e.g., energy medicine, mind/body therapies).[34]

Given all this, especially John Fetzer's abiding concern for a spiritual science, it would be impossible not to call the end product of his long search "New Age." And yet, while Fetzer's worldview was typically New Age in many regards, the fact that he managed to institutionalize his vision makes his search distinctive, both in the sense that he was one of the few New Agers who had the energy, skills, and wealth to do so and also because Fetzer's final worldview reflected a certain phase in the evolution of the New Age. From the beginning, the Fetzer Institute's mission was always firmly focused on Fetzer's desire for global spiritual transformation, and it continues to be so focused to this day. In this, however, John Fetzer and his institute have fallen out of step with more recent developments within the New Age movement. Beginning in the 1990s, precisely when the Fetzer Institute was consolidating Fetzer's vision, the New Age moved on, largely abandoning the emphasis on global transformation in favor of a consumerist hyperindividualism more responsive to the imperatives of the market than to the needs of humankind. Indeed, the New Age movement today has devolved to the point that many contemporary observers see it as a shorthand for spiritual shallowness and reject the label outright. Many prefer instead the label of "spiritual but not religious" (SBNR) to describe their understanding of Western spiritual monism, although SBNRs tend to be just as hyperindividualistic and shallow as the New Agers they decry.[35]

If John Fetzer had lived to see this turn of events, he, too, might have rejected the "New Age" label. During his lifetime, however, he was perfectly comfortable with the term, since for him, it still signified that "the path of attainment and complete personal fulfillment" was simply part of the larger process toward the creation of a new "Golden Era of Earth."[36] In other words, the defining aspect of Fetzer's understanding of the coming New Age was that he believed that personal spiritual transformation (the "freedom of the spirit") should always be in service to the collective transformation of humanity (the "community of freedom"). Indeed, if there is one theme that runs consistently from "Faith of Our Fathers" all the way to the "Founder's Statement," it is that the latter without the former would be empty, and the former without the latter impossible. Perhaps, then, Fetzer's most important legacy should be seen in the fact that, in all his metaphysical wanderings, he never lost sight of the intrinsic connection between personal and global spiritual transformation and, more than this, that he managed to create an enduring institution—the Fetzer Institute—committed to precisely this principle, thus guaranteeing that this key insight of the "old New Age" would not soon be lost.

Notes

Abbreviations

AP	John E. Fetzer Adventist Papers
BR	John E. Fetzer Broadcasting Papers
FP	John E. Fetzer Personal Papers
FI	John E. Fetzer Institute Papers
TB	Thinnes Book Project Papers
WB	Wenger Book Project Papers
FPL	John E. Fetzer Personal Library
JGC	Jim Gordon Collection

With the exception of the Jim Gordon Collection (JGC), all the above are housed in the Fetzer Archives located at the Fetzer Institute Administration Building in Kalamazoo, Michigan. Note that the John E. Fetzer Adventist Papers (AP), the Oral Histories, and the Fetzer Foundation Board Minutes, while housed at the Fetzer Archives, are uncataloged and therefore lack a seven-digit record number. The Jim Gordon Collection, which is also uncataloged, is in the possession of Jim Gordon, Inner Light Ministries, in Austin, Texas.

Preface

Epigraph: Quoted in Carol Hegedus, *John Earl Fetzer: Stories of One Man's Search* (Kalamazoo, MI: Fetzer Institute, 2004), viii.

1. Some terminological explanations are relevant at this point. I specify "spiritual" monism to differentiate it from "material" monism, the dominant worldview of the

natural sciences. Also, I avoid the term "pantheism" because of its close association with neo-paganism and other earth-focused spiritualities. Moreover, in the Old World, Western spiritual monism is known as "Western esotericism" or "the occult," while developments within this tradition in the United States go by the name "metaphysical religions." For good introductions to Western esotericism, see Wouter J. Hanegraaff, *New Age Religion and Western Culture: Esotericism in the Mirror of Secular Thought* (Albany: State University of New York Press, 1998); and Arthur Versluis, *Magic and Mysticism: An Introduction to Western Esotericism* (Lanham, MD: Rowman and Littlefield, 2007). For "metaphysical religions," see J. Stillson Judah, *The History and Philosophy of the Metaphysical Movements in America* (Philadelphia: Westminster, 1967); and Catherine L. Albanese, *A Republic of Mind and Spirit: A Cultural History of American Metaphysical Religion* (New Haven, CT: Yale University Press, 2006).

2. Philip Barlow, "A Demographic Portrait: America Writ Small?," in *Religion and Public Life in the Midwest: America's Common Denominator?*, ed. Philip Barlow and Mark Silk (Walnut Creek, CA: AltaMira, 2004), 30, 44–45.

3. There are two full-length books on Fetzer's many lives: Hegedus's engaging biography, *John Earl Fetzer*, and, focusing specifically on Fetzer's life in baseball, Dan Ewald's *John Fetzer: On a Handshake: The Times and Triumphs of a Tiger Owner* (Detroit: Wayne State University Press, 2000).

4. Although I have derived this definition from Fetzer's own statements, it accords well with the discussion of metaphysical spirituality in general found in Catherine L. Albanese, "The Subtle Energies of the Spirit: Explorations in Metaphysical and New Age Spirituality," *Journal of the American Academy of Religion* 67, no. 2 (1999): 305–25.

5. From 1984 to 1989, the lion's share of the Fetzer Foundation's program budget was devoted to science projects. FI 15 (Foundation Grants History): "John E. Fetzer Foundation History: Grants," n.d., R02.13288.

6. Judah, *History and Philosophy of the Metaphysical Movements*, 11, 21; see also Hanegraaff, *New Age Religion and Western Culture*, 62–76. For the quest to reconcile religion and science in the United States, see, for example, John Hedley Brooke, *Science and Religions: Some Historical Perspectives* (Cambridge: Cambridge University Press, 1991); Jon H. Roberts, *Darwinism and the Divine in America: Protestant Intellectuals and Organic Evolution, 1859–1900* (Madison: University of Wisconsin Press, 1988); D. H. Meyers, "American Intellectuals and the Victorian Crisis of Faith," *American Quarterly* 27 (December 1975): 585–603.

7. Hanegraaff, *New Age Religion and Western Culture*, 15, 75, 223, 303, 330, 370; Christopher Partridge, *The Re-enchantment of the West*, vol. 1 (London: T&T Clark, 2004), 32–33; Albanese, *Republic of Mind and Spirit*, 7–9.

8. For more on the rise and growth in the United States of the "spiritual but not religious" (SBNR) demographic and its connection to the New Age, see Robert C. Fuller, *Spiritual but Not Religious: Understanding Unchurched America* (Oxford: Oxford University Press, 2001); Courtney Bender, *The New Metaphysicals: Spirituality and the American Religious Imagination* (Chicago: University of Chicago Press, 2010); Elizabeth Drescher, *Choosing Our Religion: The Spiritual Lives of America's Nones* (Oxford: Oxford University Press, 2016); Linda A. Mercadante, *Belief without Borders: Inside the Minds of the Spiritual but Not Religious* (Oxford: Oxford University Press, 2014). Mercadante especially highlights the pervasiveness of spiritual monism among SBNRs (116–21).

9. Philip Jenkins, *Mystics and Messiahs: Cults and New Religions in American History* (New York: Oxford University Press, 2000), 88.

10. J. Gordon Melton with James V. Geisendorfer, *A Directory of Religious Bodies in the United States* (New York: Garland, 1977), 14.

11. Albanese, *Republic of Mind and Spirit*, 16.

1. Meeting Jesus in an Elevator

Epigraph: TB 31 (Interviews Fetzer, John E.—Early Years December 3, 1982 II), R02.14833, 5.

1. John E. Fetzer, *One Man's Family: A History and Genealogy of the Fetzer Family* (Ann Arbor: Ann Arbor Press, 1964), 98–104; John E. Fetzer, *The Men from Wengen and America's Agony* (Kalamazoo, MI: John E. Fetzer Foundation, 1971), 335–43; TB 31 (Interviews Fetzer, John E.—Early Years [First Interview], October 21, 1982 I), R02.14830, 9–12.

2. TB 31 (Interviews Fetzer, John E.—Early Years [First Interview], October 21, 1982 I), R02.14830, 13–14, 17, 23–25, 27, 30, 42–44; TB 31 (Interviews Thomas, Harriet & John E. Fetzer, October 28, 1982), R02.14837, 10; TB 31 (Interviews Fetzer John—Early Years [Trip to Lafayette] October 28, 1982), R02.14834, 1–3; TB 31 (Interviews Fetzer, John—Baseball [Lafayette], October 29, 1982), R02.14828, 7, 23; Hegedus, *John Earl Fetzer*, 15–34.

3. FP 1 (Fetzer, John E.—Diary, Dec. 1, 1914–Feb. 12, 1925): December 6, 1914, R02.13788; FP 1 (Correspondence 1926 II): John E. Fetzer to Rhea Yeager, June 29, 1926, R02.13792; Fetzer, *One Man's Family*, 107, 109–10; Fetzer, *Men from Wengen*, 343–47; TB 31 (Interviews Fetzer, John E.—Early Years [First Interview], October 21, 1982 II), R02.14831, 32–40; TB 31 (Interviews Thomas, Harriet & John E. Fetzer, October 28, 1982), R02.14837, 1–7; Hegedus, *John Earl Fetzer*, 15–40.

4. Sidney E. Mead, "In Search of God," in *The Heritage of the Middle West*, ed. John J. Murray (Norman: University of Oklahoma Press, 1958), 152–76.

5. Peter W. Williams, *America's Religions: From Their Origins to the Twenty-First Century* (Urbana: University Illinois Press, 2000), 295.

6. Fetzer, *One Man's Family*, 99.

7. TB 31 (Interviews Fetzer, John E.—Early Years [First Interview], October 21, 1982 I), R02.14830, 15; Fetzer, *Men from Wengen*, 254, 269, 286, 288, 296, 339, 355.

8. FP 19 (Fetzer, John E.—Baptismal Souvenir, 1901), R02.14180.

9. FP 1 (Fetzer, John E.—Diary, Dec. 1, 1914–Feb. 12, 1925): December 6, 1914, R02.13788; TB 31 (Interviews Fetzer, John E.—Early Years [First Interview], October 21, 1982 I), R02.14830, 16.

10. Mark Noll, "Protestants: An Enduring Methodist Tinge," in Barlow and Silk, *Religion and Public Life in the Midwest*, 49–82.

11. T. C. Rudolph, *Hoosier Faiths: A History of Indiana Churches and Religious Groups* (Bloomington: Indiana University Press, 1995), 23; James H. Madison, *Hoosiers: A New History of Indiana* (Bloomington: Indiana University Press 2014), 96–103.

12. US Bureau of the Census, *Religious Bodies: 1906 Census, Part 1: Summary and General Tables* (Washington DC: Government Printing Office, 1910), 55.

13. FP 1 (Fetzer, John E.—Diary, Dec. 1, 1914–Feb. 12, 1925): December 6, 1914, R02.13788.

14. James E. Kirby, Russell E. Richey, and Kenneth E. Rowe, *The Methodists* (Westport, CT: Praeger, 1996), 231.

15. FP 1 (Fetzer, John E.—Diary, Dec. 1, 1914–Feb. 12, 1925): December 16 and 18, 1914, R02.13788.

16. Ian M. Randall, "Methodist Spirituality" in *Ashgate Research Companion to World Methodism*, ed. William Gibson and Martin Wellings (Abingdon, UK: Ashgate, 2013), 289–306.

17. TB 31 (Interviews Fetzer, John E.—Early Years [First Interview], October 21, 1982 II), R02.14831, 11, 31.

18. Ibid., 40; Hegedus, *John Earl Fetzer*, 13, 25–32.

19. For a comprehensive overview of the flu pandemic, see John M. Barry, *The Great Influenza: The Story of the Deadliest Pandemic in History* (London: Penguin, 2005).

20. TB 31 (Interviews Thomas, Harriet & John E. Fetzer, October 28, 1982), R02.14837, 22–24; TB 31 (Interviews Fetzer, John E.—Early Years [First Interview], October 21, 1982 I), R02.14830, 14–15; TB 31 (Interviews Fetzer, John E.—Early Years, December 3, 1982 I), R02.14832, 6.

21. TB 31 (Interviews Fetzer, John E.—Early Years [First Interview], October 21, 1982 II), R02.14831, 32–40; TB 31 (Interviews Fetzer, John E.—Early Years, December 3, 1982 I), R02.14832, 4–5.

22. Fern Honeywell Martin and Paula Alexander Woods, *Greater Lafayette: A Pictorial History* (St. Louis: G. Bradley, 1994), 156.

23. The Seventh-day Adventist Church was incorporated in Battle Creek in 1863; its headquarters were relocated to Takoma Park, Maryland, in 1903–4. Richard W. Schwarz, "The Perils of Growth 1886–1905," in *Adventism in America: A History*, ed. Gary Land (Berrien Springs, MI: Andrews University Press, 1998), 105–7.

24. WB 9 (Thomas, Harriet—Interview Transcript, November 1966), R02.13768, 18–19.

25. See Grant Underwood, *The Millenarian Worldview of Early Mormonism* (Urbana: University of Illinois Press, 1999); Robert S. Fogarty, *The Righteous Remnant: The House of David* (Bowling Green, OH: Kent State University Press, 1981); Judith Cook, *Zion City, Illinois: Twentieth-Century Utopia* (Syracuse, NY: Syracuse University Press, 1996); George M. Marsden, *Fundamentalism and American Culture: The Shaping of Twentieth-Century Evangelicalism, 1870–1925* (New York: Oxford University Press, 2006).

26. See Everitt N. Dick, "The Millerite Movement, 1830–1845," in Land, *Adventism in America*, 1–28; for an estimate of the number of Millerites, see David L. Rowe, "Millerites: A Shadow Portrait," in *The Disappointed: Millerism and Millenarianism in the Nineteenth Century*, ed. Ronald L. Numbers and Jonathan N. Butler (Knoxville: University of Tennessee Press, 1993), 1–15.

27. See Godfrey T. Anderson, "Sectarianism and Organization, 1846–1864," in Land, *Adventism in America*, 29–52.

28. Rudolph, *Hoosier Faiths*, 495–97, 508–10. By this time, the church as a whole had close to two hundred thousand members. George R. Knight, *A Brief History of Seventh-day Adventism* (Hagerstown, MD: Review and Herald, 2004), 132.

29. Jane Smith, "A History of the Seventh Day Adventist Church in Lafayette, Indiana," Lafayette Seventh-day Adventist Church website, accessed July 25, 2016, http://lafayette23.adventistchurchconnect.org/article/2/about-us; founding of Adventist hospital: Ronald L. Numbers, personal communication (October 14, 2016).

30. TB 31 (Interviews Fetzer, John E.—Early Years, December 3, 1982 I), R02.14832, 6–7.

31. Ibid.

32. "WEMC: The Radio Lighthouse," *College Bulletin* 15, no. 1 (1927): 7, 9, 11–15; TB 31 (Interviews Fetzer, John—Early Years [Trip to Lafayette], October 28,

1982), R02.14834, 17–18; TB 31 (Interviews Fetzer, John E.—Early Years, December 3, 1982 I), R02.14832, 7–12; TB 31 (Interviews Clarke, C. Fred, JEF Interview Transcript, June 25, 1984), R02.14825, 7–8; Hegedus, *John Earl Fetzer*, 44–45.

33. FP 1 (Correspondence 1925 I): John E. Fetzer to Della Fetzer, July 18, 1925, R02.13789; FP 1 (Correspondence 1925 II): John E. Fetzer to Della Fetzer, August 3, 1925, R02.13790; FP 1 (Correspondence 1925 II): John E. Fetzer to Della Fetzer, August 15, 1925, R02.13790; TB 31 (Interviews Fetzer, John E.—Early Years [Trip to Lafayette], October 28, 1982), R02.14834, 16; TB 31 (Interviews Fetzer, John E.—Early Years, December 3, 1982 II), R02.14833, 19–26; Hegedus, *John Earl Fetzer*, 51–54, 110, 112.

34. FP 1 (Correspondence 1926 I): John E. Fetzer to Rhea Yeager, June 23, 1926, R02.13791; FP 1 (Correspondence 1926 II): "Wedding Announcement," July 19, 1926, R02.13792; TB 31 (John E. Fetzer Interview, October 28, 1982), R02.14834, 15–17; TB 31 (Interviews Fetzer, John E.—Early Years, December 3, 1982), R02.14832, 9; TB 31 (Interviews Fetzer, John E.—Early Years, December 3, 1982 II), R02.14833, 2–3, 13, 26, 28–29; Hegedus, *John Earl Fetzer*, 110–13.

35. FP 1 (Correspondence 1927 I): "EMC Graduation Announcement," May 20–22, 1927, R02.13794; TB 31 (Interviews Fetzer, John E.—Early Years, December 3, 1982 II), R02.14833, 27.

36. BR 1 (Speeches JEF, 1926–1927): "Faith of Our Fathers," May 22, 1927, R02.16628.

37. Ibid.

2. Fundamental Disagreements

1. TB 31 (Interviews Fetzer, John E.—Early Years, December 3, 1982 II), R02.14833, 27.

2. Ibid., 3.

3. AP: Sterling B. Slater to John E. Fetzer, May 19, 1926. NB: All correspondence is quoted verbatim from the original source and includes all original punctuation, grammar, and spelling.

4. FP 1 (Correspondence 1928 III): Della Fetzer to John E. Fetzer, August 12, 1928, R02.13797.

5. "WEMC: The Radio Lighthouse," *College Bulletin* 15, no. 1 (1927): 26, 28.

6. For the early twentieth-century controversy over evolution and the role of Seventh-day Adventism, see Ronald L. Numbers, *The Creationists: The Evolution of Scientific Creationism* (New York: Knopf, 1992).

7. AP: Thurber H. Madison to John E. and Rhea Fetzer, March 10, 1929.

8. Ibid.; AP: Thurber and Agnes Madison to John E. and Rhea Fetzer, July 7, 1929.

9. AP: Thurber H. Madison to John E. Fetzer, postmarked April 1, 1929; AP: John Kolvoord to John E. Fetzer, April 14, 1929; June 13, 1929; July 22, 1929; John Kolvoord and Moses E. Kellogg, *The Vision of the Evening and the Morning: A Study of the Prophecy of Daniel VIII* (Battle Creek, MI, 1907).

10. AP: E. S. Ballenger to John E. Fetzer, April 16, 1929. Several issues of the *Gathering Call* with Fetzer's annotations are included in the AP.

11. AP: William Norton (The Bible Institute Colportage Association of Chicago) to John E. Fetzer, July 10 and 16, 1929; many of these titles and more are extant in the AP.

12. C. I. Scofield, *Rightly Dividing the Word of Truth (2 Tim. 2:15): Being Ten Outline Studies of the More Important Divisions of Scripture* (1907; Chicago: Bible Institute Colportage Association, 1928?).

13. TB 31 (Interviews Fetzer, John E.—Early Years, December 3, 1982 II), R02.14833, 3.

14. FP 2 (Correspondence 1939) John E. Fetzer to Della Fetzer, November 10, 1939, R02.13827.

15. FP 1 (Correspondence 1928 IV): Rhea Fetzer to John E. Fetzer, October 14, 1928, R02.13798; FP 7 (Yeager Family Correspondence 1938 I): LaMont Yeager to William Yeager, September 9, 1938, R02.13926; FP 7 (Yeager Papers 1943–1944): LeVant Yeager to Loena Yeager, December 22, 1943, R02.13932; TB 12 (Research Material 1920–1944 VI): "1938," R02.14456, 6.

16. FP 7 (Yeager Papers 1939 III): LeVant Yeager to William and Loena Yeager, April 17, 1939, R02.13930.

17. FP 1 (Correspondence 1925 I): John E. Fetzer to Rhea Yeager, July 1, 1925, R02.13789; TB 12 (Research Material 1920–1944 VI): "1938," R02.14456, 6; TB 31 (Interviews Fetzer, John E.—Early Years, December 3, 1982 II), R02.14833, 17.

18. AP: Agnes Madison to John E. Fetzer and Rhea Fetzer, February 19, 1930.

19. AP: Thurber Madison to John E. Fetzer and Rhea Fetzer, March 5, 1930. Fetzer apparently announced to the Madisons his and Rhea's resignation from the Seventh-day Adventist Church in a previous letter, now lost.

20. FP 1 (Correspondence 1929): Della Fetzer to John E. Fetzer, October 23, 1929, R02.13800.

21. FP 1 (Correspondence 1930 I): Della Fetzer to John E. Fetzer, January 30, 1930, R02.13801.

22. FP 3 (Correspondence 1952): Della Fetzer to John E. Fetzer, February 12, 1952, R02.13845; FP 3 (Correspondence 1953): Della Fetzer to John E. Fetzer, July 13, 1953, R02.13845; FP 3 (Correspondence 1954): Della Fetzer to John E. Fetzer, February 1, 1954, R02.13847.

23. FP 3 (Correspondence 1944): Della Fetzer to John E. Fetzer, March 1, 1944, R02.13835.

24. Fetzer carefully lined the valise with a section of the *Chicago Daily News*, hence the precise date.

25. See FP 2 (Correspondence 1935 IV): Rhea Fetzer to John E. Fetzer, August 28, 1935, R02.13816.

26. TB 31 (Interviews Fetzer, John E.—Early Years, December 3, 1982 II), R02.14833, 4.

27. FP 11 (Contributions and Donations 1982–1986 I & II), R02.14004–5.

28. BR 14 (Broadcasting 1980 May–June): "Andrews University Commencement Speech," R02.16929.

29. According to Judy Skutch Whitson's Oral History, March 15, 2011, 17, Fetzer remained fascinated by the idea of the Last Judgment during the 1970s, and Bruce Fetzer remembers reading apocalyptic New Age books by Tuella and Benjamin Crème with his great-uncle during the 1980s. Bruce Fetzer, personal communication, October 26, 2016. Perhaps even more significantly, Fetzer responded enthusiastically when his channeler, Jim Gordon, put a New Age spin on the Book of Revelations in one of his readings. "Revelations—Jim Gordon," May 24, 1982, JGC.

30. FI 6 (Fetzer, John E.—"This I Believe," April 10, 1967), R02.13085, 1.

31. TB 31 (Interviews Fetzer, John E.—Baseball, Spirituality, February 9, 1984), R02.14826, 27.

3. Restless among the Spirits

1. BR 1 (1930 August–December): "Contract," October 7, 1930, R02.16634.

2. Hegedus, *John Earl Fetzer*, 54–55.

3. Ibid., 55–61.

4. TB 31 (Interviews Fetzer, John E.—Baseball, Spirituality, February 9, 1984), R02.14826, 24–27.

5. The two best scholarly studies of American Spiritualism are Brett E. Carroll, *Spiritualism in Antebellum America* (Bloomington: Indiana University Press, 1997);

and Ann Braude, *Radical Spirits: Spiritualism and Women's Rights in Nineteenth-Century America*, 2nd ed. (Bloomington: Indiana University Press, 2001). See also Judah, *History and Philosophy of the Metaphysical Movements*, 50–91; Albanese, *Republic of Mind and Spirit*, 177–53, 257–70; and Todd Jay Leonard, *Talking to the Other Side: A History of Modern Spiritualism and Mediumship* (New York: iUniverse, 2005).

6. Carroll, *Spiritualism in Antebellum America*, 152–76; Braude, *Radical Spirits*, 162–91.

7. Ann Braude, "News from the Spirit World: A Checklist of American Spiritualist Periodicals, 1847–1900," *Proceedings of the American Antiquarian Society* 99 (1999): 444–48.

8. Rudolph, *Hoosier Faiths*, 337–44.

9. Anna Stockinger, "The History of Spiritualism in Indiana," *Indiana Magazine of History* 20 (March–December 1924): 280–87; Louis Martin Sears, "Robert Dale Owen as a Mystic," *Indiana Magazine of History* 24, no. 1 (1928): 15–25.

10. Jenkins, *Mystics and Messiahs*, 79. By 1936, the number of official members had tapered off to twenty-eight thousand. Ibid., 253n17.

11. FP 1 (Correspondence 1930 II): Della Fetzer to John E. and Rhea Fetzer, September 25, 1930, October 17, 1930, R02.13802. For Adventist attitudes toward Spiritualism, see Ellen G. White, *The Great Controversy between Christ and Satan* (1888; Mountain View, CA: Pacific, 1950), 551–62; Ronald L. Numbers, *Prophetess of Health: Ellen G. White and the Origins of Seventh-day Adventist Health Reform* (1992; Grand Rapids, MI: Wm. B. Eerdmans, 2008), 66, 190, 281; Dick, "Millerite Movement," 26.

12. FI 6 (Fetzer, John E.—"A Talk with John Fetzer" [1986]), August 29, 1986, R02.13084, 1. This interview appeared in the 1986 Fetzer Foundation annual report.

13. For more on Tesla, see Marc J. Seifer, *Wizard: The Life and Times of Nikola Tesla* (New York: Citadel, 1998); and Richard Carlson, *Tesla: Inventor of the Electric Age* (Princeton, NJ: Princeton University Press, 2013).

14. Nikola Tesla, *My Inventions and Other Writings* (New York: Penguin, 2011), xix.

15. Ibid., 104–5.

16. Ibid., 105.

17. FI 6 (Fetzer, John E.—"A Talk with John Fetzer" [1986]), August 29, 1986, R02.13084, 1–2.

18. It must be said, however, that in "The Problem of Increasing Human Energy," while Tesla professed his continuing belief in Christianity as a moral force, he nevertheless denied the survival of individual personality after death, and by

the time of his autobiography, *My Inventions* (1919), he specifically denied ever having a supernatural experience, "for which there is absolutely no foundation." Tesla, *My Inventions*, 80–82, 105, 127. However, Fetzer was not the last person to read Tesla esoterically: see John J. O'Neil, *Prodigal Genius: The Life of Nikola Tesla* (1944; Kempton, IL: Adventures Unlimited, 2008).

19. TB 31 (Interviews Fetzer, John E.—Family, Spirituality [Lafayette], October 28, 1982), R02.14835, 6.

20. For an overview of Camp Chesterfield, see Camp Chesterfield, *Chesterfield Lives! 1886–1986: Our First Hundred Years* (Chesterfield, IN: Camp Chesterfield, 1986); see also Stockinger, "History of Spiritualism in Indiana"; Rudolph, *Hoosier Faiths*, 341–43.

21. TB 31 (Interviews Fetzer, John E.—Baseball, Spirituality, February 9, 1984), R02.14826, 34.

22. TB 31 (Interviews Fetzer, John E.—Family, Spirituality [Lafayette], October 28, 1982), R02.14835, 6.

23. The Camp Chesterfield Hotel register shows that Fetzer stayed there in 1962, 1963, and 1964. Camp Chesterfield records, accessed June 25, 2017, http://indiamond6.ulib.iupui.edu/cdm/search/collection/CampChesterfield; TB 18 (Rhea Fetzer Diaries 1968–1972): August 7, 1970; TB 18 (Rhea Fetzer Diaries 1973–1976): August 18, 1973. In a 1976 Ouija board session, when Fetzer asked if he should "see some of [his] friends at Chesterfield," he was told, "You are beyond that now, you don't need anymore evidence, do you?" Ouija Board Transcripts, July 23, 1976, JGC.

24. TB 31 (Research Notes 1983): Kaye Averitt to John E. Fetzer, memo, October 6, 1983, R02.14847: "About ½ were phonies—probably. Only went to 3 or 4 he knew." See also Bruce Fetzer Oral History, March 15, 1996, 76; Bruce Fetzer Oral History, December 12, 2002, 77–78.

25. Fetzer, *One Man's Family*, xi; TB 30 (Rhea's Diary 1966): July 17, 1966; TB 18 (Rhea Fetzer Diaries 1968–1972): August 7, 1970, August 18, 1973; "Hypathia" reading by Clifford Bias, June 21, 1971, JGC.

26. TB 31 (Interviews Fetzer, John E.—Baseball, Spirituality, February 9, 1984), R02.14826, 30–35. The spirit photographs are preserved in the Fetzer Archives: 1964 (P0324933), July 1966 (P0324934), August 11, 1967 (P0324935), August 1968 (P0324936), August 14, 1969 (P0324937), July 24, 1970 (P03249444), August 7, 1970 (P0324941), August 8, 1970 (P0324938–40), August 30, 1973 (P0324942), August 10, 1974 (P0324943). P03249444 is identified on the back as "Silverbelle," while P0324940 is identified as George Wenger and signed by Charlie Swann, the medium.

27. FP 18 (Camp Chesterfield 1962–1974): spirit readings and drawings including undated note card in Fetzer's hand; "Della Frances, Your Teacher, Indian Chief," August 15, 1962; "Dr. Fyfe, Walter, Thunder Cloud," August 24, 1963; "Running Red Fox, Pierre Goulan, Johanna Bunz Fetzer, Walter," August 1, 1964; "Your Father, John Fetzer," August 1974, R02.14165; Ouija Board Transcripts, October 3, 1978, October 11, 1978, JGC; Bruce Fetzer Oral History, December 12, 2002, 77.

28. Bruce Fetzer Oral History, March 15, 1996, 67.

29. TB31 (Interviews Fetzer, John E.—Early Years, December 3, 1982 II), R02.14833, 6; Whitson Oral History, February 10, 2011, 26; Whitson Oral History, March 30, 2011, 2–3.

30. Fetzer, *One Man's Family*, xi; Bruce Fetzer Oral History, December 12, 2002, 77.

31. TB 31 (Interviews Fetzer, John E.—Baseball, Spirituality, February 9, 1984), R02.14826, 30–32.

32. Fetzer, *Men from Wengen*, 77–78.

33. TB 31 (Interviews Fetzer, John E.—Baseball, Spirituality, February 9, 1984), R02.14826, 34.

34. Wilson Van Dusen, *The Presence of Other Worlds: The Findings of Emanuel Swedenborg* (New York: Harper and Row, 1974); see also Judah, *History and Philosophy of the Metaphysical Movements*, 34–37, 41–42; Albanese, *Republic of Mind and Spirit*, 140–44.

35. Marguerite Block, *The New Church in the New World* (New York: Swedenborg, 1984), 112–29; George R. Mathers, *Frontier Faith: The Story of the Pioneer Congregations of Fort Wayne, Indiana, 1820–1860* (Fort Wayne, IN: Allen County–Fort Wayne Historical Society, 1992), 235–41; Howard Means, *Johnny Appleseed: The Man, the Myth, the American Story* (New York: Simon and Schuster, 2011).

36. See Robert C. Fuller, *Mesmerism and the American Cure of Souls* (Philadelphia: University of Pennsylvania Press, 1982); and Craig J. Hazen, *The Village Enlightenment in America: Popular Religion and Science in the Nineteenth Century* (Urbana: University of Illinois Press, 2000).

37. On Davis, see Robert W. Delp, "Andrew Jackson Davis: Prophet of American Spiritualism," *The Journal of American History* 54, no. 1 (1967): 43–56; Catherine L. Albanese, "On the Matter of Spirit: Andrew Jackson Davis and the Marriage of God and Nature," *Journal of the American Academy of Religion* 60, no. 1 (1992): 1–17; Carroll, *Spiritualism in Antebellum America*.

38. Block, *New Church in the New World*, 133–37; Whitney R. Cross, *The Burned-Over District: The Social and Intellectual History of Enthusiastic Religion in Western New York, 1800–1850* (Ithaca, NY: Cornell University Press, 1957), 343–44;

Ann Lee Bressler, *The Universalist Movement in America, 1770–1880* (New York: Oxford University Press, 2001), 111–20.

39. In a 1988 speech, Fetzer quoted Myers: "Love is a kind of exalted, but unspecialized telepathy;—the simplest and most universal expression, of that mutual gravitation, or kinship of spirits, which is the foundation, of telepathic law." FI 6 (Fetzer, John E.—"Helping Heal the Whole Person and the Whole World," Conference Closing Remarks, June 25, 1988), R02.13068. The quote is from F. W. H. Myers, *Human Personality and Its Survival of Bodily Death* (London: Longmans, Green, 1903), 344. See also Whitson Oral History, February 10, 2011, 5–7. In addition to *The Rock of Truth or Spiritualism, the Coming World Religion* (London: Psychic, 1933), Findlay's *The Unfolding Universe* (London: Psychic, 1935) can also be found in John Fetzer's personal library.

40. Quoted in Leonard, *Talking to the Other Side*, 86. The NASC adopted the first six principles in Chicago in 1899; the seventh and eighth in Rochester, New York, in 1909; and the ninth in St. Louis, Missouri, in 1944. Ibid., 85–86.

41. James H. Ryan, *Introduction to Philosophy* (New York: Macmillan, 1924), FPL, 25–53.

42. "A Fetzer View of the Future," *Encore*, November 1980, 1 (offprint).

43. Leonard, *Talking to the Other Side*, 86; B. F. Austin, *The A.B.C. of Spiritualism* (Los Angeles: Austin, 1920), 3–4.

44. TB 31 (Interviews Fetzer, John E.—Baseball, Spirituality, February 9, 1984), R02.14826, 1, 34.

45. Whitson Oral History, February 10, 2011, 27–28.

46. TB 31 (Interviews Fetzer, John E.—Family, Spirituality [Lafayette], October 28, 1982), R02.14835, 4–6.

47. J. Gordon Melton, Jerome Clark, and Aidan A. Kelly, *The New Age Almanac* (New York: Visible Ink, 1991), 276; Jutta K. Lehman, "The Influence of the Theosophical Movement on the Revival of Astrology in Great Britain and North America in the 20th Century" (Ph.D. diss., Concordia University, 1998), 52–58.

48. FP 1 (Correspondence 1930 II): Della Fetzer to John E. and Rhea Fetzer, September 17, 1930, R02.13802; TB 13 (Research Material 1948 I): February 24, 1948, R02.14472; TB 13 (Research Material 1948 II): "Interview with JEF—TT & KTA," December 15, 1983, R02.14473, 11; TB 18 (Research Fetzer, Rhea—Diaries & Letters [Transcripts] [Restricted] 1943–1947): June 28, 1947, R02.14572; TB 31 (Interviews Fetzer, John—Family, Spirituality [Lafayette], October 28, 1982), R02.148350, 11.

49. FP 2 (Correspondence 1938 I): John E. Fetzer to Rhea Fetzer, March 26, 1938, R02.13825.

50. FP 3 (Correspondence 1948): John E. Fetzer to Folks, June 9, 1948, R02.13841.

51. FP 3 (Correspondence 1952): John E. Fetzer to Rhea Fetzer, November 20, 1952, R02.13845.

52. *Sunday Morning Star* (Wilmington, DE), April 3, 1938, 33; TB 31 (Interviews Fetzer, John E.—Baseball, Spirituality, February 9, 1984), R02.14826, 30.

53. Mitch Horowitz, *Occult America: White House Séances, Ouija Circles, Masons, and the Mystic History of Our Nation* (New York: Bantam Books, 2009), 66–79.

54. Whitson Oral History, February 4, 2011, 23–24; February 10, 2011, 23; March 30, 2011, 11–12; Bruce Fetzer Oral History, March 14, 1996, 41.

55. Hegedus, *John Earl Fetzer*, 127–29; Whitson Oral History, March 30, 2011, 3, 24–25; Lloyd Swierenga Oral History, August 6, 2012, 25. According to Bruce Fetzer, John Fetzer also kept a Ouija board at his home in Tucson. Personal communication, October 26, 2016.

56. Whitson Oral History, February 10, 2011, 25–26; March 30, 2011, 4–6.

57. FP 6 (Censored Correspondence 1934–1938): John E. Fetzer to Rhea Fetzer, March 29, 1938, R02.13898; TB 13 (Research Material 1948 II): "Interview with JEF—TT & KTA," December 15, 1983, R02.14473, 11.

58. FP 3 (Correspondence 1952): John E. Fetzer to Rhea Fetzer, November 20, 1952.

59. TB 13 (Research Material 1948 II): "Interview with JEF—TT & KTA," December 15, 1983, R02.14473, 11.

60. For the concept of the cultural *bricoleur* (Fr.: handyman), see Claude Lévi-Strauss, *The Savage Mind* (Chicago: University of Chicago Press, 1966), 16.

4. Finding Ancient Wisdom in the Midwest

1. Hegedus, *John Earl Fetzer*, 63.

2. Ibid., 62.

3. TB 12 (Research Material 1945 II & III): "Fetzer Diary of European Trip," August 2–September 11, 1945, R02.14465–66, 36–38, 54–57; TB 12 (Research Material 1945 I): "1945—ETO Tom Thinnes and JEF—2 Tapes," August 1983, R02.14464, 22–23, 26–28, 30.

4. BR 3 (Broadcasting 1945): "Dedicatory Address by John E. Fetzer Opening WJEF, Grand Rapids, Michigan Delivered from WTOP, CBS for Washington D.C.," February 5, 1945, R216670, 1–2.

5. BR 12 (Broadcasting 1974 January–June): "Anchor Lodge lifetime membership," R02.16901.

6. FP 3 (Correspondence 1944): Homer Fetzer to John E. Fetzer, March 25, 1944, R02.13835. After Homer died in Florida on January 14, 1970, Fetzer went to

considerable effort to find out which lodge he had attended in Minneapolis in order to create a memorial for him. FP 4 (Correspondence 1971): John E. Fetzer to R. E. Dahl, April 5, 1970, R02.13873; FP 4 (Correspondence 1971): Glenn L. Alt to John E. Fetzer, August 10, 1970, R02.13873; FP 4 (Correspondence 1971): John E. Fetzer to Harvey E. Hansen, August 13, 1970, R02.13873; FP 4 (Correspondence 1971): H. R. Hansen to John E. Fetzer, August 17, 1970, R02.13873; FP 4 (Correspondence 1971): John E. Fetzer to R. E. Dahl, August 19, 1970, R02.13873; FP 4 (Correspondence 1971): George E. Mokler and R. E. Dahl to John E. Fetzer, May 8, 1971, R02.13873; FP 4 (Correspondence 1971): John E. Fetzer to R. E. Dahl, April 5, 1971, R02.13873; FP 4 (Correspondence 1971): R. E. Dahl to John E. Fetzer, September 22, 1971, R02.13873; FP 4 (Correspondence 1971): John E. Fetzer to R. E. Dahl, September 26, 1971, R02.13873; BR 11 (Broadcasting 1970 January–April): "Masonic plaque inscription for Homer Fetzer," R02.16869; TB 18 (Research Fetzer, Rhea—Diaries & Letters [Transcripts] [Restricted] 1968–1972), January 16, 1970, R02.14577.

7. FP 2 (Correspondence 1937 II): John E. Fetzer to Rhea Fetzer, April 14, 1937, R02.13820: "Sykes asked me a lot of questions and I feel that he would like to vote for me and probably will in the final analysis. Governor Case leaned over backwards in going into details . . . he discussed the political side of the case. . . . He is a Shriner and alluded to my being one and gave me the Masonic sign which I have reason to believe, means a vote."

8. Jay Kinney, *The Masonic Myth: Unlocking the Truth about Symbols, the Secret Rites, and the History of Freemasonry* (New York: HarperCollins, 2009), 8.

9. Alexander Piatigorsky, *Freemasonry: The Study of a Phenomenon* (London: Harvill, 1999), 102–4; Kinney, *Masonic Myth*, 36.

10. Lynn Dumenil, *Freemasonry in American Culture, 1880–1930* (Princeton, NJ: Princeton University Press, 1984), especially 3–71; Steven C. Bullock, *Revolutionary Brotherhood: Freemasonry and the Transformation of the American Social Order, 1730–1840* (Chapel Hill: University of North Carolina Press, 1996).

11. Robert Freke Gould, *Gould's History of Freemasonry throughout the World*, vol. 6 (New York: Charles Scribner's Sons, 1936), 86.

12. Jefferson S. Conover, *Freemasonry in Michigan*, vol. 1 (Coldwater, MI: Conover, 1897), 14–173.

13. Freemasons, Grand Lodge of Michigan, *Transactions of the Grand Lodge of Free and Accepted Masons of the State of Michigan* (Port Huron: Grand Lodge of Michigan, 1899), 289–95.

14. Dumenil, *Freemasonry in American Culture*, 225; Kinney, *Masonic Myth*, 81.

15. Kinney, *Masonic Myth*, 59–70.

16. Dumenil, *Freemasonry in American Culture*, 42; see also Mark C. Carnes, *Secret Ritual and Manhood in Victorian America* (New Haven, CT: Yale University Press, 1989).

17. Dumenil, *Freemasonry in American Culture*, 42–71.

18. Ibid., 225.

19. The term "Strict Observance" was originally tied to a pseudo-masonic rite that included a number of extra degrees besides the primary three (Entered Apprentice, Fellowcraft, and Master Mason) that held some interest for freemasons in the 1700s. It died out in the late 1700s when the man who created the rite could not support any historical provenance for it. However, the use of "Strict Observance" in the name of Michigan freemasonic lodges is more aligned with the idea of strictly observing the traditional Masonic constitutions and ritual from its origins (which is still a topic of debate). It denotes an implied intention of the freemasons who chose the name for their lodge to adhere to older, more strict ritual, conduct, and Masonic principles. In other words, the brothers were going to make sure discipline and attention to detail were practiced to make sure things were done right in the lodge ceremonies and in the behavior of members according to Masonic principles. No shortcuts or mistakes.

Dirk W. Hughes, Director, Michigan Masonic Museum and Library, Grand Rapids, Michigan, personal communication, November 10, 2015.

20. Kinney, *Masonic Myth*, 107–19.

21. Ibid., 120–23.

22. Fetzer, *One Man's Family*, 196–97 (italics in original). He would, however, occasionally talk to trusted confidants about Masonry. "JEF—Jim Gordon—Arthur Douet—Austin, Texas," February 1984, JGC; Charles E. Spence Oral History, January 10, 1997, 99.

23. Kinney, *Masonic Myth*, 94–101.

24. FP 2 (Correspondence 1935 IV): Rhea Fetzer to John E. Fetzer, November 22, 1935, R02.13816; FP 2 (Correspondence 1935 IV): John E. Fetzer to Rhea Fetzer, November 23, 1935, R02.13816; FP 6 (Fetzer, Leland and Myrtle Correspondence 1964–1973): Leeland Fetzer to John E. Fetzer, October 25, 1969, R02.13914; FP 9 (Fetzer Jewelry Appraisal, 1978–1987): "Paul E. Morrison Jewelry Appraisal," August 17, 1978, R02.13956; BR 10 (Broadcasting 1966 June–December): "Royal Arch Masons Certificate" (original), R02.16837; BR 10 (Broadcasting 1968 September–December): "Masonic's 33rd Degree Awarded," *Kalamazoo Gazette*,

October 2, 1968, 13, R02.16846; BR 10 (Broadcasting 1969 June–September): W. Wallace Kent to John E. Fetzer (includes press release), June 24, 1969, R02.16850; BR 10 (Broadcasting 1969 June–September): "Supreme Council 33° Meeting in Boston," *Scottish Rite News*, September–October 1969, 5, R02.16850; BR 11 (Broadcasting 1969 September–December): "Annual Meeting of the Supreme Council, 33° Program," (September 17–25, 1969, R02.16851) (also in this file are several letters of congratulation for achieving the 33°): Garry Brown, September 25, 1969; Paul Harvey, September 26, 1969; Sol Taishoff, September 26, 1969; Richard W. Chapin, September 27, 1969; BR 12 (Broadcasting 1971): Charles Lawyer to John E. Fetzer, January 28, 1971, R02.16877; BR 12 (Broadcasting 1971): "Masonic 'birthday' card," n.d., R02.16877; BR 12 (Broadcasting 1973 June–August): "The Kalamazoo Masonic Organizations Certificate of Appreciation," June 19, 1973, R02.16891; BR 14 (Broadcasting 1981 January–February): Carl C. Worfel to John E. Fetzer, January 19, 1981, R02.16934; TB 6 (Research Material Broadcasting History [42–83] 1968 II): "Scottish Rite Record," November 7, 1968, R02.14343; TB 18 (Research Fetzer, Rhea—Diaries & Letters [Transcripts] [Restricted] 1968–1972), September 24, 1969, R02.14577; TB 18 (Research Fetzer, Rhea—Diaries & Letters [Transcripts] [Restricted] 1968–1972), September 24, 26, 1973, R02.14578; Linda Grdina Oral History, June 27, 1996, 20; Whitson Oral History, March 30, 2011, 14–15; April 7, 2011, 40.

25. Kinney, *Masonic Myth*, 127–41.

26. Albert G. Mackey, *An Encyclopedia of Freemasonry and Its Kindred Sciences Comprising the Whole Range of Arts, Sciences and Literature as Concerned with the Institution*, 2 vols. (Chicago: Masonic History, 1927), FPL. For a more recent summation of the esoteric roots of Masonic ritual, see Timothy W. Hogan, "The Hermetic Influence on Freemasonry," *Heredom* 17 (2009): 121–36.

27. Corinne Heline, *New Age Bible Interpretation*, vol. 2 (1946; La Canada, CA: New Age, 1975), FPL; for Fetzer's reading of the *New Age Bible*, see John E. Fetzer to Jim Gordon, August 30, 1982, JGC. The works of Manly P. Hall were well known in esoteric circles throughout the twentieth century. For a journalistic account of his life, see Louis Sahagun, *Master of the Mysteries: The Life of Manly Palmer Hall* (Port Townsend, WA: Process Media, 2008). It is unclear when Fetzer first read Hall. We do know, however, that sometime in the late 1970s or early 1980s, Judy Skutch Whitson gave Fetzer one of the original first editions of Manly P. Hall's *The Secret Teachings of All Ages: An Encyclopedic Outline of Masonic, Hermetic, Qabbalistic and Rosicrucian Symbolical Philosophy: Being an Interpretation of the Secret Teachings Concealed within the Rituals, Allegories, and Mysteries of All Ages* (San

Francisco: H. S. Crocker, 1928). Whitson Oral History, March 30, 2011, 15–16. There exists in the Fetzer archives copies of an announcement and personal invitation sent to Fetzer for a lecture by Manly P. Hall in Sedona, Arizona, on May 9, 1987. FI 7 (Foundation Correspondence 1987–1988): "The Sedona Center and Beacon Light Center, Inc. Welcomes Manly Palmer Hall and Marie Bauer Hall," May 9–12, 1987, R02.13115. It is not known whether Fetzer actually attended the lecture.

28. William Walker Atkinson, *The Kybalion: A Study of the Hermetic Philosophy of Ancient Egypt and Greece* (1906; Chicago: Yogi, 1936), FPL (unless otherwise noted, all subsequent citations refer to this edition); Paschal Beverly Randolph, *Soul! The Soul-World: The Homes of the Dead* (1872; Quakertown, PA: Confederation of Initiates, 1932), FPL.

29. Copies of these books in Fetzer's library with his annotations date from 1936 (*The Kybalion*) and 1932 (*Soul!*); a Chimes bookplate indicates that *Soul!* was purchased after 1964, when the Chimes Publishing Company began operation in Encinitas, California.

30. Philip Deslippe, introduction to *The Kybalion: The Definitive Edition*, by William Walker Atkinson (New York: Jeremy P. Tarcher / Penguin, 2011), 1.

31. Atkinson, *Kybalion*, 8, 16. According to Fetzer, all secret orders, including the Masonic Order, were founded "by Hermes at the time of the pyramids." John E. Fetzer to Jim Gordon, April 15, 1982, JGC.

32. See Deslippe, introduction to *The Kybalion: The Definitive Edition*, by William Walker Atkinson, 1–44. For more on New Thought, see Judah, *History and Philosophy of Metaphysical Movements*, 146–255; Albanese, *Republic of Mind and Spirit*; John S. Haller, *The History of New Thought: From Mind Cure to Positive Thinking and the Prosperity Gospel* (West Chester, PA: Swedenborg Foundation Press, 2012).

33. The others are polarity (motion is caused by the fact that everything has two opposite poles—spirit/matter, light/dark, love/hate, etc.), rhythm (like a pendulum, everything oscillates between its poles, although the adept can control this oscillation), cause and effect (everything happens according to an inflexible law, although the adept can learn to become cause, not effect), and gender (everything contains within it the poles of male and female). Atkinson, *Kybalion*, 25–41.

34. Fetzer underlined those pages linking Hermeticism with science in his copy of Atkinson, *Kybalion*, 88–90.

35. FI 6 (Fetzer, John E.—"A Talk with John Fetzer" [1986]), R02.13084, 1–2.

36. Atkinson, *Kybalion*, 121.

37. Ibid., 43–51, 62. Fetzer specifically underlined passages on this equivalence on pp. 88–89.

38. Ibid., 92.

39. Ibid., 132–33.

40. See Frances A. Yates, *The Rosicrucian Enlightenment* (London: Routledge and Kegan Paul, 1972).

41. Atkinson, *Kybalion*, 128.

42. John Patrick Deveney, *Paschal Beverly Randolph: A Nineteenth-Century Black American Spiritualist, Rosicrucian, and Sex Magician* (Albany: State University of New York Press, 1997). For Rosicrucian offshoots of Randolph's Fraternitas Rosae Crucis, see Robert Ellwood, *Religious and Spiritual Groups in Modern America* (Englewood Cliffs, NJ: Prentice Hall, 1973), 110–12.

43. *Soul!* was an expanded version of an earlier Randolph work, *Dealings with the Dead: The Human Soul, Its Migrations and Its Transmigrations* (Utica, NY: Alexander Brady, 1861); see Deveney, *Paschal Beverly Randolph*, 349–50, 359.

44. Randolph, *Soul!*, 144–47, 169, 174–89, 194, 197, 198, 209, 210–11, 215, 219–21, 227–29, 238, 241.

45. Ibid., 198, 219, 221.

46. Ibid., 219, 221.

5. The Ascended Masters' Call

1. Deveney, *Paschal Beverly Randolph*, 253–308.

2. Judah, *History and Philosophy of the Metaphysical Movements*, 92–119; Ellwood, *Religious and Spiritual Groups in Modern America*, 74–78, 98–102; Albanese, *Republic of Mind and Spirit*, 270–83, 334–44. For a good overview of the lore of Atlantis and Lemuria, see L. Sprague de Camp, *Lost Continents: The Atlantis Theme* (1954; New York: Ballantine, 1970). At some point at Camp Chesterfield, Fetzer was initiated into an order that a later Ouija board session revealed to be the Great White Brotherhood. Ouija Board Transcripts, November 26, 1976, JGC.

3. Ellwood, *Religious and Spiritual Groups in Modern America*, 99. For more on the World's Parliament of Religions, see Eric J. Ziolkowski, ed., *A Museum of Faiths: Histories and Legacies of the 1893 World's Parliament of Religions* (Atlanta: Scholars, 1993).

4. John Benedict Buescher, *Aquarian Evangelist: The Age of Aquarius as It Dawned in the Mind of Levi Dowling* (Fullerton, CA: Theosophical History, 2008); for the number of lodges, see *Supplement to the Theosophical Forum*, n.s. 2, no. 10 (1897): 1–11; for the national membership in 1926, see Gregory John Tillett,

"Appendix 4: Membership of the Theosophical Society," in *Charles Webster Lead-beater 1854–1934: A Biographical Study*, accessed June 29, 2017, http://leadbeater .org/tillettcwlappendix4.htm.

5. Judah, *History and Philosophy of the Metaphysical Movements*, 81, 136.

6. Joy Mills, *100 Years of Theosophy: A History of the Theosophical Society in America* (Wheaton, IL: Theosophical Publishing, 1987), 44, 56–57, 82–84, 88, 204.

7. C. W. Leadbeater, *The Inner Life*, vol. 1 (1910; Wheaton, IL: Theosophical Press, 1949), FPL; C. Jinarajadasa, *Theosophy and Reconstruction* (Adyar, India: Theosophical Publishing, 1919), FPL; Ernest Wood, *The Seven Rays* (1925; Wheaton, IL: Theosophical Publishing, 1967), FPL.

8. Godfré Ray King, *Unveiled Mysteries* (1934; Chicago: Saint Germain, 1939), FPL; King, *The Magic Presence* (Chicago: Saint Germain, 1935), FPL; *The "I AM" Discourses* (1935; Chicago: Saint Germain, 1940), FPL; and *Ascended Master Light* (Chicago: Saint Germain, 1938), FPL.

9. FP 1 (Correspondence 1930 II): Della Fetzer to John and Rhea Fetzer, September 17, 1930, R02.13802; FP 1 (Research 1930 II): Della Fetzer to John and Rhea Fetzer, September 25, 1930, R02.13802; FP 11 (Thomas, Harriett—Correspondence 1967–1984 I): John E. Fetzer to Harriett ("Hattie") Thomas, November 28, 1978, R02.14015; FP 11 (Harriett Thomas Correspondence 1967–1984 I): Harriet ("Hattie") to John E. Fetzer, n.d., R02.14015; FP 11: (Harriett Thomas Correspondence 1967–1984 II): Harriet ("Hattie") to John E. Fetzer, n.d., R02.14016; TB 13 (Research Material 1948 I): "Rhea Fetzer's Diary—1948," February 24, 1948, R02.14472.

10. King, *Unveiled Mysteries*, 1–32, 42, 63, 67, 88, 92, 102–6, 114, 136, 242, 251–52, 260. Although the Great Central Sun has its origins in Swedenborg, Blavatsky popularized it in her *Isis Unveiled* (1877; New York: J. W. Bouton, 1892), e.g., 29, 324 (here quoting Eliphas Lévi). Fetzer also encountered the idea in Marie Corelli's *A Romance of Two Worlds* (1886; New York: William L. Allison, 1887) (see note 17 to chapter 7).

11. *The Voice of "I AM" 1939* (1939; Schaumburg, IL: Saint Germain, 2003), 7 (September 1939), 35; see also TB 12 (Research Material 1920–1944 VII): "WKZO Daily Broadcast Report," June 12, 1940, R02.14457. The association of the Archangel Michael with the dawning New Age seems to have started with the Renaissance Hermeticist Trithemius and was popularized in the nineteenth century by Eliphas Lévi. See Christopher McIntosh, *Eliphas Lévi and the French Occult Revival* (London: Rider, 1972), 151; Jenkins, *Mystics and Messiahs*, 98–99.

12. Ellwood, *Religious and Spiritual Groups in Modern America*, 121. Throughout the 1930s, the Ballards undertook a series of national tours, giving lectures and

classes to widespread acclaim: one of their 1935 classes at Los Angeles filled the six-thousand-seat Shrine Auditorium (the Ballards often made use of Masonic venues for their classes). Perhaps because of their phenomenal popularity, the Ballards began to attract negative attention from the press. Moreover, Guy Ballard's unexpected death in 1939 and Edna's and Donald's conviction of mail fraud in 1942 hit the movement hard. The Ballards' conviction was eventually overturned in a landmark Supreme Court ruling in 1946, but the "I AM" Religious Activity (as it came to be called) never again enjoyed its early success, although the group survives to the present day. See G. Barbee Bryan, *Psychic Dictatorship in America* (Los Angeles: Truth Research, 1940); Ellwood, *Religious and Spiritual Groups in Modern America*, 121–25; Robert Ellwood, "Making New Religions: The Mighty 'I AM,'" *History Today* 38, no. 6 (1988): 18–23; Saint Germain Foundation, *The History of the "I AM" Activity and Saint Germain Foundation* (Schaumberg, IL: Saint Germain, 2003), 1–70.

13. The Masters were said to have also recovered vast quantities of Aztec and Incan gold and Spanish gold from sunken galleons at the bottom of the sea, which they stored in their caves on the American continent. Apparently, these stories led to John Fetzer's curious involvement with an old SDA classmate from Emmanuel Missionary College, Clifford Burdick. Now living in Tucson, Burdick claimed to have located such a stash of gold in northern Mexico and solicited funds from Fetzer to recover it. See FP 4 (Correspondence 1962): Clifford L. Burdick to John E. Fetzer (on letterhead of Creation Research Society), n.d., R02.13858; FP 4 (Correspondence 1962): "Affidavit of A. W. Perrine," August 29, 1962 (also bears a notary stamp and signature of Clifford Osborne dated July 8, 1966), R02.13858; BR 10 (Broadcasting 1966 January–May): Clifford L. Burdick to John Fetzer, May 12, 1966 (with business card listing his occupation as geologist), R02.16836; BR 10 (Broadcasting 1966 January–May): Wilma Beertema to Clifford L. Burdick, May 24, 1966, R02.16836. Over the years, Fetzer forwarded funds to Burdick; see Ouija Board Transcripts, August 11 and September 5, 1978, JGC; FP 18 (Burdick, Clifford—Correspondence 1978–1983 II): John E. Fetzer to C. L. Burdick, May 2, 1979, R02.14162; the signed copy with a note from Burdick is in FP 4 (Correspondence 1962): John E. Fetzer to C. L. Burdick, May 2, 19?, R02.13858. After Fetzer tried to recover his money, in 1980 he decided that Burdick was engaged in "bogus activities" and "must be stopped in his tracks." FP 18 (Burdick, Clifford—Correspondence 1978–1983 I): John E. Fetzer to Louis Barassi, December 19, 1980, R02.14161. More correspondence and documentation can be found in FP 18 (Burdick, Clifford—Correspondence

1978–1983 I–IV), R02.14161–64. See also note 93 to chapter 8. For Burdick's contributions to "scientific creationism," see Numbers, *Creationists*, 259–68.

14. King, *Unveiled Mysteries*, 16, 42, 44, 47–48, 50–51, 55, 97, 138–39, 181, 192–93, 234, 251–52, 259; King, *Magic Presence*, xii, 62–68, 75–79, 82–86, 90–91, 96, 134, 155, 178, 198, 279, 287, 304–5, 306, 321–22, 327–32, 356. Another similarity to Seventh-day Adventism was the Masters' prohibition of "narcotics, alcohol, meat, tobacco, excess sugar, salt, and strong coffee"; at one point, Ballard is fed something called "sun-cereal." King, *Magic Presence*, 148, 326. For more references to the alchemical themes underlined by Fetzer, see *Ascended Master Light*, 212–13; for the sacred destiny of the United States underlined by Fetzer, see *Ascended Master Light*, "Goddess of Liberty's Discourse," 462; for Jesus's role as Ascended Master underlined by Fetzer, see *"I AM" Discourses*, 187–88, 202, 348–56.

15. King, *Unveiled Mysteries*, 23, 33–39, 41, 75, 82, 85–85, 87, 91–96, 113, 122, 128, 166–67, 230, 233, 244, 254; King, *Magic Presence*, 182, 353. According to Catherine L. Albanese, *Unveiled Mysteries* is one of the first uses of the term "channel" in the New Age sense. Albanese, "Historical Imagination and Channeled Theology: Or, Learning the Law of Attraction," in *Handbook of Spiritualism and Channeling*, ed. Cathy Gutierrez (Leiden: Brill, 2015), 481, 490. For more on the lore of Mu, see Sprague de Camp, *Lost Continents*, 48–52.

16. Albanese, "Historical Imagination and Channeled Theology," 489.

17. King, *Unveiled Mysteries*, 88–89, 215–42; see also *"I AM" Discourses*, 106–7, for similar discussions of wealth underlined by Fetzer.

18. King, *Magic Presence*, 1–3, 175, 265–89.

19. Phylos the Tibetan, *A Dweller on Two Planets* (1905; Los Angeles, CA: Borden, 1952), FPL; the "sequel," *An Earth Dweller's Return* (1940; Los Angeles, CA: Borden, 1969), FPL, which was also extensively annotated by Fetzer; Joseph Benner, *The Impersonal Life* (1914; San Gabriel, CA: C. A. Willing, 1974), FPL. Yet another book that inspired the "I AM" Religious Activity with Fetzer markings is Will L. Carver, *Brother of the Third Degree* (1894; Alhambra, CA: Borden, 1964), FPL, purchased through the Association Sanada and Sanat Kumara (ASSK), Mount Shasta, CA. In addition to the four heavily marked volumes of the anonymous *Books of Azrael: Teachings of the Great White Brotherhood* (vol. 1: Santa Barbara, CA: J. F. Rowny, 1960?; vols. 2–4: Los Angeles: DeVorss, 1961, 1964, 1967), FPL, other "I AM"–inspired books in Fetzer's collection include Brother Philip, *Brotherhood of the Seven Rays: Secret of the Andes* (Clarksburg, WV: Saucerian Books, 1961), FPL; and Joseph Whitfield, *The Treasure of El Dorado* (1971; Washington, DC: Occidental, 1980), FPL, purchased through ASSK.

20. "The Why and Wherefore of the Treasure Box in Heaven," attributed to the spirit of Nikola Tesla (Sedona, AZ: Magnificent Consummation, 1974). This pamphlet is clipped to the inside cover of Fetzer's copy of Tuella, *World Messages for the Coming Decade: A Cosmic Symposium* (Deming, NM: Guardian Action, 1981), FPL.

21. Florence Huntley, *Harmonics of Evolution*, vol. 1 (Los Gatos, CA: Great School of Natural Science, 1956), FPL; Nancy Fullwood, *Song of the Sano Tarot* (1929; New York: Macoy, 1946), FPL, which was purchased at the Chicago Theosophical Book Concern; Vera Stanley Alder, *The Initiation of the World* (1939; London: Rider, 1957), FPL; Tuella, *World Messages for the Coming Decade* (Deming, NM: Guardian Action, 1981), FPL, purchased through ASSK; W. P. Phelon, *Our Story of Atlantis* (Quakertown, PA: Philosophical Publishing, 1937), FPL; Edgar Evans Cayce, *Edgar Cayce on Atlantis* (New York: Warner Books, 1967), FPL; Paul Brunton, *A Search in Secret Egypt* (1936; Boston: E. P. Dutton, 1959), FPL. Tom Beaver reports that he and Fetzer also read David Anrias, *Through the Eyes of the Masters: Meditations and Portraits* (London: G. Routledge and Sons, 1932), although the book does not survive in Fetzer's personal library. Tom Beaver, personal communication, October 5, 2016.

22. Fetzer, *One Man's Family*, 192. See also his remarks on the lessons of Atlantis in FI 6 (Fetzer, John E. Interview Transcript), R02.13070; FI 9 (Institute of Noetic Sciences 1981): John E. Fetzer to W. W. Harman, October 26, 1981, R02.13170; Whitson Oral History, March 30, 2011, 52–53.

23. Alice A. Bailey, *The Unfinished Autobiography of Alice A. Bailey* (New York: Lucis, 1951), FPL. For Fetzer's underlined passages, see pp. 35–38, 51–55, 72, 89, 142, 155, 162–68, 171, 254–58. The Bailey books were available at Camp Chesterfield, so Fetzer may have first encountered them there. The author has in his possession a copy of Bailey's *Discipleship in the New Age* (1954 printing) with a "Psychic Observer Book Shop, Chesterfield, Indiana, USA." book plate.

24. For Fetzer's underlined passages, see Bailey, *Unfinished Autobiography*, 40–41, 72, 142, 237–40, 288, 299.

25. Alice A. Bailey, *Initiation, Human and Solar* (1922; New York: Lucis, 1959), FPL.

26. For more on Bailey and the Arcane School, see Ellwood, *Religious and Spiritual Groups in Modern America*, 103–6; Melton, Clark, and Kelly, *New Age Almanac*, 9–12.

27. For Fetzer's underlined passages, see Bailey, *Unfinished Autobiography*, 39, 169, 191, 193, 194, 213, 239, 252, 305. Fetzer reproduced the "Great Invocation" in both of his genealogical works, *One Man's Family*, 188–89, and *Men from Wengen*, 415.

28. Lucis Trust, "The Great Invocation," accessed July 17, 2017, www.lucistrust.org/ the_great_invocation.

29. Bailey, *Initiation, Human and Solar*, 49, 50–62, 98–99, 105, 182–83 (Fetzer underlinings).

30. Ibid., 182–84 (Fetzer underlinings).

31. Ibid., 78–79 (Fetzer underlinings).

32. Ibid., 50 and chapters 7–19, with the Esoteric Catechism following (Fetzer underlinings).

33. Ibid., 118–19 (Fetzer underlinings).

34. Baird T. Spalding, *Life and Teachings of the Masters of the Far East*, 5 vols. (1924–27; Los Angeles, CA: DeVorss, 1937, 1944, 1935, 1948, 1955), FPL. A sixth volume of miscellaneous material by and about Spalding was published by DeVorss in 1996. Spalding, *Life and Teachings of the Masters of the Far East*, vol. 6 (Camarillo, CA: DeVorss, 1996).

35. See the title page of Spalding, *Life and Teachings of the Masters of the Far East*, vol. 5, where Fetzer underlined DeVorss's name, adding "Douglas K." and writing, "He is gone. Ma2-6639. Mr. Andrus now in charge." Apparently this was not the first time that the publisher was asked to supply further information, and in later editions, a "Publisher's Note" was inserted disclaiming any further knowledge of Spalding or his claims. A somewhat debunking biography of Spalding was published in 1954: David Bruton, *Baird T. Spalding as I Knew Him* (San Pedro, CA: Institute of Esoteric Philosophy, 1954), subsequently picked up for republication by DeVorss in 1980; it is not known whether Fetzer read this biography. For a more recent appraisal of Spalding and his work, see Horowitz, *Occult America*, 192–204.

36. Spalding, *Life and Teachings of the Masters of the Far East*, 1:7, 5:23, 6:17.

37. Ibid., 1:22, 143, 157.

38. Ibid., 6:14–15; *History of the "I AM" Activity*, 1–2.

39. Spalding, *Life and Teachings of the Masters of the Far East*, 1:77–79, 2:19–21.

40. Later in life, Fetzer was well acquainted with this work, as attests his well-marked copy of Levi Dowling, *The Aquarian Gospel of Jesus the Christ* (1907; Los Angeles: DeVorss, 1987), FPL. For more on Dowling and his midwestern roots, see Buescher, *Aquarian Evangelist*. Dowling himself was probably inspired in part by Nicolas Notovitch, *The Unknown Life of Jesus Christ* (1894; New York: Dover, 2008).

41. Spalding, *Life and Teachings of the Masters of the Far East*, 1:15–25, 34–42, 2:5, 7–16, 14, 4:174–85.

42. Ibid., 1:64–71.

43. Spalding was a student of New Thought, and the first volume of *Life and Teachings* was serialized in a San Francisco New Thought magazine, the *Comforter*. See Todd, "Comforter League of Light—your help needed," post to Baird T. Spalding website, June 25, 2013, www.bairdtspalding.org.

44. Spalding, *Life and Teachings of the Masters of the Far East*, 1:30, 32, 62, 3:69–81, 4:152.

45. Fetzer was especially interested in the "camera of past events," which Spalding said he was developing in collaboration with Edison and Steinmetz. Spalding, *Life and Teachings of the Masters of the Far East*, 5:14, 23–29 (see chapter 8).

46. Ibid., 1:73–74; see also 1:152–53, 2:28–29, 41.

47. Ibid., 2:29, 3:70–71, 4:142–57, 186–96, 5:47–54, 61–62.

48. For example, Bruce Fetzer remembers studying the Theosophically inspired Tuella, *World Messages for the Coming Decade*, with his great-uncle in 1981. Bruce Fetzer Oral History, March 14, 1996, 38.

49. Many of these themes appear in both of Fetzer's extended philosophical statements in *One Man's Family*, 180–97, and *Men from Wengen*, 375–416. See chapter 6.

6. Unorthodox Science

1. Hegedus, *John Earl Fetzer*, 62–77.

2. Fetzer, *Men from Wengen*, 362; BR 11 (NAB Distinguished Service Award), R02.16862–68.

3. BR 8 (Radio Free Europe—Crusade for Freedom Tour), R02.16779–83.

4. Linda Grdina, ed., "The Fetzer Institute Program History Report," unpublished internal document, October 2013, 3, Fetzer Institute Archives.

5. TB 31 (Kaye Averitt 1982–1985 I): October 15, 1982, R02.14839, 3.

6. Several of the books in Fetzer's personal library bear a *Chimes* book plate, and articles clipped from *Fate* can be found in the archives; see, for example, Henry Duskis, "The Third Eye—Now a Fact," *Fate*, January 1970, 88, FP 18 (Book Material 1969–1979 I), R02.14159; D. Scott Rogo, "The Crisis in Experimental Parapsychology," *Fate* 27, no. 6 (1974): 89–95, FI 15 (Human Dimension Institute July 1973–May 1974), R02.13293.

7. TB 7 (Broadcasting 1962 II): "Rhea Fetzer Diary," October 13–November 28, 1962, R02.14358.

8. Paul Brunton, *A Search in Secret India* (1935; Boston: E. P. Dutton, 1951), FPL; T. Lobsang Rampa, *The Rampa Story* (London: Souvenir, 1960), FPL. In 1974, Fetzer circulated "A Paraphrase of Remarks by Lobsang Rampa" to members of the Fetzer Foundation Board. Fetzer Foundation Minutes, Book 1, August 22,

1974; the "Paraphrase" itself can be found in FI 19 (Fetzer, John E.—Paraphrases of Remarks by Lobsang Rampa August 22, 1974), R02.13367.

9. TB 7 (Broadcasting 1962 II): "Rhea Fetzer's Diary," December 1, 1962, R02.14358.

10. Ibid., December 10–17, 1962, R02.14358. Fetzer also mentions meeting Shafica Karagulla "while at Luxor, deep in Upper Egypt on the River Nile" in *One Man's Family*, 195.

11. TB 13 (Research Material 1948 II): "Interview with JEF—TT & KTA," December 15, 1983, R02.14473, 6–7.

12. Ouija Board Transcripts, November 26, 1976, JGC; FI 5 (Fetzer, John E.—Jim Gordon 1980–1985 XI), (December 16, 1983, R02.13059) (the handwritten original can be found in JGC); FI 5 (Fetzer, John E.—Jim Gordon 1980–1985 XV), November 2, 1984, R02.13063; TB 31 (Interviews Fetzer, John E.—Baseball, Spirituality February 9, 1984), R02.14826, 18–20; "Background on Arizona Tape—JEF—KTA," March 15, 1984, JGC; Bruce Fetzer Oral History, March 15, 1996, 106, and December 12, 2002, 114. Fetzer would have been well primed for these stories by his previous reading: King, *Unveiled Mysteries*, 195–214; *Ascended Master Light*, 133; "*I AM*" *Discourses*, 46.

13. TB 13 (Research Material 1948 II): "Interview with JEF—TT & KTA," December 15, 1983, R02.14473, 1–7. Fetzer found a Theosophical interpretation of dowsing in Bailey, *Initiation, Human and Solar*, 130–32 (underlined by Fetzer).

14. David J. Hess, *Science in the New Age: The Paranormal, Its Defenders and Debunkers, and American Culture* (Madison: University of Wisconsin Press, 1993), ix. Another term for such phenomena was "Fortean," after Charles Fort, an early twentieth-century chronicler of anomalous events. An omnibus of Fort's writings, *The Books of Charles Fort* (New York: Henry Holt, 1941), FPL, with a few of Fetzer's annotations, was part of his personal library.

15. Lyell D. Henry, "Unorthodox Science as a Popular Activity," *Journal of American Culture* 4, no. 2 (1981): 1–22; see also Hess, *Science in the New Age*. Of course, unorthodox science is not new in American culture but finds its roots in the so-called Village Enlightenment of the early nineteenth century. See Hazen, *Village Enlightenment in America*.

16. Christopher Partridge, *The Re-enchantment of the West*, vol. 2 (London: T&T Clark, 2005), 181.

17. In Fetzer's edition of Erich von Däniken's *Chariots of the Gods* (New York: Bantam, 1973), FPL, he had copied out the following lines, which are a good description of the mind-set of the "unorthodox scientist": "It seems as if narrow-mindedness was always a special characteristic when new worlds of ideas were

beginning. But on the threshold of the twenty-first century, the research worker should be prepared for fantastic realities. He should be eager to revise laws and knowledge which were considered sacrosanct for centuries but are nevertheless called into question by new knowledge. Even if a reactionary army tries to dam up this new intellectual flood, a new world must be conquered in the name of truth and reality. . . . The word 'impossible' should have become literally impossible for the modern scientist" (30). Earlier, in his copy of Wavney Girvan's *Flying Saucers and Common Sense* (New York: Citadel, 1956), FPL, Fetzer highlighted the line, "Science has been as intolerant as religion" when it comes to new ideas (22).

18. Brenda Denzler, *The Lure of the Edge: Scientific Passions, Religious Beliefs, and the Pursuit of UFOs* (Berkeley: University of California Press, 2003); James R. Lewis, ed., *The Gods Have Landed: New Religions from Other Worlds* (Albany: State University of New York Press, 1995); Gregory L. Reece, *UFO Religion: Inside Flying Saucer Cults and Culture* (London: I. B. Taurus, 2007).

19. FP 19 ("The Flying Saucer Hoax," May 14, 1974), R02.14191, 1–2; see also TB 31 (Interviews Fetzer, John E.—Comments in Lafayette [Transcripts], November 1982), R02.14829, 10.

20. FP 3 (Correspondence 1956): Donald E. Keyhoe to John E. Fetzer, October 18, 1956, R02.13849; on Glycadis's employment, see "Lee Named No. 2 in Fetzer Command," *Broadcasting Telecasting* 45 (August 3, 1953): 60.

21. In Fetzer's copy of Gray Barker's *They Knew Too Much about Flying Saucers* (New York: University Books, 1956), FPL, he carefully marked in the bibliography those books that he had already read and those that he had yet to buy. See also FP 19 ("The Flying Saucer Hoax," May 14, 1974), R02.14191, in which he discusses his wide reading on the subject.

22. Donald E. Keyhoe, *The Flying Saucers Are Real* (New York: Fawcett, 1950), FPL; Keyhoe, *Flying Saucers from Outer Space* (New York: Henry Holt, 1953), FPL; Keyhoe, *The Flying Saucer Conspiracy* (New York: Henry Holt, 1955), FPL; Edward J. Ruppelt, *The Report on Unidentified Flying Objects* (Garden City, NY: Doubleday, 1956), FPL; Donald H. Menzel, *Flying Saucers* (Cambridge, MA: Harvard University Press, 1953), FPL. See also FP 19 ("The Flying Saucer Hoax," May 14, 1974), R02.14191, 4–11.

23. Fetzer's copy of Coral E. Lorenzen's *The Great Flying Saucer Hoax: The UFO Facts and the Interpretation* (New York: William-Frederick, 1962), FPL, is inscribed, "To John Fetzer—Best wishes and thanks for your support. Coral Lorenzen 8 Mar '62." See also FP 19 ("The Flying Saucer Hoax," May 14, 1974), R02.14191, 12–13. Over two decades' worth of the *APRO Bulletin* beginning in 1956 can be found in the Fetzer archives with Fetzer's annotations (051482–83).

24. See for example Fetzer's heavily annotated copies of Leonard G. Cramp's *Space Gravity and the Flying Saucer* (New York: British Book Centre, 1955), FPL; and Aimé Michel, *The Truth about Flying Saucers* (New York: Criterion Books, 1956), FPL, especially 197–211, both of which outline the Plantier theory of UFO propulsion; and Dino Kraspedon, *My Contact with Flying Saucers* (New York: Citadel, 1959), FPL, 57–77. See also FP 19 ("The Flying Saucer Hoax," May 14, 1974), R02.14191, 13–15.

25. John C. Sherwood, *Flying Saucers Are Watching You: The Incident at Dexter and the Incredible Michigan Flap* (Clarksburg, WV: Saucerian, 1967), FPL.

26. Reece, *UFO Religion*, 24–27.

27. Gerald R. Ford Archives, Ann Arbor, MI (Box D9: UFO Folder 1966, Press Secretary & Speech File 1947–1973).

28. A copy of the Condon Report is in Fetzer's personal library. Edward Condon and Daniel S. Gillmor, eds., *Scientific Study of Unidentified Flying Objects* (New York: Bantam, 1969), FPL. For Fetzer's negative opinion of the Condon Report, see FP 19 ("The Flying Saucer Hoax," May 14, 1974), R02.14191, 11.

29. J. Allen Hynek, *The UFO Experience: A Scientific Inquiry* (Chicago: Henry Regnery, 1972), FPL. In this book, Hynek employs for the first time the "close encounter" typology for UFO contacts.

30. Fetzer first met Hynek in Chicago through Judy Skutch Whitson. Judy Skutch Whitson Oral History, February 4, 2011, 16–18. This was probably in 1977, since Rhea Fetzer recorded that Fetzer met with Hynek in Chicago at a UFO conference in October 1977 and came back with renewed confidence in the reality of flying saucers. TB 18 (Research Fetzer, Rhea—Diaries & Letters [Transcripts] [Restricted] 1976–1979): "1977 Rhea Fetzer's Diary and Personal Correspondence," October 26, 1977, R02.14579.

31. FP 19 ("The Flying Saucer Hoax," May 14, 1974), R02.14191. Earlier, in *One Man's Family*, Fetzer predicted, "Man will one day use space travel to other planets after discovery that life forms exist almost everywhere. The strange flying phenomena of the skies will one day be proved to be the explorations by a form of intelligence operating in space" (192).

32. FP 19 ("The Flying Saucer Hoax," May 14, 1974), R02.14191, 7, 39–40. Strangely, Fetzer attributes this last quotation to Albert Einstein, when in fact it comes from Desmond Leslie and George Adamski, *Flying Saucers Have Landed* (New York: British Book Center, 1953), FPL, 222.

33. Truman Bethurum, *Aboard a Flying Saucer* (Los Angeles, CA: DeVorss, 1954), FPL; George W. Van Tassel, *I Rode in a Flying Saucer: The Mystery of the Flying Saucers Revealed* (Los Angeles: New Age, 1952), FPL; Leslie and Adamski,

Flying Saucers Have Landed; George Adamski, *Inside the Space Ships* (New York: Abelard-Schuman, 1955), FPL.

34. David Stupple, "Mahatmas and Space Brothers: The Ideologies of Alleged Contact with Mahatmas and Space Brothers: The Ideologies of Alleged Contact with Extraterrestrials," *Journal of American Culture* 7 (1984): 131–39.

35. TB 30 (Rhea's Diary 1967–1969): "Rhea Fetzer's Diaries," November 24, 1968, R02.14821; Reece, *UFO Religion*, 126–28.

36. See Stupple, "Mahatmas and Space Brothers"; Christopher Partridge, "Channeling Extraterrestrials: Theosophical Discourse in the Space Age," in Gutierrez, *Handbook of Spiritualism and Channeling*, 390–417. Beginning with Desmond Leslie and Brinsley le Poer Trench, Theosophical influences on the UFO movement led to the "ancient astronauts" theory that space aliens intervened in early human history; mistaken as gods, space aliens were thus seen as responsible for, for example, the putative technological sophistication of Lemuria and Atlantis and such ancient monuments as the Pyramids of Egypt and Mexico. Given Fetzer's fascination with ancient civilizations, books by both of these authors found their way into his library, as did those of the most famous proponent of the "ancient astronauts" theory, Eric von Däniken, whose books became a publishing sensation in the 1970s. For an overview of the "ancient astronaut" theory, see Reece, *UFO Religion*, 159–81. Annotated "ancient astronaut" books in Fetzer's personal library include Leslie and Adamski, *Flying Saucers Have Landed*; Brinsley le Poer Trench, *The Sky People* (Clarksburg, WV: Saucerian Books, 1960), FPL; Brother Philip, *Brotherhood of the Seven Rays*; von Däniken, *Chariots of the Gods*; Erich von Däniken, *Gods from Outer Space* (New York: Bantam, 1973), FPL; von Däniken, *Gold of the Gods* (New York: G. P. Putnam's Sons, 1973), FPL. At some point, Fetzer conceived an interest in the Mitchell-Kedges crystal skull, perhaps after the von Däniken–inspired TV documentary *In Search of Ancient Mysteries* (1973) popularized the theory of its alien origins. Fetzer mentions seeing *In Search of Ancient Mysteries* in his 1974 flying saucer talk. FP 19 ("The Flying Saucer Hoax," May 14, 1974), R02.14191. Fetzer attended a lecture and display of the skull in London, Ontario, sometime in the early 1980s. FI 11 (Jochmans, Joseph—Reports 1984 II): "Report #5 to the Fetzer Foundation Prepared by Joseph R. Jochmans," June 20, 1984, R02.13192. And later, Fetzer staff were encouraged to view it at the Phoenix Cultural Center while attending the ARE Symposium the week of January 18, 1987. Fetzer Board Minutes (Binder 3): "John E. Fetzer Foundation, Inc. Executive Committee Meeting," February 2, 1987. Later that year, John Fetzer sought to secure the skull for the Fetzer Institute. FI 4 (Correspondence 1987): John E. Fetzer to Hanna Mitchell-Kedges,

September 21, 1987, R02.13021; FI 4 (Fetzer, John E. Correspondence, Donna Meyer 1987): Donna Myer to John E. Fetzer, September 17, 1987, R02.13040; FI 4 (Fetzer, John E. Correspondence, Donna Meyer 1987): John E. Fetzer to Donna Meyer, October 1, 1987, R02.13040.

37. For books in Fetzer's library that discussed this idea, see Trevor James, *They Live in the Sky* (Los Angeles: New Age, 1958), FPL, 17–50; and le Poer Trench, *Sky People*, 167–74.

38. J. Gordon Melton, "New Thought and the New Age," in *Perspectives on the New Age*, ed. James R. Lewis and J. Gordon Melton (Albany: State University of New York Press, 1992), 15–29.

39. Stupple, "Mahatmas and Space Brothers," 131–39; Jennifer E. Porter, "Spiritualists, Aliens and UFOs: Extraterrestrials as Spirit Guides," *Journal of Contemporary Religion* 11, no. 3 (1996): 337–53.

40. Van Tassel, *I Rode in a Flying Saucer*; Tuella, *World Messages for the Coming Decade*; Tuella also quotes from *The Kybalion* (50). See also Reece, *UFO Religion*, 132–40.

41. Martin Gardner, *Urantia: The Great Cult Mystery* (Amherst, NY: Prometheus Books, 1995); see also Reece, *UFO Religion*, 143–45; Urantia Foundation, *The Urantia Book* (1955; Chicago: Urantia Foundation, 2008), FPL. According to the 2016 Urantia Foundation annual report, 123,813 copies of the *Urantia Book* had been distributed that year either in print or electronically. Urantia Foundation, *2016 Annual Report*, accessed June 29, 2017, www.urantia.org/sites/default/files/docs/annual_report_2016.pdf.

42. Douglas Main, "Most People Believe Intelligent Aliens Exist, Poll Says," *Newsweek*, September 29, 2015, www.newsweek.com/most-people-believe-intelligent-aliens-exist-377965.

43. As Jung put it, UFO myths were "symptoms of psychic changes which always appear at the end of one Platonic month [i.e., astrological age] and at the beginning of another. They are, it seems, changes in the constellation of psychic dominants, of the archetypes, or 'gods' as they used to be called, which bring about, or accompany, long-lasting transformations of the collective psyche." Carl Jung, *Flying Saucers: A Modern Myth of Things Seen in the Sky* (1959; Princeton, NJ: Princeton University Press, 2002), xii.

44. Harvey J. Irwin and Caroline A. Watt, *An Introduction to Parapsychology*, 5th ed. (Jefferson, NC: McFarland, 2007), 1.

45. A good example of this from Fetzer's library is R. Dewitt Miller, *You DO Take It with You* (New York: Citadel, 1957), FPL, which seamlessly integrated space aliens and UFOs into discussions of traditional paranormal topics such as spiritualism, psychic abilities, and reincarnation.

46. FI 16 (Princeton University—Jahn, Robert 1978–1986I): John E. Fetzer to Bowie Kuhn, February 22, 1979, R02.13313.

47. Gina Cerminara, *Many Mansions: The Edgar Cayce Story on Reincarnation* (1950; New York: William Sloane, 1959), FPL; Jess Stearn, *Edgar Cayce: The Sleeping Prophet* (Garden City, NY: Doubleday, 1967), FPL; Elsie Sechrist, *Dreams: Your Magic Mirror with Interpretations of Edgar Cayce* (New York: Warner Books, 1968), FPL; Cayce, *Edgar Cayce on Atlantis*. On the Cayce renaissance, see Jenkins, *Mystics and Messiahs*, 171.

48. The full passage from Jeane Dixon, *My Life and Prophecies* (New York: William Morrow, 1969), FPL: "John, president of the Detroit Tigers baseball club and president of a chain of radio and television stations in Michigan and Nebraska, is unquestionably a most realistic businessman. Yet—and this only increases his stature as a man—he has never allowed his realistic attitude to blind him to the spiritual core of life or phenomena of the psychic world. I have heard people refer to John as an 'abstract intellectual,' and though I do not share this view entirely, he nevertheless is a deep thinker" (53). For more on their friendship, see TB 18 (Research Fetzer, Rhea Diaries & Letters [Transcripts] [Restricted] 1963–1967), December 3, 1965; "books read 1969–1971" by Rhea included Dixon's *Life and Prophecies*, R02.14576; TB 18 (Research Fetzer, Rhea Diaries & Letters [Transcripts] [Restricted] 1968–1972), March 24, 1969, R02.14577; TB 30 (Research Material Fetzer, Rhea—Diary [Restricted] 1966), March 2, 1966; June 3, 1966, R02.14820; TB 31 (Interviews Fetzer, John—Baseball [Lafayette], October 29, 1982), R02.14828, 27–28; FP 4 (Correspondence 1967): James J. Fahey to John E. Fetzer, September 16, 1967, R02.13867; FP 6 (Fetzer, Leland and Myrtle Correspondence 1964–1973): John E. Fetzer to Leeland Fetzer, December 11, 1969, R02.13914: "I am glad you caught up with Jeane Dixon's book. I have known her for many years and, of course, she is a most delightful person. She has an uncanny record for accuracy in her prophetic utterances. I only hope that in our case our political leaders will heed what she has to say about the Soviet Union"; BR 10 (Broadcasting 1969 January–May): Jeane Dixon's *Open Line* newsletter, R02.16849; BR 10 (Broadcasting 1969 June–September): Jeane Dixon Children to Children Project, R02.16850; BR 11 (Broadcasting 1969 September–December): Charles H. Tower to John E. Fetzer, September 10, 1969, R02.16851; BR 11 (Broadcasting 1970 January–April): John E. Fetzer to Charles H. Tower, January 8, 1970, R02.16869; BR 12 (Broadcasting 1974 January–June): Chuck Tower to John E. Fetzer, January 13, 1974?, R02.16901.

49. John Beloff, *Parapsychology: A Concise History* (New York: St. Martin's, 1993), 125–51; Seymour H. Mauskopf and Michael R. McVaugh, *The Elusive Science:*

Origins of Experimental Psychical Research (Baltimore: Johns Hopkins University Press, 1980).

50. Shafica Karagulla, *Breakthrough to Creativity: Your Higher Sense Perception* (Los Angeles: DeVorss, 1967), FPL. The inscription in Fetzer's copy reads, "To John Fetzer, our friend from Arizona!!! With affectionate regards, Shafica and Viola." Viola was Viola Petit Neal, a clairvoyant with whom Karagulla founded the Higher Sense Perception Research Foundation in Beverly Hills, CA. Later, Karagulla became interested in Theosophy and the HSP abilities of Dora Van Gelder, a Theosophical leader in Los Angeles. "Shafica Karagulla," in *Encyclopedia of Occultism and Parapsychology*, ed. J. Gordon Melton (Detroit: Gale, 2001), 850; see also J. G. Bolen, "Interview with Shafica Karagulla," *Psychic* 4, no. 6 (1973): 6–11.

51. Karagulla, *Breakthrough to Creativity*, 97–101.

52. Irwin and Watt, *Introduction to Parapsychology*, 124–137.

53. Karagulla, *Breakthrough to Creativity*, 31.

7. Articulating a Worldview for the New Age

1. TB31 (Interviews Fetzer, John E.—Early Years December 3, 1982 II), R02.14833, 6; Ouija Board Transcripts, October 3, 1978, JGC; see also Whitson Oral History, February 10, 2011, 26; Whitson Oral History, March 30, 2011, 2–3.

2. Fetzer, *One Man's Family*, 181. Such a pessimistic assessment may have been influenced by his reading of Helmut Kuhn, *Encounter with Nothingness: An Essay on Existentialism* (Hinsdale, IL: Henry Regnery, 1949), FPL.

3. Fetzer, *One Man's Family*, 181–82.

4. Ibid., 182, 183, 185. For the "Great Invocation," see chapter 5.

5. Ibid., 188–89. Later, Fetzer put it like this:

> I start with the idea that the belief base of our social system is actually seriously flawed and that, moreover, our Western science has created this actuality which is more diminishing than ennobling. Our science repeatedly debunks fundamental values such as representing human beings as being mechanistic or mere animals; hence our resulting dilemma. I take a dim view that scientists of the present vintage can create a great deal to enlighten us concerning our deepest motivations and desires, such as our creative capabilities or enhancement, our connectedness to one another, our possibilities for living and for altruistic behavior. Frankly, I believe it will require a new breed of scientists who are highly spiritually oriented to ever make much of a contribution in this respect. FI 9 (Institute of Noetic Science

1981): John E. Fetzer to Willis H. Harmon, October 26, 1981, R02.131170.

6. Fetzer, *One Man's Family*, 185, 191–92.

7. Ibid., 195. Also mentioned by name in the list of modern authors is Murdo MacDonald-Bayne, whose 1954 book *Beyond the Himalayas* (London: L. N. Fowler) tells a story of a sojourn among the lamas of Tibet slightly less fantastical than that of Baird Spalding's *Life and Teachings of the Masters of the Far East*. None of MacDonald-Bayne's books can be found in Fetzer's extant library, but in a later document, Fetzer quotes from MacDonald-Bayne's *Spiritual and Mental Healing* (London: L. N. Fowler, 1947), 158–59. TB 30 (Broadcasting 1973 III): "John E. Fetzer Foundation Preamble," September 9, 1973, R02.14608, 19–20. Unnamed in this list is Alice Bailey, whose "Great Invocation" figures prominently in Fetzer's thought.

8. Norman Vincent Peale, *The Power of Positive Thinking* (1952; New York: Prentice Hall, 1953), FPL. Fetzer met Peale at a meeting of the National Association of Broadcasters at the Shoreham Hotel in New York on May 26, 1955. TB 13 (Research Material 1955 I): "Rhea Fetzer's Diary 1955," R02.14485. Fetzer was also a fan of Dale Carnegie, whose *How to Win Friends and Influence People* (New York: Simon and Schuster, 1936) Fetzer promised family members would "do you more good than all the pills in the world." FP 3 (Correspondence 1949): John E. Fetzer to Folks, January 13, 1949, R02.13842; see also Whitson Oral History, February 10, 2011, 19–20.

9. Claude Bristol, *The Magic of Believing* (New York: Prentice Hall, 1948), 39, 56, 62, 175–76.

10. Ibid., 29, 49, 176, 238. Some of Fetzer's language echoes Bristol's closely. E.g., compare Fetzer, *One Man's Family*, 185, with Bristol, *Magic of Believing*, 61: "The subconscious mind is beyond space and time, and is fundamentally a powerful sending and receiving station with a universal hookup. It can communicate with the physical, mental, psychic, and—according to many investigators—spiritual worlds." The idea of human beings as essentially radio sets can also be found in Guy Ballard's (King's) *Unveiled Mysteries* (see chapter 5).

11. Bristol, *Magic of Believing*, 49, 91, 116, 229. Although Bristol died in 1951, his influence on Fetzer continued through Harold Sherman. Sherman wrote *Your Keys to Happiness* (New York: G. P. Putnam's Sons, 1944), FPL. So close in ideas were Bristol and Sherman that they collaborated on *TNT: The Power within You* (New York: Prentice Hall, 1954). Although this book is not in Fetzer's library, most of Sherman's other books are. Sherman was originally from Traverse City,

Michigan. Fetzer met Sherman along with the psychic Arthur Ford at an ESP convention in Hot Springs, Arkansas, on November 24, 1968 (Sherman's ESP Research Association Foundation was located in Little Rock). TB 30 (Rhea's Diary 1967–1969): "Rhea Fetzer's Diary 1968," R02.14821, 13. Five days later, Fetzer secured a copy of Sherman's new book, *The New TNT—Miraculous Power within You* (Englewood Cliffs, NJ: Prentice Hall, 1967), FPL, which Sherman inscribed ("To John E. Fetzer—Who is LOADED with 'TNT'—and who shares with me this great and demonstrable PHILOSOPHY OF LIFE! All good wishes! Harold Sherman"). Fetzer collected three more of Sherman's books: *Your Mysterious Powers of ESP: The New Medium of Communication* (New York: World, 1969), FPL; *How to Foresee and Control Your Future* (New York: Information, Incorporated, 1970), FPL; *How to Know What to Believe* (New York: Fawcett, 1976), FPL. Interestingly, chapter 5 of this last book details Sherman's early involvement with the *Urantia Book* beginning in 1941; see also Gardner, *Urantia*, 113–60. Sherman was additionally intensely interested in UFOs and wrote regularly for *Fate* magazine (including the archetypal "little green men from Mars" stories); see Martin Gardner, *The New Age: Notes of a Fringe Watcher* (Buffalo, NY: Prometheus Books, 1988), 260–62.

12. See specifically Fetzer, *One Man's Family*, 180–88, 191. During the 1980s, Fetzer discovered the Unity Church in Tucson. The Unity Church, which developed out of the New Thought teachings of Charles and Myrtle Fillmore of Kansas City, Missouri, stressed a number of New Thought concepts that Fetzer embraced: God is all in all; we are all spiritual beings; our thinking creates the reality; affirmations are the way to create a connection to God. While nominally Christian, Unity by the 1980s had embraced the teachings of multiple religions, including Eastern traditions. Although there was a long-standing Unity Church in Kalamazoo, apparently Fetzer only attended Unity services in Tucson because he felt he could only be anonymous there. FP 12 (Fetzer Ranch 1965–1990): "Order of service from Unity Church of Tucson," February 26, 1984, R02.14022; TB 31 (Fetzer, John—Early years [Trip to Lafayette], October 28, 1982), R02.14835, 1; TB 18 (Research Fetzer, Rhea—Diaries and Letters [Transcripts] [Restricted] 1980–1981): "1980 Rhea Fetzer's Diary and Personal Correspondence," March 2, 1980, R02.14580, 3.

13. FP 18 (Book Material 1969–1979 IV): "This I Believe," undated version, R02.14160.

14. Most prominent of these are Alice Bailey, Guy Ballard, Baird Spalding, and Nancy Fullwood (see chapter 5). Another influence was the Theosophist Mabel Collins's *The Idyll of the White Lotus* (1890; New York: Theosophical Publishing, 1907),

116, two stanzas of which Fetzer included with slight modifications in both versions of "This I Believe" and in *The Men from Wengen and America's Agony*, 409–10. "This I Believe," undated version, R02.14160, 24; FP 6 (Fetzer, John E.—"This I Believe" April 10, 1967): "This I Believe," revised April 10, 1967, R02.13085, 13. *The Idyll of the White Lotus*, however, is not extant in Fetzer's personal library.

15. "This I Believe," undated version, R02.14160, 1. Fetzer's source for the then-latest cosmological theories was C. P. Gilmore, "The Birth and Life of the Universe," *New York Magazine*, June 12, 1966, 26–27, 85–89. FP 18 (Book Material 1969–1979 II): "The Birth and Life of the Universe," R02.14158.

16. "This I Believe," undated version, R02.14160, 1. See Spalding, *Life and Teachings of the Masters of the Far East*, 3:26, 78. The confusion over universes and galaxies is original to Spalding.

17. "This I Believe," undated version, R02.14160, 2. This description comes almost directly from Corelli, *Romance of Two Worlds*, 189–90, although no copy is extant in Fetzer's personal library. Marie Corelli (1855–1924) was a successful English novelist; while her book had roots in Spiritualism, *A Romance of Two Worlds* proved popular with Theosophists. For more on Corelli's *A Romance of Two Worlds*, see J. Jeffrey Franklin, "The Counter-Invasion of Britain by Buddhism in Marie Corelli's 'A Romance of Two Worlds' and H. Rider Haggard's 'Ayesha: The Return of She,'" *Victorian Literature and Culture* 31, no. 1 (2003): 19–42; and Jill Galvan, "Christians, Infidels, and Women's Channeling in the Writings of Marie Corelli," *Victorian Literature and Culture* 31, no. 1 (2003): 83–97.

18. "This I Believe," undated version, R02.14160, 3. See Spalding, *Life and Teachings of the Masters of the Far East*, 3:77–80.

19. "This I Believe," undated version, R02.14160, 3–4. There follows here a rather confused discussion about how the DNA of each cell is controlled by "enzymes [that] arrive across interstellar space." Apparently, Fetzer had read a *Reader's Digest* book that referenced advances in cytology (Reader's Digest Association, *Our Amazing World of Nature: Its Marvels and Mysteries* [New York: Reader's Digest Association, 1969], 25) and, perhaps inspired by the idea of the extraterrestrial origins of life popular in UFO circles, he extrapolated "space enzymes."

20. "This I Believe," undated version, R02.14160, 4–5.

21. Ibid., 4–7. While New Thought and parapsychological concepts are still much in evidence here (for example, the statements about "affirmative and negative power of thoughts," "supply," and telepathy), Fetzer's religious anthropology is also based on the ancient Indian idea of the seven chakras of the human body, typically pictured as seven whirling discs or wheels of energy, each radiating a distinct color

when receiving *prana* (subtle energy) from the cosmos. Much of Fetzer's discussion of the chakras ("seven centers") and their abilities to channel the wisdom of the cosmos and reflect it back, can be traced to his reading of Bailey's *Initiation, Human and Solar*, 30, 99, 200–202; Spalding's *Life and Teachings of the Masters of the Far East*, 3:35–40; and King's *Unveiled Mysteries*, 82–83.

22. "This I Believe," undated version, R02.14160, 10, 14–15. See Bristol, *Magic of Believing*, 24; Peale, *Power of Positive Thinking*, 50–69; Spalding, *Life and Teachings of the Masters of the Far East*, 3:141. The first affirmation is a variation on the French psychologist Émile Coué's "Every day in every way, I am getting better and better" (although Fetzer may have encountered it in MacDonald-Bayne's *Spiritual and Mental Healing*, 85–86); and the second is from Spalding, *Life and Teachings of the Masters of the Far East*, 5:97. The television analogy is apparently Fetzer's, although it also appears in the channeled texts of Ernest Norman of the UFO religion Unarius ("Man is a television receiver"), but there is no evidence that Fetzer knew these texts firsthand; see Diana G. Tumminia, *When Prophecy Never Fails: Myth and Reality in a UFO Religion* (New York: Oxford University Press, 2005), 403.

23. "This I Believe," undated version, R02.14160, 19. See Fetzer's annotations in Fullwood, *Song of the Sano Tarot*, 14–16, 21–22, 92–93; see also Bristol, *Magic of Believing*, 49.

24. "This I Believe," undated version, R02.14160. See Bailey, *Initiation, Human and Solar*.

25. "This I Believe," undated version, R02.14160, 21–23. See King, *Unveiled Mysteries*; Spalding, *Life and Teachings of the Masters of the Far East*, 1:22, 23, 29–32, 35, 45, 48, 62, 63, 65, 140, 143, 145, 146, 150–56; 2:67, 73–77, 131–32; 3:116, 148–57; 4:33, 40–41, 52, 76, 82–83, 139, 143, 147, 181; 5:96–97. The "single eye" is a reference to Matt. 6:22–23: "The light of the body is the eye: if therefore thine eye be single, thy whole body shall be full of light. But if thine eye be evil, thy whole body shall be full of darkness" (KJV).

26. "This I Believe," undated version, R02.14160, 15–16, 19. See Fullwood, *Song of the Sano Tarot*, vi.

27. "This I Believe," undated version, R02.14160, 16. See Bailey, *Initiation, Human and Solar*, 20–62, especially charts on xiv, 48–49; Fullwood, *Song of the Sano Tarot*, xiv.

28. "This I Believe," undated version, R02.14160, 20. See Spalding, *Life and Teachings of the Masters of the Far East*, 1: 62–63: "It is in this way that we can return all things to the Universal Mind Substance, from which they sprang, and bring them back or return them perfect into outer form or manifestation. . . . We must realize

that the inner alchemist, God within, has taken hold of this and has transmuted, refined, and perfected that which seemed imperfect, that which we brought forth and are now returning."

29. "This I Believe," undated version, R02.14160, 25.

30. Ibid., 17; see also 11. This is an idea that Fetzer must have encountered as far back as his first introduction to Spiritualism and Theosophy, but it recurs clearly in Spalding, *Life and Teachings of the Masters of the Far East*, 1:133–34.

31. "This I Believe," undated version, R02.14160, 17. Reincarnation is a theme throughout the works of Alice Bailey, Guy Ballard, and Edgar Cayce, but the idea that reincarnation is a choice and can be avoided seems to have come from Spalding, *Life and Teachings of the Masters of the Far East*, 4:116, as indicated by Fetzer's annotations and note to himself on the first page of the book. The "Divine Monitor" is a term from the *Urantia Book*; see, for example, 196:3.34 (2097.2).

32. "This I Believe," undated version, R02.14160, 25–26. See Spalding, *Life and Teachings of the Masters of the Far East*, 3:64: "There is slowly rising from the ashes of orthodoxy the actual temple not made by hands, eternal in heaven, in man. A great new race of thinkers is coming to the fore with Herculean strides. Soon the tides will surge over the earth to sweep away the debris of delusion which has been strewn over the paths of those who are struggling along under the load of evolution."

33. "This I Believe," undated version, R02.14160, 26. See Spalding, *Life and Teachings of the Masters of the Far East*, 4:204: "The Quantum Theory is the approach of Science to this basic fact of life and there can be no true science, religion, social structure, or successful living outside the undefeatable and indissoluble oneness of all things."

34. "This I Believe," revised April 10, 1967, R02.13085, 1.

35. Tom Beaver, personal communication, July 7, 2015.

36. Fetzer, *Men from Wengen*. "America's Agony" was subsequently published separately in 2007 by the Fetzer Institute with the references to the Wenger family edited out: Fetzer, *America's Agony* (Kalamazoo, MI: Fetzer Institute, 2007).

37. Fetzer, *Men from Wengen*, 375–78. For a good discussion of the origins of "Washington's Vision," see J. L. Bell, "The Truth of *Washington's Vision*," *Boston 1775* (blog), December 30, 2006, http://boston1775.blogspot.com/2006/12/truth-of-washingtons-vision.html. Where did Fetzer first learn of it? A typescript version of "Washington's Vision," which Fetzer used to prepare *America's Agony*, exists in the Fetzer archives. FP 18 (Book Material; 1969–1979 III): "WORDS OF LIFE General Washington's Vision," R02.14159. Internal clues in the typescript indicate that this version came from a tract series called "Words of Life,"

published by the Pentecostal Christian Worker's Union in the 1910s. Interestingly, based on a premillennial gloss in the penultimate paragraph that does not appear in the original newspaper version (and was dropped by Fetzer), this tract was also the source used by the I AM Religious Activity: a pamphlet containing this version of "General Washington's Vision" is still published by the Saint Germain Press today. According to G. Barbee Bryan, *Psychic Dictatorship of America* (Los Angeles: Truth Research Publications, 1940), 176–77, Guy Ballard incorporated "Washington's Vision" into the teachings of the I AM Religious Activity in 1937. From then on, "Washington's Vision," said to have been delivered by the Goddess of Liberty, became a staple of the I AM movement. Fetzer may have first become aware of it through the I AM teachings since one of the books in Fetzer's collection bearing his annotations, *Ascended Master Light*, directly refers to it. See Kuthumi's discourse, December 19, 1937, 324; Goddess of Liberty's Discourse, October 13, 1937, 462. "Washington's Vision" was also reprinted in Masonic newspapers during the nineteenth century. See, for example, *Quarterly Bulletin of the Iowa Masonic Library* 1, no. 1 (1898): 34. So it is possible that Fetzer encountered it through this source as well; indeed, the three trials could be glossed as the first three degrees of Freemasonry.

38. Fetzer, *Men from Wengen*, 379–81. In addition to "Washington Vision" and his Adventist background, Fetzer felt that the peril to the country was clear when it was compared to the rise and fall of the Roman Empire. His source for this was Brady Black, "Roman History Offers Parallels That Are Chilling," reprinted from the *Cincinnati Enquirer*, May 19, 1969, 1–3. FP 18 (Book Material 1969–1979 I): "Roman History Offers Parallels That Are Chilling," R02.14157. Fetzer believed Roman history epitomized the so-called Tytler Cycle. *Men from Wengen*, 280: "From Bondage to Spiritual Faith," etc. It is not clear where Fetzer first encountered the Tytler Cycle; for what little information there is on the Tytler Cycle, see "Alexander Fraser Tytler," Wikipedia, accessed July 29, 2016, http://en .wikipedia.org/wiki/Alexander_Fraser_Tytler.

39. Fetzer, *Men from Wengen*, 385–90.

40. Ibid., 391–93.

41. Ibid., 395–410. Fetzer observes that many members of the younger generation are hoping to achieve this connection to God through drugs but find that such "chemically-induced mystical experience is more like a road block than a discovery that leads to cosmic experience" (394); however, see note 79 to chapter 8.

42. Fetzer, *Men from Wengen*, 411–16. Again, as an indication of his debt to Theosophy, Fetzer includes the same stanzas of *Idyll of the White Lotus* by Collins (409–10) and the "The Great Invocation" of Bailey (415). In addition, he

quotes A. J. Rydholm (391), a writer for the *Beacon*, the Arcane School journal edited by Foster Bailey. See Theosophical Society in Australia, "The Beacon
1922—Continuing, New York, Lucis Trust, Foster Bailey," accessed July 29, 2016,
www.austheos.org.au/indices/BEACON.HTM. And at the very end of "America's Agony," he cites a New Age paean (416), which, while attributed to Flora R.
Mathews, can be traced back to Peter Ballbusch. See "The Perfect Storm Series
#5: Bush & Co Wrecking the World," Earth Rainbow Network, March 10, 2005,
www.cedp.ca/Archives2006/PerfectStorm5.htm, where "Flora Ruth floraruth
@w3az.net" cites the same passage and adds, "This was spoken through Peter
Ballbusch, a trance channel, on 4-14-63 (not a typo error) [*sic*] and recorded by
me." Ballbusch was a psychic, Anthroposophist, and student of Edgar Cayce. See
Peter Ballbusch, *The Body Is a Shell* (Hollywood, CA: White Knight, 1956).

43. Fetzer, *Men from Wengen*, 409.

44. The phrase is from Partridge, *Re-enchantment of the West*, 2:11.

45. See Paul Heelas and Linda Woodhead, *The Spiritual Revolution: Why Religion Is
Giving Way to Spirituality* (Oxford, UK: Blackwell, 2005).

8. The Science of Spirit

1. FI 15 (Fetzer Institute Programs, Human Dimensions Institute, April 1972–June
1973): John E. Fetzer to Helen Neuman, February 6, 1973, R02.13292.

2. FI 9 (Institute of Noetic Sciences 1979–1980): John E. Fetzer to Dorothy Lyddon,
August 1, 1979, R02.13169.

3. Douglas Dean and John Mihalasky, "Testing for Executive ESP," *Psychic* 6, no. 1
(1974): 21–33. See also Nancy Kool, "Enlightenment and the Oldest Tiger,"
Monthly Detroit, April 1981, 34–41.

4. "JEF—Jim Gordon—Arthur Douet—Austin, Texas," February 1984, JGC: "I
think that's my [Fetzer's] biggest problem with pendulums—getting my own
mind out of the way because I can make a pendulum do anything that I want to
think it should do"; see also Hegedus, *John Earl Fetzer*, 95–96; Whitson Oral History, March 9, 2011, 8–12; Bruce Fetzer, personal communication, October 26,
2016.

5. Board Meeting Minutes (Binder 1): November 9, 1972. In addition to John and
Rhea Fetzer, the original board consisted of Carl E. Lee, Robert C. Van Horn,
Arthur F. Homer, Bruce L. Fetzer, and A. James Ebel.

6. Board Meeting Minutes (Binder 1): December 14, 1972.

7. Board Meeting Minutes (Binder 1): January 20, 1973.

8. Board Meeting Minutes (Binder 1): February 8, 1973. For a time, Fetzer maintained membership in the American Society for Psychical Research. FI 7 (Foundation Correspondence 1976–1980): "Receipts for JEF membership in American Society for Psychical Research from 1976 to 1980," R02.13109.

9. Board Meeting Minutes (Binder 1): February 8, 1973.

10. Alan Vaughan, "In Pursuit of the Whole at the Human Dimensions Institute," *Psychic*, March–April 1972, 9–14. Fetzer requested information from the institute. FI 15 (Human Dimension Institute April 1972–June 1973): John E. Fetzer to Gentlemen, April 26, 1972, R02.13292.

11. The roster of speakers at the institute for 1973 included Edgar D. Mitchell and William A. McGarry of the Edgar Cayce Foundation, both of whom Fetzer eventually funded. See fliers in FI 15 (Human Dimension Institute April 1972–June 1973), R02.13292.

12. FI 15 (Human Dimension Institute April 1972–June 1973): John E. Fetzer to Jeanne Pontius Rindge, March 14, 1973, R02.13292.

13. FI 15 (Human Dimension Institute April 1972–June 1973): Jeanne Pontius Rindge to John E. Fetzer, June 14, 1973, R02.13292. The letter was to acknowledge her meeting with Fetzer in Kalamazoo shortly before. Fetzer encouraged her to visit Camp Chesterfield, but since the "two sensitives" Fetzer recommended were not available, it is not clear that she made the trip. Alice Bailey, *Esoteric Healing* (New York: Lucis, 1953).

14. Board Meeting Minutes (Binder 1): May 31, 1973.

15. Board Meeting Minutes (Binder 1): September 12, 1973.

16. Board Meeting Minutes (Binder 1): "John E. Fetzer Foundation Report" (aka the "Spalding Memo"), n.d., 1–20.

17. Ibid., 1. Fetzer also discussed Anderson's theory directly with the foundation board. Board Meeting Minutes (Binder 1): August 27, 1973.

18. Fetzer was especially impressed with this camera since Spalding reported that the first images recorded were of Washington's first inaugural. "John E. Fetzer Foundation Report," 12. This appears in Spalding, *Life and Teachings of the Masters of the Far East*, 5:24–55. In Fetzer's personal comments, he referred to an unverified report that an English TV station had picked up a TV program from a Texas station broadcast years before, suggesting that once transmitted, a program continues to "bounce around in space" indefinitely, perhaps as do the vibrations generated by all past events (the similarity of Spalding's claim to the Theosophical idea of the *akashic* records is obvious). As for sound projection, this was perhaps borne out for Fetzer empirically by his later involvement in the Muzak Corporation.

19. Board Meeting Minutes (Binder 1): November 21, 1973; Board Meeting Minutes (Binder 1): "Compilation of Replies to Spalding Memorandum," November 21, 1973, 1–9.

20. "Compilation of Replies to Spalding Memorandum." The last comment was from John Artley of Duke University. FI 15 (Duke University and Psychical Research Foundation 1973–1974): John Artley to John E. Fetzer, November 12, 1973, R02.13282. Fetzer himself never lost faith in the veracity of Spalding, although he did check with the Ouija board as to whether he should continue to trust *Life and Teachings of the Masters of the Far East*; the spirits said yes. Ouija Board Transcripts, July 16, 1976, JGC.

21. "John E. Fetzer Foundation Report," 1–3.

22. R. A. McConnell, "Parapsychology: Its Future Organization and Support," *Journal of the American Society of Psychical Research* 68, no. 2 (1974): 169–81. Fetzer mentions receiving the paper from McConnell in a letter. FI 15 (Human Dimension Institute July 1973–May 1974): John E. Fetzer to Jeanne Pontius Rindge, April 26, 1974, R02.13293.

23. McConnell, "Parapsychology," 171, 175.

24. Board Meeting Minutes (Binder 1): "[Digest of Comments on] 'Parapsychology: Its Future Organization and Support' by R. A. McConnell," n.d., 1–6.

25. While the digest of comments on McConnell's paper does not include names, Rindge's comments originated in a still-extant letter to John Fetzer. FI 15 (Human Dimension Institute July 1973–May 1974): Jeanne Pontius Rindge to John E. Fetzer, May 17, 1974, R02.13293. A photocopy of the Rogo paper can also be found here. D. Scott Rogo, "The Crisis in Experimental Parapsychology," *Fate* 27, no. 6 (1974): 89–95. Rindge's quote is taken from p. 94.

26. Stacy Horn, *Unbelievable: Investigations into Ghosts, Poltergeists, Telepathy, and Other Unseen Phenomena from the Duke Parapsychology Laboratory* (New York: HarperCollins, 2009), 79, 81.

27. FI 15 (Human Dimension Institute April 1972–June 1973): Jeanne Pontius Rindge to John E. Fetzer, October 2, 1974, R02.13294. According to Board Meeting Minutes (Binder 1): October 11, 1974, Fetzer planned to meet with

> Sir George Trevelyan, Director of the Wrekin Trust, London; Colonel Marcus McCausland, organizer of the "Health for the New Age" London; Sir John Sinclair, head of the Human Development Trust, London; Harry Edwards, head of the Center of Burrows Lea Shere, London; Dr. Kenneth Cummings, Director of the Burswood Health Center, London; Nancy Magor and Michael Eastcote, operators of

the "Center for the Tibetan Work," London; Lady Muriel Dowding, widow of Marshall Dowding, who is supporting parapsychology, London; Dr. Paul Beard, President of the College of Psychic Science, London; Bernard Nesfield-Cookson, director of Hawkwood College, London; Dr. Carlo Suares, a well-known author on ancient energy codes, Paris, France; and Dr. Hans Bender, head of the Parapsychology Institute at the University of Freiburg, West Germany.

28. TB 18 (Research Fetzer, Rhea—Diaries & Letters [Transcripts] [Restricted] 1973–1976): "1974 Rhea Fetzer's Diary and Personal Correspondence," October 17–18, 1974, R02.14578; "Intrigue at Luxor," n.d., JGC. McCausland wrote Fetzer asking for funds to help underwrite Health for the New Age, arguing that even Rhine has understood the connection between laboratory research into ESP and parapsychology and alternative forms of healing; Fetzer sent him a check for $500. FI 4 (Fetzer, John E.—Correspondence, Health for a New Age [1977–1978]): Marcus McCausland to John E. Fetzer, December 20, 1977, R02.13031. Unfortunately, there is very little biographical information available for Marcus McCausland. For Grant, see Joan Grant, *Speaking from the Heart: Ethics, Reincarnation and What It Means to Be Human*, edited by Nicola Bennett, Jane Lahr, and Sophia Rosoff (New York: Overlook/Duckwood, 2007). For Twigg, see Ena Twigg with Ruth Hagy Brod, *Ena Twigg: Medium* (1972; London: Star, 1974). Fetzer met with Twigg once more, on July 25, 1977, when she communicated with Fetzer's deceased father and mother. "Interview with Ena Twigg in London," July 25, 1977, JGC; TB 18 (Research Fetzer, Rhea—Diaries & Letters [Transcripts] [Restricted] 1976–1979): "1977 Rhea Fetzer's Diary and Personal Correspondence," July 25, 1977, R02.14579.

29. TB 18 (Research Fetzer, Rhea—Diaries & Letters [Transcripts] [Restricted] 1963–1967): "1974 Rhea Fetzer's Diary and Personal Correspondence," October 25, 1974, R02.14578. For more on Bender, see Martin Ebon, "Hans Bender: A Life in Parapsychology," *Journal of Religion and Psychical Research* 18, no. 4 (1995): 187–95. Fetzer also met with parapsychologists in Japan in 1972 while on his goodwill trip with the Tigers. TB 18 (Research Fetzer, Rhea—Diaries & Letters [Transcripts] [Restricted] 1968–1972): "1972 Rhea Fetzer's Diary and Personal Correspondence," November 2, 1972, R02.14577; TB 30 (Broadcasting 1973 I): Sadao Nakamichi to John E. Fetzer, January 17, 1973, R02.14806.

30. Board Meeting Minutes (Binder 1): "Memorandum of Executive Committee to Trustees," December 2, 1974. One result of the trip, however, was the creation by Fetzer of the Jefferson Charitable Trust at the Credit Suisse Bank in Zurich,

Switzerland, and Hamilton, Bermuda, for the purpose of funding parapsychological research in Europe; apparently the trust was not a success, and Fetzer moved to dissolve the Bermuda account in 1976. FI 10 (Jefferson Charitable Trust 1974–1976), R02.13186.

31. Board Meeting Minutes (Binder 1): "John E. Fetzer Foundation: Contributions Made—Year Ended 7/31/73." For the early funding history, see FI 15 (Foundation Grants History): "John E. Fetzer Foundation History: Grants," n.d., R02.13288.

32. "John E. Fetzer Foundation History: Grants," n.d., R02.13288. Correspondence between Fetzer and the Human Dimensions Institute can be found in FI 15 (Human Dimensions Institute [April 1972–February 1977]), R02.13292–95. Some of the speakers were Kenneth Pelletier, Karl Zurn, and Edgar Mitchell. TB 18 (Research Fetzer, Rhea—Diaries & Letters [Transcripts] [Restricted] 1976–1979): "1976/1979 Rhea Fetzer's Diary and Personal Correspondence," November 8, 1976, May 13, 1979, R02.14579; BR 13 (Broadcasting 1979 April–November): "John E. Fetzer introduction of Ed Mitchell at Kalamazoo College," May 14, 1979, R02.16919; Board Meeting Minutes (Binder 1): "Memorandum of Executive Committee to the Trustees John E. Fetzer Foundation, Inc.," May 30, 1979.

33. "John E. Fetzer Foundation History: Grants," n.d., R02.13288. Correspondence between Fetzer and the parapsychologists at Duke University and the Psychical Research Foundation can be found in FI 2 (Duke University—Artley, John 1973–1975), R02.12996; FI 15 (Duke University and Psychical Research Foundation, 1973–1980), R02.13282–84; and correspondence between Fetzer and Princeton University's PEAR lab in FI 16 (Princeton University—Jahn, Robert, 1978–86), R02.13313–25. See also Robert G. Jahn, "Psychic Process, Energy Transfer, and Things That Go Bump in the Night," *Princeton Alumni Weekly*, December 4, 1978, S-1–12, a copy of which was sent to John E. Fetzer (January 2, 1979) and can be found in Board Meeting Minutes (Binder 1). See also Fetzer Foundation Projects (1979–1981 Binder): "John E. Fetzer Foundation, Inc. Project Summary Presentation Duke University Psychical Research Foundation Project 1979–1980," December 1982.

34. FI 16 (Princeton University—Jahn, Robert [1978–1988 I]): John E. Fetzer to William G. Bowen, January 9, 1979; John E. Fetzer to Bowie Kuhn, January 9, 1979; John E. Fetzer to Bowie Kuhn, February 22, 1979, R02.13313.

35. FP 4 (Correspondence 1967): Charles LeVant Yeager to John E. Fetzer, April 3, 1967, R02.13867.

36. FP 4 (Correspondence 1969 X): Charles LeVant Yeager to John E. Fetzer, April 1, 1969; John E. Fetzer to Charles LeVant Yeager, April 7, 1969, R02.13870. Early in Yeager's career, he became an expert on the use of the electroencephalograph (EEG). See FP 7 (Yeager Papers 1939 III): "An Ode to a Brain Wave," n.d., R02.13930.

37. TB 18 (Research Fetzer, Rhea—Diaries & Letters [Transcripts] [Restricted] 1968–1972): "1970 RYF," May 4, 1970, R02.14577; TB 18 (Research Fetzer, Rhea—Diaries & Letters [Transcripts] [Restricted] 1973–1976): "1973 Rhea Fetzer's Diary and Personal Correspondence," February 27, 1973, R02.14578.

38. TB 18 (Research Fetzer, Rhea—Diaries & Letters [Transcripts] [Restricted] 1973–1976): "1974 Rhea Fetzer's Diary and Personal Correspondence," September 30, 1974, R02.14578.

39. Board Meeting Minutes (Binder 1): "John E. Fetzer Foundation: Contributions Made—Year Ended 7/31/73"; FI 15 (Foundation Grants History): "John E. Fetzer Foundation History: Grants," n.d., R02.13288. Later in 1978, the Fetzer Foundation funded another biofeedback researcher at UCSF: "The additional grant to the University of California for $8,400 is to support the work of Dr. Alan S. Gevins, Director of the EEG Systems Laboratory. The purpose of this research is to scientifically produce a model of cognitive functioning based on the traditional esoteric sources. This model will be used to develop an understanding of what the processes of altered states of consciousness really are. Mr. Brian Cutillo of MIT who is an expert in translations of Indian Sanskrit will be employed as an Associate Specialist in the EEG Systems Laboratory. There is considerable material in the Indian culture giving explanations of the process of cognition. It is necessary to secure translations, which Mr. Cutillo can precisely formulate and carefully define." Board Meeting Minutes (Binder 1): "Memorandum of Executive Committee to Trustees John E. Fetzer Foundation," September 11, 1978, April 4, 1979. See also Fetzer Foundation Projects (1979–1981 Binder): "John E. Fetzer Foundation, Inc. Project Summary Presentation University of California Langley Porter Institute EEG and Higher Cortical Functions Project 1979–1982," December 1982.

40. FI 14 (Hardt Project—Hardt, James, Dr. [UCSF] 1982 I): James V. Hardt to John E. Fetzer, n.d., R02.13276; FI 14 (Hardt Project—Hardt, James, Dr. [UCSF] 1980 I): "James V. Hardt, 'The Fetzer Foundation's Biofeedback Project: Long Term Training in EEG Feedback,'" n.d., R02.13272.

41. FI 14 (Hardt Project—Hardt, James, Dr. [UCSF] 1979 I): James V. Hardt to John E. Fetzer, June 30, 1979, R02.13271.

42. FI 14 (Hardt Project—Hardt, James, Dr. [UCSF] 1979 I): James V. Hardt to John E. Fetzer, postcard, May 23, 1979, R02.13270; FI 14 (Hardt Project—Hardt, James, Dr. [UCSF] 1984–86): Maureen Sansing to John E. Fetzer, April 9, 1984, R02.13280; Board Meeting Minutes (Binder 1): "Annual Report: Long Term EEG Feedback Training Sponsored by the Fetzer Foundation," n.d. but likely 1975.

43. FI 14 (Hardt Project—Hardt, James, Dr. [UCSF] 1980 II): James V. Hardt to John E. Fetzer, September 8, 1980, R02.13273: "I'd promised you a description of the work undertaken in the last two weeks which were a part of the 'Key Person' portion of the full proposal. The day I returned from Yosemite I met with Gunnar Hurtig (a Fetzer Program Trainee), and one of his friends. This friend, Joe Akerman, is an investment advisor for the electronics industry and controls the flow of venture capital into new enterprises. Since he manages a fund of $40 million, he would seem to be within the scope of Key Persons in science, government and industry. His training, now completed, was most extraordinary. He was open, trusting, and willing to grow, and I was thrilled and blessed to facilitate and to attend the birth of a new high being. By session #4 (of 7), he was going into such high alpha states that his Luminous Body (Astral Body) was clearly visible to him. It floated off 5 or 6 feet—attached to him by the Silver cord and he marveled and wondered at it. This run drew upon the full range of insight I have developed over the years of doing this training as I was called upon to help interpret the meaning of the mystical communications. For example, I had to interpret for him the meaning that when he and not the Luminous Body was seen floating on the end of the cord, that he was being told not to seek the transcendent 'out there,' but rather to look within, to know that he and his Luminous Body were one. At just the right moments the words of Jesus came through me to him: 'The kingdom of Heaven is within you,' and this guided him in exploring deeper into his higher self. The transformation in this Fetzer trainee (Joe Akerman) was beautiful to behold and I guess we may be hearing more of him. Because he is a Key Person, his new consciousness will quickly influence decisions about the growing edge of electronic technology. I feel a little like Johnny Appleseed—spreading the Light and sharing the Spirit, and all the while filled with joy that you and the Fetzer Foundation are helping to make it possible, helping the growth of the new higher consciousness." Fetzer responded, "Your description of the Joe Akerman experience and the 'luminous body' certainly portends a high order of alternate consciousness and the fact that his 'joining' gave him this new insight is pushing electronic technology into its rightful place." FI 14 (Hardt Project—Hardt, James, Dr. [UCSF] 1980 II): John E. Fetzer to James V. Hardt, October 7, 1980,

R02.13273. See also FI 14 (Hardt Project—Hardt, James, Dr. [UCSF] 1982 I): James V. Hardt to John E. Fetzer, n.d., R02.13276.

44. FI 14 (Hardt Project—Hardt, James, Dr. [UCSF] 1980 I): James V. Hardt to John E. Fetzer, July 16, 1980, R0313272.

45. FI 14 (Hardt Project—Hardt, James, Dr. [UCSF] 1981 I): John E. Fetzer to Lynne Dailey, May 4, 1981, R02.13274.

46. FI 14 (Hardt Project—Hardt, James, Dr. [UCSF] 1976): John E. Fetzer to Charles LeVant Yeager, October 22, 1976, R02.13267; FI 14 (Hardt Project—Hardt, James, Dr. [UCSF] 1978): John E. Fetzer to James V. Hardt, May 16, 1978, R02.13269; FI 14 (Hardt Project—Hardt, James, Dr. [UCSF] 1979 II): John E. Fetzer to James V. Hardt, December 27, 1979, R02.13271; FI 14 (Hardt Project—Hardt, James, Dr. [UCSF] 1981 I): John E. Fetzer to Lynne Dailey, May 4, 1981, R02.13274; FI 14 (Hardt Project—Hardt, James, Dr. [UCSF] 1988): James V. Hardt to Victor B. Eichler, June 11, 1988, R02.13281. See also Fetzer Foundation Projects (1979–1981 Binder): "John E. Fetzer Foundation, Inc. Project Summary Presentation University of California EEG Biofeedback Project 1979–1982," December 1982.

47. FI 15 (Foundation Grants History): "John E. Fetzer Foundation History: Grants," n.d., R02.13288; Board Meeting Minutes (Binder 1): "John E. Fetzer Foundation, Inc. Executive Committee Report," July 10, 1975; Board Meeting Minutes (Binder 1): "Memorandum of Executive Committee to Trustees John E. Fetzer Foundation," January 8, 1976, July 2, 1976, October 21, 1976, January 14, 1977, February 10, 1978, July 18, 1978. See also Richard Williams Oral History, May 13, 2011; and Fetzer Foundation Projects (1979–1981 Binder): "John E. Fetzer Foundation, Inc. Project Summary Presentation Western Michigan University Institute for Holistic Medicine 1979–1981," December 1982. In addition, it should be mentioned that in 1978, a new initiative, called the New Frontiers Program, was funded at Kalamazoo College under the leadership of Wen Chao Chen and Carl Butters. The program was designed to promote "the reawakening of [the] holistic way of thinking," including holistic health. Board Meeting Minutes (Binder 1): "Memorandum of the Executive Committee to the Trustees John E. Fetzer Foundation, Inc.," October 11, 1978. Edgar Mitchell's visit on May 13–14, 1979, kicked off the New Frontiers Program. Board Meeting Minutes (Binder 1): "Memorandum of the Executive Committee to the Trustees John E. Fetzer Foundation, Inc.," May 30, 1979. The last mention of funding of the New Frontiers Program occurs in Board Meeting Minutes (Binder 2): "John E. Fetzer Foundation Statement of Earnings and Contributions Made for the Second Quarter Ended January 31, 1981." See also Fetzer Foundation Projects

(1979–1981 Binder): "John E. Fetzer Foundation, Inc. Project Summary Presentation Kalamazoo College New Frontiers Program 1979–1981," December 1982.

48. Edgar D. Mitchell, *Psychic Exploration: A Challenge to Science*, ed. John White (New York: G. P. Putnam's Sons, 1974), 13. A signed copy of this book is in Fetzer's personal library: "To John—with the hope that this is the first of many landmarks in Noetics that we can make together—with warmest affection Ed Mitchell."

49. Edgar D. Mitchell Oral History, September 29, 2011, 24–25; TB 31 (Interviews Fetzer, John—Early Years [Trip to Lafayette], October 28, 1982), R02.14834; FP 5 (1973 I): Rhea Fetzer to Harriet ("Hattie") Thomas, May 3, 1973: "We had an interesting time in Detroit last week-end. Edgar Mitchell, the astronaut, was there to lecture an organization on 'Psychic Phenomenon,' and we spent quite a bit of time with him. John had corresponded with him several times, and they both have the same interest in parapsychology. They had lots of good conversation, and he and his public relations director had dinner with us Friday before his speech and lunch on Saturday with us before the ballgame. He also went to the ballgame with us. . . . He has a scientific interest in consciousness research and is working to find some of the answers to unsolved questions. When we see you, John can tell you much more of this. . . . It was hard to believe that he had ever walked on the moon." See also Whitson Oral History, February 4, 2011, 1–10.

50. Mitchell Oral History, September 29, 2011, 25; FI 9 (Institute of Noetic Science 1979): "List of Attendees Quail Roost Conference Center, December 9–12, 1978," R02.13168; FI 9 (Institute of Noetic Sciences 1979–1980): John E. Fetzer to Dorothy Lyddon, August 1, 1979, R02.13169. For more on Whitson, see later in this chapter. For more on Ferguson, see Melton, Clark, and Kelly, *New Age Almanac*, 400–401. A signed copy of *The Aquarian Conspiracy* (Los Angeles: J. P. Tarcher, 1980) exists in the Fetzer archives ("For John Fetzer with love and admiration Marilyn Ferguson").

51. FI 15 (Foundation Grants History): "John E. Fetzer Foundation History: Grants," n.d., R02.13288; Board Meeting Minutes (Binder 1): "Memorandum of Executive Committee to Trustees John E. Fetzer Foundation, Inc.," April 30, 1976. In 1976, the Fetzer Foundation gave $10,000 to IONS for a variety of programs, and the following year, gave $5,000 to support the work of Robert Jahn at PEAR.

52. FI 9 (Institute of Noetic Sciences 1979–1980): "IONS Board of Directors Roster," September 1979, R02.13169.

53. FI 9 (Institute of Noetic Sciences 1979–1980): John E. Fetzer to Dorothy Lyddon, August 1, 1979, R02.13169. Edgar Mitchell believed their differences were due primarily to the fact that IONS was more concerned with exploring the nature

of consciousness, while Fetzer was more interested in establishing the survival of consciousness after death. Mitchell Oral History, September 29, 2011, 27, 35.

54. FI 16 (Princeton University—Jahn, Robert 1978–1986 IV): John E. Fetzer to Brenda Dunne, October 8, 1981, R013318; Board Meeting Minutes (Binder 2): "Memorandum of Executive Committee to Trustees John E. Fetzer Foundation, Inc.," July 17, 1981.

55. For example, see FP 1 (Correspondence 1928 IV): John E. Fetzer to Rhea Fetzer, October 3, 1928; John E. Fetzer to Rhea Fetzer, October 11, 1928, R02.13798.

56. FI 7 (Foundation Correspondence 1989): "Draft of Memorandum by John E. Fetzer," February 4, 1989. See also FP 1 (Fetzer, John E.—Diary Dec. 1, 1914–Feb. 12, 1915): December 21, 1914, December 25, 1915, R02.13788.

57. Existing transcripts for the Ouija board sessions start on May 18, 1976, and end on May 18, 1982, JGC. Fetzer also wrote up narratives of his time in Egypt ("Intrigue at Luxor and Beyond," JGC) and as St. John of the Cross ("St. Maria Teresa and St. John of the Cross, Carmelites, Part I"; "Maria Teresa and Juan, Part II," JGC); Mary Teresa was one of Fetzer's spirit guides identified at Camp Chesterfield (see chapter 3). A footnote in "Intrigue at Luxor and Beyond" credits the 1974 meeting with Twigg with initiating the Ouija board sessions with Ibrahim. (Curiously, in the original version, Fetzer is named explicitly, but in subsequent versions, he identified himself only as "a well-known radio, television, and baseball executive.") With regard to his occasional skepticism, e.g., Fetzer wrote a letter to "American Archaeologists" working in Luxor to ask about the validity of some Egyptian names that had come through. John E. Fetzer to American Archaeologists, February 17, 1975, JGC. A response from Kent R. Weeks from the Oriental Institute at the University of Chicago politely informed him that "neither name sounds particularly Egyptian, ancient or modern." Kent R. Weeks to John E. Fetzer, March 1, 1975, JGC.

58. Ellwood, *Religious and Spiritual Groups in Modern America*, 231–35; Melton, Clark, and Kelly, *New Age Almanac*, 69.

59. Dean and Mihalasky, "Testing for Executive ESP," 30.

60. Probably Jack Forem, *Transcendental Meditation: Maharishi Mahesh Yogi and the Science of Creative Intelligence* (New York: E. P. Dutton, 1973), FPL, an annotated copy of which exists in the Fetzer archives.

61. TB 31 (Interviews Fetzer, John E.—Baseball, Spirituality, February 9, 1984), R02.14826, 21–22; TB 30 (Research Material Broadcasting [1–14] 1975 I): "1975 Rhea Fetzer's Diary and Personal Correspondence," April 5, 8, 11, 1975, R02.14813. The Ouija board confirmed for Fetzer that TM was a useful practice. Ouija Board Transcripts, July 16, 1976, JGC.

62. FP 5 (1975 I): John E. Fetzer to Dr. and Mrs. Charles L. Yeager, May 23, 1975, R02.13877; Gordon Anderson Oral History, June 23, 1988, 70–72; Francis Morse Oral History, November 10, 1995, 28–30; Alice Sloane Oral History, December 28, 1995, 29–31 (Sloane gives a good description of how TM was introduced at spring training. She reported that the players most interested were Bill Freehan, Ron LeFlore, and Verne Ruhl). "Use of Transcendental Meditation Helps Tigers," *Lakeland Ledger*, April 27, 1975; "Tigers on Spiritual Route to Success," *Highpoint Enterprise*, April 27, 1975; "TM Benefits Athletic Ability," *Los Angeles Times*, June 19, 1975; Rev. L. A. Schroeder, "Transcendental Mediation, Address to Michigan District Teachers' Convention South Haven, Michigan," 1977, http://essays.wls.wels.net/bitstream/handle/123456789/2998/SchroederTM.pdf.

63. TB 30 (Research Material Broadcasting [1–14] 1975 I): "1975 Rhea Fetzer's Diary and Personal Correspondence," March 28–29, 1975, R02.14813.

64. BR 13 (Broadcasting 1975 February–May): John E. Fetzer to Messrs. Lee and Anderson, April 15, 1975, R02.16905.

65. For an insider's account of *A Course in Miracles*, see Robert Skutch, *Journey without Distance: The Story behind "A Course in Miracles"* (1984; Mill Valley, CA: Foundation for Inner Peace, 1996). See also Jon Klimo, *Channeling: Investigations on Receiving Information from Paranormal Sources* (Los Angeles: Jeremy P. Tarcher, 1987), 37–42.

66. Hanegraaff, *New Age Religion and Western Culture*, 37–38; Whitson Oral History, February 10, 2011, 48–49; March 3, 2011, 5–12; A Course in Miracles Archives, "About the Publisher: The Foundation for Inner Peace," accessed June 29, 2017, http://acim-archives.org/Organizations/about_FIP.html.

67. *A Course in Miracles: Text* (New York: Foundation for Inner Peace, 1975), vii, 359, FPL; *A Course in Miracles: Workbook for Students* (New York: Foundation for Inner Peace, 1975),1, FPL. *A Course in Miracles: Manual for Teachers* (New York: Foundation for Inner Peace, 1975) can also be found in Fetzer's personal library.

68. Klimo, *Channeling*, 39.

69. Whitson Oral History, March 30, 2011, 45, 47, 49–50. Copies with Fetzer's annotations of Jane Roberts, *Seth Speaks: The Eternal Validity of the Soul* (Englewood Cliffs, NJ: Prentice Hall, 1972), FPL, and *The Nature of Personal Reality: A Seth Book* (Englewood Cliffs, NJ: Prentice Hall, 1974), FPL, exist in Fetzer's personal library, as do the *Urantia Book* and Levi Dowling's *Aquarian Gospel of Jesus*. Seth was reported to be an "energy personality essence no longer focused in physical matter" who channeled a wide range of metaphysical material to Jane

Roberts from 1963 to 1984; that the channelings began with a Ouija board probably attracted Fetzer. Roberts, *Seth Speaks*, 5, ix.

70. Whitson Oral History, February 4, 2011, 6–10; March 3, 2011, 12–46; March 9, 2011, 1–3; March 15, 2011, 14–22; March 30, 2011, 10–11, 18. Some pages from the *Course* manuscript originally sent by Whitson to Fetzer and bearing his annotations can be found in the JGC.

71. FI 12 (James Keating 1973–1976 II): James Keating to John E. Fetzer, December 2, 1976; John E. Fetzer to James Keating, December 17, 1976, R02.13216; FI 15 (Duke University Psychical Research Foundation): John E. Fetzer to William Joines, November 12, 1976, R02.13283; FI 15 (Duke University Psychical Research Foundation 1975–1978): Lynne Daily to John Fetzer, memos, June 8, 1977, January 25, 1978, R02.13283; FP 5 (Correspondence 1978 I): Alice Yeager to John E. Fetzer, January 11, 1978, R02.13886; Bobbie Lee Smythe to John E. Fetzer, March 13, 1978, R02.13886; FP 5 (Correspondence 1978 III): John E. Fetzer to Elouise Ebel, October 25, 1978, R02.13888; FP 5 (Correspondence 1980 I): Alice Yeager to Rhea and John E. Fetzer, June 18, 1980, R02.13891; FI 14 (Hardt Project—Hardt, James, Dr. [UCSF] 1978): James Hardt to Lynne Dailey, February 6, 1979, R02.13269, FI 14 (Hardt Project—Hardt, James, Dr. [UCSF] 1979 II): John E. Fetzer to James Hardt, December 27, 1979, R02.13271; FI 14 (Hardt Project—Hardt, James, Dr. [UCSF] 1980 I): John E. Fetzer to James Hardt, June 2, 1980, R02.13272; FI 16 (Princeton University, Robert Jahn 1978–1986 IV): Lynne Daily to Brenda Dunne, July 25, 1980, and Lynne Daily to Robert Jahn, July 9, 1982, R02.13316; TB 31 (Interviews Fetzer, John—Sale of the Tigers [October 14, 1983]), R02.14836, 44; Bruce Fetzer Oral History, March 14, 1996, 37.

72. Carolyn Dailey Oral History, November 16, 2011, 3, 7, 12, 25–26, 29. Fetzer's copies of *A Course in Miracles*, extant in the archives, are original 1975 hardback editions published by the Foundation for Inner Peace. Fetzer even found the *Miracle* materials applicable to baseball, as he revealed in a talk he gave at an IONS board meeting at Asilomar, California, in July 1978. TB 18 (Research, Fetzer, Rhea—Diary & Letters [Transcripts] [Restricted] 1976–1979): "1978 Rhea Fetzer's Diary and Personal Correspondence," July 9, 1978, R02.14579. Hegedus relates that as late as 1987, John Fetzer was meeting with foundation staff to discuss *A Course in Miracles*. Hegedus, *John Earl Fetzer*, 212.

73. FP 5 (Correspondence 1978 III): John E. Fetzer to Elouise Ebel, October 25, 1978, R02.13888. Of course, Fetzer constantly sought confirmation of his positive evaluation of *Course* through the Ouija board. See for example Ouija Board Transcripts, July 16, 1976, August 7, 1979, JGC. He also asked Jesus if he were

indeed the author of the texts; the answer was yes. Ouija Board Transcripts, August 26, 1976, November 17, 1976, JGC.

74. Whitson Oral History, February 4, 2011, 7–8, 12.

75. Board Meeting Minutes (Binder 1): "John E. Fetzer Foundation, Inc. Annual Meeting," August 2, 1976.

76. Apparently, Fetzer's meeting with Helen Schucman hinged on the fact that he had used the word "shoehorn" in a letter to Whitson asking for the meeting; unbeknownst to Fetzer, Schucman had uttered the word "shoehorn" in a recent dream that she considered highly significant, although for reasons she did not explain. After this, Fetzer became somewhat obsessed with learning the symbolic meaning of "shoehorn." "Helen Schucman's Dream" ("I am standing in a small, rectangular room . . ."), n.d., JGC; Ouija Board Transcripts, November 11, 1976, December 17, 1979, May 21, 1979, August 7, 1979, August 24, 1979, JGC; "Interpretation of Schucman Dream by Kenneth Killick," June 6, 1979, JGC; Kenneth Killick to John E. Fetzer, June 19, 1979, JGC; Whitson Oral History, March 3, 2011, 19, 22–24, 26.

77. Whitson Oral History, February 4, 2011, 12–21, 26–29, 36–37; March 9, 2011, 23–32; April 7, 2011, 24–38; TB 18 (Research, Fetzer, Rhea—Diary & Letters [Transcripts] [Restricted] 1976–1979): "1978 Rhea Fetzer's Diary and Personal Correspondence," April 6 and July 1–6, 1978, R02.14579; FI 9 (Institute of Noetic Sciences 1979): "List of Attendees: Quail Roost Conference Center," December 9–12, 1978, R02.13168. Marilyn Ferguson in her *Aquarian Conspiracy* wrote about the Quail's Roost Conference, citing it as the epitome of New Age leadership and networking (202–5), and although the attendees are not mentioned by name, Fetzer was clearly "the owner of a major-league baseball team" (203). The agenda for this meeting (reproduced in *The Aquarian Conspiracy*) echoed many of the themes of Fetzer's "America's Agony":

> We tend to share a conviction that this nation, and industrialized society in general, is experiencing profound transformation. We perceive that the next decade could be perilous if we fail to understand the nature and transcendent potential of the transformation. We agree that at the heart of this transformation is a change in the basic social paradigm, including fundamental beliefs and values underlying the present form of the industrial economy. In our own positions in government, business, education, or professional life, we sense a deep need for the society to find its spiritual moorings, its sense of destiny, of right direction. We seek the support and comradeship of others of

like mind, confident that when minds are joined in common search and purpose, the effect is amplified. We recognize that our country was guided in its initial decades by this kind of joining of minds in common purpose. It is in keeping with these shared convictions that the meeting be quite unstructured. There will be no chairperson. There is no agenda. There will be no speeches. Simply come prepared to share your deepest hopes and concerns. We have no specific expectations for what may emerge from this meeting. (203)

78. TB 18 (Research, Fetzer, Rhea—Diary & Letters [Transcripts] [Restricted] 1976–1979): "1978 Rhea Fetzer's Diary and Personal Correspondence," March 30, 1978, R02.14579; Whitson Oral History, April 7, 2011, 2–5. It so happened that when Fetzer phoned Whitson, she was hosting a dinner party. About the incident, Fetzer later wrote, "There was a very strange coincidence in connection with all of this. I called a friend in San Francisco who along with me for years has been interested in parapsychological matters. I found her at a house party with 35 guests. While a lot of the people there were friends of hers, most of them did not know Rhea or me. In any event, they stopped their proceedings, held hands and sent a silent prayer to Rhea. Shortly after that Rhea improved remarkably." FP 5 (Correspondence 1978 I): John E. Fetzer to Homer L. Fetzer, April 18, 1978, R02.13886.

79. Whitson Oral History, March 9, 2011, 24–44; March 30, 2011, 55; Hegedus, *John Earl Fetzer*, 142–43; Hegedus Interviews Binder: "Judy Whitson notes," n.d.; Fetzer, *Men from Wengen*, 394. According to Whitson, the LSD experience confirmed Fetzer's long-standing hesitancy to trust his spiritual gifts, a hesitancy stemming from his belief that during a past life in Egypt, he had abused such gifts. Whitson, personal communication, November 1, 2016. Apparently, Fetzer had earlier been in communication with Willis Harman, who supplied him with two of his academic articles on psychedelic drugs: Willis W. Harman, "The Issue of Consciousness Raising Drugs," *Main Currents in Modern Thought* 20, no. 1 (1963): 5–13; Harman, "Some Aspects of the Psychedelic-Drug Controversy," *Journal of Humanistic Psychology*, Fall 1963, 93–107. These can be found in the JGC with an attached memo from Harman to Fetzer dated July 10 (1978): "Here are a couple of the papers I mentioned (along with some the things Mike Murphy gave me to give you)."

80. Lloyd Swierenga Oral History, August 6, 2012, 7–8.

81. FI 12 (Keating, James 1973–1976 I): John E. Fetzer to James B. Keating, January 25, 1973, R02.13215; John E. Fetzer to Sister Mary J. Bader, February 5,

1973, R02.13215; Sister Mary L. Bader to John E. Fetzer, February 19, 1973, R02.13215; James Keating Oral History, April 28, 2011, 4–11.

82. FI 15 (Foundation Grants History): "John E. Fetzer Foundation History: Grants," n.d., R02.13288; FI 12 (Keating, James 1973–1976 I): James Keating to John E. Fetzer, September 5, 1973, R02.13215; Keating Oral History, April 28, 2011, 22, 42–44.

83. See, for example, FI 12 (Keating, James 1973–1976 I): James Keating to John E. Fetzer, April 19, 1974, May 1, 1975, March 22, 1976, R02.13215; FI 12 (Keating, James 1973–1976 II): James Keating to John E. Fetzer, December 2, 1976, R02.13216. See also FI 12 (Keating, James 1973–1976 I): "Proposal for a Mid-West Center for Research and Development of Psychic Sciences," May 10, 1974, R02.13215.

84. FI 12 (Keating, James 1973–1976 I): "Proposal for a Mid-West Center for Research and Development of Psychic Sciences," May 10, 1974, R02.13215; FI 12 (Keating, James 1973–1976 I): James Keating to John E. Fetzer, September 5, 1973, May 1, 1975, March 22, 1976, June 1, 1976, R02.13215; Keating Oral History, April 28, 2011, 8, 14, 20–21, 31–33. Swierenga was the president of a company called CLEAR (Creative Logic Ethic Adaptation & Returns). Board Meeting Minutes (Binder 2): "Report to Board of Trustees John E. Fetzer Foundation, Inc.," March 22, 1984; Kenneth Killick (see the following text in this chapter) was vice president of this company. FI 9 (Inner Light Ministries [1979–1990]): "Business Card of Kenneth Killick," R02.13156.

85. Keating Oral History, April 28, 2011, 8, 14, 16–17, 20, 31–33; Spence Oral History, December 18, 1996, 13–14, 18–22. Information on Killick is sparse: in addition to an incomplete copy of his résumé in the Fetzer archives (FI 12 [James Keating, 1973–1976 II]: "Kenneth Killick Resume," n.d., R02.13216), details in the paragraph following are from Dean Hardy, Mary Hardy, Marjorie Killick, and Kenneth Killick, *Pyramid Energy: The Philosophy of God, the Science of Man* (Allegan, MI: Delta-K Pyramid Products of America, 1987), FPL, 2, 4–6, 58, 109, 146–51, 329–30, 340, 351–56. An inscribed copy of this book exists in Fetzer's personal library ("John, To a friend of Light—May your wishes lead humanity into the Christed Light of the Father. Love & Light, Mary Hardy"). It was probably a copy of this book that Fetzer sent to Brenda Dunne, the wife and colleague of Robert Jahn's, in 1979. FI 16 (Princeton University—Robert Jahn [PK research] 1978–1986 III): Brenda Dunne to John E. Fetzer, n.d. but before November 1, 1979, R02.13315. *Pyramid Energy* incorporates and expands on two earlier books by Mary Hardy, Dean Hardy, and Kenneth Killick: *Pyramid Energy Explained* (Allegan, MI: Delta-K Pyramid Products

of America, 1979), FPL; and *Pyramid Energy and the Second Coming* (Allegan, MI: Delta-K Pyramid Products of America, 1981), FPL, both of which, with Fetzer's extensive underlining, can also be found in Fetzer's personal library, the former bearing an inscription from James Keating (May 1975) and the latter from Mary Hardy. Fetzer had long been interested in pyramids, not only Egyptian but also those of Central America: "To build the Pyramids as they did [in Mexico and Guatemala], they had to have advanced knowledge of trigonometry, calculus, and artistic development comparable to anything we know in our day." FP 3 (Correspondence 1951): John E. Fetzer to Folks, April 14, 1951, R02.13844.

86. FI 12 (James Keating, 1973–1976 II): "Kenneth Killick Resume," n.d., R02.13216.

87. Hardy et al., *Pyramid Energy*, 2, 4, 21, 109, 148–51, 60–61, 329–30; Keating Oral History, April 28, 2011, 32–35; Swierenga Oral History, August 6, 2012, 4; Spence Oral History, December 18, 1996, 13–14. Killick was also adept at constructing medicine wheels. Hardy et al., *Pyramid Energy*, 185–201.

88. FI 12 (Keating, James 1973–1976 I): James Keating to John E. Fetzer, May 1, 1975; John E. Fetzer to James Keating, May 12, 1975; James Keating to John E. Fetzer, June 1, 1976, R02.13215.

89. According to Mary Hardy's account, she and her husband, Dean, and their two young sons were then returning home from a trip to Indiana. Tired from their day traveling, they had decided to stop to take a break and get some exercise when they saw what they thought were headlights but that then "stretched out and disappeared." They then felt a strong but invisible presence and, after checking their watches, found that they had lost some forty-five minutes of time. Hardy et al., *Pyramid Energy*, 3–4.

90. Hardy et al., *Pyramid Energy*, 2, 3–7, 9–10, 27–35, 67, 110, 132–45, 156–84, 149, 326; Dean Hardy, "New Construction Technique for Maximum Pyramid Energy," *Journal for Borderland Research* 32, no. 4 (1976): 7–9. Local newspapers quickly picked up the story: Walt Lockwood, "A Peak at the Secrets of the Pyramids," *Grand Rapids Press*, August 28, 1977; Jan Weist, "Allegan Family . . . It's Like 'Star Wars,'" *Detroit News*, September 8, 1978 (copies of both articles can be found in JGC). The Hardys were also featured as a case study of "unorthodox science" in Henry, "Unorthodox Science as a Popular Activity."

91. FI 12 (Keating, James 1973–1976 II): James Keating to John E. Fetzer, September 28, 1976, December 2, 1976; John E. Fetzer to James B. Keating, December 17, 1976, R02.13216; Ouija Board Transcripts, June 13, 1977, JGC; Keating Oral History, April 28, 2011, 23–24, 28–34, 36–37; Dean and Mary Hardy Oral History, May 11, 2011, 1–56. Fetzer visited the pyramids on several occasions. E.g.

Ouija Board Transcripts, June 13, 1977, July 3, 1979, July 16, 1980, JGC; TB 18 (Research, Fetzer, Rhea—Diary & Letters [Transcripts] [Restricted] 1976–1979): "1979 Rhea Fetzer's Diary and Personal Correspondence," October 10–13, 1979, R02.14579; Jim Keating to John E. Fetzer, undated notecard with mimeographed articles by the Hardys, JGC.

92. Swierenga Oral History, August 6, 2012, 4–6, 15–16; Michael Gergely Oral History, May 9, 1998, 76–78, 97, 106–7; TB 18 (Research Fetzer, Rhea—Diaries & Letters [Transcripts] [Restricted] 1980–1981): "1980 Rhea Fetzer's Diary and Personal Correspondence," October 25, 1980, December 7, 1980, R02.14580. With regard to Killick's engineering experience, Fetzer had great interest in the AVRO car project, illustrating it in his 1974 UFO talk with a plate taken from Leonard G. Cramp's *Space Gravity and the Flying Saucer*; Killick also apparently claimed to have built a subtle-energy "health machine" based on Atlantian designs. Ouija Board Transcripts, July 2, 1980, JGC.

93. FI 12 (James Keating, 1973–1976 II): John E. Fetzer to Kenneth Killick, October 4, 1980, R02.13216. Fetzer also told Killick about his dealings with Clifford Burdick (see note 13 to chapter 5) and his "exploratory program in Mexico which seemingly is dealing with fabulous amounts of gold hidden away in secret passages by earlier Indian tribes." While Fetzer was now sure that Burdick was a con man, he apparently was still confident that the gold actually existed.

94. Indeed, a copy of a letter concerning the Great Seal of the United States was blind copied to Killick, indicating Fetzer wanted Killick's input. FI 9 (Institute of Noetic Science 1981): John E. Fetzer to Willis H. Harmon, March 24, 1981, R02.13170.

95. Bruce Fetzer Oral History, March 14, 1996, 50–51; Monday Night Group Oral History (Carolyn Dailey, Bruce Fetzer, Mike Gergely, Sister Elizabeth Reis), August 3, 2011, 10–12, 69; Richard Williams Oral History, May 13, 2011, 17–20; Denise Killick, daughter of Kenneth Killick, personal communication, May 31, 2016; Bruce Fetzer, personal communication, October 26, 2016. For an indication of Fetzer's changed attitude toward Killick, see John E. Fetzer to Jim Gordon, November 4, 1981, JGC; John E. Fetzer to Jim Gordon, September 3, 1982, JGC. In an undated letter to which the November 4, 1981, letter was probably a response, Jim Gordon (see chapter 9) warned Fetzer not to have further dealings with Killick, claiming that Killick had been an adversary when Fetzer was ruler of Atlantis in a past life. Jim Gordon to John E. Fetzer, n.d., JGC. In 1982, Fetzer asked the Ouija board, "Has Kenneth gone over the horizon for good?"; the reply was yes. Ouija Board Transcripts, May 18, 1982, JGC.

96. FI 7 (Foundation Correspondence 1981–1984): Kenneth Killick to Carolyn Dailey, October 3, 1981, R02.13110. Apparently, this was a retyped copy of a handwritten original. The letter also mentions that attached to it was "the promised outline that may be useful in firming up the direction of the 'John Earl Fetzer Foundation.'" An undated "John E. Fetzer Foundation Statement of Purpose" follows it in the file, but it is not clear that this is the outline referred to. It is divided between "personal goals," which call on the "Masters of Light" to help individuals to find the "I AM" within and redeem them from the cycle of rebirth to allow them to become "channels of Light, channels of the Spirit"; and "overall goals of the Foundation," namely, to follow the "Trinity principle" ("the *Father*, service to humanity; the *Son*, study to balance the mental and emotional; and the *Holy Spirit*, meditation to bring forth the Light of the soul in man") and to use "spiritual energies" for "bringing about physical healing on an individual level." See also Spence Oral History, December 18, 1996, 28, 34. Of Killick's later psychic career, little is known; he committed suicide in 1998. Denise Killick, personal communication, May 31, 2016.

9. Fetzer's Psychic Advisor

1. TB 31 (Interviews Fetzer, John—Early years [Trip to Lafayette], October 28, 1982), R02.14835, 9–10, 26.

2. The foundation had already benefited from substantial stock holdings and business ownerships that Fetzer donated to it in the 1970s. Bruce Fetzer Oral History, March 15, 1996, 74–76. But these were not liquid assets.

3. Bruce Fetzer contends that with each sale, John Fetzer suffered a major health crisis. Bruce Fetzer Oral History, December 11, 2002, 48.

4. Hegedus, *John Earl Fetzer*, 98.

5. TB 31 (Fetzer Interview, October 14, 1983): "Selling the Tigers," October 14, 1983, R02.14836, 42–44; Sloane Oral History, December 28, 1995, 41; Bruce Fetzer Oral History, March 15, 1996, 74–76; Whitson Oral History, March 9, 2011, 23; Spence Oral History, December 18, 1996, 52–53.

6. Fetzer had actually transferred controlling interest in the Detroit Tigers to the foundation, so the foundation board, which was well aware of Fetzer's desire to sell, voted to allow him to negotiate with Monaghan and voted to approve the sale. Board Meeting Minutes (Binder 2): "John E. Fetzer Foundation, Inc. Annual Minutes," August 16, 1982, August 1, 1983, September 12, 1983, September 12, 1983, October 5, 1983; and "Special Meeting Board of Trustees John E. Fetzer

Foundation, Inc.," December 20, 1983. See also James R. Gordon Oral History, November 16, 1996, 98–99.

7. Board Meeting Minutes (Binder 2): "Regarding Sale of Fetzer Television Companies, Report of Executive Committee to Trustees John E. Fetzer Foundation," July 17, 1985; "John E. Fetzer Foundation, Inc. Annual Meeting," August 1, 1985; and "Report of Executive Committee to Trustees John. E. Fetzer Foundation, Inc.," November 8, 1985; Fetzer, *America's Agony*, 83.

8. Bruce Fetzer Oral History, March 15, 1996, 83.

9. Kool, "Enlightenment and the Oldest Tiger," 34–41.

10. FP 6 (Correspondence 1981): John E. Fetzer to Harriet ("Hattie") Thomas, April 23, 1981, R02.13895; FP 11: (Harriett Thomas Correspondence 1967–1984 II): Harriet ("Hattie") Thomas to John E. Fetzer, n.d., R02.14016.

11. Hegedus, *John Earl Fetzer*, 138–39. Hegedus cites 1973 as the date of the publication of *A Course in Miracles* and 1974 as the year Fetzer received it from Whitson and the beginning of the *Course* group; however, this is incorrect, since Whitson did not receive the *Course* manuscripts until 1975 (see chapter 8).

12. For Gergely's relationship with John Fetzer, see Gergely Oral History, May 9, 1998, 68–76.

13. Most of the following information is taken from Gordon Oral History, November 14–15, 1996.

14. Gordon Oral History, November 14, 1996, 23–24, 37, 61–62. IPM was founded in 1964 by Francisco Coll; see James R. Lewis, *Encyclopedia of Cults, Sects, and New Religious Movements* (Amherst, NY: Prometheus Books, 2002), 418. For Bateman, see Diane Ladd, *Spiraling through the School of Life* (Carlsbad, CA: Hay House, 2006), 83–84.

15. Hamid Bey, *My Experiences Preceding 5,000 Burials* (1938; Whitefish, MT: Kessinger, 2006). See also Lewis, *Encyclopedia of Cults, Sects, and New Religious Movements*, 256–57.

16. Gordon Oral History, November 14, 1996, 37–53. Some of Gordon's Coptic lectures and channelings of Hamid Bey can be found in the Fetzer Archives. FI 5 (Fetzer, John E.—Jim Gordon 1980–1985 II, V, VI), R02.13050, 53, 54.

17. Gordon Oral History, November 15, 1996, 53–65.

18. FI 5 (Fetzer, John E.—Jim Gordon 1980–1985 XIV): "Conversation with Jim Gordon," August 26, 1981, R02.13062; FI 5 (Fetzer, John E.—Jim Gordon 1980–1985 XIV): Archangel Michael to John E. Fetzer, January 5, 1982, R02.13062 (the handwritten original can be found in the JGC).

19. Gordon Oral History, November 15, 1996, 53–66, 83–84; Gergely Oral History, May 9, 1998, 82–90. Gergely, too, was convinced of Gordon's psychic powers,

having experienced Gordon's ability to travel astrally. Gergely Oral History, May 9, 1998, 92–96.

20. Jim Gordon to John E. Fetzer, July 22, 1983, JGC; John E. Fetzer to Jim Gordon, July 27, 1983, JGC; FI 5 (Fetzer, John E.—Jim Gordon 1980–1985 XI): "Channeling," September 21, 1983, R02.13059 (the handwritten original can be found in the JGC); Gordon Oral History, November 15, 1996, 66–82, 88. Gordon continued to lecture for the Coptic Fellowship of America until 1986. Gordon Oral History, November 15, 1996, 52. John Fetzer was already aware of the Coptic Fellowship before he met Gordon, having had come across Hamid Bey's memoir, *My Experiences Preceding 5,000 Burials*, in the bibliography for James, *They Live in the Sky*, 271; moreover, for a time, Killick's Michigan branch of Les Initiés partnered with the Coptic Fellowship and Spiritual Frontiers Fellowship in Grand Rapids. See the materials in FI 9 (Inner Light Ministries 1979–1990), R02.13156. Fetzer also attended at least one Coptic Fellowship Conference in Albion in May 1982. John E. Fetzer to Jim Gordon, July 27, 1983, JGC; Bruce Fetzer, personal communication, November 10, 2015. In part, this was to hear Jim Gordon speak, but it was also because Fetzer was intrigued by Coptic ideas: his extensively annotated copies of the 104 lessons of *The Sacred Teachings of the Coptic Fellowship of America* are in the Fetzer Institute's library; Fetzer reportedly took initiation in the Coptics' ministerial order of Ankh. Bruce Fetzer, personal communication, November 10, 2015. And he continued to make donations to the Coptic Fellowship until at least 1989. FP 11 (Contributions and Donations 1987–1990): John Davis to John E. Fetzer, February 15, 1989, R02.14006. Moreover, a document exists that suggests that Jim Gordon envisioned a close working relationship between the Coptics and the Fetzer Foundation. "Jim Gordon in JEF's Office," July 16, 1984, JGC.

21. For a good overview of channeling in the United States during this period, see Klimo, *Channeling*.

22. Gordon Oral History, November 15, 1996, 71–72; FI 5 (Fetzer, John E.—Jim Gordon 1980–1985 XIV): Archangel Michael to John E. Fetzer, January 5, 1982, R02.13062 (the handwritten original can be found in the JGC). Gordon also encouraged Fetzer to record his dreams, which they would discuss; several of these recorded dreams are preserved. FP 10 (Fetzer, John E.—Dreams 1972–1985 I–III), R02.13986–88. Gordon sent Fetzer a lengthy paper on dreams and dream interpretation. "Dreams by Jim Gordon," May 6, 1982, R02.13050. Later, Gordon gave a seminar in dreams and dream interpretation to the Fetzer Foundation staff. "Seminar on Dreams and Meditation with JEF Staff," August 22, 1985, JGC.

23. Much of the information for this paragraph is from the Monday Night Group Oral History (Carolyn Dailey, Bruce Fetzer, Mike Gergely, Sister Elizabeth Reis), August 3, 2011; see also Gordon Oral History, November 15, 1996, 70–71; and Gergely Oral History, May 9, 1998, 100–107.

24. Zolen was the widow of Gergely's deceased law partner, and it was Zolen who recommended Gergely to Fetzer as personal attorney. Gergely Oral History, May 9, 1998, 68–69, 72, 89–90.

25. Cleora Daily Oral History, October 5, 2011, 1–13; Hardy et al., *Pyramid Energy*, 231. Daily at some point cast Fetzer's horoscope: "Decatur, Indiana, March 25, 1901 at 7pm (which is a guess). Pluto moon Neptune conjunction in Gemini . . . means real sensitivity. Emotional need in communication. Dual nature . . . private re his spiritual life. Conjunct pluto. Emotional need to work with the Public. Venus = romantic idealist. Libra rising—likes to keep things harmonious." Hegedus Interviews Binder: "Cleora Daily Notes," n.d.

26. Fetzer later took Silva mind training from José Silva himself in Detroit. Monday Night Group Oral History, August 3, 2011, 47–48. Much Silva Mind Control material can be found in the Fetzer archives: see FP 11 (Reis, Sister Elizabeth [1981–1985 I–VI]), R02.14008–13. Fetzer also completed Sister Liz's "Art of Listening" workshop on January 28, 1984, accompanied by the Monday Night Group and Jim Gordon. FP 11 (Reis, Sister Elizabeth [1981–1985 I]), R02.14009. It was during this workshop that Jim Gordon had an astral experience and identified the chapel at Nazareth College as one of a few "Interdimensional Teletransport Systems" in the world. FI 5 (Fetzer, John E.—Jim Gordon 1980–1985 X): untitled, January 28, 1983, R02.13058.

27. Bruce Fetzer Oral History, March 14, 1996, 21–48; December 11, 2002, 1–13; December 12, 2002, 67–75.

28. John E. Fetzer to Jim Gordon, January 5, 1982, JGC; FI 5 (Fetzer, John E.—Jim Gordon 1980–1985 XI): "Channeling," June 18, 1983, R02.13059 (the handwritten original is in the JGC); John E. Fetzer to Jim Gordon, July 27, 1983, JGC.

29. John E. Fetzer to Jim Gordon, November 15, 1982, JGC; Monday Night Group Oral History, August 3, 2011; Gordon Oral History, November 15, 1996, 71, 155; Gergely Oral History, May 9, 1998, 107–111; Bruce Fetzer Oral History, December 12, 2002, 70; Sister Elizabeth Reis and Carolyn Dailey, personal communication, November 5, 2016. A copy of the ritual with Gordon's comments can be found in FI 5 (Fetzer, John E.—Jim Gordon 1980–1985 I): "Special Meditation," n.d., R02.13049. Gordon started developing the ritual back in 1970. "Meditation 'The Master in the Heart,'" Spring 1970, JGC.

30. Most of the Ouija board sessions made reference to the idea of group reincarnation, but for an explicit statement by Fetzer, see Ouija Board Transcripts, May 21, 1981, JGC; for Jim Gordon's confirmation, see Jim Gordon to John E. Fetzer, October 17, 1981, JGC; FI 5 (Fetzer, John E.—Jim Gordon 1980–1985 XIV): "J. Gordon," December 20, 21, 1981, R02.13062; John E. Fetzer to Jim Gordon, October 7, 1981, JGC; FI 5 (Fetzer, John E.—Jim Gordon 1980–1985 XIV): Archangel Michael to John E. Fetzer, January 5, 1982, R02.13062 (the handwritten original can be found in the JGC); Jim Gordon to John Fetzer, January 20, 1982, JGC; FI 5 (Fetzer, John E.—Jim Gordon 1980–1985 XIV): Jim Gordon to John E. Fetzer, March 2, 1982, R02.13059 (the handwritten original can be found in the JGC); FI 5 (Fetzer, John E.—Jim Gordon 1980–1985 XI): Jim Gordon to John E. Fetzer and all, August 24, 1982, R02.13059 (the handwritten original can be found in the JGC); Jim Gordon to John E. Fetzer, September 13, 1982, JGC; Jim Gordon to Mike Gergely, 1982, JGC; FI 5 (Fetzer, John E.—Jim Gordon 1980–1985 X): Cato and Jesus to the Foundation, May 1983, R02.13058; FI 9 (Inner Light Institute 1984 I): "Inner Light Establishment Jim Gordon," July 16–20, 1984, R02.13154. In an interview with Kaye Averitt in 1984 in response to the question, "Were you together before?" Fetzer said, "Yes. We've been associated innumerable times before. When you understand the principles of reincarnation, all of your groupies come back, they all find each other in life after life. They all come back about the same time, and fulfill different capacities each time they come back. Just as it did with Lynne [Carolyn Dailey], with you and innumerable people around me. We've all been associated before." TB 31 (Interviews Fetzer, John E.—Family, Spirituality [Lafayette], October 28, 1982), R02.14835, 10; see also Whitson Oral History, March 30, 2011, 32, 36.

31. FI 5 (Fetzer, John E.—Jim Gordon 1980–1985 XIV): "J. Gordon," December 20, 21, 1981, R02.13062; FI 5 (Fetzer, John E.—Jim Gordon 1980–1985 XI): Jim Gordon to John E. Fetzer, March 2, 1982, R02.13059; FI 5 (Fetzer, John E.—Jim Gordon 1980–1985 XI): Jim Gordon to John E. Fetzer, June 4, 1982, R02.13059 (the handwritten original can be found in JGC). In one 1982 channeling session, Jim Gordon put the foundation's mission in the context of the prophecies of the Book of Revelation, to which Fetzer responded enthusiastically: "So this is putting our whole thrust of activity into focus, much more into focus with me personally because now we are apparently identified with all these events on a world basis and this is something I have not had a part of my envisionment as what was to happen. I knew that we were going to principally be dealing with the holistic health thrust of instrumentation. I didn't realize that

the foundation itself might be active on this world basis, of the new Jerusalem." "Revelations—Jim Gordon," May 24, 1982, JGC.

32. FI 5 (Fetzer, John E.—Jim Gordon 1980–1985 X): "Jim Gordon—Cato and High Master," July 12, 1983, R02.13058; FI 5 (Fetzer, John E.—Jim Gordon 1980–1985 X): memo from John E. Fetzer, May 1983, R02.13058. See also FI 5 (Fetzer, John E.—Jim Gordon 1980–1985 XV): "Channeling," November 2, 1984, R02.13063. In a later channeling, this parallel between the founding of the nation and the founding of the foundation was reiterated by none other than Abraham Lincoln himself. FI 5 (Fetzer, John E.—Jim Gordon 1980–1985 X, XVI): "Channeling," November 3–4, 1984, R02.13058, 64.

33. FI 5 (Fetzer, John E.—Jim Gordon 1980–1985 XI): Jim Gordon to John E. Fetzer, March 4, 1982, R02.13059 (the handwritten original can be found in the JGC); FI 5 (Fetzer, John E.—Jim Gordon 1980–1985 XI): Channeling from Michael to John E. Fetzer, April 29, 1982, R02.13059 (handwritten original can be found in JGC); FI 5 (Fetzer, John E.—Jim Gordon 1980–1985 XI): Jim Gordon to John E. Fetzer, June 4, 1982, R02.13059; FI 5 (Fetzer, John E.—Jim Gordon 1980–1985 XI): "Jim Gordon," July 12, 1982, R02.13059; FI 5 (Fetzer, John E.—Jim Gordon 1980–1985 XI): Jim Gordon to John E. Fetzer, August 13, 1982, R02.13059; FI 5 (Fetzer, John E.—Jim Gordon 1980–1985 XI): Jim Gordon to John E. Fetzer and all, August 24, 1982, R02.13059; FI 5 (Fetzer, John E.—Jim Gordon 1980–1985 XI): "Jim Gordon," October 28, 1982, R02.13059; FI 5 (Fetzer, John E.—Jim Gordon 1980–1985 XI): Jim Gordon to John E. Fetzer, February 10, 1983, R02.13059; FI 5 (Fetzer, John E.—Jim Gordon 1980–1985 X): Cato and Jesus to the Foundation, May 1983, R02.13058; FI 7 (Foundation Correspondence 1981–1984): "Potential Goals from Channeling," n.d., R0.213110; FI 5 (Fetzer, John E.—Jim Gordon 1980–1985 XVI): "Channeling," January 24, 1985, R02.13064.

34. FI 5 (Fetzer, John E.—Jim Gordon 1980–1985 XI): "Archangel Michael Channeling," August 13, 1982, R02.13059; FI 5 (Fetzer, John E.—Jim Gordon 1980–1985 XI): "Archangel Michael Channeling," August 14, 1982, R02.13059 (the handwritten original can be found in the JGC).

35. FI 7 (Foundation Correspondence 1981–1984): "Statement of Purpose," n.d., R0.213110. According to Bruce Fetzer, the "Statement" "was channeled by Jim Gordon, and edited by John Fetzer. Carolyn Dailey, Chuck Spence, Bruce Fetzer, and the Monday night group reviewed it and thought it was consistent with the early vision of the Foundation." Bruce Fetzer to Rob Lehman, memo, "History of the Fetzer Foundation Commitment," revised September 6, 2006.

36. FI 5 (Fetzer, John E.—Jim Gordon 1980–1985 XIV): Jim Gordon to John E. Fetzer, February 5, 1982, R02.13062; FI 5 (Fetzer, John E.—Jim Gordon 1980–1985 XI): Jim Gordon to John E. Fetzer, March 2, 4, 1982, R02.13059 (the handwritten original can be found in the JGC).

37. FI 5 (Fetzer, John E.—Jim Gordon 1980–1985 XI): "Channeling," September 21, 1983, R02.13059 (the handwritten original can be found in the JGC).

38. The Masters of the Inner Light made their appearance in the following channelings: FI 5 (Fetzer, John E.—Jim Gordon 1980–1985 XI): Cato to John E. Fetzer, January 26, 1983, R02.13059 (the handwritten original can be found in the JGC); FI 5 (Fetzer, John E.—Jim Gordon 1980–1985 XI): Inner Masters of Light to John E. Fetzer, February 9, 1983, R02.13059 (the handwritten original can be found in the JGC); FI 5 (Fetzer, John E.—Jim Gordon 1980–1985 XI): Cato to John E. Fetzer, February 23, 1983, R02.13059 (the handwritten original can be found in the JGC). See also FI 9 (Inner Light Institute 1984 I): "Inner Light Establishment Jim Gordon," July 16–20, 1984, R02.13154: "We [Masters of the Inner Light] have gone through many of the lessons of the lower planes as well as the inner planes of spirit, and have merged back into at-one-ment in God. In that full at-one-ment, we have become co-creators, co-manifesters in the light of God, in the full awareness of God. In that state, we have move beyond God itself" (16). It is interesting to note that the council of the Masters of the Inner Light was run much like a board meeting, complete with council chambers and agendas; this was something to which Fetzer could obviously relate. E.g. FI 5 (Fetzer, John E.—Jim Gordon 1980–1985 XV): "Channeling," November 2, 1984, R02.13063. Later, Gordon in his channelings would apparently refer to the Masters of the Inner Light as the "Silent Ones." FI 5 (Fetzer, John E.—Jim Gordon 1980–1985 XVII): "Channeling," January 28, 1985, R02.13065.

39. Gordon was first paid a consulting fee beginning in June 1982. Board Meeting Minutes (Binder 2): "Report of Executive Committee to Trustees John E. Fetzer Foundation, Inc.," June 23, 1982; and "John E. Fetzer Foundation Statement of Earnings and Contributions made for Year ended [July 31, 1982]." Regarding Inner Light Publications, see Jim Gordon to John E. Fetzer, June 17, 1983, JGC; Lynne Dailey to John E. Fetzer, June 30, 1983, JGC; Board Meeting Minutes (Binder 2): "Report to Executive Committee to Trustees John E. Fetzer Foundation, Inc.," July 25, 1983, August 1, 1983; John E. Fetzer to Jim Gordon, July 27, 1983, JGC; Board Meeting Minutes (Binder 2): "Research Grant Application and Grant Proposal (Historical Documentation and Publication of Spiritual Healing Doctrines and Techniques)," July 21, 1983; and "Memorandum of Executive Committee to the Trustees John E. Fetzer Foundation, Inc.," August 19, 1983.

One of the books was to be on ancient Egypt and have illustrations by the noted painter of esoteric subjects Arthur Douët. Board Meeting Minutes (Binder 2): "Report of Executive Committee to Trustees John E. Fetzer Foundation, Inc.," January 19, 1984; see also FI 5 (Fetzer, John E.—Jim Gordon 1980–1985 XV): "Channeling," November 2, 1984, R02.13063. A chapter of this book can be found in the Fetzer archives. FI 5 (Fetzer, John E.—Jim Gordon 1980–1985 I): "Angels in Egypt," July 19, 1984, R02.13049.

40. FI 5 (Fetzer, John E.—Jim Gordon 1980–1985 XI): Jim Gordon to John E. Fetzer, July 21, 1984, R02.13059 (the original handwritten letter can be found in the JGC); see also FI 9 (Inner Light Institute 1984 I): "Inner Light Establishment Jim Gordon," July 16–20, 1984, R02.13154. An earlier channeling from Cato had already made this distinction between Fetzer's physical mission and Gordon's spiritual one, although Cato assured Fetzer that he was nevertheless a "Master in the Spirit but in service in the physical." FI 5 (Fetzer, John E.—Jim Gordon 1980–1985 XI): "Channeling," September 21, 1983, R02.13059 (the handwritten original can be found in the JGC).

41. For the creation of the Inner Light Institute (sometimes called the International Institute for Inner Light [III]), see FI 9 (Inner Light Institute 1984 I): "Inner Light Establishment Jim Gordon," July 16–20, 1984, R02.13154; FI 5 (Fetzer, John E.—Jim Gordon 1980–1985 XIV-XV): "Channeling," October 30, 1984, R02.13062, 63; FI 5 (Fetzer, John E.—Jim Gordon 1980–1985 XV): "Channeling," November 2, 1984, R02.13063; FI 5 (Fetzer, John E.—Jim Gordon 1980–1985 X, XVI): "Channeling," November 3–4, 1984, R02.13058, 64; FI 9 (Inner Light Institute 1984 II): Bruce F. Fetzer to John E. Fetzer, December 4, 1984 (amended December 10), R02.13155; FI 5 (Fetzer, John E.—Jim Gordon 1980–1985 XVI-XVII): "Channeling," January 24, 29, 1985, R02.13064–65. To save time and effort in securing tax-exempt status, Fetzer secured control from Lloyd Swierenga of the Michigan branch of Les Initiés and converted this into the Inner Light Institute. FI 9 (Inner Light Institute 1984 II): John E. Fetzer to Jerry Luptak, December 12, 1984, R02.13155; FI 7 (Foundation Correspondence 1985–1986): John E. Fetzer to David York, January 8, 1985, R02.13111; FI 1 (ARE Clinic 1985–1989 III): EMD to JDL, January 30, 1986, R02.12976; Swierenga Oral History, August 6, 2012, 17. Financial and other materials from Les Initiés can be found in the Fetzer archives. FI 9 (Inner Light Ministries 1979–1990), R02.13156; and FI 9 (Inner Light Ministries Bank Statements 1979–1981, 1982–1984, 1985–1987), R02.13157–59. For Inner Light Ministries, see FI 9 (Inner Light Ministries & Fetzer Foundation Jim Gordon, July 1985): "Jim Gordon Inner Light Ministries and Fetzer Foundation," July 31, 1985,

R02.13163; Board Meeting Minutes (Binder 3): Addenda #1 to "John E. Fetzer Foundation, Inc. Board of Trustees Meeting," February 27, 1988; and "John E. Fetzer Foundation, Inc. Executive Committee Phone Meeting," September 15, 1988; FI 9 (Inner Light Ministries Hawaii Property 1990 II): John E. Fetzer to Jay Fishman, September 6, 1990, R02.13161; FI 9 (Inner Light Ministries Hawaii Property 1990 II): Jim Gordon to John E. Fetzer, September 14, 1990, R02.13161; Gordon Oral History, November 15, 1996, 129–31. Further correspondence concerning the donation of the Hawaii real estate to Inner Light Ministries can be found in FI 9 (Inner Light Ministries Hawaii Property 1990 I–III), R02.13160–62.

42. FI 5 (Fetzer, John E.—Jim Gordon 1980–1985 XIV): "Channeling," December 21, 1981, R02.13062; FI 5 (Fetzer, John E.—Jim Gordon 1980–1985 XI): Michael to John E. Fetzer, April 29, 1982, R02.13059 (handwritten original can be found in JGC); Jim Gordon to John E. Fetzer, September 13, 1982, JGC; FI 5 (Fetzer, John E.—Jim Gordon 1980–1985 X): Cato and Jesus to the Foundation, May 1983, R02.13058; FI 5 (Fetzer, John E.—Jim Gordon 1980–1985 IV): "Master Paul the Venetian Channeling," January 13, 1984, R02.13052 (the handwritten original can be found in the JGC); FI 5 (Fetzer, John E.—Jim Gordon 1980–1985 XIV–XV): "Cato," October 30, 1984, R02.13062, 63; FI 5 (Fetzer, John E.—Jim Gordon 1980–1985 X, XVI): "Channeling," November 3–4, 1984, R02.13058, 64; FI 5 (Fetzer, John E.—Jim Gordon 1980–1985 XVII): "Channeling," January 29, 1985, R02.13065. In a February 1984 channeling session in Tucson, Fetzer asked if Little Fox was the same being as Running Red Fox, who was identified as one of his spirit guides at Camp Chesterfield; he was told no, but both Indians had lived in the Tucson area. FI 5 (Fetzer, John E.—Jim Gordon 1980–1985 IV): "JEF Tape," February 1984, R02.13052, 15. Kuthumi (Koot Hoomi), Paul the Venetian, El Morya, and Hilarion are Masters originally found in the Theosophical tradition. See, for example, Anrias, *Through the Eyes of the Masters*.

43. FI 5 (Fetzer, John E.—Jim Gordon 1980–1985 X): Cato and Jesus to the Foundation, May 1983, R02.13058; FI 5 (Fetzer, John E.—Jim Gordon 1980–1985 XVI): "Channeling," January 24, 1985, R02.13064. The planet Clarion, permanently hidden from the earth by the moon, was first mentioned in the UFO classic by Truman Bethurum *Aboard a Flying Saucer*, a book Fetzer had in his personal library.

44. For the influence of the Coptic Fellowship of America, see Gordon's channelings of Hamid Bey (May 22, 23, 1981) in FI 5 (Fetzer, John E.—Jim Gordon 1980–1985 V–VI) "Channeling," R02.13053–54 and Gordon's essays

"Reincarnation" in FI 5 (Fetzer, John E.—Jim Gordon 1980–1985 II), R02.13050; "The World Beyond," "Master Disciple Relationship," and "The Coptic Order: Past, Present, and Future" in FI 5 (Fetzer, John E.—Jim Gordon 1980–1985 VI), R02.13054; and "Mysticism" in FI 5 (Fetzer, John E.—Jim Gordon 1980–1985 VII), R02.13055. Channeled discussion of the *Urantia Book* can be found in FI 5 (Fetzer, John E.—Jim Gordon 1980–1985 XVII): "Channeling," January 29, 1985, R02.13065. Also mentioned in the channelings: Rudolf Steiner (Anthroposophy) (FI 5 [Fetzer, John E.—Jim Gordon 1980–1985 X, XVI]): "Channeling," November 3–4, 1984, R02.13058, 64; Rosicrucians and Self-Realization Fellowship (SRF) (FI 5 [Fetzer, John E.—Jim Gordon 1980–1985 XV–XVI]: "Channeling," November 5, 1984, R02.13063–64).

45. See Mark Juergensmeyer, *Radhasoami Reality: The Logic of a Modern Faith* (Princeton, NJ: Princeton University Press, 1991); and Andrea Diem-Lane, *The Guru in America: The Influence of Radhasoami on New Religions* (Walnut, CA: Mt. San Antonio College, 2015).

46. "There are now three great Masters on the Earth who represent these 3 aspect[s] of truth. The Father is represented by the Eleven Ring Master of the Great Temple of the Coptic, the Son is represented by the Dalai Lama of Tibet, and the Holy Spirit is represented by the Rahdi Soami Charn Singh of India." "The Coptic Order: Past, Present, and Future," n.d., in FI 5 (Fetzer, John E.—Jim Gordon 1980–1985 VI), R02.13054.

47. Both volumes were in Fetzer's personal library and extensively annotated: Brunton, *Search in Secret India*; Julian Johnson, *The Path of the Masters: The Science of Surat Shabd Yoga: The Yoga of the Audible Life Stream* (1939; Punjab, India: Radha Soami Satsang Beas, 1972), FPL. The latter was a gift of Mike Wunderlin, who was also initiated in the tradition of Surat Shabd Yoga. Tom Beaver, personal communication, June 6, 2016.

48. Gordon Oral History, November 15, 1996, 153–55.

49. Ibid., 155–56; Cleora Daily Oral History, August 13, 2013, 13–17; Monday Night Group Oral History, August 3, 2011, 83–84. For more on SUN, see J. Gordon Melton, ed., *Encyclopedia of American Religions* (Farmington Hills, MI: Gale, 2003), 819. For more on MSIA, see Diem-Lane, *Guru in America*, 64–73; James R. Lewis, *Seeking the Light: Uncovering the Truth about the Movement of Spiritual Inner Awareness and Its Founder, John-Roger* (Los Angeles: Mandeville, 1998).

50. Lewis, *Seeking the Light*, 19–91 (Lewis estimates that the membership of MSIA in 1998 was "between five and six thousand"; 163); Glenn A. Rupert, "Employing

the New Age: Training Seminars" in *Perspectives on the New Age*, ed. James R. Lewis and J. Gordon Melton (Albany: State University of New York Press, 1992), 127–35.

51. FI 5 (Fetzer, John E.—Jim Gordon 1980–1985 XI): Jim Gordon to John Fetzer (Channeling), July 21, 1984, R02.13059; FI 5 (Fetzer, John E.—Jim Gordon 1980–1985 XIV–XV): "Tucson channelings," October 30, 1984, R02.13062, 63; FI 5 (Fetzer, John E.—Jim Gordon 1980–1985 XV): "Channeling," November 2, 1984, R02.13063; FI 5 (Fetzer, John E.—Jim Gordon 1980–1985 XV–XVI): "Channeling," November 5, 1984, R02.13063–64; FI 5 (Fetzer, John E.—Jim Gordon 1980–1985 XVII): "Channeling," January 28, 1985, R02.13065; FI 5 (Fetzer, John E.—Jim Gordon 1980–1985 XVII): "Channeling," January 30, 1985, R02.13065.

52. James R. Gordon Oral History, November 15, 1996, 150, 155–57; Cleora Daily Oral History, August 13, 2013, 13–20. Fetzer's initiations by and attitude toward John-Roger: Tom Beaver, personal communication, June 6, 2016; Bruce Fetzer, personal communication, October 26, 2016. Insight workshops: FP 14 (Insight II Opening Heart Seminar): "Registration Form for Insight II" and "Insight II Intake Form," November 11–15, 1987, R02.14087. Contributions to MSIA: FP 15 (Correspondence 1987): George Cappannelli and Alexandra McMullen to John Fetzer, October 29, 1987, R02.14099. Board and soul awareness: FI 6 (Fetzer, John E.—Remarks to Foundation Board Revised [April 24, 1989]): "Remarks to Foundation Board," March 3–4, 1989, R02.13080. Doubts about John-Roger: FP 10 (Fetzer, John E.—Dreams 1972–1985 II) "September 30 [1986?], am," R02.13986–87; Jim Gordon, personal communication, October 22, 2016.

53. FI 7 (Foundation Correspondence 1985–1986): Valerie Eisenberg to Milton G. Crane, January 15, 1986, R02.131111; FI 7 (Foundation Correspondence 1986 I): John E. Fetzer to Margaret H. Zolen, June 4, 1986, R02.131113. Fetzer had already been weakened by a bout of the shingles earlier that year: FP 10 (Fetzer, John E.—Dreams 1972–1985 III): "April 14, 15, 19; May 22 1985," R02.13988.

54. FI 7 (Foundation Correspondence 1986 II): Margaret and Frank Zolen to John E. Fetzer, May 27, 1986, R02.13113; FI 7 (Foundation Correspondence 1986 II): Margaret Zolen to the "Core Group" of the Fetzer Foundation, n.d., R02.13113; FI 7 (Foundation Correspondence 1986 II): John E. Fetzer to Margaret H. Zolen, June 4, 1986, R02.13113; Monday Night Group Oral History, August 3, 2011, 62–63.

55. FI 5 (Fetzer, John E.—Jim Gordon 1980–1985 X, XVI): "Channeling," November 3–4, 1984, R02.13058, 64; Bruce Fetzer, personal communication, October 20, 2015.

10. Building for the New Age

1. Carolyn Dailey Oral History, January 12, 2011; Monday Night Group Oral History, October 13, 2011, 25, 35–36.

2. Board Meeting Minutes (Binder 2): "Executive Committee Meeting Memorandum to Trustees John E. Fetzer Foundation," October 2, 1981.

3. Spence Oral History, December 18, 1996, January 10, 1997.

4. Board Meeting Minutes (Binder 2): July 11, 1983; "Report to the Board of Trustees John E. Fetzer Foundation, Inc.," March 22, 1984; and "John E. Fetzer Foundation, Inc. Annual Meeting," August 1, 1984; Bruce Fetzer Oral History, December 11, 2002, 36–39.

5. Board Meeting Minutes (Binder 2): "Executive Committee Meeting Memorandum to John E. Fetzer Foundation, Inc.," October 2, 1981; and "Report to the Board of Trustees John E. Fetzer Foundation, Inc.," March 22, 1984.

6. See the definition quoted in FI I (ARE Clinic 1985–1989 III): "Harvey Grady to Clinic Staff and Interested Persons," September 12, 1986, R02.12976.

7. For a brief history of energy medicine in the United States, see Catherine L. Albanese, "Energy Medicine: The Spiritual Culture of an Emerging Paradigm," *Odyssey* 3 (2000): 12–36. For more on the general history of alternative medicine in the United States, see James C. Whorton, *Nature Cures: The History of Alternative Medicine in America* (Oxford: Oxford University Press, 2002).

8. Board Meeting Minutes (Binder 2):"Memorandum of Executive Committee to Trustees Meeting John E. Fetzer Foundation, Inc.," September 16, 1981.

9. FI 16 (Princeton University—Jahn, Robert 1978–1986 IV): John E. Fetzer to Brenda Dunne, October 8, 1981, R013318.

10. Board Meeting Minutes (Binder 2): "Report of Executive Committee to Trustees John E. Fetzer Foundation, Inc.," February 24, 1983; FI 7 (Foundation Correspondence 1981–1984): "Potential Goals from Channeling," n.d., R0.213110; Bruce Fetzer Oral History, September 12, 2002, 72. Gordon was also asked about the current staffing of the foundation, but the Masters remained noncommittal. FI 5 (Fetzer, John E.—Jim Gordon 1980–1985 X, XVI): "Channeling," November 3–4, 1984, R02.13058, 64.

11. This does not mean that funding of all purely parapsychological research was stopped; funding of Robert Jahn of PEAR continued throughout the decade, and George Meek's Spiricom, a device to communicate electronically with the dead, was also funded at this time (see the next section in this chapter).

12. Board Meeting Minutes (Binder 2): July 11, 1983. A year later, the mission was restated: "The John E. Fetzer Foundation supports and provides research and

education regarding the interrelationships between the physical, mental, emotional and spiritual dimensions in fostering human potential." Moreover, the goals now specifically referred to "energy field research" as the primary focus of the foundation. Board Meeting Minutes (Binder 2): August 1, 1984. This mission statement and its goals were later amended in 1987, substituting "energy medicine" for "energy field research." Board Meeting Minutes (Binder 2): February 2, 1987.

13. In 1982, the foundation also funded "bio-energetic/synergistic research" with a local "aura-balancing" firm called Sansa Limited, but the project was terminated after a year. Board Meeting Minutes (Binder 2): June 23, 1982, November 12, 1982. There is evidence that aura balancing was used to treat Rhea Fetzer's dementia, but how this was related to the aforementioned project is not known. Jim Gordon Channelings Binder: Nancy Lee (Meisterheimer) to John Fetzer, August 5, 1980. See also John E. Fetzer to Jim Gordon, August 30, 1982, JGC; and Cleora Daily Oral History, August 13, 2013, 12.

14. Copies of Herbert Benson, *The Relaxation Response* (New York: Avon Books, 1975), FPL, and Herbert Benson, *Beyond the Relaxation Response: How to Harness the Healing Power of Your Personal Beliefs* (New York: Times Books, 1984), FPL, are extant in the Fetzer archives. The latter has Fetzer's annotations and is inscribed, "For John E. Fetzer with thanks and appreciation for your support. Herbert Benson, M.D. May 29, 1984."

15. Herbert Benson Oral History, March 28, 2012, 5–6; Hegedus, *John Earl Fetzer*, 164–66. This was the New Frontiers Program, referred to in note 47 to chapter 8.

16. FI 14 (Benson, Herbert, Dr.—Harvard Medical School 1980): Herbert Benson to John E. Fetzer, May 8 and September 30, 1980, R02.13261; FI 14 (Benson, Herbert, Dr.—Harvard Medical School 1982 I): Herbert Benson to John E. Fetzer, July 14, 1982, R02.13263; FI 14 (Benson, Herbert, Dr.—Harvard Medical School 1982 II): Herbert Benson to Fetzer Foundation Trustees, July 27, 1982, R02.13264; Herbert Benson, John W. Lehmann, M. S. Malhotra, Ralph F. Goldman, Jeffrey Hopkins, and Mark D. Epstein, "Body Temperature Changes during the Practice of g Tum-mo Yoga," *Nature* 295 (January 21, 1982): 234–36.

17. Hegedus, *John Earl Fetzer*, 166.

18. FI 14 (Benson, Herbert, Dr.—Harvard Medical School 1983): Robert M. Leeds to Chuck Spence, January 21, 1983, R02.13265; FI 14 (Benson, Herbert, Dr.—Harvard Medical School 1983–1986): Herbert Benson to Chuck Spence, May 26, 1983, R02.13266.

19. FI 15 (Foundation Grants History): "John E. Fetzer Foundation History: Grants," n.d., R02.13288; Benson Oral History, March 28, 2012, 11.

20. Richard Williams Oral History, May 13, 2011, 2–3, 15–16.

21. A. T. Barker, ed., *The Mahatma Letters to A. P. Sinnett*, 2nd ed. (1923; London: Rider, 1948), 455.

22. FI 16 (Menninger Foundation—Green, Elmer, Dr. 1983–1989 II): "Elmer Green, 'Progress Notes on the New Psychophysics: on 'Energy Physics,'" unpublished paper, November 1, 1984, R02.13307.

23. Elmer E. Green, "Copper Wall Research: Psychology and Psychophysics," *Subtle Energies & Energy Medicine* 10, no. 3 (1999): 238–43; FI 16 (Menninger Foundation—Green, Elmer, Dr. 1983–1989 I): Charles E. Spence to Roy W. Menninger, November 16, 1983, R02.13306; FI 16 (Menninger Foundation—Green, Elmer, Dr. 1983–1989 III): Roy W. Menninger to John E. Fetzer, August 7, 1987, R02.13308.

24. FI 10 (Institute of Noetic Science 1983): John E. Fetzer to Paul Temple, September 19, 1983, R02.13172; Board Meeting Minutes (Binder 2): September 21, 1983; FI 10 (Institute of Noetic Science 1983): Lynne Dailey to George Strom, November 16, 1983, R02.13172; FI 10 (Institute of Noetic Science 1983): Charles E. Spence to Barbara McNeill, November 16, 1983, R02.13172.

25. FI 10 (Institute of Noetic Science 1984 I): Charles E. Spence to Barbara McNeill, January 19, 1984, R02.13173; Board Meeting Minutes (Binder 2): January 19, 1984; FI 15 (Life Beyond Death Research Foundation 1982–1984 I-1982–1984 IV), R02.13300–13303. See also George W. Meek, *After We Die, What Then?* (Columbus, OH: Ariel, 1987), FPL, 157–58, 161–62, 170.

26. FI 10 (Institute of Noetic Science 1984 II): "Inner Mechanisms of the Healing Response," R02.13174; FI 10 (Institute of Noetic Science 1984 II): Lynne (Carolyn) Dailey to Foundation Staff, July 6, 1984, R02.13174; Board Meeting Minutes (Binder 2): February 1, 1985; FI 10 (Institute of Noetic Science 1985 II): "John E. Fetzer Foundation, Inc. Project Report Summary IONS—Mechanisms of Healing," October 10, 1985, R02.13179; FI 10 (Institute of Noetic Science 1985 II): "A Report on Recent Activities of The Inner Mechanisms Program," September 1984–July 1985, R02.13179; FI 10 (Institute of Noetic Science 1986–88): Brendan O'Regan to John E. Fetzer, March 23, 1988, R02.13180.

27. Board Meeting Minutes (Binder 2): May 16, 1984, August 1, 1984; FI 7 (Foundation Correspondence 1985–1986): John E. Fetzer to Shafica Karagulla, January 13, 1986, R02.13111; FI 7 (Foundation Correspondence 1985–1986): Shafica Karagulla to John E. Fetzer, January 21, 1986, R02.13111. Karagulla passed away two months later on March 12, 1986. "Shafica Karagulla," 850; see also Bolen, "Interview with Shafica Karagulla." Apparently, Karagulla was working on a book manuscript at the time, which ended up with the Theosophical Society in

Wheaton, Illinois. The foundation at one point offered to help underwrite its editing and publication. FI 13 (Schumaker, Jim 1986): Jim Schumaker to John E. Fetzer and Chuck Spence, September 10, 1986, R02.13247; and Jim Schumaker to Dora Kunz, September 11, 1986, R02.13247. The manuscript was eventually published as Shafica Karagulla and Dora van Gelder Kunz, *The Chakras and the Human Energy Fields* (Wheaton, IL: Theosophical Publishing, 1989), FPL, with Fetzer Foundation funding credited on p. xi.

28. FI I (ARE Clinic 1985–1989 II): Edward M. Deron to Harvey Grady, September 10, 1985, R02.12975; FI I (ARE Clinic 1985–1989 II): "Edward M. Deron to I.R.S.," September 11, 1985, R02.12975; FI 2 (ARE Clinic Board of Trustees Manual 1984–1985 I): "The ARE Clinic Manual for Board Members," n.d., R02.12977; FI 2 (ARE Clinic Board of Trustees Manual 1984–1985 II): "The ARE Clinic—Its Ideals, Purposes and Goals," R02.12978; William A. McGarey, *The Edgar Cayce Remedies* (New York: Bantam, 1983), 263–64; Analea McGarey, *Born to Heal: The Life Story of Holistic Health Pioneer Gladys Taylor McGarey, MD* (Scottsdale, AZ: Inkwell, 2003); Gladys McGarey Oral History, January 26, 2012; Harvey Grady Oral History, January 27, 2012. Earlier in 1928, the Edgar Cayce hospital had been founded in Virginia Beach, Virginia, but it did not survive the Depression. K. Paul Johnson, *Edgar Cayce in Context: The Readings: Truth and Fiction* (Albany: State University of New York Press, 1998), 7–8.

29. Board Meeting Minutes (Binder 2): May 16, 1984, August 1, 1984, February 1, 1985; and "Report of the Executive Committee to the Board of Trustees Meeting John E. Fetzer Foundation, Inc.," November 1, 1984, February 3, 1986; FI I (ARE Clinic 1985–1989 I): "Proposal for John E. Fetzer Energy Research Institute Continuation—Second Year," n.d., R02.12974; Board Meeting Minutes (Binder 3): "John E. Fetzer Foundation, Inc. Executive Committee Meeting," November 1, 1986, February 2, 1987; FI I (ARE Clinic 1985–1989 III): William A. McGarey to John E. Fetzer, June 1, 1987, R02.12976; FI I (ARE Clinic 1985–1989 III): "A Covenant Relationship between ARE Clinic and the John E. Fetzer Foundation," June 1, 1987, R02.12976; Linda Grdina Oral History, June 27, 1996, 24; Grady Oral History, January 27, 2012, 9–11, 12, 13, 16, 29.

30. Grady Oral History, January 27, 2012, 15–16; FI I (ARE Clinic 1985–1989 I): "Proposal for John E. Fetzer Energy Research Institute Continuation—Second Year," n.d., R02.12974; FI I (ARE Clinic 1985–1989 I): "Minutes of Plant Growth Project Planning Meeting," March 30, 1985, R02.12974. Later that year, Maxey was brought to Kalamazoo to prepare a proposal for the broader study of electromagnetic effects on biological systems. Board Meeting Minutes

(Binder 2): "Report of the Executive Committee to the Board of Trustees John E. Fetzer Foundation, Inc.," November 8, 1985. Engineers contracted from the Florida Institute of Technology created the "environmental bubble" necessary for the project. Board Meeting Minutes (Binder 2): "Report of the Executive Committee to the Board of Trustees John E. Fetzer Foundation, Inc.," February 3, 1986; FI I (ARE Clinic 1985–1989 I): "Proposal for John E. Fetzer Energy Research Institute Continuation—Second Year," n.d., R02.12974. The funding for this project was suspended at the May 5, 1986, board meeting until the "medical research staff have reviewed the program," an apparent reference to the anticipated staff of the future John E. Fetzer Medical Institute (see later in this section). See also material in FI 11 (John Fetzer Life-Science Laboratory 1985 II), R02.13194.

31. Hiroshi Motoyama, "Acupuncture Meridians," *Science & Medicine* 6, no. 4 (1999): 48–53; FI I (ARE Clinic 1985–1989 I): "Proposal for John E. Fetzer Energy Research Institute Continuation—Second Year," n.d., R02.12974. Apparently, the Fetzer Foundation board had already joined Motoyama's association in 1982. Board Meeting Minutes (Binder 2): December 30, 1982.

32. FI I (ARE Clinic 1985–1989 I): "Proposal for John E. Fetzer Energy Research Institute Continuation—Second Year," n.d., R02.12974. Later FEMRI projects included research into Kirlian photography for aura diagnosis, the medicinal value of castor-oil packs, and the evaluation of something called the Cayce Impendence Device for the treatment of hypertension: FI I (ARE Clinic 1985–1989 III): Harvey Grady to Clinic Staff and Interested Persons, September 12, 1986, R02.12976. See the following research reports prepared for FEMRI: "Kirlian Corona Discharge Photography: A Method of Physiological Monitoring," December 1988 (0388); "Immunomodulation through Castor Oil Packs," December 1988 (0488); "Study of Cayce Impendence Device," December 1988 (0588), all of which can be found in the Fetzer Archives.

33. FI 7 (Foundation Correspondence 1989): "Draft of memorandum," January 4, 1989, R02.13116.

34. The Pathoclast was sold by Elliot C. L. Maynard of the Borderland Sciences Research Foundation of Vista, California. FI 12 (Pathoclast—Maynard, C. L.), R02.13232.

35. Fetzer reportedly had the Lakhovsky device built specifically to cure the cancer of a friend, probably Janice Anders, a member of the *Course in Miracles* group (see chapter 8). Hegedus, *John Earl Fetzer*, 176–78. Further research on the Lakhovsky Multiple Wave Oscillator was carried out by FEMRI: FI I (ARE Clinic 1985–1989 III): Harvey Grady to Clinic Staff and Interested Persons, September 12, 1986, R02.12976; FI 12 (Lakhovsky, George [Lakhovshy Device]

1988 I): "The Lakhovsky Multiple Wave Oscillator: Electromagnetic Waves in Healing," Fetzer Energy Medicine Research Institute Report, December 1988, #0188, R02.13217. See also FI 2 (Robert Beck [Lakhovsky Device] 1985–1986), R02.12981; and other materials in FI 12 (Lakhovsky, George [Lakhovshy Device] 1988 I–III), R02.13217–19. Fetzer had already read about the Lakhovsky device in Alder, *Initiation of the World*, 194–96.

36. T. M. Srinivasan, ed., *Energy Medicine around the World* (Phoenix: Gabriel, 1988) (based on the papers presented at the Madras Energy Medicine Conference held from February 27 to March 1, 1987); Srinivasan, "Pulsed Magnetic Field Coil," *Energylines* 2, no. 3 (1989): 1–4 (uncataloged in Fetzer Archives); T. M. Srinivasan, "MED (FAME) Device: Psychophysiological Correlates," in *Energy Fields in Medicine: A Study of Device Technology Based on Acupuncture Meridians and Chi Energy*, ed. Michael A. Morton and Carrie Dlouhy (Kalamazoo, MI; John E. Fetzer Foundation, 1989), 338–49 (this book was based on the research presented at the "Energy Fields, Meridians, Chi and Device Technology Roundtable," held at the Fetzer Foundation May 11–14, 1989). For Srinivasan's CV, see FI 18 (President's Office Lehman, Rob Board of Trustees Correspondence October 1989), R02.13351. See also Board Meeting Minutes (Binder 3): "John E. Fetzer Foundation, Inc. Executive Committee Meeting," November 1, 1986, February 2, 1987, May 17, 1987, September 30, 1989; FI I (ARE Clinic 1985–1989 III): William A. McGarey to John E. Fetzer, April 8, 1987, R02.12976; Grady Oral History, January 27, 2012, 15, 24; Williams Oral History, May 13, 2011, 15, 33; Vic Eichler Oral History, March 30, 2012, 11–12; Swierenga Oral History, August 6, 2012, 29, 30, 33; McGarey Oral History, January 26, 2012, 17–18. For John Fetzer's interest in an in-house lab, see Board Meeting Minutes (Binder 1): "Report of Executive Committee to Trustees John E. Fetzer Foundation, Inc.," January 6, 1982; Board Meeting Minutes (Binder 3): "John E. Fetzer Foundation, Inc. Executive Board of Trustees' Meeting," March 3–4, 1989; FI 6 (Fetzer, John E.—Research in Foundation Laboratory [January 9, 1989]): "Research in Foundation Laboratory," January 9, 1989, R02.13082; FI 6 (Fetzer, John E.—"Thoughts on Research," [October 4, 1989]), R02.13086. In the latter memo, Fetzer wrote that he believed that Edison and Einstein were willing and waiting to aid in this research from beyond the grave, an idea perhaps taken from Jim Gordon's channelings. FI 5 [Fetzer, John E.—Jim Gordon 1980–1985 XIV–XV]: "Channeling," October 30, 1984, R02.13062, 63, although this idea also appears in Tuella, *World Messages for the Coming Decade*, 58.

37. FI 5 (Fetzer, John E.—Jim Gordon 1980–1985 XV): "Channeling," November 2, 1984, R02.13063; FI 5 (Fetzer, John E.—Jim Gordon 1980–1985 X, XVI): "Channeling," November 3–4, 1984, R02.13058, 64.

38. FI I (ARE Clinic 1985–1989 I): "Proposal for John E. Fetzer Energy Research Institute Continuation—Second Year," n.d., R02.12974; FI 11 (John Fetzer Life-Science Laboratory 1985 I–III), R02.13193–95.

39. FI 11 (John E. Fetzer Medical Institute June–July 1985–July 1986), R02.13196–R02.13204; FI I (ARE Clinic 1985–1989 I): "Memorandum from Jay S. Ruffner (Lewis and Roca, Lawyers)," June 5, 1985, R02.12974; FI I (ARE Clinic 1985–1989 I): Harvey Grady to Charles Spence, June 6, 1985, R02.12974; FI I (ARE Clinic 1985–1989 I): John E. Fetzer to Staff Committee, June 26, 1985, R02.12974; FI I (ARE Clinic 1985–1989 I): Chuck Spence to Harvey Grady, June 5, 1985, R02.12974; FI I (ARE Clinic 1985–1989 III): "Memorandum [RE: John E. Fetzer Foundation, Inc. (JEFF)]—Control of Directors of ARE," n.d., R02.12976. Apparently, following the legal advice of Ruffner as to the best way to create permanent ties to the ARE Clinic (if not to take it over outright), the Fetzer board approved the establishment of the John E. Fetzer Medical Institute, which was duly incorporated in the state of Michigan. Board Meeting Minutes (Binder 2): "Report of the Executive Committee to the Board of Trustees Meeting John E. Fetzer Foundation, Inc.," September 9, 1985, November 8, 1985, February 3, 1986.

40. Grady Oral History, January 27, 2012, 11.

41. FI 5 (Fetzer, John E.—Jim Gordon 1980–1985 XI): "Channeling," November 18, 1983, R02.13059 (the handwritten original can be found in JGC).

42. Deb Berkenhauer, "Fetzer Business Center to be Dedicated in November," *Western Herald*, August 29, 1983; "FetCen: An Inside Look at Western's Newest Facility," *Western Herald*, November 18, 1983; FI 5 (Fetzer, John E.—Jim Gordon 1980–1985 IV): "Channeling," January 13, 1984, R02.13052. Jim Gordon commissioned the painter Arthur Douët to document the ensoulment of the building; the painting exists in the Fetzer Archives (A04.26425).

43. Board Meetings Minutes (Binder 2): "Report of the Executive Committee to Trustees John E. Fetzer Foundation, Inc.," January 19, 1984.

44. FI 5 (Fetzer, John E.—Jim Gordon 1980–1985 XI): "Dear Children of Light," December 16, 1983, R02.13059 (the handwritten original can be found in JGC). More channeled advice, this time about possible architects, came in FI 5 (Fetzer, John E.—Jim Gordon 1980–1985 IV): "Channeling," February 1984, R02.13052.

45. According to the *Proceedings of the 5th National Coptic Convention*, Potawatomi Inn, Angola, Indiana, August 24–26, 1979 (author's collection), both Gordon and

Jochmans presented papers at the convention. For more on Jochmans's work for the foundation, see Board Meeting Minutes (Binder 2): "Report to the Executive Committee to Trustees John E. Fetzer Foundation, Inc.," January 19, 1984; FI 10 (Jochmans, Joseph 1983–1985 II): "Fetzer Foundation Advisory Group—Joe Jochmans," January 9, 1984, R02.13188; FI 10 (Jochmans, Joseph 1983–1985 I): "Conversation with Joey Jochmans [in] Kalamazoo," January 11, 1984, R02.13187; FI 10 (Jochmans, Joseph 1983–1985 I): Charles E. Spence to Joseph R. Jochmans, January 20, 1984, R02.13187; FI 11 (Jochmans, Joseph—Reports 1984 I): "Pendulum and Dowsing Readings—Recommendations and Observations," March 3, 1984, R02.13191; FI 11 (Jochmans, Joseph—Reports 1984 I): "Report #2 to the Fetzer Foundation Prepared by Joseph R. Jochmans," April 24, 1984, R02.13191; "Report #3 to the Fetzer Foundation Prepared by Joseph Jochmans," May 18, 1984, JCG; FI 11 (Jochmans, Joseph—Reports 1984 I): "Report #4 to the Fetzer Foundation Prepared by Joseph R. Jochmans," June 8, 1984, R02.13191; FI 11 (Jochmans, Joseph—Reports 1984 II): "Report #5 to the Fetzer Foundation Prepared by Joseph R. Jochmans," June 20, 1984, R02.13192; Bruce Fetzer Oral History, March 15, 1996, 84–88; Daily Oral History, August 13, 2012, 15, 35; Monday Night Group Oral History, October 13, 2011, 36–42, 54, 73, 83; Swierenga Oral History, August 6, 2012, 21. Jochmans was born in Chicago in 1950. Like Fetzer, he was a Seventh-day Adventist and attended Andrews University; he also attended another Adventist institution briefly before dropping out to become a "spiritual anthropologist" lecturing to such groups as the Coptics, Spiritual Frontiers Fellowship, Unity, the American Society of Dowsers, and the E.S.P. Forum of Battle Creek. Jochmans was also a student of the Edgar Cayce material and lectured to ARE groups. FI 10 (Jochmans, Joseph 1983–1985 I): "Conversation with Joey Jochmans [in] Kalamazoo," January 11, 1984, R02.13187; FI 10 (Jochmans, Joseph 1983–1985 III): untitled biography, R02.13189. In the '70s, Jochmans began channeling the being AEI (aka Jalandris), whose messages he self-published as the *Books of AIE*, which Fetzer ordered and read. FI 7 (Foundation Correspondence 1981–1984): Valerie Eisneberg to Inner Isis, April 17, 1984; Susan B. Roenick (Inner Isis) to John E. Fetzer, n.d., R02.13110; for descriptions of the books, see the brochure in FI 11 (Jochmans, Joseph 1983–1985 IV), R02.13190. In addition, Jochmans was also involved with Dean and Mary Hardy and their Allegan pyramids. "Mary Hardy Letter for Unity," n.d., JGC. Jochmans died in 2013. "Jochmans, Joseph Robert," *Lincoln (NE) Journal Star*, November 17, 2013, http://journalstar.com/lifestyles/announcements/obituaries/jochmans-joseph-robert/article_b4b2fc28

-0481-5e47-b8a9-b6afc998d2f7.html. For more on ley lines, see Philip Heselton, *The Elements of Earth Mysteries* (Shaftesbury, UK: Element, 1998).

46. Board Meeting Minutes (Binder 2): May 16, 1984; "Report #3 to the Fetzer Foundation Prepared by Joseph Jochmans," May 18, 1984, JCG; Board Meeting Minutes (Binder 2): August 1, 1984. For Gordon's channelings regarding Dustin Lake property, see FI 5 (Fetzer, John E.—Jim Gordon 1980–1985 XI): "Channeling," May 18, 1984, R02.13059 (the handwritten original can be found in the JGC); see also FI 5 (Fetzer, John E.—Jim Gordon 1980–1985 XVII): "Channeling," May 22, 1985, R02.13065, in which Cato identified Dustin Lake as a site sacred to the local Native Americans in the past.

47. Board Meeting Minutes (Binder 2): August 1, 1984, August 1, 1985; and "Report of the Executive Committee to Board of Trustees John E. Fetzer Foundation, Inc.," November 1, 1984, February 1, 1985, May 1, 1985, November 8, 1985; Swierenga Oral History, August 6, 2012.

48. FI 5 (Fetzer, John E.—Jim Gordon 1980–1985 XI): "Channeling," May 18, 1984, R02.13059 (the handwritten original can be found in the JGC). In order to ensure the cooperation of the devas, on May 28, 1985, Swierenga, Bruce Fetzer, Carolyn Dailey, and Chuck Spence performed at the building site a simple ceremony outlined by Jim Gordon. Lloyd Swierenga to John E. Fetzer, Lynne (Carolyn) Dailey, and Bruce Fetzer, June 6, 1985, JGC; FI 5 (Fetzer, John E.—Jim Gordon 1980–1985 XVII): "Channeling," May 22, 1985, R02.13065.

49. FI 11 (Jochmans, Joseph—Reports 1984 I): "Guiding Design Principles for the Fetzer Foundation Centers prepared by Joseph R. Jochmans," n.d., R02.13191. The terms "terramonics" and "archemonics" were Jochmans's own creation. FI 10 (Jochmans, Joseph 1983–1985 II): "Fetzer Foundation Advisory Group—Joe Jochmans," January 9, 1984, R02.13188, 7–8. According to Jochmans,

> Terramonics is the placement of structures within a landscape so as to be in perfect balance with its multi-dimensional energy systems. Determining this involves using such geomantic tools as dowsing instruments and pendulums, map dowsing, field dowsing, kiniesiology muscle-testing, meditation visualization, and supportive divinatory arts—astrology, feng-shui, I Ching, Tarot, runes, lithomancy, etc. These geomantic tools are utilized to determine the location within the landscape of both present and future distribution of earth energy ley-lines, water lines, water domes, ley and/or water line crossings, aquastats, track-lines, geostats, down shoots, earthing points, fusion points, solar-lunar-celestial alignments, ore veins, ancient sites

physical and etheric, ancient and future (intent) psychic imprints, inter-dimensional gateways, earth fracture zones, devic and/or nature spirit centers and man-made forms—buried electric and telephone cables, water and gas and sewage pipes, etc. The geomancer's work will be to take all these aspects into account, as well as the proper balance adjustments for all earth, life, mind and cosmic forces focused within the land, in determining the proper placement of a structure or structures, and ascertaining its best purpose within such an environment. Archemonics focuses attention on how the structure, once placed, may be designed to enhance its inherent purpose.

"Guiding Design Principles," 1. In addition to the three amethysts buried on the property by Jochmans ("Report #3 to the Fetzer Foundation Prepared by Joseph Jochmans," May 18, 1984, JCG) and the many large crystals on display in the finished building, Fetzer later had a grid of twelve quartz crystals planted "to create an energy field around the building"; and elsewhere on the property, a medicine wheel in the shape of a Star of David was constructed "to prevent ley energies from causing disturbance within the building and contribute to a greater internal energy balance." Jim Herweg to Bruce Fetzer, July 27, 1988, JGC.

50. Board Meeting Minutes (Binder 2): February 1, 1985; and "Report of the Executive Committee to Board of Trustees John E. Fetzer Foundation, Inc.," May 1, 1985. For greater details of the planning process for the building, see Bill Hamill Oral History, May 8, 1988.

51. FI 52 (HEPY Interview with JEF): "Proposed Administration Building Meeting with John Fetzer, Tuesday, January 8, 1985," R1627871; Bruce Fetzer Oral History, March 15, 1996, 89–91. For more on the connection between Freemasonry and Egyptian symbolism, see Erik Hornung, *The Secret Lore of Egypt: Its Impact on the West* (Ithaca, NY: Cornell University Press, 2001), 116–27.

52. FI 13 (Symbolism—Administration Building 1987): "JEFF Administration Building Symbolism Talk by Jim Gordon in Associate Staff Meeting," September 11, 1987, R02.13250; FI 13 (Symbolism—Administration Building 1987): "Fetzer Foundation Administration Building Symbolism [Lloyd Swierenga]," Spring 1987, R02.13250; FI 13 (Symbolism—Administration Building 1987): "Fetzer Foundation Administration Building Symbolism at Board Meeting," November 7, 1987, R02.13250; FI 9 ("Information on Crystals" 1988): "John E. Fetzer Foundation Information in Crystals Prepared by Carol Hegedus primarily from information dictated by Rosemarie, Crystal Resources," R02.13153; Hamill Oral History, May 8, 1988, 16–17. Again, many of the building's motifs (triangles,

twin pillars, Egyptian iconography, etc.) can also be read Masonically. Akram Elias, personal communication, April 22, 2016. The solar disk above the entrance and Isis and Nephthys at the building's exit were copied from the innermost shrine of the tomb of King Tutankhamen, according to notations found on photos of the originals in the Fetzer Archives (cabinet 5, drawer 1). The copper disk was placed to mark the point where the altitude bisected the base of the triangle of the building, and the entire building and cooling tower had been carefully sited so that the sunlight through the obelisk would strike this precise spot on Fetzer's birthday. Bruce Fetzer, personal communication, October 26, 2016. The obelisk also functions to house the Administration Building's air-conditioning system, which, for aesthetic reasons, the architects did not want to place on the roof of the building.

53. John E. Fetzer to Jim Gordon, January 5, 1982, JGC; FI 5 (Fetzer, John E.— Jim Gordon 1980–1985 XIV): Jim Gordon to John E. Fetzer, March 2, 1982, R02.13059 (the handwritten original can be found in the JGC); FI 13 (Symbolism—Administration Building 1987): "JEFF Administration Building Symbolism Talk by Jim Gordon in Associate Staff Meeting," September 11, 1987, R02.13250.

54. FI 5 (Fetzer, John E.—Jim Gordon 1980–1985 XVII): "Channeling," May 22, 1985, R02.13065; Gordon Oral History, November 15, 1996, 93–94; FI 13 (Symbolism—Foundation Logo 1986): "Symbolism of Foundation Logo [prepared by] J. Andersen," May 27, 1986, R02.13251; FI 13 (Symbolism—Foundation Logo 1986): "Symbolism of Foundation Logo (for Public)," May 27, 1986, R02.13251; FI 6 (Fetzer, John E.—Remarks to Foundation Board Revised [April 24, 1989]): "Remarks to Foundation Board," March 3–4, 1989, R02.13080.

55. FI 13 (Symbolism—Administration Building 1987): "JEFF Administration Building Symbolism Talk by Jim Gordon in Associate Staff Meeting," September 11, 1987, R02.13250, 14–15; FI 13 (Symbolism—Administration Building 1987): "Fetzer Foundation Administration Building Symbolism [Lloyd Swierenga]," Spring 1987, R02.13250, 6–7.

56. Board Meeting Minutes (Binder 2): "Report of Executive Committee to Trustees John E. Fetzer Foundation, Inc.," February 3, 1986; Board Meeting Minutes (Binder 3): "John E. Fetzer Foundation, Inc. Executive Committee Meeting," November 1, 1986; FI 9 (Hall of Records Discussion 1987): "Kirk Newman—Jan Andersen Discussion about the Hall of Records," March 20, 1987, R02.13150; FI 22 (Publications "Hall of Records" 1988): "Hall of Records Booklet," 1988, R02.20405.

57. Jim Gordon to John E. Fetzer, with note from L.D. (Carolyn Dailey) attached, 1981, JGC; John E. Fetzer to Jim Gordon, January 5, 1982, JGC; Jim Gordon to John E. Fetzer, January 20, 1982, JGC; Jim Gordon to John E. Fetzer, July 18, 1983, JGC; John E. Fetzer to Jim Gordon, July 27, 1983, JGC; "Conversation with Jim Gordon," December 29, 1983, JGC; FI 5 (Fetzer, John E.—Jim Gordon 1980–1985 XVII): "Channeling," January 24, 1985, R02.13065; Hamill Oral History, May 8, 1988, 20; Janis Claflin Oral History, November 13–14, 1996, 92; Janis Claflin Oral History, June 16, 2011, 30–31.

58. FI 22 (Publications "Hall of Records" 1988): "Hall of Records Booklet," 1988, R02.20405; Keating Oral History, April 28, 2011, 49.

59. Mark Lehner, *The Egyptian Heritage Based on the Edgar Cayce Readings* (Virginia Beach, VA: ARE, 1974), 93–102 (in the Fetzer Archives); Johnson, *Edgar Cayce in Context*, 67, 91, 94–95; Jalandris (Joseph Jochmans), *The Hall of Records: Hidden Secrets of the Pyramid and Sphinx* (San Francisco, CA: Holistic Life Travels, 1980); Joseph Robert Jochmans, *The Hall of Records Part One*, 4 vols. (N.p.: n.p., 1985) (both Jochmans's volumes are in the Fetzer Archives); FI 10 (Jochmans, Joseph 1983–1985 I): "Conversation with Joey Jochmans [in] Kalamazoo," January 11, 1984, R02.13187, 17–21; FI 10 (Jochmans, Joseph 1983–1985 II): "Fetzer Foundation Advisory Group—Joe Jochmans," January 9, 1984, R02.13188, 15, 33–34. Jim Gordon also suggests that John Fetzer associated the Hall of Records with Manly P. Hall's discussion of the Masonic myths of Enoch's secret underground vaults, which the patriarch constructed to preserve ancient wisdom from the biblical flood. Gordon, personal communication, October 21, 2016.

60. FI 9 (Hall of Records Discussion 1987): "Hall of Records Discussion [with John E. Fetzer, Tom Beaver, and Jan Andersen]," April 8, 1987, R02.13150. Occasionally, Fetzer would get tangible evidence that what he hoped for had indeed occurred: for example, in response to one visitor's comments, Fetzer wrote, "Thanks kindly for writing as you did concerning your experience in the Hall of Records. It gives one a lot of courage to understand that there are many others on this planet who understand and experience the force of energy when environmental situations bring things into focus. There are many things about the Hall of Records, as well as the building itself where the Foundations exists, that are highly energized and have real depth of meaning to those who understand. Glad to count you as one who does." FI 4 (Correspondence 1988–1997): John E. Fetzer to Desaix Riordan, July 8, 1988, R02.13022. The Hall of Records was removed from the Fetzer Administration Building in the early 1990s and replaced with a display on the life of John E. Fetzer.

61. Board Meeting Minutes (Binder 2): "Report of the Executive Committee to Board of Trustees John E. Fetzer Foundation, Inc.," February 3, 1986.

62. Hegedus, *John Earl Fetzer*, 197. For an example of the variety of details attended to by Swierenga, see Board Meeting Minutes (Binder 3): "John E. Fetzer Foundation, Inc. Executive Committee Meeting," November 1, 1986.

63. FI 7 (Foundation Correspondence 1985–1986): Valerie Eisenberg to Milton G. Crane, January 15, 1986, R02.131111; FI 7 (Foundation Correspondence 1986 I): John E. Fetzer to Margaret H. Zolen, June 4, 1986, R02.131113; Grady Oral History, January 27, 2012, 18–23.

64. FI 7 (Foundation Correspondence 1985–1986): John E. Fetzer to All Staff, February 3, 1986, R02.13111; FI 2 (*Encore* Dec. 1980): "Mind Body and Spirit Are One Says Rev. Dave McShane," *Encore* 8, no. 3 (1980): 9–11, R02.12997; FI 4 (Fetzer, John E. Correspondence 1986): John E. Fetzer to Jim Gordon, October 29, 1986, R02.13020; Bruce Fetzer Oral History, March 15, 1996, 92–94.

65. Bruce Fetzer Oral History, March 15, 1996, 95–96; Hegedus, *John Earl Fetzer*, 198–99.

66. FI 1 (Administration Building Associate Dedication [March 25] 1987), R02.12951.

67. Ibid.

68. FI 1 (Administration Building Dedication 1988 II): "Dedication of the John E. Fetzer Foundation World Headquarters," June 25, 1988, 4:00 p.m., R02.12954.

11. The Last of the Nine Lives

1. Gordon Oral History, November 15, 1996, 161; Tom Beaver Oral History, June 19, 1997.

2. FI 18 (President's Office, Olds, Glenn Correspondence from John Fetzer 1987+1989): John E. Fetzer to Glenn A. Olds, December 1, 1987, R02.13354.

3. Bruce Fetzer Oral History, March 14, 1996; 42; Claflin Oral History (November 13–14, 1996), 56–57; Whitson Oral History (March 3, 2011), 35.

4. FI 7 (Foundation Commitment): "John E. Fetzer Foundation Commitment," n.d., R02.13108.

5. Grdina Oral History, June 27, 1996, 17; Board Meeting Minutes (Binder 3): November 7, 1987. According to Bruce Fetzer, the commitment "was developed by the advisory core group (Lloyd Swierenga, Chuck Spence, Bruce Fetzer, Carolyn Dailey) and personally edited and approved by John Fetzer. It was used to open every staff meeting. As the foundation staff grew to over 40 employees, job applicants were asked to read it and comment on it during the interview process.

The practice was abandoned with the hiring of Glenn Olds." Bruce Fetzer to Rob Lehman, memo, "History of the Fetzer Foundation Commitment," revised September 6, 2006.

6. Hanegraaff, *New Age Religion and Western Culture*, 189–94; for Alice Bailey, Guy Ballard, and Baird Spalding, see chapter 5; for Edgar Cayce, see Johnson, *Edgar Cayce in Context*, 29, 39, 46, 47, 58, 84; for Jim Gordon and John-Roger, see chapter 9; for John Davis, see, e.g., Davis, "Prophecy of the Second Coming: Birth of Christ Within," in *Proceedings of the 5th National Coptic Convention*, August 24–26, 1979, 1–9 (author's collection); Joey Jochmans: FI 11 (Jochmans, Joseph—Reports 1984 II): "Report # 5 to the Fetzer Foundation Prepared by Joseph R. Jochmans," June 20, 1984, R02.13192.

7. The commitment was also featured in the covenant signed with the ARE Clinic. FI I (ARE Clinic 1985–1989 III): "A Covenant Relationship between ARE Clinic and the John E. Fetzer Foundation," June 11, 1987, R02.12976. It should be pointed out that, in order that the commitment not be misunderstood by employees as an orthodox Christian statement, a special memo, "Definition of Christ Consciousness," was circulated:

> We ask to be attuned with the light and consciousness of the Christ so that all our efforts will remain clearly focused on our mission of service to others. In using the word "Christ," we are referring not to an individual person, but to the cosmic energy and intelligence which is responsible for helping humanity progress spiritually. The Christ is an office which carries spiritual authority in much the same way as a governor heads political authority in a state. As more than one person can fill the office of governor, so can more than one Christed entity fill the office of Christ. When we use the words "Christ Consciousness," we are referring to the principle of divine love which permeates and governs each individual's soul. These words also refer to a state of spiritual awareness which recognizes that humanity is one, ultimately guided and purified by this divine love. Every soul on earth has the potential to reach this level of spiritual awareness. At the Foundation, our goal is to emulate and express the Christ Consciousness in our daily lives.

> FI 7 (Foundation Correspondence 1986 II): "Definition of Christ Consciousness," May 27, 1986, R02.13113.

8. Board Meeting Minutes (Binder 3): "John E. Fetzer Foundation, Inc. Special Meeting," May 1, 1987.

9. Janis Claflin reported that she had urged Fetzer to create just such a professional board in order to smooth the foundation's transition after his death. Claflin Oral History, November 13–14, 1996, 34–35, 44–45, 57, 77–79.

10. Board Meeting Minutes (Binder 3):"Fetzer Foundation Statement of Purpose," Addenda #4.

11. FI 6 (Fetzer, John E.—Institute Status): "Institute Status Dictation," June 27, 1988, R02.13069; FI 6 (Fetzer, John E.—Memo to Board of Trustees): "Foundation Purpose," July 15, 1988, R02.13071; FI 6 (Fetzer, John E.—Remarks to Foundation Board Revised [April 24, 1989]): "Remarks to Foundation Board," March 3–4, 1989, R02.13080; Board Meeting Minutes (Binder 3): March 3–4, 1989; FI 6 (Fetzer, John E.—Research in Foundation Laboratory [January 9, 1989]), R02.13082; FI 6 (Fetzer, John E.—Research in Foundation Laboratory [January 9, 1989]): "Memorandum," March 15, 1989, R02.13082; FI 4 (Founder's Statement Notes): "The Founders Statement," September 30, 1989, R02.13047 and R02.137048.

12. Bruce Fetzer Oral History, March 15, 1996, 97–99; Beaver Oral History, June 19, 1997, 48–51; Hamill Oral History, May 8, 1998, 34–35; Claflin Oral History, November 13–14, 1996, 34–39, 42–45, 48–52, 62–69.

13. FI 18 (President's Office, Olds, Glenn Correspondence from John Fetzer 1987+1989): John E. Fetzer to Glenn A. Olds, December 1, 1987, R02.13354; Board Meeting Minutes (Binder 3): "John E. Fetzer Foundation, Inc. Special Meeting," May 1, 1987; "John E. Fetzer Board of Trustees Meeting John E. Fetzer Foundation (November 6–8, 1987)" (separate binder): "Glenn A. Olds CV"; "Kalamazoo Declaration: A Mailer to Conference Delegates Presented to Fetzer Foundation Board of Trustees," November 4, 1988 (separate binder); FI 6 (Fetzer, John E.—Institute Status): "Institute Status Dictation," June 27, 1988, R02.13069; FI 6 (Fetzer, John E.—Memo to Board of Trustees): "Foundation Purpose," July 15, 1988, R02.13071; Board Meeting Minutes (Binder 3): July 23, 1988, November 5, 1988, June 24, 1989; FI 18 (President's Office, Olds, Glenn Final Correspondence August 1989): Glenn A. Olds to Board Members, August 23, 1989, R02.13355; Gordon Oral History, November 15, 1996, 126–35; Claflin Oral History, November 13–14, 1996, 45–48, 52, 66, 70, 81–85, 101–103; Beaver Oral History, June 19, 1997, 51–53; Bruce Fetzer Oral History, December 12, 2002, 105–13. Fetzer and Olds also came to loggerheads because Olds wanted to cut down trees to facilitate his view of the lake; Fetzer, however, asked him not to do so because of "troll activities around the place," obviously a reference to one of the devas spoken about by Gordon and Jochmans. FI 18

(President's Office, Olds, Glenn Correspondence from John Fetzer 1987+1989): John E. Fetzer to Glenn A. Olds, June 1, 1989, R02.13354.

14. FI 11 (Lehman, Robert 1988): "Curriculum Vitae Robert F. Lehman," January 16, 1988, R02.13214. For an example of his leadership style, see FI 18 (President's Office Lehman, Rob Introductory Remarks, July 14, 1989): "Introductory Remarks to the Fetzer Foundation Staff by Rob Lehman," July 14, 1989, R02.13350. See also Gordon Oral History, November 15, 1996, 137–44.

15. John E. Fetzer Foundation Board of Trustees Meeting, January 26–27 (separate binder): John E. Fetzer Foundation Board of Trustees Meeting, June 22–23 (separate binder): Lou Leeberg to Rob Lehman, memo, January 8, 1990; and Lou Leeberg to Rob Lehman, memo, May 15, 1990; Hegedus, *John Earl Fetzer*, 216–18, 220–21, 223–24.

16. Also named to the board of the Memorial Trust were Michael Gergely, Bruce Fetzer, Tom Beaver, and Louis Leeburg, an investment advisor to the Fetzer Foundation since 1989. The Memorial Trust also held an endowment for the support of Inner Light Ministries and for the upkeep of the Clovelly house. "John E. Fetzer Institute, Inc. Minutes of the Board of Trustees Meeting Executive Session," June 26–28, 1991 (separate binder); Beaver Oral History, June 19, 1997, 68; Hegedus, *John Earl Fetzer*, 225–26; Bruce Fetzer Oral History, December 12, 2002, 115–17.

17. FI 9 (Hologram Dedication—Rob Lehman's Remarks 1990): "[Rob Lehman's] Remarks in Honor of Vincent's Sculpture," November 13, 1990, R02.13151; FI 9 (Hologram Dedication—Rob Lehman's Remarks 1990): "Comments Taken from Tape of Hologram Dedication," November 13, 1990, R02.13151. Fetzer had probably been introduced to Mariani through Jim Gordon. Jim Gordon, "Information on Spirit, Strobe, and Sonar," July 27, 1985, JGC.

18. Gordon Oral History, November 15, 1996, 162; Beaver Oral History, June 19, 1997, 53–55; Bruce Fetzer Oral History, December 12, 2002, 113–14; Hegedus, *John Earl Fetzer*, 221–25.

19. Gordon Oral History, November 15, 1996, 162; Beaver Oral History, June 19, 1997, 53–54; Bruce Fetzer Oral History, December 12, 2002, 113–14.

20. Gordon Oral History, November 15, 1996, 161–71; Beaver Oral History, June 19, 1997, 56–59.

21. See John E. Fetzer Institute Board of Trustees Meeting, February 13–17, 1991 (separate binder).

22. Gordon Oral History, November 15, 1996, 171–75.

23. TB 30 (Broadcasting [1–16] 1974 I): John E. Fetzer to Ed Kirby, March 18, 1974, R02.14809; TB 30 (Broadcasting [58–98] 1974 III): John E. Fetzer to

Reed Andress, December 21, 1973, R02.14812; BR 14 (1980 *Encore*—November, 1980): "A Fetzer View of the Future," *Encore*, November 1980, 11, R02.16932; FI 4 (Fetzer, John E.—Encore Interview Transcript 1988): "Interview Fetzer, John Encore 1988," January 27, 1988, 16, R02.13045; FP 5 (Correspondence 1977 II): John E. Fetzer to Svea Yeager, March 14, 1977, R02.13883; Whitson Oral History, March 15, 2011, 41–45.

24. Linda Grdina, ed., "The Fetzer Institute Program History Report," unpublished internal document, October 2013, 1–13, Fetzer Institute Archives.

25. Ibid., 15–20.

26. Ibid., 21–44.

27. As mentioned in note 22 to chapter 9, at the encouragement of Jim Gordon, Fetzer kept a dream diary for a couple of years:

> 5:18 am, Labor Day, 1983: I had a dream of a new religion that was being given to the world and I was in a great meeting and I gave the address concerning this new religion, it had a short name that I don't remember. I do remember that I was inspired and I talked for about 20 minutes and the words that flowed out had a depth of meaning that I can't explain, except to say that the inspiration as they flowed I seem[e]d to be speaking under the impact of a mighty force. I remember after the meeting was over walking down the street with some of the people that were in the audience and we would discuss the thing further and as we walked down the street we all concluded that possibly this was the religion of the future and it was a new hope for mankind. It was an experience a different kind of an experience, that really can't be put into words. That's the way I felt as a result of being in the pulpit and speaking in its behalf. That's all I can say.

> FP 10 (Fetzer, John E.—Dreams 1972–1985 II): "Dreams," September 5, 1983, R02.13987.

28. FI 6 (Fetzer, John E.—"Helping Heal the Whole Person and the Whole World," Conference Closing Remarks [June 25, 1988]), R02.13068.

29. Board Meeting Minutes (Binder 3): September 30, 1989; FI 4 (Founder's Statement Notes): "The Founders Statement," September 30, 1989, R02.13047 and R02.137048. Technically, it was still the Fetzer Foundation at the time of this statement, but I use "Institute" to avoid confusion. The phrase "avatar symmetry" is probably a misremembering of the "Avatar of Synthesis," a cosmic being first spoken of by Alice Bailey in her *Externalisation of the Hierarchy* (New York: Lucis,

1957, 312, 662–63, 648, 650) and widely adopted by later New Age theorists. Benjamin Crème describes Bailey's Avatar of Synthesis thus:

> A great cosmic Being, the Avatar of Synthesis, entered our planetary life through the Christ. He embodies the energies of will, love and intelligence, plus another energy for which we have as yet no name. This entity can come only as low as the mental plane, and from that level he pours his fourfold energy through the Christ, and thus into the world. Together with the Buddha, who brings in the wisdom energy from cosmic levels, these great Beings form a triangle whose energies the Christ channels to us. In this coming time, he will be known as the "Point within the Triangle." The will of the Avatar, his synthesizing force, the love of the spirit of peace or equilibrium and the wisdom of the Buddha, focused through the Christ, will transform—and are now transforming—this world.

Benjamin Crème, "The Esoteric Work of the Christ," Share International Archives, accessed July 21, 2016, www.shareintl.org/archives/M_mission/Mm_bcesoteric.htm. Jim Gordon remembers talking with John Fetzer about the "avatar symmetry" as a manifestation of the Christ Consciousness or unconditional love. Gordon, personal communication, October 23, 2016. Judy Skutch Whitson remembers talking to Fetzer about the same being, whom she likened to one of thirty-six Lamed Vovniks of Jewish lore (see chapter 8). Whitson, personal communication, November 30, 2016.

30. Fetzer Institute, "About Us," accessed October 26, 2016, http://fetzer.org/about-us.

31. See the fund's website, www.fetzer-franklin-fund.org (accessed July 22, 2016). The fund is named in part for Winston ("Wink") Franklin, a longtime board member of both the Memorial Trust and IONS.

32. Again, I specifically characterize this cosmo-theology as Western *spiritual* monism to differentiate it from Western *materialist* monism (see note 1 to the preface).

33. Wouter J. Hanegraaff, "The New Age Movement and Western Esotericism," in *Handbook of the New Age*, ed. Darren Kemp and James R. Lewis (Leiden: Brill, 2007), 25–49; Steven Sutcliffe, "The Origins of 'New Age' Religion between the Two World Wars," ibid., 51–75. For extended discussions of this history, see also Hanegraaff, *New Age Religion and Western Culture*; and Steven Sutcliffe, *Children of the New Age: A History of Spiritual Practices* (New York: Routledge, 2003).

34. Hanegraaff, "New Age Movement and Western Esotericism," 31–38.

35. See Hanegraaff, *New Age Religion and Western Culture*; John A. Saliba, *Christian Responses to the New Age Movement: A Critical Assessment* (London: G. Chapman, 1999), vii; Sutcliffe, *Children of the New Age*; J. Gordon Melton, "Beyond Millennialism: The New Age Transformed," in Kemp and Lewis, *Handbook of New Age*, 78–97; Adam Possamï, "Producing and Consuming New Age Spirituality: The Cultic Milieu and the Network Paradigm," in Kemp and Lewis, *Handbook of New Age*, 151–65; Mercadante, *Belief without Borders*, 71, 237–43.

36. See Fetzer's "New Age Epilogue," in *Men from Wengen*, 411–16; Ouija Board Transcripts, November 18, 1976, July 2, 1980, JGC.

Bibliography

Primary Sources

Adamski, George. *Inside the Space Ships*. New York: Abelard-Schuman, 1955.

Alder, Vera Stanley. *The Initiation of the World*. 1939. London: Rider, 1957.

Anrias, David. *Through the Eyes of the Masters: Meditations and Portraits*. London: G. Routledge and Sons, 1932.

Ascended Master Light. Chicago: Saint Germain, 1938.

Atkinson, William Walker. *The Kybalion: A Study of the Hermetic Philosophy of Ancient Egypt and Greece*. 1906. Chicago: Yogi, 1936.

Austin, B. F. *The A.B.C. of Spiritualism*. Los Angeles: Austin, 1920.

Bailey, Alice A. *Esoteric Healing*. New York: Lucis, 1953.

———. *Externalisation of the Hierarchy*. New York: Lucis, 1957.

———. *Initiation, Human and Solar*. 1922. New York: Lucis, 1959.

———. *The Unfinished Autobiography of Alice A. Bailey*. New York: Lucis, 1951.

Ballbusch, Peter. *The Body Is a Shell*. Hollywood, CA: White Knight, 1956.

Barker, A. T., ed. *The Mahatma Letters to A. P. Sinnett*. 1923. 2nd ed. London: Rider, 1948.

Barker, Gray. *They Knew Too Much about Flying Saucers*. New York: University Books, 1956.

Benner, Joseph. *The Impersonal Life*. 1914. San Gabriel, CA: C. A. Willing, 1974.

Benson, Herbert. *Beyond the Relaxation Response: How to Harness the Healing Power of Your Personal Beliefs*. New York: Times Books, 1984.

———. *The Relaxation Response*. New York: Avon Books, 1975.

Benson, Herbert, John W. Lehmann, M. S. Malhotra, Ralph F. Goldman, Jeffrey Hopkins, and Mark D. Epstein. "Body Temperature Changes during the Practice of g Tum-mo Yoga." *Nature* 295 (January 21, 1982): 234–36.

Bethurum, Truman. *Aboard a Flying Saucer*. Los Angeles: DeVorss, 1954.

Bey, Hamid. *My Experiences Preceding 5,000 Burials*. 1938. Whitefish, MT: Kessinger, 2006.

Blavatsky, Helena. *Isis Unveiled*. 1877. New York: J. W. Bouton, 1892.

———. *The Secret Doctrine*. 2 vols. London: Theosophical Publishing, 1888.

Bolen, J. G. "Interview with Shafica Karagulla." *Psychic* 4, no. 6 (1973): 6–11.

Books of Azrael: Teachings of the Great White Brotherhood. Vol. 1: Santa Barbara, CA: J. F. Rowny, 1960?; vols. 2–4: Los Angeles: DeVorss, 1961, 1964, 1967.

Bradshaw, Wesley. "Washington's Vision." *National Tribune* 4, no. 12 (1880): 1.

Bristol, Claude. *The Magic of Believing*. New York: Prentice Hall, 1948.

Bristol, Claude, and Harold Sherman. *TNT: The Power within You*. New York: Prentice Hall, 1954.

Brother Philip. *Brotherhood of the Seven Rays: Secret of the Andes*. Clarksburg, WV: Saucerian Books, 1961.

Brunton, Paul. *A Search in Secret Egypt*. 1936. Boston: E. P. Dutton, 1959.

———. *A Search in Secret India*. 1935. Boston: E. P. Dutton, 1951.

Bruton, David. *Baird T. Spalding as I Knew Him*. San Pedro, CA: Institute of Esoteric Philosophy, 1954.

Bryan, G. Barbee, *Psychic Dictatorship in America*. Los Angeles: Truth Research Publications, 1940.

Camp Chesterfield. *Chesterfield Lives! 1886–1986: Our First Hundred Years*. Chesterfield, IN: Camp Chesterfield, 1986.

Carnegie, Dale. *How to Win Friends and Influence People*. New York: Simon and Schuster, 1936.

Carver, Will L. *Brother of the Third Degree*. 1894. Alhambra, CA: Border, 1964.

Cayce, Edgar Evans. *Edgar Cayce on Atlantis*. New York: Warner Books, 1967.

Cerminara, Gina. *Many Mansions: The Edgar Cayce Story on Reincarnation*. 1950. New York: William Sloane, 1959.

Collins, Mabel. *The Idyll of the White Lotus*. 1890. New York: Theosophical Publishing, 1907.

Condon, Edward, and Daniel S. Gillmor, eds. *Scientific Study of Unidentified Flying Objects*. New York: Bantam, 1969.

Coptic Fellowship of America. *The Sacred Teachings of the Coptic Fellowship of America: Lessons 1–104*. N.p.: Coptic Fellowship of America, n.d.

Corelli, Marie. *A Romance of Two Worlds*. 1886. New York: William L. Allison, 1887.

Course in Miracles, A: Manual for Teachers. New York: Foundation for Inner Peace, 1975.

Course in Miracles, A: Text. New York: Foundation for Inner Peace, 1975.

Course in Miracles, A: Workbook for Students. New York: Foundation for Inner Peace, 1975.

Cramp, Leonard G. Space Gravity and the Flying Saucer. New York: British Book Centre, 1955.

Dasgupta, Shashi Bhusha. Aspects of Indian Religious Thought. Calcutta: A. Mukherjee, 1957.

Davis, John. "Prophecy of the Second Coming: Birth of Christ Within." Proceedings of the 5th National Coptic Convention, August 24–26, 1979, 1–9.

Dean, Douglas, and John Mihalasky. "Testing for Executive ESP." Psychic 6, no. 1 (1974): 21–33.

Dixon, Jean. My Life and Prophecies. New York: William Morrow, 1969.

Dowling, Levi. The Aquarian Gospel of Jesus the Christ. 1907. Los Angeles: DeVorss, 1987.

Ebon, Martin. "Hans Bender: A Life in Parapsychology." Journal of Religion and Psychical Research 18, no. 4 (1995): 187–95.

Ferguson, Marilyn. The Aquarian Conspiracy: Personal and Social Transformation in the 1980s. Los Angeles: J. P. Tarcher, 1980.

Fetzer, John E. America's Agony. Kalamazoo, MI: Fetzer Institute, 2007.

———. The Men from Wengen and America's Agony. Kalamazoo, MI: John E. Fetzer Foundation, 1971.

———. One Man's Family: A History and Genealogy of the Fetzer Family. Ann Arbor, MI: Ann Arbor Press, 1964.

Findlay, Arthur. The Rock of Truth or Spiritualism, the Coming World Religion. London: Psychic, 1933.

———. The Unfolding Universe. London: Psychic, 1935.

Forem, Jack. Transcendental Meditation: Maharishi Mahesh Yogi and the Science of Creative Intelligence. New York: E. P. Dutton, 1973.

Fort, Charles. The Books of Charles Fort. New York: Henry Holt, 1941.

Freemasons, Grand Lodge of Michigan. Transactions of the Grand Lodge of Free and Accepted Masons of the State of Michigan. Port Huron, MI: Grand Lodge of Michigan, 1899.

Fullwood, Nancy. Song of the Sano Tarot. 1929. New York: Macoy, 1946.

Gilmore, C. P. "The Birth and Life of the Universe." New York, June 12, 1966, 26–27, 85–89.

Girvan, Wavney. Flying Saucers and Common Sense. New York: Citadel, 1956.

Grant, Joan. Speaking from the Heart: Ethics, Reincarnation and What It Means to Be Human. Edited by Nicola Bennett, Jane Lahr, and Sophia Rosoff. New York: Overlook/Duckwood, 2007.

Green, Elmer E. "Copper Wall Research: Psychology and Psychophysics." *Subtle Energies & Energy Medicine* 10, no. 3 (1999): 238–43.

Hall, Manly P. *The Secret Teachings of All Ages: An Encyclopedic Outline of Masonic, Hermetic, Qabbalistic and Rosicrucian Symbolical Philosophy: Being an Interpretation of the Secret Teachings Concealed within the Rituals, Allegories, and Mysteries of All Ages.* San Francisco: H. S. Crocker, 1928.

Hardy, Dean. "New Construction Technique for Maximum Pyramid Energy." *Journal for Borderland Research* 32, no. 4 (1976): 7–9.

Hardy, Dean, Mary Hardy, Marjorie Killick, and Kenneth Killick. *Pyramid Energy: The Philosophy of God, the Science of Man.* Allegan, MI: Delta-K Pyramid Products of America, 1987.

Hardy, Mary, Dean Hardy, and Kenneth Killick. *Pyramid Energy and the Second Coming.* Allegan, MI: Delta-K Pyramid Products of America, 1981.

———. *Pyramid Energy Explained.* Allegan, MI: Delta-K Pyramid Products of America, 1979.

Harman, Willis W. "The Issue of Consciousness Raising Drugs." *Main Currents in Modern Thought* 20, no. 1 (1963): 5–13.

———. "Some Aspects of the Psychedelic-Drug Controversy." *Journal of Humanistic Psychology*, Fall 1963, 93–107.

Heline, Corinne. *New Age Bible Interpretation.* Vol. 2. 1946. La Canada, CA: New Age, 1975.

Heselton, Philip. *The Elements of Earth Mysteries.* Shaftesbury, UK: Element, 1998.

Huntley, Florence. *Harmonics of Evolution.* Vol. 1. Los Gatos, CA: Great School of Natural Science, 1956.

Hynek, J. Allen. *The UFO Experience: A Scientific Inquiry.* Chicago: Henry Regnery, 1972.

"I AM" Discourses, The. 1935. Chicago: Saint Germain, 1940.

Jahn, Robert G. "Psychic Process, Energy Transfer, and Things That Go Bump in the Night." *Princeton Alumni Weekly*, December 4, 1978, S-1–12.

Jalandris (Joseph R. Jochmans). *The Hall of Records: Hidden Secrets of the Pyramid and Sphinx.* San Francisco: Holistic Life Travels, 1980.

James, Trevor. *They Live in the Sky.* Los Angeles: New Age, 1958.

Jinarajadasa, C. *Theosophy and Reconstruction.* Adyar, India: Theosophical Publishing House, 1919.

Jochmans, Joseph Roberts. *The Hall of Records Part One.* 4 vols. N.p.: N.p., 1985.

Johnson, Julian. *The Path of the Masters: The Science of Surat Shabd Yoga: The Yoga of the Audible Life Stream.* 1939. Punjab, India: Radha Soami Satsang Beas, 1972.

Jung, Carl. *Flying Saucers: A Modern Myth of Things Seen in the Sky*. 1959. Princeton, NJ: Princeton University Press, 2002.

Karagulla, Shafica. *Breakthrough to Creativity: Your Higher Sense Perception*. Los Angeles: DeVorss, 1967.

Karagulla, Shafica, and Dora van Gelder Kunz. *The Chakras and the Human Energy Fields*. Wheaton, IL: Theosophical Publishing, 1989.

Keyhoe, Donald E. *The Flying Saucer Conspiracy*. New York: Henry Holt, 1955.

———. *The Flying Saucers Are Real*. New York: Fawcett, 1950.

———. *Flying Saucers from Outer Space*. New York: Henry Holt, 1953.

King, Godfré Ray (Guy Ballard). *The Magic Presence*. Chicago: Saint Germain, 1935.

———. *Unveiled Mysteries*. 1934. Chicago: Saint Germain, 1939.

Kolvoord, John, and Moses E. Kellogg. *The Vision of the Evening and the Morning: A Study of the Prophecy of Daniel VIII*. Battle Creek, MI, 1907.

Kool, Nancy. "Enlightenment and the Oldest Tiger." *Monthly Detroit*, April 1981, 34–41.

Kraspedon, Dino. *My Contact with Flying Saucers*. New York: Citadel, 1959.

Kuhn, Helmut. *Encounter with Nothingness: An Essay on Existentialism*. Hinsdale, IL: Henry Regnery, 1949.

Ladd, Diane. *Spiraling through the School of Life*. Carlsbad, CA: Hay House, 2006.

Leadbeater, C. W. *The Inner Life*. Vol. 1. 1910. Wheaton, IL: Theosophical Press, 1949.

Lehner, Mark. *The Egyptian Heritage Based on the Edgar Cayce Readings*. Virginia Beach, VA: ARE, 1974.

le Poer Trench, Brinsley. *The Sky People*. Clarksburg, WV: Saucerian Books, 1960.

Leslie, Desmond, and George Adamski. *Flying Saucers Have Landed*. New York: British Book Center, 1953.

Lorenzen, Coral E. *The Great Flying Saucer Hoax: The UFO Facts and the Interpretation*. New York: William-Frederick, 1962.

MacDonald-Bayne, Murdo. *Beyond the Himalayas*. London: L. N. Fowler, 1954.

———. *Spiritual and Mental Healing*. London: L. N. Fowler, 1947.

Mackey, Albert G. *An Encyclopedia of Freemasonry and Its Kindred Sciences Comprising the Whole Range of Arts, Sciences and Literature as Concerned with the Institution*. 2 vols. Chicago: Masonic History, 1927.

McConnell, R. A. "Parapsychology: Its Future Organization and Support." *Journal of the American Society of Psychical Research* 68, no. 2 (1974): 169–81.

McGarey, Analea. *Born to Heal: The Life Story of Holistic Health Pioneer Gladys Taylor McGarey, MD*. Scottsdale, AZ: Inkwell, 2003.

McGarey, William A. *The Edgar Cayce Remedies*. New York: Bantam, 1983.

Meek, George W. *After We Die, What Then?* Columbus, OH: Ariel, 1987.

Menzel, Donald H. *Flying Saucers*. Cambridge, MA: Harvard University Press, 1953.

Michel, Aimé. *The Truth about Flying Saucers*. New York: Criterion Books, 1956.

Miller, R. Dewitt. *You DO Take It with You*. New York: Citadel, 1957.

Mitchell, Edgar D. *Psychic Exploration: A Challenge to Science*. Edited by John White. New York: G. P. Putnam's Sons, 1974.

Motoyama, Hiroshi. "Acupuncture Meridians." *Science & Medicine* 6, no. 4 (1999): 48–53.

Myers, F. W. H. *Human Personality and Its Survival of Bodily Death*. London: Longmans, Green, 1903.

Notovitch, Nicolas. *The Unknown Life of Jesus Christ*. 1894. New York: Dover, 2008.

O'Neil, John J. *Prodigal Genius: The Life of Nikola Tesla*. 1944. Kempton, IL: Adventures Unlimited, 2008.

Peale, Norman Vincent. *The Power of Positive Thinking*. 1952. New York: Prentice Hall, 1953.

Phelon, W. P. *Our Story of Atlantis*. Quakertown, PA: Philosophical Publishing, 1937.

Phylos the Tibetan. *A Dweller on Two Planets*. 1905. Los Angeles: Borden, 1952.

———. *An Earth Dweller's Return*. 1940. Los Angeles: Borden, 1969.

Rampa, T. Lobsang. *The Rampa Story*. London: Souvenir, 1960.

Randolph, Paschal Beverly. *Dealings with the Dead: The Human Soul, Its Migrations and Its Transmigrations*. Utica, NY: Alexander Brady, 1861.

———. *Soul! The Soul-World: The Homes of the Dead*. 1872. Quakertown, PA: Confederation of Initiates, 1932.

Reader's Digest Association. *Our Amazing World of Nature: Its Marvels and Mysteries*. New York: Reader's Digest Association, 1969.

Rhine, J. B. *Extra-Sensory Perception*. Boston: Boston Society for Psychic Research, 1934.

———. *New Frontiers of the Mind: The Story of the Duke Experiments*. New York: Farrar and Rhinehart, 1937.

Roberts, Jane. *The Nature of Personal Reality: A Seth Book*. Englewood Cliffs, NJ: Prentice Hall, 1974.

———. *Seth Speaks: The Eternal Validity of the Soul*. Englewood Cliffs, NJ: Prentice Hall, 1972.

Rogo, D. Scott. "The Crisis in Experimental Parapsychology." *Fate* 27, no. 6 (1974): 89–95.

Ruppelt, Edward J. *The Report on Unidentified Flying Objects*. Garden City, NY: Doubleday, 1956.

Ryan, James H. *Introduction to Philosophy*. New York: Macmillan, 1924.

Saint Germain Foundation. *The History of the "I AM" Activity and Saint Germain Foundation*. Schaumberg, IL: Saint Germain, 2003.

Scofield, C. I. *Rightly Dividing the Word of Truth (2 Tim. 2:15): Being Ten Outline Studies of the More Important Divisions of Scripture*. 1907. Chicago: Bible Institute Colportage Association, 1928(?).

Sechrist, Elsie. *Dreams: Your Magic Mirror with Interpretations of Edgar Cayce*. New York: Warner Books, 1968.

Sherman, Harold. *How to Foresee and Control Your Future*. New York: Information, Incorporated, 1970.

———. *How to Know What to Believe*. New York: Fawcett, 1976.

———. *The New TNT—Miraculous Power within You*. Englewood Cliffs, NJ: Prentice Hall, 1967.

———. *Your Keys to Happiness*. New York: G. P. Putnam's Sons, 1944.

———. *Your Mysterious Powers of ESP: The New Medium of Communication*. New York: World, 1969.

Sherwood, John C. *Flying Saucers Are Watching You: The Incident at Dexter and the Incredible Michigan Flap*. Clarksburg, WV: Saucerian, 1967.

Skutch, Robert. *Journey without Distance: The Story behind "A Course in Miracles."* 1984. Mill Valley, CA: Foundation for Inner Peace, 1996.

Spalding, Baird T. *Life and Teachings of the Masters of the Far East*. 5 vols. 1924–27. Los Angeles: DeVorss, 1937, 1944, 1935, 1948, 1955.

———. *Life and Teachings of the Masters of the Far East*. Vol. 6. Camarillo, CA: DeVorss, 1996.

Srinivasan, T. M., ed. *Energy Medicine around the World*. Phoenix: Gabriel, 1988.

———. "MED (FAME) Device: Psychophysiological Correlates." In *Energy Fields in Medicine: A Study of Device Technology Based on Acupuncture Meridians and Chi Energy*, edited by Michael A. Morton and Carrie Dlouhy, 338–49. Kalamazoo, MI: John E. Fetzer Foundation, 1989.

Stearn, Jess. *Edgar Cayce: The Sleeping Prophet*. Garden City, NY: Doubleday, 1967.

Supplement to the Theosophical Forum, n.s. 2, no. 10 (1897): 1–11.

Tesla, Nikola. *My Inventions and Other Writings*. New York: Penguin, 2011.

Tuella. *World Messages for the Coming Decade: A Cosmic Symposium*. Deming, NM: Guardian Action, 1981.

Tumminia, Diana G. *When Prophecy Never Fails: Myth and Reality in a UFO Religion*. Oxford: Oxford University Press, 2005.

Twigg, Ena, with Ruth Hagy Brod. *Ena Twigg: Medium*. 1972. London: Star, 1974.

Urantia Foundation. *The Urantia Book*. 1955. Chicago: Urantia Foundation, 2008.

Van Tassel, George W. *I Rode in a Flying Saucer: The Mystery of the Flying Saucers Revealed*. Los Angeles: New Age, 1952.

Vaughan, Alan. "In Pursuit of the Whole at the Human Dimensions Institute." *Psychic*, March–April 1972, 9–14.

von Däniken, Erich. *Chariots of the Gods*. New York: Bantam, 1973.

———. *Gods from Outer Space*. New York: Bantam, 1973.

———. *Gold of the Gods*. New York: G. P. Putnam's Sons, 1973.

Voice of "I AM" 1939, The. 1939. Schaumburg, IL: Saint Germain, 2003.

White, Ellen G. *The Great Controversy between Christ and Satan*. 1888. Mountain View, CA: Pacific, 1950.

Whitfield, Joseph. *The Treasure of El Dorado*. 1971. Washington, DC: Occidental, 1980.

"Why and Wherefore of the Treasure Box in Heaven, The." Attributed to the spirit of Nikola Tesla. Sedona, AZ: Magnificent Consummation, 1974.

Wood, Ernest. *The Seven Rays*. 1925. Wheaton, IL: Theosophical Publishing, 1967.

Secondary Sources

Albanese, Catherine L. "Energy Medicine: The Spiritual Culture of an Emerging Paradigm." *Odyssey* 3 (2000): 12–36.

———. "Historical Imagination and Channeled Theology: Or, Learning the Law of Attraction." In *Handbook of Spiritualism and Channeling*, edited by Cathy Gutierrez, 480–502. Leiden: Brill, 2015.

———. "On the Matter of Spirit: Andrew Jackson Davis and the Marriage of God and Nature." *Journal of the American Academy of Religion* 60, no. 1 (1992): 1–17.

———. *A Republic of Mind and Spirit: A Cultural History of American Metaphysical Religion*. New Haven, CT: Yale University Press, 2006.

———. "The Subtle Energies of the Spirit: Explorations in Metaphysical and New Age Spirituality." *Journal of the American Academy of Religion* 67, no. 2 (1999): 305–25.

Anderson, Godfrey T. "Sectarianism and Organization, 1846–1864." In *Adventism in America*, edited by Gary Land, 29–52. Berrien Springs, MI: Andrews University Press, 1998.

Barlow, Philip. "A Demographic Portrait: America Writ Small?" In *Religion and Public Life in the Midwest: America's Common Denominator?*, edited by Philip Barlow and Mark Silk, 21–48. Walnut Creek, CA: AltaMira, 2004.

Barry, John M. *The Great Influenza: The Story of the Deadliest Pandemic in History*. London: Penguin, 2005.

Bell, J. L. "The Truth of *Washington's Vision*." *Boston 1775* (blog), December 30, 2006. http://boston1775.blogspot.com/2006/12/truth-of-washingtons-vision.html.

Beloff, John. *Parapsychology: A Concise History*. New York: St. Martin's, 1993.

Bender, Courtney. *The New Metaphysicals: Spirituality and the American Religious Imagination*. Chicago: University of Chicago Press, 2010.

Block, Marguerite. *The New Church in the New World*. New York: Swedenborg, 1984.

Braude, Ann. "News from the Spirit World: A Checklist of American Spiritualist Periodicals, 1847–1900." *Proceedings of the American Antiquarian Society* 99 (1999): 399–462.

———. *Radical Spirits: Spiritualism and Women's Rights in Nineteenth-Century America*. 2nd ed. Bloomington: Indiana University Press, 2001.

Bressler, Ann Lee. *The Universalist Movement in America, 1770–1880*. New York: Oxford University Press, 2001.

Brooke, John Hedley. *Science and Religions: Some Historical Perspectives*. Cambridge: Cambridge University Press, 1991.

Buescher, John Benedict. *Aquarian Evangelist: The Age of Aquarius as It Dawned in the Mind of Levi Dowling*. Fullerton, CA: Theosophical History, 2008.

Bullock, Steven C. *Revolutionary Brotherhood: Freemasonry and the Transformation of the American Social Order, 1730–1840*. Chapel Hill: University of North Carolina Press, 1996.

Carlson, Richard. *Tesla: Inventor of the Electric Age*. Princeton, NJ: Princeton University Press, 2013.

Carnes, Mark C. *Secret Ritual and Manhood in Victorian America*. New Haven, CT: Yale University Press, 1989.

Carroll, Brett E. *Spiritualism in Antebellum America*. Bloomington: Indiana University Press, 1997.

Conover, Jefferson S., *Freemasonry in Michigan*. Vol. 1. Coldwater, MI: Conover, 1897.

Cook, Judith. *Zion City, Illinois: Twentieth-Century Utopia*. Syracuse, NY: Syracuse University Press, 1996.

Cross, Whitney R. *The Burned-Over District: The Social and Intellectual History of Enthusiastic Religion in Western New York, 1800–1850*. Ithaca, NY: Cornell University Press, 1957.

Delp, Robert W. "Andrew Jackson Davis: Prophet of American Spiritualism." *Journal of American History* 54, no. 1 (1967): 43–56.

Denzler, Brenda. *The Lure of the Edge: Scientific Passions, Religious Beliefs, and the Pursuit of UFOs*. Berkeley: University of California Press, 2003.

Deveney, John Patrick. *Paschal Beverly Randolph: A Nineteenth-Century Black American Spiritualist, Rosicrucian, and Sex Magician*. Albany: State University of New York Press, 1997.

Dick, Everitt N. "The Millerite Movement, 1830–1845." In *Adventism in America*, edited by Gary Land, 1–28. Berrien Springs, MI: Andrews University Press, 1998.

Diem-Lane, Andrea. *The Guru in America: The Influence of Radhasoami on New Religions*. Walnut, CA: Mt. San Antonio College, 2015.

Drescher, Elizabeth. *Choosing Our Religion: The Spiritual Lives of America's Nones*. Oxford: Oxford University Press, 2016.

Dumenil, Lynn. *Freemasonry in American Culture, 1880–1930*. Princeton, NJ: Princeton University Press, 1984.

Ellwood, Robert S. "Making New Religions: The Mighty 'I AM.'" *History Today* 38, no. 6 (1988): 18–23.

———. *Religious and Spiritual Groups in Modern America*. Englewood Cliffs, NJ: Prentice Hall, 1973.

Ewald, Dan. *John Fetzer: On a Handshake: The Times and Triumphs of a Tiger Owner*. Detroit: Wayne State University Press, 2000.

"Fetzer View of the Future, A." *Encore*, November 1980.

Fogarty, Robert S. *The Righteous Remnant: The House of David*. Bowling Green, OH: Kent State University Press, 1981.

Franklin, J. Jeffrey. "The Counter-Invasion of Britain by Buddhism in Marie Corelli's 'A Romance of Two Worlds' and H. Rider Haggard's 'Ayesha: The Return of She.'" *Victorian Literature and Culture* 31, no. 1 (2003): 19–42.

Fuller, Robert C. *Mesmerism and the American Cure of Souls*. Philadelphia: University of Pennsylvania Press, 1982.

———. *Spiritual but Not Religious: Understanding Unchurched America*. Oxford: Oxford University Press, 2001.

Galvan, Jill. "Christians, Infidels, and Women's Channeling in the Writings of Marie Corelli." *Victorian Literature and Culture* 31, no. 1 (2003): 83–97.

Gardner, Martin. *The New Age: Notes of a Fringe Watcher*. Buffalo, NY: Prometheus Books, 1988.

———. *Urantia: The Great Cult Mystery*. Amherst, NY: Prometheus Books, 1995.

Gould, Robert Freke. *Gould's History of Freemasonry throughout the World*. Vol. 6. New York: Charles Scribner's Sons, 1936.

Haller, John S. *The History of New Thought: From Mind Cure to Positive Thinking and the Prosperity Gospel*. West Chester, PA: Swedenborg Foundation Press, 2012.

Hanegraaff, Wouter J. "The New Age Movement and Western Esotericism." In *Handbook of the New Age*, edited by Darren Kemp and James R. Lewis, 25–49. Leiden: Brill, 2007.

———. *New Age Religion and Western Culture: Esotericism in the Mirror of Secular Thought*. Albany: State University of New York Press, 1998.

Hazen, Craig J. *The Village Enlightenment in America: Popular Religion and Science in the Nineteenth Century*. Urbana: University of Illinois Press, 2000.

Heelas, Paul, and Linda Woodhead. *The Spiritual Revolution: Why Religion Is Giving Way to Spirituality*. Oxford, UK: Blackwell, 2005.

Hegedus, Carol. *John Earl Fetzer: Stories of One Man's Search*. Kalamazoo, MI: Fetzer Institute, 2004.

Henry, Lyell D. "Unorthodox Science as a Popular Activity." *Journal of American Culture* 4, no. 2 (1981): 1–22.

Hess, David J. *Science in the New Age: The Paranormal, Its Defenders and Debunkers, and American Culture*. Madison: University of Wisconsin Press, 1993.

Hogan, Timothy W. "The Hermetic Influence on Freemasonry." *Heredom* 17 (2009): 121–36.

Horn, Stacy. *Unbelievable: Investigations into Ghosts, Poltergeists, Telepathy, and Other Unseen Phenomena from the Duke Parapsychology Laboratory*. New York: HarperCollins, 2009.

Hornung, Erik. *The Secret Lore of Egypt: Its Impact on the West*. Ithaca, NY: Cornell University Press, 2001.

Horowitz, Mitch. *Occult America: White House Séances, Ouija Circles, Masons, and the Mystic History of Our Nation*. New York: Bantam Books, 2009.

Irwin, Harvey J., and Caroline A. Watt. *An Introduction to Parapsychology*. 5th ed. Jefferson, NC: McFarland, 2007.

Jenkins, Philip. *Mystics and Messiahs: Cults and New Religions in American History*. New York: Oxford University Press, 2000.

Johnson, K. Paul. *Edgar Cayce in Context: The Readings: Truth and Fiction*. Albany: State University of New York Press, 1998.

Judah, J. Stillson. *The History and Philosophy of the Metaphysical Movements in America*. Philadelphia: Westminster, 1967.

Juergensmeyer, Mark. *Radhasoami Reality: The Logic of a Modern Faith*. Princeton, NJ: Princeton University Press, 1991.

Kemp, Daren, and James R. Lewis, eds. *Handbook of New Age*. Leiden: Brill, 2007.

Kinney, Jay. *The Masonic Myth: Unlocking the Truth about Symbols, the Secret Rites, and the History of Freemasonry*. New York: HarperCollins, 2009.

Kirby, James E., Russell E. Richey, and Kenneth E. Rowe. *The Methodists*. Westport, CT: Praeger, 1996.

Klimo, Jon. *Channeling: Investigations on Receiving Information from Paranormal Sources*. Los Angeles: Jeremy P. Tarcher, 1987.

Knight, George R. *A Brief History of Seventh-day Adventism*. Hagerstown, MD: Review and Herald, 2004.

Land, Gary, ed. *Adventism in America: A History*. Berrien Springs, MI: Andrews University Press, 1998.

"Lee Named No. 2 in Fetzer Command." *Broadcasting Telecasting* 45 (August 3, 1953): 60.

Lehman, Jutta K. "The Influence of the Theosophical Movement on the Revival of Astrology in Great Britain and North America in the 20th Century." Ph.D. diss., Concordia University, 1998.

Leonard, Todd Jay. *Talking to the Other Side: A History of Modern Spiritualism and Mediumship*. New York: iUniverse, 2005.

Lévi-Strauss, Claude. *The Savage Mind*. Chicago: University of Chicago Press, 1966.

Lewis, James R. *Encyclopedia of Cults, Sects, and New Religious Movements*. Amherst, NY: Prometheus Books, 2002.

———, ed. *The Gods Have Landed: New Religions from Other Worlds*. Albany: State University of New York Press, 1995.

———. *Seeking the Light: Uncovering the Truth about the Movement of Spiritual Inner Awareness and Its Founder, John-Roger*. Los Angeles: Mandeville, 1998.

Lewis, James R., and J. Gordon Melton, eds. *Perspectives on the New Age*. Albany: State University of New York Press, 1992.

Madison, James H. *Hoosiers: A New History of Indiana*. Bloomington: Indiana University Press, 2014.

Main, Douglas. "Most People Believe Intelligent Aliens Exist, Poll Says." *Newsweek*, September 29, 2015. www.newsweek.com/most-people-believe-intelligent -aliens-exist-377965.

Marsden, George M. *Fundamentalism and American Culture: The Shaping of Twentieth-Century Evangelicalism, 1870–1925*. New York: Oxford University Press, 2006.

Martin, Fern Honeywell, and Paula Alexandra Brooks. *Greater Lafayette: A Pictorial History*. St. Louis: G. Bradley, 1994.

Mathers, George R. *Frontier Faith: The Story of the Pioneer Congregations of Fort Wayne, Indiana, 1820–1860*. Fort Wayne, IN: Allen County–Fort Wayne Historical Society, 1992.

Mauskopf, Seymour H., and Michael R. McVaugh. *The Elusive Science: Origins of Experimental Psychical Research*. Baltimore: Johns Hopkins University Press, 1980.

McIntosh, Christopher. *Eliphas Lévi and the French Occult Revival*. London: Rider, 1972.

Mead, Sidney E. "In Search of God." In *The Heritage of the Middle West*, edited by John J. Murray, 152–76. Norman: University of Oklahoma Press, 1958.

Means, Howard. *Johnny Appleseed: The Man, the Myth, the American Story*. New York: Simon and Schuster, 2011.

Melton, J. Gordon. "Beyond Millennialism: The New Age Transformed." In *Handbook of New Age*, edited by Darren Kemp and James R. Lewis, 78–97. Leiden: Brill, 2007.

———, ed. *Encyclopedia of American Religions*. Farmington Hills, MI: Gale, 2003.

———. "New Thought and the New Age." In *Perspectives on the New Age*, edited by James R. Lewis and J. Gordon Melton, 15–29. Albany: State University of New York Press, 1992.

Melton, J. Gordon, Jerome Clark, and Aidan A. Kelly. *New Age Almanac*. New York: Visible Ink, 1991.

Melton, J. Gordon, with James V. Geisendorfer. *A Directory of Religious Bodies in the United States*. New York: Garland, 1977.

Mercadante, Linda A. *Belief without Borders: Inside the Minds of the Spiritual but Not Religious*. Oxford: Oxford University Press, 2014.

Meyers, D. H. "American Intellectuals and the Victorian Crisis of Faith." *American Quarterly* 27 (December 1975): 585–603.

Mills, Joy. *100 Years of Theosophy: A History of the Theosophical Society in America*. Wheaton, IL: Theosophical Publishing, 1987.

"Mind Body and Spirit Are One Says Rev. Dave McShane." *Encore* 8, no. 3 (1980): 9–11.

Noll, Mark. "Protestants: An Enduring Methodist Tinge." In *Religion and Public Life in the Midwest: America's Common Denominator?*, edited by Philip Barlow and Mark Silk, 49–82. Walnut Creek, CA: AltaMira, 2004.

Numbers, Ronald L. *The Creationists: The Evolution of Scientific Creationism*. New York: Knopf, 1992.

———. *Prophetess of Health: Ellen G. White and the Origins of Seventh-day Adventist Health Reform*. 1992. Grand Rapids, MI: Wm. B. Eerdmans, 2008.

Numbers, Ronald L., and Jonathan N. Butler, eds. *The Disappointed: Millerism and Millenarianism in the Nineteenth Century*. Knoxville: University of Tennessee Press, 1993.

Partridge, Christopher. "Channeling Extraterrestrials: Theosophical Discourse in the Space Age." In *Handbook of Spiritualism and Channeling*, edited by Cathy Gutierrez, 390–417. Leiden: Brill, 2015.

———. *The Re-enchantment of the West*. Vol. 1. London: T&T Clark, 2004.

———. *The Re-enchantment of the West*. Vol. 2. London: T&T Clark, 2005.

Piatigorsky, Alexander. *Freemasonry: The Study of a Phenomenon*. London: Harvill, 1999.

Porter, Jennifer E. "Spiritualists, Aliens and UFOs: Extraterrestrials as Spirit Guides." *Journal of Contemporary Religion* 11, no. 3 (1996): 337–53.

Possamï, Adam. "Producing and Consuming New Age Spirituality: The Cultic Milieu and the Network Paradigm." In *Handbook of New Age*, edited by Darren Kemp and James R. Lewis, 151–65. Leiden: Brill, 2007.

Randall, Ian M. "Methodist Spirituality." In *Ashgate Research Companion to World Methodism*, edited by William Gibson and Martin Wellings, 289–306. Abingdon, UK: Ashgate, 2013.

Reece, Gregory L. *UFO Religion: Inside Flying Saucer Cults and Culture*. London: I. B. Taurus, 2007.

Roberts, Jon H. *Darwinism and the Divine in America: Protestant Intellectuals and Organic Evolution, 1859–1900*. Madison: University of Wisconsin Press, 1988.

Rowe, David L. "Millerites: A Shadow Portrait." In *The Disappointed: Millerism and Millenarianism in the Nineteenth Century*, edited by Ronald L. Numbers and Jonathan N. Butler, 1–15. Knoxville: University of Tennessee Press, 1993.

Rudolph, T. C. *Hoosier Faiths: A History of Indiana Churches and Religious Groups*. Bloomington: Indiana University Press, 1995.

Rupert, Glenn A. "Employing the New Age: Training Seminars." In *Perspectives on the New Age*, edited by James R. Lewis and J. Gordon Melton, 127–35. Albany: State University of New York Press, 1992.

Sahagun, Louis. *Master of the Mysteries: The Life of Manly Palmer Hall*. Port Townsend, WA: Process Media, 2008.

Saliba, John A. *Christian Responses to the New Age Movement: A Critical Assessment*. London: G. Chapman, 1999.

Schwarz, Richard W. "The Perils of Growth 1886–1905." In *Adventism in America: A History*, edited by Gary Land, 77–111. Berrien Springs, MI: Andrews University Press, 1998.

Sears, Louis Martin. "Robert Dale Owen as a Mystic." *Indiana Magazine of History* 24, no. 1 (1928): 15–25.

Seifer, Marc J. *Wizard: The Life and Times of Nikola Tesla*. New York: Citadel, 1998.

"Shafica Karagulla." In *Encyclopedia of Occultism and Parapsychology*, edited by J. Gordon Melton, 850. Detroit: Gale, 2001.

Sprague de Camp, L. *Lost Continents: The Atlantis Theme*. 1954. New York: Ballantine, 1970.

Stockinger, Anna. "The History of Spiritualism in Indiana." *Indiana Magazine of History* 20 (March–December 1924): 280–87.

Stupple, David. "Mahatmas and Space Brothers: The Ideologies of Alleged Contact with Mahatmas and Space Brothers: The Ideologies of Alleged Contact with Extraterrestrials." *Journal of American Culture* 7 (1984): 131–39.

Sutcliffe, Steven. *Children of the New Age: A History of Spiritual Practices*. New York: Routledge, 2003.

———. "The Origins of 'New Age' Religion between the Two World Wars." In *Handbook of the New Age*, edited by Darren Kemp and James R. Lewis, 51–75. Leiden: Brill, 2007.

Underwood, Grant. *The Millenarian Worldview of Early Mormonism*. Urbana: University of Illinois Press, 1999.

US Bureau of the Census. *Religious Bodies: 1906 Census, Part 1: Summary and General Tables*. Washington, DC: Government Printing Office, 1910.

Van Dusen, Wilson. *The Presence of Other Worlds: The Findings of Emanuel Swedenborg*. New York: Harper and Row, 1974.

Versluis, Arthur. *Magic and Mysticism: An Introduction to Western Esotericism*. Lanham, MD: Rowman and Littlefield, 2007.

Whorton, James C. *Nature Cures: The History of Alternative Medicine in America*. Oxford: Oxford University Press, 2002.

Williams, Peter W. *America's Religions: From Their Origins to the Twenty-First Century*. Urbana: University of Illinois Press, 2000.

Yates, Frances A. *The Rosicrucian Enlightenment*. London: Routledge and Kegan Paul, 1972.

Ziolkowski, Eric J., ed. *A Museum of Faiths: Histories and Legacies of the 1893 World's Parliament of Religions*. Atlanta: Scholars, 1993.

Index

Note: Italicized page numbers refer to figures.

Arminianism, 7

Arnold, Kenneth, 97

Ascended Master Light (1938), 74, 237n12, 249n37

Aspects of Indian Religious Thought (Dasgupta 1957), 94

Association for Research and Enlightenment (ARE), 50, 104, 145, 182

Astrology, 36, 51–52, 161, 270n25, 286n49

Atkinson, William Walker, 66–67

Atlantis, 72, 77, 79, 89, 112, 130, 164, 169, 183, 187, 193, 234n22, 240n36, 266n95

Aura, human, 69, 76, 107, 136, 157, 158, 160, 163, 164, 166, 177, 279n13, 282n32

Austin, B. F., 49

AVRO car, 149, 266n92

Bader, Sister Mary L., 148

Bailey, Alice, 79–86, 111, 129, 144, 156, 163, 199, 234n23, 244n7, 245n14, 247n21, 248n31, 294n29

Bailey, Foster, 80–81

Ballard, Donald, 75, 232n12

Ballard, Edna, 74–77, 85, 231n12

Ballard, Guy, 74–78, 85, 95, 199, 231n12, 244n10, 245n14, 248n31, 249n37

Ballbusch, Peter, 250n42

Ballenger, E. S., 25–26

Baptist Church, 5, 11, 31

Bateman, Cash, 157, 160

Beaver, Tom, xv, 197–98, *199*, 202, 204, 293n16

Belier, Henry G., 104

Bender, Hans, 135

Benner, Joseph, 79

Benson, Herbert, 179–80

Berteema, Wilma, 51

Bethurum, Truman, 100

Bey, Hamid, 157, 269n20

Bias, Clifford, 41

Biederwolf, William Edward, 27

Biofeedback, 121, 136–40, 179, 180, 184, 255n39

Blavatsky, Helena Petrovna, 71–73, 75, 80, 231n10

Book of Revelation (New Testament), 10–11, 220n29, 271n31

Books of Azrael (1960?–1967), 79

Bourdages, Gaston and Joe, 149

Bradshaw, Wesley, 119

Breakthrough to Creativity (Karagulla 1967), 106–8, 243n50

Bristol, Claude, 112–13, 244nn10–11

British Society of Psychic Research, 135

Broner, Len, 14

Bronson Methodist Hospital, 135, 138

Brunton, Paul, 79, 94, 95, 170

Buddha and Buddhism, 39, 72, 80, 93, 94, 124, 155–56, 168, 295n29

Bulwer-Lytton, Edward, 68

Burdick, Clifford, 232n13, 266n93

Butters, Curt, 156, 257n47

Camp Cassadaga, Spiritualist (Florida), 41

Camp Chesterfield, Spiritualist (Indiana), xiii, 40–52, 67, 73, 79, 93, 103, 193, 222n23, 230n2, 234n23, 251n13, 259n57, 275n42

Camp Lily Dale, Spiritualist (New York), 41

Douët, Arthur, 274n39, 284n42

Douët, Dawn, 193

Dowie, John Alexander, 10

Dowling, Levi, 86, 144, 235n40, 260n69

Dowsing, 96, 107, 186–87, 237n13;
286n49

Doyle, Sir Arthur Conan, 168

Duke University, 105, 127, 128, 129, 136

Dutch Reformed Church, x

Dweller on Two Planets, A (Phylos the
Tibetan 1905), 79

Eckankar, 170

Edgar Cayce: The Sleeping Prophet (Stearn
1967), 104

Edgar Cayce on Atlantis (Cayce 1967), 79

Edgar D. Mitchell and Associates, 127

Edison, Thomas, 117, 168, 236n45,
283n36

Einstein, Albert, 117, 130, 239n32,
283n36

Eisenberg, David, 205

Eisenhower, Dwight D., 56, *58*

El Haren, 51

Ellwood, Robert, 76, 78, 142

Emerson, Ralph Waldo, 37

Emil, 86–88

Emmanuel Missionary College, 13–18,
19, 23–24, 31, 33, 232n13; KFGZ,
13; WEMC, "the Radio Lighthouse,"
13–19, *16, 20,* 21–24, 33

Encyclopedia of Freemasonry, An (Mackey
1927), 65

Energy medicine, 107, 176, 182–85, 187,
189, 205, 211

"Enlightenment and the Oldest Tiger"
(Kool 1981), 155

Esalen Institute, 146

Esoteric Healing (Bailey 1953), 129

Euclid, 65

Evangelical Christianity, x, 4–8, 27, 37, 40

Evolution of humanity, spiritual, 1, 73,
85–87, 102, 124, 155, 164, 169, 177,
211

Extra-Sensory Perception (Rhine 1934),
106

Extrasensory perception (ESP), 93, 103–4,
106–7, 112, 126, 130, 136, 148, 253n28

Ezekiel (biblical prophet), 99

Fate (magazine), 93, 106, 133, 236n6,
245n11

Federal Communications Commission
(FCC), 34, 59

FEMRI Acupuncture Meridian
Evaluator (FAME), 184

Ferguson, Marilyn, 139, 146, 262n77

Fetzer, Bruce, 162, *172,* 173, 176, 177,
220n29, 225n55, 236n48, 272n35,
293n16

Fetzer, Della Frances Winger Evans,
2–3, *2,* 6, 8, 10, 12–13, 17, 23–24, 27,
30–31, 36–38, 40, 42, 93, 118

Fetzer, Harriet ("Hattie") Evans, *2,* 3, 10,
36, 74, 155–56

Fetzer, Homer, 2, 58, 225n6

Fetzer, Johanna Bunz, 42

Fetzer, John A., 1–6, 9, 42, 110

Fetzer, John E., avatar symmetry, 208,
294n29; community of freedom, 206,
208, 212; death, attitudes toward,
204–5; dreams, 8, 158, 207, 262n76,
269n22, 294n27; "Faith of Our
Fathers" (1927), 15–18, 212; "Flying

Saucer Hoax, The" (1974), 99–100;
"Founder's Statement" (1989), 208–9,
212; freedom of the spirit, xii, 30, 70,
168, 206, 208, 212; genealogy, spiritual
importance of, 42, 52, 110, 118, 123,
141; group reincarnation, 77, 164,
271n30; "Helping to Heal the Whole
Person and the Whole World" (1988),
207–8; Jesus experience as child, 8;
LSD experience, 146–48, 249n41,
263n79; *Men from Wengen and
America's Agony, The* (1971), 42–43,
118–23, *119*, *122*, 124; New Age
worldview, x–xiii, 117, 121, 123–24,
128, 207, 210–12; *One Man's Family*
(1964), 42, 64, 110–13, 118, 142; past
lives, 141, 154, 164, 193, 263n79,
266n95; pendulum, 126–27, 187,
250n4, 286n49; "Spalding Memo,"
129–31; spirit, Fetzer's definition
of, xi; spirit guides, 41–42, 259n57,
275n42; spirit photography, 43, *44*;
"This I Believe" (1967), 113–18,
125–26; Tom Swift books, 76, 140,
184; wealth, responsible use of, xiii,
76–78, 92, 121, 198, 211
Fetzer, Rhea Yeager, 15, *16*, 19, 23,
25–28, 31, 33–34, 36, 51, 56, 93–95,
105, 106, 142, 145, 146, 153, 161, 176,
187, 197, 202, 263n78, 279n13
Fetzer, Walter Adam, 3, 42
Fetzer Broadcast House, 91, *94*, *119*,
156, 158, 160, 162, 175, 187
Fetzer Broadcasting Company (later
System), 55, 91, 154, 162; "590 Case,"
34, 59; KOLN-TV (Lincoln, NE), 91;
WJEF (Grand Rapids, MI), 55, *56*,

57, 91, 98; WKZO (Kalamazoo, MI),
33–35, *35*, 51, 55, 76; WKZO-TV3
(Kalamazoo, MI), 91
Fetzer Business Center (Western
Michigan University), 185–86, 284n42
Fetzer Energy Medicine Research
Institute (FEMRI), 183–85, 282n32
Fetzer Foundation, x, xi, 92, 108, 125–40,
145, 148–49, 151–52, 154–68, 171,
173, 175–202; administration building
(aka World Headquarters), 185–96,
192, 197, 200, 202, 206, 213, 287n52,
289n60; Associates program, 200;
Courage to Teach program, 206;
creation and incorporation, 92–93,
125–26; endowment from sale of
Fetzer businesses, 185; Fetzer Energy
Medicine conference (1987), 184;
"Fetzer Foundation Statement of
Purpose" (1987), 200, 267n96, 272n35;
Fetzer Franklin Fund, 209, 295n31;
Fetzer Trust, 125; Helping Heal the
Whole Person and the Whole World
conference (1988), 200, *201*, 207; in-
house laboratory, 185, 200, 205, 208,
283n36; "John E. Fetzer Foundation
Commitment," 198–99, 290n5, 291n7;
logos, 165, *165*, 191–93, *193*; mission,
evolution of, 125–27, 154, 160, 164–67,
175–79, *179*, 181, 187, 201, 205–9,
278n12; New Frontiers program,
257n47, 279n15; organization and
staffing, early, 125, 175–76, 278n10;
Pioneers program, 200; professional
board, creation of, 200; "Statement
of Mission and Goals and Program
Overview" (1983), 177–78, 272n35

Fetzer Institute, xi, xii, xiv, 73, 123, 201, 202, 205–6, 209, 211–12; Common Work (1997), 206; Fetzer Global Gathering (Assisi, Italy, 2012), 207; name change to Institute, 201; Seasons (retreat center), 206

Fetzer Memorial Trust, 202, 207, 209, 293n16

Fidrych, Mark ("the Bird"), 126–27

Field, Reverend George, 45

Findlay, Arthur, 47

Forbes (magazine), ix

Ford, Gerald R., 99, 142

Fort, Charles, 237n14

Fouche, Leonard, 156

Foundation for Inner Peace, 143, 146

Foundation for Parapsychological Investigation, 143

Foundation for Research on the Nature of Man, 127–28

Founding Fathers, US, 17, 61, 87, 165, 190

Fox Sisters, 36, 46

Francis I, 193

Franklin, Benjamin, 17, 61, 117, 190

Fraternitas Rosae Crucis, 68

Freemasonry, xiii, 58–65, 66, 68, 71, 76, 82, 83, 89, 95, 109, 118, 190, 191, 193, 209, 226n7, 229n31, 232n12, 249n37, 288n52, 289n59; Anchor Lodge in Strict Observance (S.O.) No. 87 of the Free and Accepted Masons, 58, 60–62, 227n19; Detroit Masonic Temple, 60, 100; Hiram Abiff, 63–64; Kalamazoo No. 22 Masonic Lodge, 60–61; Knights Templar, 64; Saladin Lodge of the Shriners, 64, 226n7; Scottish Rite, *62*, 64, 118; Solomon's Temple, 63–64; York Rite, 64

Fuld, William, 52

Fullwood, Nancy, 79, 245n14

g Tum-mo yoga, 180

Galen, 46

Garfield, James A., 17

Garland, Hamlin, 1

Garrett, Eileen, 128

Gathering Call, The (journal), 26, *26*

Geller, Uri, 145

Gergely, Michael, 157–58, 160, 161, *188*, 270n24, 293n16

German Brethren ("Dunker") Church, 6

German Triangle, 5

Gladstone, William, 17

Glycadis, Bruce, 98

Goleman, Daniel, 206

Gordon, Jim, 157–73, *162*, 176–78, 181, 184–87, 191, 194, 198–99, 201, 202, 204, 220n29, 266n95, 269n20, 270n26, 272n35, 273n39, 274n40, 278n10, 283n36, 289n59, 292n13, 294n27, 295n29; "Master of the Heart" meditation, 163, 166, 170, 270n29; Masters of the Inner Light, 168, 185, 273n38; "Potential Goals from the Channelings" (1983), 177–78, *179*

Grady, Harvey, 182–83

Grant, Joan, 135

"Great Invocation, The" (Bailey 1922), 81, 111, 163, 234n27, 244n7, 249n42

Great White Brotherhood, 72, 75, 78, 79, 83, 86, 101, 141, 149, 230n2

Green, Elmer, 180–81

Grenfell, Wilfred, 18